# ORISSA

AND

# ITS EVANGELIZATION

# ORISSA

AND

# ITS EVANGELIZATION;

INTERSPERSED WITH SUGGESTIONS

RESPECTING THE MORE EFFICIENT CONDUCTING

OF

# INDIAN MISSIONS.

**BY AMOS SUTTON, D.D.**

GYAN

*Published by*

GYAN

Gyan Publishing House
5, Ansari Road
Daryaganj, New Delhi-110002
Phone: 011-47034999, 9811692060
E-mail: books@gyanbooks.com

*Distribution Network*
gyanbooks.com
India, USA, Canada, UK, Australia, France



ISBN: 978-81-212-7957-4 (PB)
First Published, 1850

2nd Impression 2023

*Printed at:* Gyan Press, Delhi.



**ORISSA AND ITS EVANGELIZATION**
Author: AMOS SUTTON

# NORTHERN STATIONS OF THE ORISSA MISSION.

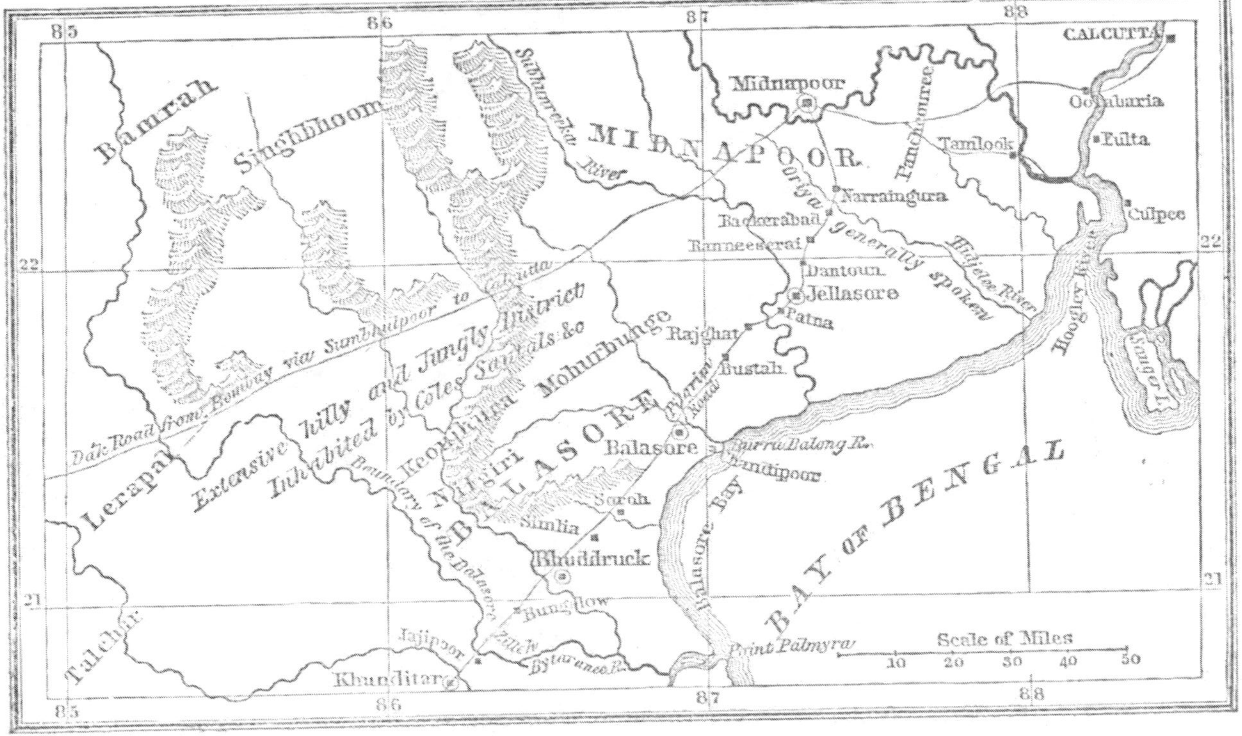

SOUTHERN & CENTRAL STATIONS OF THE ORISSA MISSION.

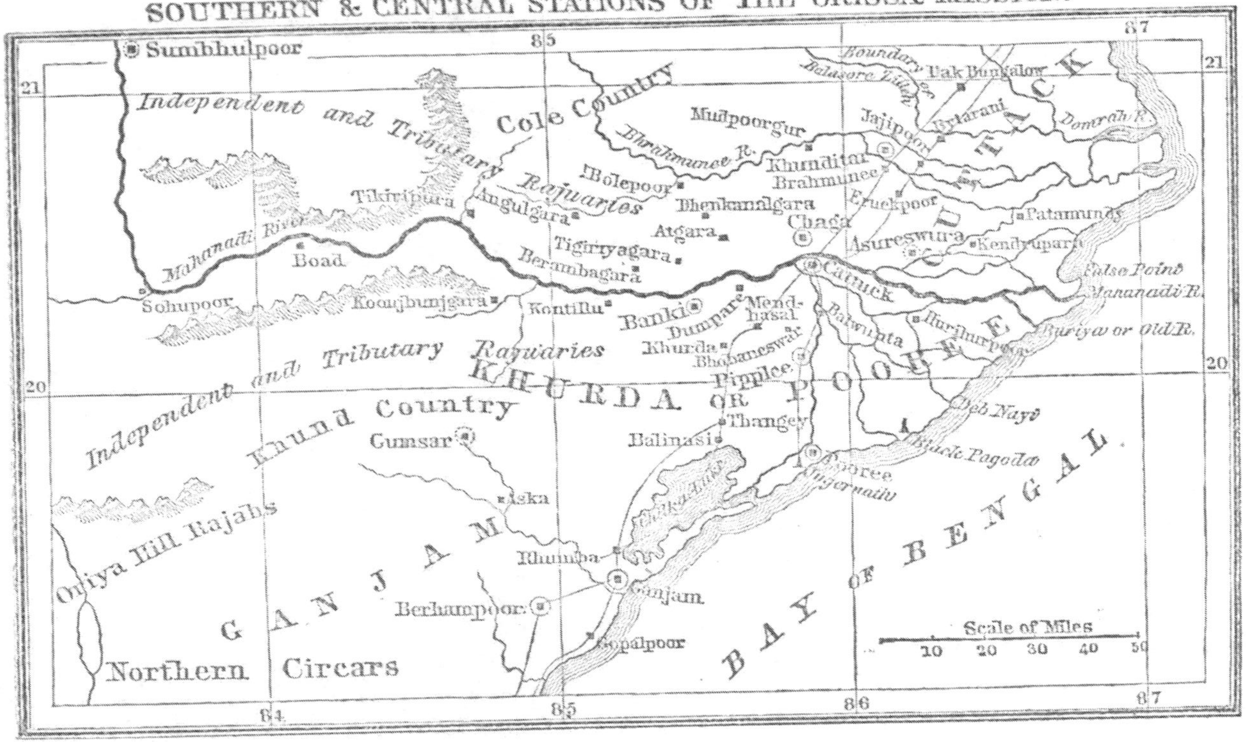

# ORISSA

AND

# ITS EVANGELIZATION;

INTERSPERSED WITH SUGGESTIONS

RESPECTING THE MORE EFFICIENT CONDUCTING

OF

# INDIAN MISSIONS.

By AMOS SUTTON, D.D.,

Missionary to Orissa.

DERBY:
WILKINS & SON.
1850.

# PREFACE.

At the farewell services connected with the author's departure from England, he was requested, by a formal request of the audience, to present once more to the churches of Christ the claims of the Orissa Mission. This request he has now endeavored to meet. The opportunities afforded him for accomplishing his task have been by no means of the most favorable kind. A few days, during his voyage to America—a few hours, during his almost daily journeys and preachings, with now and then a brief interval, which would otherwise have been devoted to relaxation, or the sweets of friendly intercourse with those from whom he expects soon to be separated for ever, are all the leisure he has been able to command. The subject-matter of the book has, however, been daily on his mind; what he has craved, has been time for a more lucid arrangement of his facts, and for attempting to clothe his ideas in their more appropriate garb. But in this, as in most other cases, he must be content to be a practical man, leaving it for those who enjoy the sweets of literary leisure, to charm by the graces of their style and entrance by the music of their sentences.

The writer has not attempted a regular account of the daily detail of missionary labor. This, for the first twelve years of the Mission, he has already given in the NARRATIVE OF THE ORISSA MISSION, published in 1833. The impression made on his mind by the various speakers when the above-named vote was taken, was, that a distinct account of the character and extent of the field of labor, the means employed in its cultivation, the results attained, and what further help is required, was called for at his hands. He has, while keeping these objects distinctly in view, endeavored to place before the reader such reflections and suggestions as in his opinion may subserve the more efficient conducting of Indian Missions generally.

The writer is not willing to suppose that he has spent five-and-twenty years in missionary life, without having gained some information or cherished some ideas which may be of service to the cause he loves. He shrinks not, therefore, from the responsibility of adding another book to the number already published on Indian Missions.

India, as a field for missionary labor, is as yet very imperfectly appreciated. Fully does the writer agree with Mr. Lacroix, in asserting, that there is not another country on the face of the earth, which is so truly prepared for missionary operations. Ardently does he hope, that the claims of this vast field may be more vividly portrayed and more urgently presented before the Christian community, so that the precious opportunity, now given us for seeking India's evangelization, may be improved; and improved too with a promptitude and zeal commensurate with its unspeakable importance. Here the writer can do no more than suggest a few hints respecting those claims which he thinks deserve devout consideration.

1. As to the extent of the field.

The missionary field of India extends from the Indus to the Brahmaputra, and from the Himalaya mountains to the sea; embracing an area of about 1600 miles by 1400, or at least a million of square miles. The whole of this vast region is, in its length and breadth, fully open to the missionary of the cross. Besides which, on the boundaries of this field are doorways, opening into the regions stretching far away to the east, west and north; that is, toward Birma and its neighboring countries; toward Persia, with its adjacent states; toward Thibet and Tartary, with vast tracts unknown. It may be safely asserted, that there is no field of labor, of equal extent, so spread open before the missionary. And this vast field is under the control of a Christian government, which will afford to all denominations of laborers the most ample toleration.

2. As to statistical enumeration.

We wish not to detract from the claims of China, with her three hundred and fifty millions; but, as a matter of fact, we must not forget that we have free access to many more Hindoos than Chinese. Besides, India affords us free intercourse with, not her one hundred and fifty millions of indigenous population merely, but with the professors of all the dominant religious creeds prevalent in Asia; that is, of the systems of religious belief held by two-thirds of the population of the globe.

A hundred and fifty millions of human beings is a mass of which few can form any adequate idea. Now, for this whole multitude, there are probably not two hundred foreign missionaries; that is, one to about every 800,000 people! These laborers in India are so very unequally distributed, that there are several whole kingdoms, and many populous districts, where there is no missionary at all. The attention of the reader is directed to such places as Oude, Gualior, Nipaul, Cashmere, to several large districts in Bengal, Orissa, and others in the south and western parts of India.

3. India in interesting associations presents unrivalled claims. It is associated with the most prominent historical facts; with the invasion of Darius, Alexander, and Mahmoud; with the reign of the Bactrian kings, the ravages of the Affghan, the Turk, and the Persian Moslem; it was the earliest scene of European commercial enterprize; the theatre of British valor and supremacy; the first field of modern missions, and still is connected with a variety of kindred subjects of unparalleled interest.

But it is also doubtless one of the earliest abodes of man; its language, its philosophy, its idolatries, its ancient cities and kingdoms, its numerous tribes and castes, its early attainments in civilization, its wealth and natural productions, all combine to make India deserving of the attention of every philanthropist.

4. As a centre of influence for all Asia, it invites the special consideration of the Christian church.

In this land originated those gigantic systems of Pantheism which have overspread the eastern world, and are even now exerting an influence on Europe. India, too, seems marked out by the hand of God as the centre of those evangelical operations which shall influence the nations to an equal, if not to a greater extent. There, under the most favored circumstances, may be raised up and trained the men who shall be fitted to preach the gospel to the adherents of their own peculiar creed in every part of the eastern world.

5. The wants and woes of India present a claim on Christian benevolence, which it seems utterly impossible to overstate, or urge with too much earnestness and pathos. For myself, I confess that I utterly break down in all my attempts to represent this claim, and constantly come away from the public meeting, eeling that I have fallen shamefully short in this matter. I avail myself of the appeal of a brother missionary, when addressing my countrymen.—"Think," he exclaims, "think that yonder, under the rule of your own Queen, a full sixth of Adam's children dwell! Take a little leisure, and say, of every six infants, one first sees the light there; to what instruction is it born? Of every six brides, one offers her vows there; to what affection is she destined? Of every six families, one spreads its table there; what love unites their circle? Of every six widows, one is lamenting there; what consolation shall soothe her? Of every six orphan girls, one is wandering there; what charities will protect her? Of every six wounded consciences, one is smarting there; what balm, what physician, does it know? Of every six men that die, one is departing there; what haven is in his eye?" Christians in every land, India appeals to you! Will you help her, by helping to send her the gospel? "If thou forbear to deliver them that are drawn unto death, and those that are ready to be slain; if thou sayest, Behold, we knew it not; doth not He that pondereth the heart consider it? and he that keepeth thy soul, doth he not know it? and shall not He render to every man according to his works?"

6. While India generally thus lifts up her voice,

and pleads with Christendom in language so pathetic and importunate, Orissa, the site of the Mission whose operations are more particularly described in the following pages, presents her own special plea. Some account of its extent, statistics, history, with its present social, civil, and moral condition, will follow these prefatory remarks; but, apart from all these, it has, in consequence of its relative position with respect to the whole of India, a peculiar claim on the sympathy of the whole Christian church. It is to India what Jerusalem was to the whole land of Israël. It is the holy land of the Hindoos. As the Israelites went up to worship at Mount Zion, so do the inhabitants of the various provinces of India go on pilgrimages to the great temple of Jugernath. For many years has the writer stood within the precincts of that "mighty pagod," and witnessed the pilgrims flocking in from all parts of Hindoosthan, on foot, on horseback, on oxen, on camels, on elephants, in litters, palanquins, vehicles of all sorts; and decked out in all the varied costumes of India's multitudinous race. For hundreds of miles, yea, upward of a thousand, have they come to worship at that monstrous idol's shrine. This peculiar feature in our field of labor, shows that missionary efforts there have a special importance, and have more or less bearing on similar labors in every part of India. Some interesting cases of conversion, at far distant stations, have occurred among Jugernath's votaries, which connect the evangelical efforts of brethren in the farthest verge of India with those of the missionaries on the plains of Orissa.

# CONTENTS.

## UNEXPLAINED ORIYA WORDS.

Most of the Native words used in this volume are explained as they occur. The following have either been overlooked, or occur so frequently, that it may be of service to the reader to give an explanation of them in this place. It will be observed, that the same words are occasionally spelled in various ways. This variation, however, chiefly refers to the vowels. Most writers endeavor to represent the Indian vowel sounds as nearly as they can, without any reference to system. A system, however, has of late years come into use, based on philological accuracy. Few ordinary readers of Indian books are acquainted with it, and hence the old mode of writing words commonly prevails. Both methods are used in this work. Thus we write Hindoo or Hindu—Juggernath or Jagarnáth—Pooree or Purí—Hunooman or Hanumán, &c. These examples may assist the reader in other cases.

Anná; sixteenth of a rupee.
Bhobuneswar; land of God.
Bharan; a land measure.
Bazar; a street or place of business.
Baboo; a gentleman.
Boishnob; a devotee.
Bruhmagyan; divine knowledge.
Byraggee; a devotee.
Cowrie; small money shell.
Chandala; an outcaste.
Cápara; a cloth, clothes.
Curree; hot spiced stew.
Debta; an idol, or god.
Dursuna; sight of an idol.
Ghat; a landing-place.
Gunga; the Ganges.
Gunja; a strong narcotic.
Gooroo; spiritual guide.
Hackery; bullock cart.
Hunuman; monkey god.
Hurre bol; cry hurre, huzza.
Kahan; 1280 cowries.
Killah; a fort, and attached district.
Koss; two or three miles.
Khetra; a sacred district.
Khunjaree; a small tabor.
Lota; a water-pot.
Langora; a tail.
Mala; necklace, or rosary.
Muntra; a sacred sentence.
Mahal; region, district.
Nautch; a dance.
Paddy; rice in the husk.
Phalgoon; February and March.
Poorana; ancient poem.
Poita; a sacred thread.

Prasad; holy food, favor.
Pariah; the lowest caste.
Pice, or Poisa; pence.
Pooja, Poojah; worship.
Pan; a fragrant leaf, a caste.
Pandavas; five ancient heroes.
Raja; a prince.
Rajpootra; royal race; a tribe.
Ranee; a queen.
Ryot; a tenant.
Rupee; about two shillings.
Sahi; a ward of a town.
Seer; two-and-a-half pounds.
Shastra; authoritative book.
Tonjohn; an open sedan.
Yug, or Jug; age, era.
Zemindar; a landholder.
Zemindaree; an estate.

---

## ILLUSTRATIONS.



---

NOTE. In drawing up the historical part of his work, the writer has been greatly indebted to Mr. Stirling.

# ORISSA, AND ITS EVANGELIZATION.

## CHAPTER I.

Orissa, its geography—Soil, scenery and productions, climate, population, &c.

ORISSA, or the country of Ootkul, the site of the mission whose operations we purpose in the following pages to describe, has always constituted a part of the great Indian Empire. In the enumeration of the original orthodox tribes of Hindoos, its inhabitants have always been mentioned with respect, and its brahmuns placed in the foremost rank.

There is a very general persuasion among the Hindoos* that in very ancient times the whole of India was really or nominally subject to a supreme sovereign, or Lord Paramount, who held his court somewhere in the northwest provinces, usually at Delhi. To this supreme monarch four principal thrones, or monarchies, established in as many divisions of the empire, were immediately dependent, while all inferior rajas were, in their turn, subject to these four principal rulers. These were severally denominated Narapati, or Lord of Men; Chatrapati,

* See Stirling's History of Cuttack.

or Lord of the Umbrella, or insignia of state; Aswapati, or Lord of the Cavalry; Gajapati, or Lord of Elephants. The first of these princes is supposed to be the ancient sovereign of the Dakhina, or southern part of India; the second, the Mahratta or Deogiri rajas; the third, the celebrated Rajputra monarchs; and the fourth, the sovereign rulers of Orissa, including the eastern provinces generally.

Should it be contended that no proof has been found of such a sovereignty ever having existed, still it must be admitted that we may safely infer from widely and long extended tradition, that the sovereigns of Orissa sustained a rank much above the general character of Hindoo rajas.

I have spoken of the Gajapati sovereigns as ruling over the eastern provinces of the empire, and this statement agrees with the inscription on the coin and seal engraved by the order of Anunga Bhim Deb, A. D., 1180, or thereabouts, and which is used by the raja of Orissa at the present time. It reads as follows:—"The illustrious hero Gajapati, Lord of Gour, Supreme Monarch over the rulers of the tribes of Ootkul, Kernata, and the nine forts, a divinity terrible as Bhairaba to the wicked, the protector of the grants enjoyed by the pious; king of kings; like the Lord of a thousand arms in the field of battle by his unequalled might, and a comet to the martial race."

This seems to support firmly the persuasion that the empire of Orissa extended to the Hoogly river on one side, and to the Carnatic on the other, at some part of its greatest prosperity; it is confirmed by existing monuments at both extremes of the kingdom; and is, moreover, a claim which would scarcely have been put forth in this manner, had there existed no real foundation for such a claim. Orissa then, we think, may fairly be ranked among the most powerful of ancient Indian sovereignties. We must not however suppose the terms Kurnata and Gour (the Carnatic and Bengal) to embrace the whole extent of country to which these names now apply. Probably the Orissa monarchs never held *permanent* possession of any part of the country southward of the modern province of Guntoor, or east of the Hoogly. We shall notice the gradual curtailment of the boundaries of the empire hereafter, but meantime we proceed to point out the limits of Orissa as now understood.

In general terms, the whole country of Orissa may be stated as situated on the western shore of the Bay of Bengal, and including within the square formed by drawing a line from the 18th and 23d degrees of north latitude, at right angles with the 80th and 88th degrees of east longitude. In other words, it extends from the southern banks of the Hoogly river to the northern borders of the Godavari, both of which streams it touches at a few points, though receding far from it at others; while it stretches from the sea-shore, two thirds of its length, back to the chain of hills which separates it from Gundwani, Chota Nagpore, and the Cole country toward Midnapore.

From a poem entitled the "Hero of Conjeveram," it would appear that in ancient days the Orissian monarchy extended as far south as Raj Mahendry, while from the name of a ghat, or landing place, situated above Chinsurah in Bengal, it is supposed that the rulers of Orissa once extended their dominions to that spot. The Oriyas themselves say that the proper boundary of Orissa, northward, is a small temple standing on the bank of a stream called Naradaole, and that it is three koss from a village called Subariya, or ten koss to the north-east of

Midnapore. From this point, probably, the limits of the empire ran in a direct line to the Orissa Ghat, above Chinsurah on the Ganges.

On the other hand, the original country of Ootkul, it is asserted, was bounded on the north by the Kansbans river, which crosses the great road about a koss southward of Soro, and on the south by the Rasikulia or Ganjam river. Certain it is that within these limits, at the present day, the Oriya language is spoken in its greatest purity, and the Oriya manners and customs, weights and measures, every where prevail; while to the north of these limits the Bengali accent and terminations to some nouns and verbs are current, just as on the south of Ganjam the Oriyas vary the pronunciation of certain words after the fashion of the Telingas or Teloogoos.

The Bengali language, however, does not preponderate until we cross the Kaliya Gye or Injellee river, to the southward of Naraingara; nor does the Telinga, excepting along the sea-shore, until we reach the banks of the Godavari. Small communities may be found beyond these boundaries among whom the Oriya language and the Oriya manners and customs prevail, and who are in fact Oriyas. While in Calcutta there is a community of at least 20,000 to 30,000 Oriyas, employed chiefly as Palkee bearers, house servants, caulkers, gardeners, &c.

Whatever may have been the real original boundaries of Orissa, they have long since undergone various alterations. Partly from the practice of apportioning certain districts to the descendants of the royal house of Orissa, and partly to suit the convenience of the collectors of revenue under various administrations, the province of Orissa has suffered numerous curtailments. The whole of the hill regions are parcelled out to some thirty Gurjat rajas, and indeed some portions of the plains also, as, for instance, those of Al, Konika, Domrá, Murichpoor, &c. The whole country north of the Subanreeka has been transferred to the Midnapore division of Bengal, and all south of the Khurda district and Chilka lake has been annexed to the Ganjam collectorate, under the Madras Presidency. The remainder, called the Mogulbundi, comprises the modern province of Orissa. Thus reduced to its narrowest limits, it is divided into three zillas or civil districts, called the north or Balasore division; the central or Cuttack division; and the southern, or Pooree, or Khurda division of Cuttack. Over this portion of Orissa, which is in fact the best and most populous, the Honorable Company hold absolute sway, while most of the Gurjat rajas are tributary.

From these different views of the extent and limitations of the province at various periods, the reader, it is hoped, will be able to distinguish between Orissa, when spoken of generally in its largest sense, or when referred to in its modern, limited extent. We shall, in a subsequent chapter, consider more particularly the present state of the province as it respects its civil and moral condition; and in this, endeavor to describe its physical aspect, soil, rivers, climate, animal, vegetable and mineral productions and population, with such other matters as may suggest themselves as we proceed.

Were a traveller to commence his journey through Orissa at Kedgeree, that is from the banks of the Hoogly river, near the sea, he would first enter upon a low, swampy tract of country, intersected in all directions by rivers and streams, and covered with low jungle, and tall coarse grass. These jungles swarm with wild hogs, tigers, buffaloes and other destructive animals, while the rivers abound with fish and alligators. Here the voice of numerous flocks of water fowl is heard in all directions, and vast herds of cattle are seen grazing on the open plains. The tangled brushwood and numberless creeping plants every where threaten to oppose the progress of the pedestrian, but, at the same time, their verdant foliage and gay flowers pleasingly divert his attention from the toil of the way. In this tract of country great quantities of very fine salt are manufactured, and the population consists, to a great extent, of the Molunghees, employed in its manufacture. Here and there may be seen a cowherd, watching his scattered herd of tame buffaloes, whose fierce looks and wild stare are enough to frighten a person unaccustomed to these animals, while from almost every tree and bush, the soft cooing of the turtle dove diffuses a pleasing pensiveness over the mind.

As the traveller proceeds, he will discern, in all directions, little villages seated amidst embowering trees, as though the intention of the rural population was to render their naturally lonely home yet more obscure and screened from the eye of strangers. This belt of jungle being past, the traveller, if he continue his course along the sea-shore, will soon emerge from his sheltered pathway and enter upon a widely extended tract of barren sand. Here the sun seems to pour down his rays in a perpetual stream, and the parched traveller looks around him in vain for some friendly tree or some refreshing shade. The surface of the sand is frequently covered by a long and strong creeper, bearing a bright reddish flower, which diffuses itself in all directions, forming a kind of net work over which it is difficult to walk. Here and there a stunted palm, or a tuft of coarse beni grass is to be seen, and occasionally a small temple varies the otherwise dull uniformity of the scene.

In this region the inexperienced traveller may be often deceived by the mirage or sultry vapor, spreading before him like a widely extended lake bestudded with verdant islands, but which, in reality, are the elevated sand hills surrounded by this mirage in a kind of giratory movement, but which does not rise high enough to overtop them. Such probably are the delusive appearances of water noticed by travellers on the deserts of Arabia and Africa.

This tract of sand continues, to a greater or less extent in breadth, all the way to Ganjam; occasionally a few fishermen's huts may be seen built upon the sea-shore, while at Chandipore and Pooree are the bungalows belonging to Europeans; otherwise the whole tract seems abandoned, of necessity, to the straggling herds of deer, which manage to pick up a subsistence from the sweet spiral grass and wild thyme growing on the sand.

The sea, however, produces an abundance of delicious fish, of which upwards of sixty kinds are enumerated, and the salt waters from the various creeks, and especially from the Chilka lake, yield a rich harvest of excellent salt.

Throughout the whole of this district, the people are more or less familiarized to the sight of various sea-going vessels, to which the inland population are strangers; and occasionally a stately merchant ship may be seen from the coast on its way to or from Calcutta, ploughing the blue waves of the Bay of Bengal.

If, however, instead of pursuing his course along the sandy shore, the traveller incline towards his right hand, that is, towards the north-west, he will soon enter upon an open country generally every where cultivated, but occasionally he will observe tracts of jungle or vast plains, at present simply devoted to pasturage for innumerable herds of cattle. Along the banks of rivers, and in a few favored spots, will be seen patches of tobacco plants, mustard seed, linseed, and various kinds of pulse, but the prevailing produce in the cultivated portions is rice. To a person passing through the province between the months of August and November, the whole tract here referred to will appear like one continuous rice field; from koss to koss, yea, from one day's travel to another, and, if a pedestrian, even from one week's to another, he will see scarcely any thing but rice, rice, rice, rice, in apparently endless continuation. In some parts of the province, however, wheat is grown, and towards the hills, fields of ragge and kangu, small farinaceous seeds, are to be seen.

As the traveller proceeds southwards, though still inclining towards the west, he will be gratified with large topes of mangoe trees, and here and there, by the wayside, the banyan spreads its umbrageous arms, inviting the weary traveller to its refreshing shade. The villages occupied by the brahmuns and the more wealthy individuals, are adorned with the towering cocoanut and the graceful areca, while, in all directions, may be seen the bel tree, the jaka, the jam, the custard apple, the kendoo, and wild plum trees of numerous kinds.

Over the thatched cottages of the peasantry may be seen climbing the kudoo and the spinage vine, and around the premises tall plantations of the castor-oil tree. Gardens, properly speaking, are not often met with; the Oriya seldom extends his ideas of culinary cultivation beyond the baigun khait, (egg plant field,) a few brinjals, kutchus, various kinds of sag, and the universal plantain.

Beyond this extended plain, the most part of which is evidently of alluvial formation, and which is usually designated the Mogulbundi, stretches far away the Nila giri, or blue hills of Orissa. As the traveller enters the province from the north-eastern extremity, he obtains the first sight of the hills a few miles before he reaches Balasore, and they thenceforth continue to form a distinct feature in the scenery of the country, very pleasingly contrasting with the dull sameness of the plains of Bengal.

At Balasore the hills project boldly forward to within five or six miles of the great road, and as the traveller approaches Cuttack, isolated mountains, in a few instances, are seen to the southward of the road; the chain then again recedes till it reaches the borders of the Chilka, where they once more stretch down to its very shores, and at Ganjam a low ridge appears actually to run out into the sea. The range then stretches away to the westward, across the Dakhin towards Bombay.

The whole of the hill district on the southern side, from Balasore to Raj Mahendry, has been parcelled out among what are termed the Gurjat rajas, who all claim to be descended from the ancient sovereigns of Orissa, and to whom, probably, these respective rajuaries were formerly entrusted, not as their own bona fidé inheritance, but as zemandari estates.

As the traveller approaches the hills, he finds himself every where surrounded by gradually thickening jungles, large clumps of thorny bamboos, and not unfrequently, immense plats of the tall, coarse beni grass, which is usually used for thatch. It is, however, but for a short distance, that man can penetrate into these interminable jungles; they gradually become so dense, that, excepting where the hand of man, or oftener the kind hand of nature has opened a road, it would seem as if all approach to the neighboring hills was interdicted. The writer has, however, scaled the highest rocky elevation opposite to Balasore, and visited the festival held on the Kapilas purbata, the largest mountain seen north-west of Cuttack. A more favorable view of the hill scenery may be obtained by sailing some forty or fifty koss up the Mahanuddee. Although designated a chain of hills, no such thing has come under the writer's observation. As the mountains are approached, they are seen to consist rather of irregular groups, or isolated hills, assuming all manner of fantastic shapes, and suggesting to the mind of the traveller a resemblance to elephants, and other creatures. Many of these hills have "peaked and waving summits, which seem to cross each other at all angles," and most of them are covered with vegetation to the very top.

From these hills, vast quantities of useful timber might be obtained; and the quantity actually brought into Cuttack, and some other places, for home consumption and for exportation, is not inconsiderable, though immeasurably below what it might and ought to be.

These hills and jungles abound with all kinds of wild animals, which afford abundant sport for the European residents in the province.

"The greatest height of the hills seen from the Mogul bunda, may be about 2,000 feet; their ordinary elevation may vary from 300 to 1,000 feet. Ranges occur further back, it is said, of greater loftiness and regularity; the prevailing color of the rock being a kind of coarse red granite, studded with quantities of imperfectly formed garnets. In the neighborhood of Bhobaneswer, however, what are called the Khundagiri, a few isolated hills of white and varied sandstone, occur. It is said that these hills exhibit the same geological characteristics as the Himalaya mountains, and singular enough is the current tradition, that these rocks were dropped by the celebrated Hunumán in his journeys to and fro for materials to build the bridge called Seta bund rameswar, viz:—from the main land of the peninsula, to Lunka, or Ceylon."

But we have detained the reader long enough with this general description of the physical aspect of Orissa, and must proceed to notice briefly its soil, rivers, climate, animals, productions and population.

Were it in the writer's power, it would be entirely out of place to enter into scientific details in this introductory chapter. For the best information hitherto published in relation to Orissa, the reader is referred to Mr. Stirling's work. We have simply to observe that the hills afford abundance of iron ore. Coal has been discovered in several places, and some of the rivers are said to have golden sands.

Lime-stones, called ghenti, are found scattered over the whole face of the country in the neighborhood of the hills, and among the hills themselves, are said to be more abundant still. These are collected and burnt, and furnish most of the lime used in the province, except, indeed, near the coast, where an excellent lime is made from the shells cast on the beach by the tide.

The soil of Orissa, generally speaking, is said to be of a hungry and unfruitful description. The writer apprehends this is too unfavorable and sweeping a statement. The flourishing state of the Sasuna or Brahmun villages, plainly show that much of the comparative unproductiveness of Orissa, generally, is to be ascribed to a want of judicious and sufficient cultivation of the land, rather than to any inherent sterility.

Orissa is, for the most part, a well watered province,

or, rather, it should be said that Providence, by a liberal bestowment of rivers and streams, has furnished the means, which might be improved to spread fertility over the land. As the traveller proceeds through the province from north to south, his progress is arrested by numerous streams which cross his path. Of these, the Subanrikha, the Bara Bolong, the Kansbans, the Solandi, the Boitarani, the Khursua, the Brahmuny, the Mahanuddee, the Katjoory, the Khusbhadra, the Doya, &c., are the chief. Some of these, after throwing off numerous branches, which spread into endless ramifications, unite, and pour their accumulated waters through their respective estuaries into the bay of Bengal. Many of the streams swell into large rivers in the rainy season, but gradually subside during the succeeding months, till, in the hot season, many become quite dry, leaving a vast bed of dry, coarse sand. All, or nearly all, become fordable at a few koss distance from the sea. The largest river is the Mahanudi, which is said to take its rise near Bustar, and after passing Sonepore, where it receives the waters of the Téalnadi, flows onward to Cuttack, where it, in turn, throws off the branch called the Katjoori, and shortly after the Birupa, all of which again divide, and subdivide, till, after endless meanderings, they find their way to the sea.

These rivers, however, with which Orissa is so amply supplied, minister but a fraction of the good they might impart, and often prove positively injurious. With great advantage to the interest of all parties, reservoirs might be excavated, or secured by embankments, which should retain these fructifying streams for the benefit of the parched crops, instead of allowing them to rush headlong to the sea, sometimes in such vast masses that they overflow their banks, and carry, not fertility, but destruction before them. A precaution of this kind would doubtless do much to avert those dreadful famines, such as a few years since spread so much misery through the land.

The *climate* of Orissa, as it respects salubrity, should be spoken of in reference to the three natural divisions of the province, viz:—the eastern angle formed by the sea and the Ganges; the Mogulbundi; and the hilly districts. The first may be designated as unhealthy; and especially so for the inhabitants of the inland portion of the province.. Nevertheless, after emerging from the jungly districts, and entering upon the sandy beach, a residence there for a few months during the hot season, is by Europeans generally deemed beneficial. The bungalows at Pipplee, Bularam Gherry, Gopalpore and Pooree, are sufficient evidence of the estimation in which the salubrious sea-breezes are held by Europeans. Natives unaccustomed to the sea air do not esteem it salutary, and are anxious to escape from it.

The Mogulbundi generally must be deemed healthy, and in the writer's estimation it is very superior to Bengal; the refreshing sea breezes blow daily over the land, especially during the hottest part of the year; and by those who have resided longest in the province, the climate of Orissa is, for a tropical climate, deemed decidedly salubrious.

The hilly and jungly tracts of India are generally considered unhealthy, especially to Europeans, and the residents of the plains. The Gurjat people are, however, a hardy, vigorous race, and afford no reason to suppose that the climate is to them in any measure prejudicial, but rather the reverse. The experiment yet remains to be made, whether the hills at Balasore, if cleared of their jungles (not an insuperable task), might not afford a sanatarium equal to Darjeeling, at all times easily accessible.

Those awful scenes of mortality to which the province has been exposed during the past twenty years, have been—when not actually induced by it—greatly augmented by the pilgrimage to Jugernath. The wretched victims of this superstition carry back with them the seeds of disease all over the country; and some years their route may be traced with awful distinctness by the scourge which accompanies them. The villages from which no pilgrims go, remain healthy; while those who have sent any of their inhabitants to the Jattra are visited in return by the destructive cholera. Under all circumstances, these hundreds of thousands of pilgrims from a distance must be fed, and, in times of scarcity, augment that scarcity. Still, were the resources of the province properly developed, and an outlet for its produce afforded by an improvement of the water communication with Calcutta, Orissa would be well able to bear this continued draft upon her resources.

*The indigenous animals of Orissa*, may be classified as domestic and wild. Under the former head may be ranked a miserable kind of small pony, cows, draft and pack bullocks, buffaloes, sheep, goats, hogs, asses and dogs. All the above animals are far below the European standard. Of poultry, there are abundance of common fowls; ducks, geese, pigeons, and in some places a few guinea-fowls and turkeys are raised.

In the jungles are found elephants, tigers, leopards, bears, ant-eaters, hyenas, jackalls, foxes, wild buffaloes, the gyall, spotted deer, hog deer, moose deer, elk, hares, porcupines, otters, apes, peacocks, partridges, quail, snipe, wild fowl and water fowl of all kinds.

Every where, vermin and reptiles in endless variety abound.

For a list of the useful trees and plants which the province produces, the reader may consult the appendix to the Oriya dictionary;* here it may be sufficient to remark, that the wood most commonly employed for building, is sál; for doors and furniture, peásal; for furniture, boxes &c., peásal and sisoo; also kurma, ghimera, panoos, and some others.

Bamboos of various kinds flourish all over the country, but are finest on or near the hills.

All over the province, a vast variety of flowering and odoriferous creepers abound, now twining round the wild corunda, and other lowly shrubs, and now swinging in pendant branches from the tops of the tallest trees. Every where the eye is delighted with their various and lovely tints, and the olfactory nerves regaled with their delicious fragrance; among plants of this kind, the panchangalia, or gloriosa superba is every where conspicuous. The native gardens abound with marigolds; various kinds of hybiscus, jasmines, &c.

The chief produce of the country is rice, of which there are two principal crops, called the biáli and sareda. Besides these two, there are various kinds which we do not stop to notice. Next to the rice cultivation, may be mentioned in their order, pulse of various kinds, maize, wheat, millet, and vegetable oil seeds, mustard seed and castor oil plant. Then may follow sugar cane, tobacco, cotton, and about Jellasore only, indigo. There are several nurseries for the pan leaf, or piper betel, near

---

* While the writer is penning this part of his little work, he believes that more than one of the talented medical practitioners in the province, are engaged in studying the botanical and materia medica resources of the province.

Pooree and Cuttack. Turmeric, and various kinds of drugs for dyeing, and others of an intoxicating nature, also, are raised in various parts of the province, especially in the hill districts.

The vegetable list comprises the baigoon, bhindee turai, kutchoo or saroo, yams, pumpkins, kudoos, cucumbers, watermelons, sweet potatoes, potatoes, onions, lunka murich, or capsicums, and various kinds of sag.

The ordinary fruits are mangoes, oranges, lemons, jam, jaka, guava, custard apple, pine apple, kendoo, pomegranate, cashew nut, bél fruit, cocoa nut, plantains, and wild plums of various kinds.

The chief articles of exportation are timber, rice, lakh, tasser, or wild silk, wax, honey, Indian pitch, vegetable dyes, salt, skins, horns, resins and oil.

Orissa has not wanted her poets and panegyrists to sing the praises of her verdant hills and fruitful plains, her golden rivers and balmy odors, and to paint her with all the extravagance of eastern hyperbole, as the garden of the gods, a very land of Beulah—such eulogiums, no European or American visitor will be disposed to adopt; yet he may nevertheless find many a pleasant scene, and lovely landscape, on which he will love to gaze, and often, perchance, exclaim,

——"every prospect pleases,
And only man is vile."

He may even, perhaps, with the writer, when long absent from its sunny plains, sigh again to gaze upon its natural beauties, to recline beneath its banias' shade, and feel that Orissa only needs the gospel to make it a happy land.

*Population.* Independently of the express declaration of sacred writ, the laborious researches of learned men have left little room for the most skeptical to doubt that all the various divisions of the human family may be traced up to Noah and his three sons, who were preserved from the universal deluge, in the ark. But whether the Hindoos are descended directly, or by intermarriage, from the progeny of Shem, Ham or Japhet, it may be longere mankind agree to decide; or, which is not improbable, whether they have descended directly from the great patriarch himself. However that may be, it is pretty certain that the original inhabitants of Orissa were not Hindoos. The first occupants of the soil, were, in all probability, the ancestors of the Khundra, Sabara, Cole, and other mountain tribes. In proportion as the primeval family hive became overstocked, swarms of adventurers issued forth to choose for themselves a home; these, with the Babel builders, gradually spread themselves over Armenia, Assyria, Tartary, and doubtless in very early ages, crowded the western banks of the Indus. Thence, it is conjectured, those who now bear the name of Hindoos, probably from the above named river, first spread themselves over the fertile plains of India, and coming in successive masses, might give rise to the ancient division of castes. Anon, others—as is plain by the names of the Pandavas—found their way over the mountain passes from Indo-Scythia, and served to augment the growing population of India. As these new and more civilized races extended themselves, the aboriginal inhabitants retired to their unenvied retreat among the hills; where, to this day, they have perpetuated their race, and stood aloof from the language and religion of their conquerors. And there in all probability they will thus remain, till the influence of Christianity pervades their jungles and fastnesses, making them blossom as the rose. Then shall these outcasts of humanity be reunited to the redeemed family of God, and their bosoms glow with all the blissful hopes of a glorious immortality.

I have already mentioned the various boundaries, which, at different periods, have been assigned to Orissa, and I might now refer to the widely differing estimates which have been given of its population; but I must candidly admit that no sufficient data have yet been furnished to enable me to give any very definite statement in this matter. I will, however, give what I deem the nearest approximation to truth. In order, however, to reconcile some of the conflicting statements which have been put forth, it may be useful to remember that sometimes reference is had only to the subjects of the Honorable Company's Government, sometimes to the whole population of Orissa proper, sometimes to the whole extent of the province, including hill rajas, wild tribes, &c. My statements have reference to the whole field of our missionary operations. This we deem to be commensurate, not only with the Oriya language wherever spoken, but those tribes and countries bordering on Orissa, which it is probable will only be reached through the labors of the Orissa missionaries.

We commence, then, with Midnapore. This is the name, both of a city and a district; and is supposed to be next to Burdwan, the most populous district under the Bengal presidency. The portion of its population coming within the widest sphere of the Orissa mission, may be estimated at 2,000,000

Next in order is the Balasore district, or northern division of Cuttack, 600,000

Then the central division of Cuttack, or Cuttack proper, 1,200,000

Next the southern division, or Pooree, Khurda, &c., 500,000

| | |
|---|---|
| More southerly, is the Ganjam collectorate, including Berhampore and Goomsur, | 1,000,000 |
| The independent and tributary rajuaries, twenty-nine in number, | 1,000,000 |
| The aboriginal races of Coles, Khunds, Santals, &c., not included in the above estimate, | 1,000,000 |
| Europeans and East Indians in all the divisions of the province, | 500 |
| | 7,300,500 |

It is probable that the northern and southern divisions of Cuttack are underrated as to present amount of population. The writer has received from government functionaries, and from writers in the same office, such widely differing statistics of the same town and district, that he feels mistrustful of all enumerations of the population yet given to the public.

## CHAPTER II.

### A sketch of Orissian history.

The dawn of authentic history breaks upon our sight as the mists of fables and marvels clear away. Most nations are ambitious of claiming for themselves a very remote origin, and as they have no true record of the early ages to which they would fain go back, in order to substantiate their claim, they have recourse to invention.

The Oriyas have not only done this, but have claimed as their local sovereigns the same celebrated characters as are mentioned in the ancient poems of upper India; and whom, indeed, the Hindoos generally claim as common property. It is thus they all attempt to supply the want of genuine and authentic history. Thus we have the names of Judhisthira, Parakhita, Janamajaya and Bhoja, and these are mixed up with other names which may possibly have belonged to real Oriya sovereigns. The following specimen of ancient Oriya history will suffice to show the worthlessness of such statements. These names, barbarous as they seem to persons unacquainted with Indian history, are perfectly familiar to those who have made it their study.

"From the commencement of the Kalijoog to the fall of Vicramaditya, thirteen rajas are made to reign for the monstrous term of 3,173 years, or 244 for each reign, viz. :—

| | | | |
|---|---|---|---|
| Judhistira, | 12 years. | Asoka, | 150 years. |
| Pareekhita, | 357 " | Bajranath, | 107 " |
| Janmajaya, | 516 " | Jarasanka, | 115 " |
| Sankara, | 410 " | Hansá, | 122 " |
| Gōtama, | 373 " | Bhoj, | 127 " |
| Mahindra, | 215 " | Vicramaditya, | 135 " |
| Ashti, | 134 " | Total, | 3,173 years." |

After this the era of Salibahana, which dates from A. D., 77, in Orissa, is used in all the accounts, and we come to reigns of a probable length. The rajcharitra or history of the kings, says, Karmajit son of the above, ruled over Orissa and died the era of Salibahana 65. Then follows

| | | | |
|---|---|---|---|
| Bata Kesari, | 51 years. | Bhim, | 37 years. |
| Tribhobana, | 43 " | Subhan, | " |
| Nirmul, | 45 " | Indra, | " |

During the reign of Subhan Deo, there is said to have been an invasion of the Yavanas, headed by Raktabahu, who drove the raja to the jungles, where he died. His son and successor, Indra Deo, was captured and put to death, and the Yavanas ruled Orissa for 146 years; thus were completed years 396 of the Sacábda.

Two memorable events are said to have occurred during the invasion by Raktabahu. The first was the carrying off the image of Jugernath to Sonepoor Gopalli, where it was buried and a bir tree planted over it; and the other was the formation of the Chilka lake by an irruption of the ocean. Both are embellished by the Oriya historian with many remarkable circumstances, which, in the nature of things, it is impossible could have occurred, and which therefore we shall not repeat.

The probability is, that the whole of the above is pure fiction, intended to fill up the gap occasioned by the want of authentic records prior to the accession of the Kesari Bansa rajas in A. D., 473. At all events, this is the earliest period from which we can, at present, date the true history of Orissa.

Lest the reader of these sketches should however cling to the idea that the Orissian records are worthy of credit, it may be remarked that the same names are claimed by nearly every petty sovereignty in India, and, of course, they could not belong to all. That the time in which they are said to have reigned, is opposed to ascertained facts, —raja Bhoja having lived in the 9th or 10th century, while the date assigned to the invasion of the Yavanas,* supposing by this term the Mussulmans be intended, is long anterior to the birth of Mahomed, the founder of that sect. The first recorded invasion of Mahomed was in the year of Christ 1000, and, moreover, that invasion only extended to the province of Mooltan.

It is a remarkable fact, that while the Hindoos have, from the earliest ages, been devoted to literary pursuits, and have produced grammarians, metaphysicians and poets of the first order, they have entirely neglected their own history. Even the Mahabharut and the Ramayuna, the national histories of the Hindoos, contain few facts elucidatory either of the origin of the Hindoo race, their settlement in India, or their progress in occupying the land. We are left to infer, from a few ambiguous expressions and a few obscure ceremonies, that the ancestors of the Hindoo family came from the north-west of the Indus, and gradually supplanted the original inhabitants of the land, who are supposed to have been the ancestors of the Bheels, Coles, Goands, Sabaras, and other mountain or jungle tribes.

We read in an ancient inscription on a pillar at Buddal, of the eradicated race of Ootkul; but who these were, or who were the eradicators, is at present mere conjecture.

Amidst this general neglect of history, perhaps the

* As the Oriyas have mixed up many matters connected with Upper India in their so called annals of the province, it is not improbable that some reference is here made to the invasion of Alexander and the Bactrian Greeks.

brahmuns of Orissa have been least blameworthy. They have certainly preserved in the Mundali Panji and Raj Charitra, a record of events of a much more ancient date than is to be found in most parts of India, (always excepting Cashmere,) and from these records, aided by collateral testimony, the materials for this brief sketch are drawn.

### THE KESARI RACE OF RAJAS.

The founder of this dynasty was Jajati Kesari, a warlike and energetic prince, but of his origin and pedigree we are not informed. He is said to have expelled the Yavanas from his dominions, who then retired to their own country ; but neither are we apprized who these Yavanas were, nor where their country was situated. Jajati built a fort and palace at Jajipoor, where he held his court, and where the last faint vestiges of a royal residence are yet discernible. The most important event of this reign is said to have been the recovery of the image and the restoration of the worship of Jugernath. It is however very questionable whether this is not an improved version of the Kali pahar affair, mentioned hereafter, foisted into the ancient records with a view of establishing a much more ancient date for this worship than genuine history warrants.

Towards the close of this reign, the building of the temples at Bhobaneswar commenced, and in A. D., 520, the raja Jajati Kesari closed his mortal career.

He was succeeded by Lalata Indra Kesari, who completed the building of the great temple at Bhobaneswar, A. D., 657, and dedicated the same to Mahadaiv, under the title of Ling Raj Bhobaneswera. He also founded there a large and populous city containing seven sahis and forty-two streets, which became the capital of the raj. The ruins of two extensive palaces, belonging to the rajas of the Kesari line, are still shown near Bhobaneswer. There is also a superb tank, called the Binda Sagara, on the north, and another, surrounded by small antique looking temples, on the east, which serve, in connection with surrounding ruins, to attest the former magnificence of the place.

After the death of Lalata Indra thirty-two princes, extending through a period of 455 years, sat upon the throne of the Gaja Patis; but with the exception of a few stories relating to Jugernath and Bhobaneswar, nothing of their history is recorded. Cuttack is said to have been founded by Raja Nirupe Kesari, A. D., 989, and the stone rivetment to have been constructed by Markat Kesari, A. D., 1006. While Madhab Kesari is said to have built the fortress at Sarangara.

Different accounts are given of the extinction of the Kesari family. The Raj Charitra says that the last of the line died childless, while the Bansa Boli says that he was deposed by a southerner named Churang Deb, who was instigated to invade the province by Basudeb Banpati, a brahmun, and powerful officer of the court. All, however, agree in placing the extinction of this race of princes in A. D., 1131, or A. S., 1054.

### THE GANGA-BANSA (RACE) OF RAJAS.

Churang or Sarang Deb, or as he is also called Chor Ganga, conquered Cuttack 13th Aswin, 1131, and thus ascended the throne of Orissa. With him began the race of princes called Ganga-bansa, who ruled the country for 400 years. This is the most brilliant and important portion of Orissa history.

Churang Deb sat upon the throne of Orissa for twenty years. He is said to have been a worshipper of Devi, to the neglect of all other gods and goddesses. He built a sáhi and tank at Pooree, which was called after his name, and to him is ascribed the building of a fort and palace at Choudwar and also at Sarangara. He is moreover said to have commenced the record at Pooree, called the Mandala Panji.

His son, Gungeswara Deb succeeded, A. D., 1151. His dominions extended from the Godavari to the Ganges. He had five Cataks or royal residences, viz., Jajipoor, Choudwar, Amrabati, Chatua and Biranasi, that is the modern Cuttack. Amrabati is said to have been situated near the Kishna, and may have been the original seat of the Gunga race of princes. This, too, may have occasioned the frequent intercourse, both friendly and adverse, between the Gajapati princes and those of Telingana and the Carnatic. This raja is said to have committed incest with his own daughter, and, as an expiation, to have dug the splendid tank called Kousala Gunj, situated between Pipply and Khurda. Such were the morals of the Gajapati rajas in those days.

After two short and unimportant reigns, Anung Bhim Deb, the most illustrious of the Ganga-bansa princes, ascended the throne of Orissa. He resided, during the early part of his reign, at Jajipoor, but from some omen was subsequently induced to build a magnificent palace on the site of Fort Barabatti, where he afterwards chiefly held his court. Partly from his own inclination, and partly to expiate the offence of killing a brahmun, he built numerous temples, bridges, tanks, wells and ghats. He also founded 460 sasans or brahmun villages. But his most celebrated work was the erection of the great temple of Jugernath, under the superintendence of his minister, Paramhans Bajpoi, at an expense of from thirty to forty lacks of rupees. The date of its completion was A. D., 1196, when the worship was either established or reëstablished with great splendor.

Under the superintendence of his ministers, Damodarbara Pundit and Iswar Patnaik, he is said to have measured the whole of his dominions, extending from the Godavari to the Hoogly, and from Sonepoor to the sea. The results were as follows :—

| | |
|---|---|
| Total contents, (each batti containing 20 bighas,) . . . . . . . . . . . | 62,28,000 |
| Deduct for beds of rivers, hills and sites of towns, &c., with other waste land, . . . | 14,80,000 |
| Battis, . . | 47,48,000 |

Of this, 24,30,000 battis were reserved for the personal expenses of the raja, and the remaining 23,18,000 battis were assigned for the support of his chiefs, armies, officers of state and establishment generally.

He ordered the seal to be struck which bears the inscription already referred to, and which is still used by the Khurda rajas.

Many of the titles of persons of distinction now in general use, as Sawant, Mungraj, Bara Jenna, Patsahani, Bara Punda, &c., were introduced at that period. Other important changes and arrangements, whose influence may even now be traced, are ascribed to Raja Anung Bhim Deb, which may excite our regret that a more full and accurate account of his reign and personal character have not been transmitted to posterity.

Anung Bhim Deb was succeeded by his son, Rajeswara Deb, who reigned thirty-five years. After which Narsing Deb, surnamed Langora, ascended the throne, A. D., 1236. He was a prince of great celebrity in the annals of Orissa, as well as in its legends and romances.

He was remarkable for his strength and skill in athletic exercises, and from some peculiarity in his dress or personal appearance, received his singular cognomen of Langora. He was also engaged in warlike enterprises, especially towards the Deccan. It was this raja who built the Kanarac Pagoda or Temple of the Sun, and which was completed under the direction of his minister, Shibar Santra, A. D., 1277.

Five other rajas, all named Nara Singh, succeeded Langora raja, and six with the title of Bhanu, which are sometimes represented as a separate family, called the Suryabansa. Their reigns are not remarkable for any great or stirring events, though it should never be forgotten, that such reigns are often productive of the greatest amount of happiness to the people. There are, however, still traces of their public spirit, such as the Atara nalah bridge at Pooree, built A. D., 1300, by Kabir Narsingh Deb, which may corroborate the above remark.

A dreadful famine occurred early in the 14th century, when paddy rose to the then enormous price of 120 kahans of couries for a bharan, sixty times the ordinary selling price of that age. It is said that, ordinarily, clear rice sold for ten couries a ser, and cotton, one pan, ten gundas a ser.

The last of the Bhanu rajas being childless, adopted as his son and successor a youth of the Suraj bansi tribe of Rajputs, named Kapila Santra. He became the celebrated Kapil Indra Deb, and ascended the throne, A. D., 1451. He spent his reign in military expeditions, and resided chiefly at Kimedy and Raja Mandry. Among his conquests are mentioned a fort called Kondjuri, perhaps Condapilly, and places called Maligunda and Malka or Malanca, perhaps Maha Lanka or Ceylon, as he is mentioned having pursued his victories to Ramas bridge or Setabund Rameswara. His history is embellished, by the native chroniclers, with a variety of supernatural occurrences, even in his boyhood, which were prophetic of his future greatness.

During this reign the Moguls appear to have first come in contact with Orissa, and from the history of the Bahmani sovereigns of Kalberga we are enabled to supply the omissions which occur in the Oriya annals. A long and harrassing campaign disturbed the declining years of Kapila Indra Deb, in which he was frequently worsted by the Mussulmans. He was at length instructed by Shri Jugernath to elect Pursottom, his youngest and illegitimate son, as his successor, much to the annoyance of his other six sons. The favored youth accompanied the raja in his last expedition to the banks of the Kistna, where Kapila Indra Deb shortly after died.

The election of Pursottom Rai, the intrigues of his brothers to effect his destruction, his miraculous preservation by Jugurnath, and his conquest of Conjeveram, are fully detailed in an original poem called Kanji Kaberi Pothi, and which, with the exception of a few passages, deserves to be printed for the use of Oriya students.

The substance of the above poem is as follows. Pursottom Deb was the accepted candidate for the hand of the beautiful daughter of the Conjeveram raja. In making inquiries, however, into the customs of the royal house of Orissa, the southern chief ascertained that the Gajapati princes were in the habit of sweeping the car of Jugernath at the commencement of the ruth Jattra. He was a worshipper of Gunesh, and could not but view with disgust so humiliating a ceremony; he, therefore, broke off the alliance. The Gajapati monarch, on his part, determined to revenge the insult, and swore to obtain the lady by force and marry her to a real sweeper.

After a long struggle, in which the gods took part with their respective votaries, Conjeveram fell before the armies of Orissa. The chief escaped, but the beautiful Padmini was captured and carried in triumph to Pooree. Conformably with his oath, Pursottom made over the lady to his minister with instructions to marry her to a chandala. The minister, however, and the people generally commisserated her misfortunes, and at the next ruth Jattra, as the raja was performing the usual ceremonies, the minister produced the lady, saying to the raja, "You are the sweeper to whom I present the princess." The raja yielded to the general wish, and married the beautiful Padmabati. She subsequently brought forth a son and then mysteriously disappeared. Pursottom Deb died soon after, leaving this child as his successor, having reigned twenty-five years.

### PARTAB RUDRA DEB.

This prince, the mysterious son of Padmabati, ascended the throne of the Gajapatis, A. D., 1503. He was learned, devout, warlike, and eminent in all royal virtues. He was, however, so impressed with a sense of the learning and skill of the Buddhists, that he for a long time was a warm supporter of that sect. His Rani, on the other hand, as zealously espoused the cause of the brahmuns. In order to test their relative skill, a snake was carefully concealed in a closed jar, and the vessel brought before a large assembly at the palace. Both parties were then asked what the jar contained. The brahmuns replied, it contains only earth; and, on examination, such was found to be the case. This miracle entirely changed the raja's views, and he now became a violent opposer of the Buddhists, and burned all their books excepting the Amára Coss and Bira Singh. It is added, that about this time Choitanya Maha-probhu came into the province and performed many miracles before the raja. In all probability this is the key to the whole story, and henceforward Buddhism declined and the tenets of Choitanya spread rapidly through Orissa. Perhaps, however, what are called Buddhists were really Jains, who have still a temple dedicated to Parushnath at Khundi Giri.

Partab Rudra died, A. D., 1524, having reigned twenty-one years, and with him ended the glory of the Ganga-bansa dynasty. Pressed at both extremities by the vigor and enterprise of the Mahommedans of Bengal and Telingana, the downfall of the Orissian monarchy was further hastened by famine, intestinal commotions, and a series of bloody contests for the supreme dignity. Partab Rudra left thirty-two sons. The eldest of these reigned five years, and was then murdered by the powerful minister, Gobinda Bidyadhar. Another son succeeded, but was murdered at the close of a year. The minister then butchered the remaining thirty sons, and other persons of eminence, and thus waded up to his neck in blood to the throne. He assumed the title of Raja Gobind Deb, A. D., 1533, and reigned for seven years.

Two remarkable personages became celebrated during this period, Mukund Harichandar, the Telinga, who subsequently became raja, and was the last independent sovereign of Orissa ; the latter, Danya Bidyadhor, though not himself a raja, was the parent of rajas, and, in fact, the ancestor of the third and titular branch of the Gajapatis of Orissa, known, in after times, as the rajas of Khurda.

After the short and turbulent reigns of Partab Chakra Deb and Narsingh Jenna, Mukund Hurichandar, the governor of Cuttack ascended the throne, A. D., 1550, under the well-known title of Telinga Mukund Deb. All the native accounts concur in describing their last independent raja as a man of courage and ability. In the early part of his reign he was employed in constructing temples, tanks and other works of superstition or public utility. He founded a ghat and temple at the sacred spot called Tribeni, on the Hoogly, which, with the town of that name, formed the extreme verge of his dominions. Whilst so occupied, frequent communications are said to have passed between him and the court of Delhi. Soloman Gurjani, the governor of Bengal, having assembled an army to invade Orissa, the raja built a strong fortress to oppose him, in which he was successful for this time. Telinga Mukund Deb was however defeated and killed by the terrific Kálapahar, A. D., 1558. Two titular princes were subsequently set up, who both fell into the hands of the conquerors, and were by them put to death. An anarchy of twenty-one years' duration then ensued, during which the Affghan Mohammedans possessed the whole open country, and there was no raja.

## KALAPAHARA.

The several accounts which have been handed down, of the character and deeds of this scourge of Orissa, differ widely in the details, though the main facts are well known and attested. The Hindoos say of this dreaded enemy of their religion and images, that he was originally a brahmun, but lost caste through a contrivance of the princess Gaura, who was smitten with the manly beauty of his person. He then married her, turned Mussulman, and became a relentless persecutor of the faith from which he had apostatized. Many dire omens preceded and announced his invasion of the province; amongst others, a large stone fell from the top of the great temple at Pooree, and when he entered the sacred Khetra, a general darkness overspread the four corners of the land. At the sound of his wonder working kettle-drum, the ears and feet of the idols would drop off for many koss all around, and, in short, that nothing could resist his infernal agency.

The Mussulmans say that Makand Deb, apprehending the designs of the governor of Bengal, encamped with a large army on the Ganges; but Kálapahara, turning his position, got ahead of him into Orissa, and before any force could be brought to oppose him, began to plunder the country, and attack the temples with relentless fury. A battle at length took place at Jajipore, in which the raja lost his life. The Affghan chief then went on to Sumbhulpore, where he was put to death by some traders; others say that as he passed the great temple at Bhobaneswar, a swarm of bees issued from the seat of the idol and stung him to death. Again it is said that Makand Deb being unable to oppose his powerful foe, fled to the dominions of the king of Delhi, where he shortly after died. All accounts, however, agree in speaking of the cruel excesses committed by the Affghan conqueror, and the wide destruction of images and temples occasioned by this furious persecutor.

The adventures of the great image of Jugernath, form a curious episode in the history of this important period. According to the Mandala Panji, "when the priests at Pooree saw the turn which matters were taking, they for the third time placed the god in a covered cart and buried him in a pit at Parákud, on the Chilka Lake. Kálapahara, however, was not to be so cheated out of so rich a prize; and having traced out the place of concealment, he dug up the image, carried him off as far as the Ganges on an elephant, breaking in pieces as he went, every image he could find. On arriving at the banks of the Hoogly, he kindled a large fire, and threw the idol on the burning pile; but immediately all his limbs dropped off, and he perished miserably. A bystander exclaimed, 'This is a punishment for insulting the god of Orissa,' and snatching the burning image from the flames, threw it into the river. Besar Mahanti, a faithful worshipper of Jugernath, watched the whole proceeding; and as the half burned image floated down the stream, he managed unperceived to extract the sacred part, and brought it carefully to Orissa, when it was placed in the custody of the Khandait of Kujang." The first part of this account is probably substantially correct; the latter part is opposed to better accredited statements.

### BHOI BANSA RAJAS.

At the close of the twenty-one years of anarchy, A. D., 1580, the ministers and principal men of the country recovered in some measure from their confusion, and chose as their chief, Ranai Raotra, son of Danaye Bidyadhor, whom they raised to the rank of maharaja of Orissa, under the title of Ramchandra Deb. With him begins the third and titular race of sovereigns called the Bhoi Bansa, or Zemindara race. The election was confirmed by Sewai Jye Singh, general of the Emperor Akber, who about this time visited the province, and who shortly after retired, favorably impressed with his visit, and leaving a large share of authority in the hands of its native princes. The town of Midnapore was at this time made the northern boundary of Orissa.

Ramchandra Rajas' first care was to recover the sacred deposit extracted from the old image of Jugernath—have a new body prepared — and the worship reëstablished according to the original order. Both the worship and the peace of the province were, however, soon after disturbed by an invasion from the southern Mussulmans.

A. D., 1582. The celebrated Dewan of the empire, Raja Toder, or Toral Mall, visited the province on revenue affairs, and introduced the Báre Dasti Padiki or rod of twelve spans. The Mogul settlement of Orissa was not, however, completed till A. D., 1592, when Raja Man Singh assumed charge of the administration. The two sons of Makand Deb, the eldest named Ram Chandra Rai, and the second Chakóri Bhowerber, continued to give much trouble, until at length Man Singh made the following arrangement. To Ram Chandra Deb were assigned Khurda, with Pooree, and certain Mahals, in Zemandari tenure free of all tribute, with the title of Maha Raja, and the Mussulman dignity of commandership of three thousand five hundred. He was also allowed to exercise the sovereignty over 129 killas, or jurisdictions of the Khetris of Orissa, including all the present Cuttack tributary Mehals south of the Mahanadi, and the estates Goomsur, Moherry, &c., reaching to the borders of Kimidy in Ganjam. To Ram Chandra Rai, eldest son of Telinga Makand Deb was assigned as a Zemandari Killa, Al, with its dependencies; and to Chakóri Bhowerber, Sarengura on the same tenure. Both were acknowledged as rajas, and had the control of the Killajat estates in different parts of the district.

To the raja of Khurda, the title of sovereignty has in modern times always been assigned. He is still the sole fountain of honor in the province, and all deeds drawn out in the Oriya language, bear the ank or date of the reigning prince. Ram Chandra Deb enjoyed his station and dignities for twenty-nine years, and his memory is still cherished with veneration. From his time, however, the history of the province ceases to be identified with the Gajapati Maharajas, and becomes involved with the perpetual conflicts of the Mahrattas and the Mussulmans, until Orissa passes under the paternal care of Britain.

The dominion of the Khurda rajas was not finally extinguished till A. D., 1804, when a most unprovoked rising against the newly established English Government, drew down upon Raja Makand Deb the vengeance of the British power. He was conquered, captured, and sent prisoner to Midnapore, while his remaining territory of Khurda was brought under the management of the British collectors. Since that period, the representatives of the Gajapati princes have been officially acknowledged only as private landholders ; but the liberal policy of government, enables them to pass their days in honorable retirement within the sacred limits of the Shri Khettra.

The following is a list of Bhoi Bansa rajas.

| | | | |
|---|---|---|---|
| Ramchundra Deb, | 1530 | Kishen Deb, | 1715 |
| Parsottem Deb, | 1609 | Gopinath Deb, | 1720 |
| Narsingh Deb, | 1630 | Ram Chandra Deb, | 1727 |
| Ganga Dhar Deb, | 1655 | Birkishore Deb, | 1743 |
| Balbhadra Deb, | 1656 | Dirb Singh Deb, | 1786 |
| Makand Deb, | 1664 | Mukand Deb, | 1793 |
| Dirb Sing Deb, | 1692 | Ram Chundra Deb, | 1818 |

## MAHRATTAS AND MUSSULMANS.

The Affghans did not disappear from the field as disturbers of the peace of Orissa, until A. D., 1611; when, having been defeated by Shujat Khan from Bengal, they at length settled peaceably in the different villages. Their descendants now form a considerable portion of the population of Orissa, under the name of Pathans.

Meantime the Khurda rajas had to maintain a conflict

with the turbulent Khandaits, till many of their rajuaries became annexed to Khurda.

Under the administration of Mohammed Taki Khan, the Naib, A. D., 1725 to 1735, most of the country north of the Subhanreeki was annexed to Bengal, while the Nizams Government obtained the entire country included between the estates called Tikully Raghunathpoor and the Chilka Lake, thus greatly reducing the revenues and authority of the Khurda rajas.

But the greatest of all calamities was now, A. D., 1743, impending over Orissa. Suddenly the Berar Mahrattas entered the province under Bhaskar Pundit, and swept the whole country up to the walls of fort Barabatti. nor did they again discontinue their plundering depredations, until finally expelled by the British, in 1803. We cannot in these brief accounts enter into the detail of Mahratta misrule, oppression, and bloodshed; but confine ourselves to a simple enumeration of the successive Soobadhars who obtained the apparent chief authority in the province.

The first, and most energetic, was Sheo Bhat Santia, who exercised a precarious and disputed authority for about eight years, viz :—to A. D., 1771.

In 1767, Narain Deb, the Zemendar of Kimedy, attempted to wrest the sceptre of the Gajapatis from the hands of Birkishore Deb. The alarmed prince called in the aid of the Mahrattas, and being unable to discharge the sum contracted for, had eventually to surrender the best portion of his dominions as security, but which he never again recovered.

In 1771 or 2, Sher Bhat was violently expelled from his government, and succeeded by Bhabani Kalna Pundit, with whom he long kept up a harassing conflict.

1775. Bhabani was recalled and Sambha Ji Ganesh

appointed his successor. His administration is remembered for its bitterness and oppressive character.

1778. Baba Ji Naik, a Mahajan, received the appointment of Soobadhar. He was opposed and imprisoned by Madhaji Hari, but again recovered his liberty in 1782, and stepped from his prison to a throne. After much intrigue, he was, however, recalled, and Madhaji allowed to return to the office of Soobadhar. In 1785, Raja Ram Pundit succeeded to the office, and by his local knowledge and respectable talents, imparted a degree of stability and character to his administration. He was the first governor who imposed a tribute on the raja of Khurda, and in other respects interfered with his authority and revenue.

In 1781, Chimina Ji Bapu came with a large army to Cuttack, under the pretence of demanding arrears of Chout from the Bengal Government. It is said that he, in connection with Raja Ram Pundit, made a final arrangement with the British officers, by which the latter agreed to pay up in full of all demands 27,00,000 rupees.

Raja Ram Pundit retired in 1800, and was succeeded first by his son Sadasáho, and after him Chimna Bala; affairs, however, were chiefly managed by Inka Ji Sukdeb, and Bala Ji Kunwar, the commander of the fort Barabatti, and principal military officer. In this state, things were found in 1803, when the province was conquered by the English armies.

# CHAPTER III.

## Present social and moral condition of Orissa.

Let us ere we close our brief sketches of Orissa, turn aside from the contemplation of war and its devastating effects, to take a general survey of those abiding features of the country which human conquests leave untouched, and of those permanent characteristics of its people which no changing dynasties can affect. While successive races of indigenous sovereigns have sat upon the throne of Orissa, and these have been supplanted by the Telinga and the Mussulman—and these again in their turn have been ousted by the Mahratta and European—the majority of the inhabitants of the land have continued to follow the same pursuits as their ancestors; to observe the same rites; to live in the same kind of mud walled cottage; to be content with the same frugal fare; and to hand down in long succession the same mode of existence to their descendants. Doubtless as to all the main features of their character, and the general purposes of their existence, the Oriyas are nearly the same as were their ancestors hundreds and perhaps thousands of years ago!

He must be less than human, who can contemplate the living representatives of this long succession of departed progenitors without deep emotion. Man, wherever found, and under whatever adventitious circumstances, is still our brother. He is bone of our bone, and flesh of our flesh; "for God hath made of one blood all nations to dwell upon the face of the earth." When shall the claims of this universal brotherhood be felt! when shall man cease to war with man, and all behold in each a "brother and a friend!" Oh, may the day soon dawn, when thus all men every where as children of the same common parent—shall love and serve the same God—seek each other's welfare—and all walk in the same peaceful path towards the same happy, eternal home!

The Hindoos generally have preserved the same costume, and observe the same customs as were noticed by the attendants of Alexander. No doubt the ancient institution of caste has had the effect of perpetuating from age to age these peculiar characteristics. The Oriyas adhere most tenaciously to this institution. Every portion of the inhabitants of the land have their distinct place assigned them in the social economy. From this position they cannot be displaced, or displace themselves, but by some act involving the deepest disgrace and social degradation. Every man is jealous of his caste. He esteems it, as the word Játi implies, his birthright. It is to him, honor, reputation, rank, and often the regulator of his religion. He esteems it his divinely appointed position among his fellow men. The lowest seem even more tenacious of caste than the highest; and entertain no idea of disgrace being attached to what we deem an inferior position in the social scale.

The original castes were four; Brahmun, Khetra, Boisya and Sudra. The three first were probably of equal rank in each other's estimation; though they had diverse duties assigned them. All wore the sacred thread, and in the earliest ages seem to have had free intercourse with each other. The Brahmuns were not so much priests, as the depositories and teachers of divine knowledge. The Khetras were to win, govern and protect kingdoms. The Boisya to engage in commerce; and the Sudras to serve all the three superior races.

Probably the first three classes were the conquerors, and the last, the conquered.

In process of time, the pure Khetras and Boisyas have become nearly if not quite extinct. Various subdivisions arising from intermarriages have taken place, and in common parlance, nearly all below the brahmuns have been denominated Sunkara burna, or mixed races. The Oriyas recognize beside the lower castes, thirty-four divisions of the mixed tribes, who all rank as Sudras, though there is a separate division called by that name. These thirty-four are designated Chatees pathuck, or thirty-four tribes of learners, whose business is to acquire some trade or means of livelihood. The following list may convey an idea both of these divisions and the leading trades or professions in Orissa.

1 Mali, or Gardener.
2 Lohari—Smith.
3 Sankari—Worker in shells.
4 Tanti—Weaver.
5 Kumhar—Potter.
6 Kansári—Brazier.
7 Barhai—Carpenter.
8 Chitrakar—Painter.
9 Roopkari—Image maker.
10 Pathariya—Stone cutter.
11 Sonar—Goldsmith.
12 Kewut—Fisherman.
13 Boidya—Physician.
14 Mahanti—Writer.
15 Gowala—Cowkeeper.
16 Bhandari—Barber.
17 Gowria—Confectioner.
18 Baniya—Druggists and money changers.
19 Chasa—Husbandman.
20 Naik—Astrologer.
21 Teli—Oilman.
22 Tiur—Fisherman.
23 Chamár—Leather dresser.
24 Sundi—Liquor seller.
25 Dhoba—Washerman.
26 Magora, or Sikhari—Huntsman.
27 Shewala—Toddy seller.
28 Pátra—Cloth seller.
29 Dom—Mat maker.
30 Tula Bhaniya—Cotton beater.
31 Kandra—Watchman.
32 Chunari—Lime seller.
33 Bouria, &c.—Laborer.
34 Pan—Cain workers, horse keepers, &c.

These professions are sometimes differently stated.

Even the low castes, or no castes, have their various minute subdivisions, to which each rigorously adheres.

Loss of caste is not sinking from a higher to a lower class, but from caste to no caste. There is no resting place for the fallen, but the base of the social system. None but a Hindoo understands what is meant by the fearful term outcaste. It is to be esteemed as "the offscouring of all things."

The regular castes of Oriyas have ever been esteemed genuine Hindoos. Their brahmuns are mentioned in the Pooranas as being of a pure and orthodox class, and are proportionably proud and bigoted. There are, however, numerous grades of them; some classes cultivate the soil, and seem to have nothing to distinguish them, but the sacred thread and the name of brahmun. Altogether, the brahmuns are supposed to constitute a third part of the population; but this is probably an overstatement. The other classes of the Oriya population of the plains, rank under some of the general subdivisions of Soodras. The Mussulmans are called Pathans, and are, for the most part, descendants of the Affghan race; they constitute perhaps a tenth part of the whole population, and occasionally add a few to their number by conversion from among the Hindoos. I believe such conversions are more frequent among females than males, and arise chiefly from concubinage, or some kind of illicit intercourse. At least several such instances have come to my knowledge.

The mountain tribes are by some supposed to be the aborigines of the country, who have been driven to their present retreat among the jungles and fastnesses of the hills by the early conquerors of India. But of this they seem to retain no idea. They can scarcely be said to have any *system* of religion among them, though, as is the case among all barbarous tribes, some few rude ceremonies and superstitious practices are observed. The

Coles, Khunds, Santals, Sabaras, and various branches of the Cole tribes, differ considerably in their appearance, language and manners, from their more civilized neighbors; and we hope in a subsequent chapter, to furnish a few particulars of the chief divisions of these mountain tribes.

There is no leading trade or manufacture in the province, unless the making of salt may be so designated. Vast quantities of this valuable article, of the best and purest kind, are manufactured both at the northern and southern extremities of the province. But it is a government monopoly, and is conveyed to Calcutta in small vessels under contract, made chiefly with Europeans. The people who are employed in making the salt, are called Molunghees. The province, too, furnishes great numbers of ship carpenters, boat builders, and caulkers. Cuttack and Ganjam furnish capital house carpenters and joiners, and very good blacksmiths.

The gold and silversmiths of Cuttack, are celebrated for their skill in making all manner of ornaments, such as are worn both by Hindoos and Europeans. A Hindoo woman, if she has saved a few rupees, generally expends them in ornaments, which she keeps as her peculiar property. I believe the whole list of articles mentioned by Isaiah 3 : 18–24, may be found among the decorations of the Oriya ladies. Poor women wear bracelets of varnished clay, lac, glass, brass or bell metal; occasionally bone ornaments are seen.

The houses of the people are generally built of mud, with bamboos for rafters, and thatch covering. They are very rarely more than one story high, and are built in a quadrangular form. In villages, streets and bazars, they are often built in one continuous line; and for a temporary residence, a single house, somewhat like a stable, is run up. Occasionally they have gardens attached to these cottages, and the writer thinks they have of late years become much more common than they were twenty years ago—a cheering sign of peace and prosperity.

The houses are kept clean by the females, who very frequently smear both walls and floor with a mixture of cow-dung and earth. When well done, they are far from presenting a despicable appearance. It is said they contrast very favorably with the cabins of the Irish peasantry.

The people generally are naturally affable, cheerful, and fond of social converse. You will constantly see clusters of them sitting on the sunny side of a house or wall, in the early morning, engaged in friendly conversation; or at other times under the shade of a neighboring tree, or idol's temple. Some of them may be seen playing at cards, or a kind of chess; and among the lower classes, clusters of them meet at the low spirit shops, or toddy trees. People of the shoemaking and currier castes, and also washermen, as perhaps other low classes, are fond of uniting for a feast and carouse. In these cases they usually purchase a hog, or goat, and adjourn to a neighboring clump of trees, where they kill and cook the animal, and then sing, smoke, and revel till midnight. Similar feasts, without flesh, usually, are common in some parts of the country, when all castes unite in a midnight revel, under the name of true fellowship, but carefully abstain from all allusions to it in the daytime.

The principal opportunities for general display and enjoyment, are the idol and bathing festivals. On these occasions they stream forth in their gayest attire from all parts of the land; the fathers and brothers often carrying the little ones astride on the hip or shoulder, and the women following them in crowds. The latter are usually dressed either in white cotton cloths, with gay red or blue borders, or else in red, yellow or blue silks. The mixture of these colors in the various groups really presents a pretty appearance. The worship, if so it may be called, is soon despatched, and the leading object seems to be pleasure or gain. The brahmuns, shopkeepers, musicians and mendicants, are immersed in the cares of getting money, while the people generally abandon themselves to whatever amusements they can find; such as listening to or looking at the musical performances on drums, trumpets, cymbals, &c., accompanied by most extravagant caperings and gesticulations; or listening to the most obstreperous singing; or, perchance, seated in crowds witnessing a kind of theatrical exhibition. At the night festivals, I suppose there is abundance of what is called by St. Peter, revellings, banquetings and abominable idolatries.

They have no national gatherings or meetings for benevolent purposes, such as are common in Christian lands. Public spirit is a thing unknown, and, with the exception of the car festival at Jugernath, there is nothing of a general gathering of the people for any purpose. And that is rather the general meeting of the Hindoos of all India than of the Oriyas.

The whole tendency of Hindoo idolatry is to encourage duplicity and licentiousness. The wonder is that the people of India, generally, are not far more depraved than they are. Still, as a matter of fact, the writer is disposed to believe that there is in Orissa considerably more of conjugal fidelity, of sterling home virtues and domestic happiness, coupled with more general respectability of character, than has been ascribed to the Hindoos generally. It is impossible to visit the people in their villages, or even to witness the gatherings of the people at the above named festivals, and contemplate the comfortable looking and respectably attired family groups, without arriving at this conclusion. Wherein the conservative principle rests, may perhaps admit of controversy ; but I do not think that experienced missionaries in Orissa will dissent from my opinion. When brought under the influence of Christianity, they are a truly amiable, interesting and loveable people.

Children of both sexes generally go quite naked for three or four years, and very frequently much longer. They are usually betrothed before they reach their twelfth year, and often in mere infancy. The marriage ceremony usually takes place by the time the female has reached her fourteenth year. Marriage is an important affair, and the negociation is usually conducted by a professed match-maker. Great care is taken to select a suitable partner as to caste, degree of consanguinity, and various other particulars. The parties seldom see each other till the knot is irrevocably tied. Girls are (with the exception of a very few in the highest rank, and those devoted to prostitution,) universally untaught to read or write. We shall refer to this matter hereafter.

At twelve years of age, brahmunical lads are invested with the sacred thread. Education commences at an early period, and, for the common people, closes atfr om twelve to fourteen years of age. Many, however, continue their studies till twenty years of age.

Rev. Eli Noyes has furnished the following account of some peculiarities of the Hindoos, which may here find an appropriate place.

"As many questions are asked with respect to the manners, customs and peculiarities of the Hindoos and their country, we have thought it best to devote a part of this number in answering them.

"I. What kind of dwellings have the Hindoos?

"*Ans.* The most common are small huts about ten feet wide and fifteen feet long, the walls of which are built of mud, which is so adhesive that when dried by the powerful heat of a tropical sun becomes very hard, and may be washed with water within and without. The roof consists of bamboos and long grass, called thatch. The thatch is bound so firmly to the bamboos as to shed all rain. The roof usually projects five or six feet all around, protecting the walls from the drenching rains, which otherwise would wash them down. A complete Hindoo house consists of two apartments, and sometimes of four, like what is described above, standing so as to enclose an area fifteen or twenty feet square, which is uncovered. Several families or branches of the same family frequently occupy such a dwelling, and all meet in this open court to talk over the news of the day and transact their business. These houses seldom have any windows, in consequence of which they are rather gloomy.

"2. Another kind of house differs from the first in having walls built of sticks, or split bamboos, and plastered outside and in with mud. Some belonging to the poorer classes have no plastering at all. The Santals and all other hill tribes generally inhabit such tenements.

"3. A third kind of house has walls of mud and the roofs covered with coiled brick, called tiles, fastened to bamboos. These are more frequently used for stores and granaries. As the tiles attract the heat of the sun, they are hot almost to suffocation.

"4. A fourth kind is called a bungalow, the walls of

which are usually built of brick, burnt or unburnt, plastered with lime outside and in, and whitewashed. The roof is covered with the bamboo and thatched, with projecting eaves so as to form a veranda eight or ten feet all around the building, or at least on two sides. Such are the kind of houses in which many of the Europeans live, and in such our missionaries are now living.

"5. Another house differs from the last mentioned only in having a flat roof of masonry, like the houses in Palestine. Such was the house upon which Peter went to pray, and where he had a vision. The roofs of the houses in Calcutta form a delightful place of retirement during the cool of the day. Standing on one of the highest, a person may look over the city of palaces almost as far as the extent of vision.

"TENTS.

"1. Those of wealthy natives, rajas and some Europeans, are very capacious and expensive. They are usually made of strong canvass lined with colored calico. Some of them contain two or three rooms from twenty to twenty-five feet square. A camp ground, where a regiment of soldiers have pitched their tents, presents a very imposing appearance. The missionaries sojourn in tents the most of the time during the cold season, which lasts four months, for the purpose of preaching in the villages and for the distribution of books. The tents are much smaller than those of other Europeans.

"2. The tents of the common people consist only in a piece of cloth spread over a pole that lies horizontally on two sticks inserted in the earth.

"3. Another kind is made of mats woven with grass or tatties, a kind of curtain made of the palm leaf. These are such as are used by jugglers and gypsies. A certain wandering class of people, called goonies, who go about exhibiting snakes, and who profess to have the power of charming them, spend their days in these frail tenements.

"II. What household furniture have the Hindoos?

"The furniture, like that in the most of Eastern countries, is very simple. They have no chairs, but sit on the floor or upon a rush mat, which article they also use for table and bed. But few houses contain any thing that resembles a bedstead. A brown earthen vessel, called a handy, is used for boiling their rice, and plates made of the same material are in common use. Some, however, have brass plates, and almost all have a brass vessel, holding about a quart, called a lota, used for various purposes. Many have a leather bottle made of an entire goat skin. Such were the bottles used by the Jews, to which our Lord refers when he speaks against putting new wine into old bottles lest the bottles should burst. The new wine would expand by effervescence, and the old leather, incapable of yielding to its pressure, must be rent asunder.

"III. How do the Hindoos dress?

"The dress of the Hindoos consists of two pieces of cloth, one wound around the lower part of the body, the other piece they frequently bind around the loins when they commence a journey or engage in any thing that requires muscular exertion. The Jews had such a custom, to which frequent allusion is made in the Scriptures. The Israelites were to eat the Passover with their loins girt and their staves in their hands, all ready to leave Egypt. These garments are generally of white cotton, which material grows in considerable abundance in their country. Their dresses are, however, frequently stained with yellow, purple, or red. Silks and a kind of cloth made of silk, called tussa, are in common use. They generally go bareheaded, but sometimes wear a cloth wound up in the form of a turban. They frequently wear a sort of wooden sandal, called paduka, and shoes made of leather embroidered with gold and silver thread. They are always down at the heel, and appear very clumsy. The Hindoos always take off their shoes, as a token of respect or reverence, when they enter a temple, a house, or even when they salute a person. Such a custom is doubtless alluded to when God says to Moses, 'Put thy shoes from off thy feet, for the place whereon thou standest is holy ground.'

"The female costume differs but little from that of the male. They only wear one cloth long enough to cover their shoulders and head as well as their body. They have a squeamish custom of covering the face when they pass by a man. A Hindoo lady, in full attire, must have rings on her wrists and in her ears and nose. Many wear five or six pounds of brass and iron as ornaments.

"The respectable Hindoos pride themselves much in keeping their persons and garments clean. They wash their clothes oft, bathe their bodies daily before eating by baptizing themselves in water, and they also anoint themselves with oil.

"Their fashion of dress differs but little amongst the different classes, and is invariably the same from age to age.

"The natives distil a kind of spirit, something like New England rum, from rice. This is called mada. The sap of a species of palm tree is also much used as an intoxicating drink. When first drawn from the tree, it is almost like new milk, sweet and pleasant and not injurious. After standing about twelve hours, it becomes like new cider. When a day old, it has fermented, and becomes a spirit which the natives call tadee. A drug or gum, called gunja, they also use to chew and smoke. But the practice of chewing and smoking *opium* is more common, and the effects produced by it more deleterious than any thing else. A great quantity of this drug is sold by the East India Company and their agents, who monopolize the sale of it. Numbers of the poor natives use it so constantly, that they are all the time stupefied from the effects of it. They think they cannot live if deprived of this their beloved poison. Indeed so much have they accustomed themselves to the use of it, that the physicians say if they were to be deprived of opium they could not live; and, in consequence of this, Government allows the prisoners in all the jails a certain quantity of this deadly drug every day. Even the beggars who go about the country, poor and miserable as they are, have their opium daily."

"SALUTATIONS.

"The Hindoos are very full of compliments. There are several ways in which they salute each other.

"1. The most common method is by raising the right hand to the forehead and repeating the word salam, which is an Arabic word and signifies peace. This is done both at meeting and parting.

"2. Another method is by putting the palms of the hands together, raising them to the forehead and repeating the word namascara, which signifies salutation. This is practised by all our Hindoo Christians, and by those who are intimate friends.

"3. Another mode is by raising both hands to the head and prostrating the body, repeating the word dundabut, which signifies obeisance. This is the manner in which soodras salute brahmuns. The brahmun at the same time extends his hand and pronounces a blessing, if he is in the mood of blessing, otherwise he pays no attention to the object before him."

The following extract from a work just published in England, by William J. B. Lawrie, Lieut. of Madras Artillery, and entitled, "Orissa, the Garden of Superstition and Idolatry," may not be deemed inappropriate in this place. The work itself contains very little that we have not ourselves presented, in some form or other, to the Christian public; but we hail the writer as a fellow laborer in the same great cause of benevolence. We cannot indeed subscribe to all his opinions, nor endorse all his statements; but, on the whole, we recommend his work to all who are interested in the severance of British connection with the temple of Jugernath.

The writer remarks, "Orissa may be compared to a huge caldron, which has been boiling for many hundreds of years, into which ignorance, stupidity and bigotry have cast so many poisonous ingredients, that it is difficult to say when the contents will become purified and good.

"Its early history is perhaps more wrapped in obscurity than that of any other province. Ignorance, oppression and superstition, garnished with the deceitful trappings of romance, either by or through the means of self-interested potentates, have for many ages gilded the misery which has been endured by its poor, deluded inhabitants. Filth, and every abomination of the earth, have been converted by the heathen poets into sacred streams, and fragrant flowers, and fruits of exquisite flavor. Idolatry has sanctioned these descriptions as well suited to her purpose. And yonder!—leaning against the threshold of the small temple, over which he presides,—behold the bigoted brahmun, with a countenance seeming to glory as it were in his fallen state. If you ask him concerning any of the beautiful and wonderful remains of the former greatness of his country, he knows nothing about them, save what consists in a few words; like the reply to the question respecting ruins in the *Antiquary*,—'They were made by the monks lang syne.'

"It is related by the annalists of Orissa, that, 'When the famous Sivai Jay Singh, the General of Akber, marched with an army into the country in A. D., 1580, he was struck with amazement at the sight of its sacred river, the Mahanuddi, its vast crowds of brahmuns, its lofty temples of stone, and all the wonders of the ancient capital, Bhuvaneswar, and exclaimed, 'This country is not a fit subject for conquest and schemes of human ambition. It belongs wholly to the gods, and is one entire tirth, or place of pilgrimage.' He accordingly interfered little in its affairs, and soon returned to Hindustan. We imagine, from this burst of admiration, that the 'General of Akber' proceeded no further than Bhobanéser (as we shall term it, according to the modern pronunciation,) which certainly is, even at the present day, a wonderful sight to see. Imagine a vast space of some two or three miles in extent, abounding with beautiful temples, some entire, some in ruins; the former, as it were, representing the brahmunical scientific genius and vivid imagination of former ages; the latter, emblematic of these gifts now fallen to decay. But more of this ancient 'city' hereafter,—a powerful illustration of the freedom of Hindoo intellect checked by a pitiful fanaticism and the stern resolution of millions to pass a useless life.

"Orissa is entirely indebted for its celebrity to its temples, places of pilgrimage, and its brahmunical insti-

tutions. But, among these, the Hindoos look upon the name, *Jagannáth*, the Lord of the world, as the inspiring soul of all; and the town of Púrí, or Púrí Jagannáth, owes its importance entirely to its connection with the temple. This Mecca of Hindustan is resorted to by pilgrims from every quarter of India. It is, as is well known, the chief seat in eastern India of brahmunical power, and the principal stronghold of Hindoo superstition."

In 1849, Messrs. Lacoix and Mullins, of the London Missionary Society, visited Orissa. Their object was to be present at the car festival of Jugernath, and then inquire into our missionary proceedings and success. They were so interested in what they witnessed, that they, on their return to Orissa, both preached and published on the subject. It is with reluctance the writer refrains from inserting lengthened extracts from their lectures on Orissa. In this place, however, he contents himself with a few sentences introductory to their account of the rise and progress of our mission, as they support the statements already given.

"Hindooism exists in full force in Orissa. Oriya versions of the shastras have been made, and all the abominable legends and stories of the gods are well known. The worship of Jugernath is universal; the land abounds with temples, and the constant visits of the people to his great shrine, their intercourse with the Pándas,* and familiarity with the stories of Krishna, have stamped them with the grossest immorality. The effects which constant intercourse with Europeans has produced on the Bengalles are scarcely seen in Orissa. English education, for which there is such a demand in Bengal, has

* Pilgrim hunters.

there had no influence. Every thing is still purely native, and the people must be approached through their own language and in their own way. This fact will show the wisdom of the plans followed by the Orissa missionaries for the spread of the gospel."

The writer must reserve for another chapter a more particular inquiry into the actual religious systems from time immemorial prevalent in Orissa, and here close his brief survey of its geography, history, and statistics. But he cannot do so without casting one long, sad look over its past dense, dark night. How deeply have its people been sunk, age after age, in the most revolting heathenism. What myriads have lived and died "without God," "without Christ," "without hope." Over its dark regions no heavenly gospel light has shined; to its benighted multitudes, no herald of the cross has proclaimed, "This is the way, walk ye in it." For its weary wanderers after rest, no Sabbath has dawned, an emblem of a better rest on high,—all has been darkness and desolation and death! But we may not pierce the veil which shrouds the past and hides the mystery of Divine Providence from our gaze. Enough for us to know that the Judge of all the earth will do right. The picture, however, brightens with glorious hope. The people who sat in darkness have seen a great light, and upon them who sit in the region of the shadow of death light is springing up.

"Yes, it shall come! e'en now my eyes behold
In distant view the wished for age unfold;
Lo, o'er the shadowy days that roll between,
A wandering gleam foretells the ascending scene!
Oh doom'd victorious from thy wounds to rise,
Dejected India lift thy downcast eyes,
And mark the hour whose faithful steps for thee
Through times prest ranks brings on the Jubilee."

# CHAPTER IV.

## Hindooism as seen in Orissa.

Hindooism is a term commonly applied to the system of religion professed and practised by the multitudinous population of India; a system all but infinite in extent, and unparalleled in intricacy.

In its widest extent, it embraces Buddhism and Brahmunism; two gigantic systems, which, in their diversified ramifications, constitute the religion of 600,000,000 of the earth's population. Buddhism has its most numerous votaries scattered or crowded throughout Ceylon, Thibet, Burma, Siam, Cochin China and China Proper; while Brahmunism is limited, by its own sacred books, to India in all its extent, viz.,—between the Indus and Brahmaputra, and to the whole land between the Himálayas and the sea.

Which of these two systems is the more ancient has long been disputed. This point the writer makes no pretensions to decide. To him, modern Buddhism appears evidently to have sprung out of Brahmunism, and is thus spoken of in those Pooranas which describe the occasion of Vishnu's ninth incarnation. But whether there was not a more ancient system than either, out of which both arose, is at least very probable. Buddhism evidently down to a very recent date had extensive influence in Orissa. All that now remains of it are the caves of Khundigiri, near Bhobaneswer, and the Jain temple, dedicated to Parushnath.

In this paper we confine ourselves to Hindooism as seen in Orissa and the neighboring districts. But this brief notice must necessarily embrace the essentials of the Hindoo religion wherever seen. Still there are local variations, which, in many particulars, render an account of Hindooism in one part of India inapplicable to Hindooism in another part of India. This consideration explains many of the objections raised against Mr. Ward's View of the Hindoos, a book which would have been more correctly entitled a View of the Bengallees. For to them alone it is, in its widest extent, fully applicable.

Were a perfect stranger to Christianity to visit England or America, supposing him to possess a sincere desire to become acquainted with it, there are two ways in which he might seek to accomplish his object. First by attentive observation and inquiry respecting its present practical embodiment, as seen in the avowed creed,—publicly acknowledged rites and ceremonies of worship, the institutions arising out of it,—and its influence on the several classes of its professors. Secondly, finding as he would, considerable variety in the faith and practice of professed Christians, and each contending for the divine authority of his own peculiarities, he might then have recourse to the sacred book, the authority of which all equally acknowledge, and to which they respectively appeal as the decider of all controversy. This method we may pursue in our view of Hindooism in Orissa.

Supposing, then, a stranger to enter Orissa from its north-east extremity, that is, from the Ganges, in the vicinity of Injellee, or Kedgeree, he would perceive a great number of temples of evidently very ancient structure, and various forms; many of them small, square stone edifices—others larger, of a conical form—and some of far humbler pretensions, and constructed of more perishable materials. As he prosecuted his way along the coast, he would come to the celebrated black pagoda, a splendid mass of ruins, said to have been built by Langora Nursing Deb, A. D., 1241, or thereabouts, and dedicated to the sun. Here he could not fail to be deeply impressed with the evidence afforded of the antiquity and magnificence of Hindooism in Orissa. He might then travel more into the centre of the land, and following a westerly course, he would arrive at Jajipoor. Here he would see temples of a different order, of unfathomable antiquity, yet evidently constructed of the ruins of temples more ancient than they. In the neighborhood, he would gaze with astonishment on elaborately sculptured colossal images, hurled from their thrones, lying neglected amidst sand and bushes, mutilated by every Goth who chooses to collect such trophies of Hindooism—but yet in their degradation and neglect, reading to him many an impressive lesson on Hindooism as it was. As our traveller passes on in his tour through the land, he would journey by the way of Cuttack to Bhobaneswar. Here he would contemplate with renewed wonder—perhaps with sentiments of awe—the stupendous proofs which present themselves, not only of the antiquity of Hindooism, but of the extensive and firm hold it must have had on the inhabitants of this land in bygone days. Here, amidst the ruins of hundreds of temples, splendid reservoirs of water, the caves and palace of Khundigiri, or, it may be, the crowds who still visit the festivals of Bhobaneswar, he might meditate long and deeply on the extended sway of Brahmunism in India. But our traveller must pass on, and in another day's journey reach the great emporium of Orissian idolatry—the place where Satan's seat is—the purlieus of Jugernath's temple. And here, with all his former impressions of the deep antiquity and powerful former sway of Hindooism, will be mingled sad and solemn thoughts respecting its still extensive prevalence, comparatively unimpaired vigor, and wretched, blasting influence. As the crowds come up in endless succession to worship at that polluted shrine, will his heart sink within him as he reflects that thus it has been from generation to generation, while multitudes on multitudes, as numerous as the dew drops of the morning, have risen into life and passed away, without God, without Christ, and without hope—the victims of this accursed superstition. These, although the principal, are by no means the only sites of idolatrous worship in Orissa. There are many other large temples and collections of temples in various parts of the province, both in the hills and on the plains; while every village has its place of worship, of some kind or other, and nearly every district its place of annual gathering, either for bathing, or in honor of some local deity or temple.

The idols most popular in Orissa, are Vishnoo, as Jugernath, or Krishna, or Rama—Mahadaiv, in the form of the Lingum, under an endless variety of local appellations, and as Hunuman. The female deities, also, are extensively worshipped, especially the consort of Vishnoo, as Lukshmee, Seeta, Radha Krishnoo, and various fanciful names—while Kalee, the consort of Sira, is worshipped as Bhobanee throughout the hill districts, among the Khunds, and many tribes in the plains. The village gods belong chiefly to the two latter classes, under various local appellations. These gods or deities are not unfrequently represented by a mere heap of stones, a stump of a tree, or an ant hill besmeared with red paint.

Some of these idols are exquisitely made, while others are of the coarsest and most clumsy workmanship imaginable. This remark especially applies to the wooden idols.

The revenues of some of the principal temples are shared by certain families, who have a right to officiate in course, and receive the offerings, as well as divide the endowments. In many cases there is but one attendant brahmun, or devotee, but in the case of Jugernath's temple, there is a large establishment of rulers, priests, pilgrim hunters, musicians, dancing women, cooks, and servants of all kinds. There are 640 officers of the temple; 300 or 400 families of cooks; upwards of 100 dancing girls; and 3,000 hereditary priests; besides other classes of privileged persons, who by this craft get their gain. Similar establishments, on a much smaller scale, are found at Bhobaneswar, Jajipoor and other places.

The offerings usually presented to the idols, are fruits, flowers, water, grain, money, jewels, garments, &c., &c.; while to the goddess Kalee, bloody sacrifices are presented, such as kids, rams, buffaloes, fowls; and as among the Khunds, and other hill tribes, human beings.

The principal public festivals, are those held in honor of Jugernath, not only at Pooree, but in various parts of the province; those in honor of Rama as the conqueror of the ten headed sovereign of Ceylon; those in honor of Durga when the image is paraded through the streets with all sorts of bacchanalian riot; those in honor of Mahadaiv at various celebrated temples, as at Singha Nath, on the Mahanuddee—Ling Raj, at Bhobaneswar—and all over the country at the hook swinging festival, and other acts of torture.

In order to give the reader an idea of the character of these festivals, a condensed account of some of the most popular is inserted. For a more elaborate statement, the reader is referred to Mr. Ward's work on the Hindoos, and similar books.

As the worship of Jugernath is referred to in the chapter relating to Pooree, we omit all reference to it in this place, and notice only the most popular festivals and holidays, common alike to Bengal and Orissa. We make our extracts chiefly from the Christian Herald, of Calcutta.

### *Sibaràtri*—6th March.

The Hindoo system is very different from the Christian in the number and appointed times of its religious festivals. The Christian has one day in seven set apart for rest from labor and the worship of God; and the experience of all ages and countries has shown this distribution of time to be the most perfect, and answering best the ends of such an institution.

The Hindoos have no particular day of rest, but keep numerous festivals, which frequently last several days consecutively, and are held at the most irregular distances of time; so that often weeks together pass by without any; whilst at other periods, nearly a whole month is occupied by a series of holidays, which follow each other in rapid succession. It is scarcely necessary to observe, that such an arrangement cannot be beneficial to the people. It is injurious to their health, and tends to create the idle and dissipated habits so prevalent among the natives.

The festival of Sibaràtri (or the night of Sib), is celebrated in honor of Sib the destroyer, the third person of the Hindoo triad. On the 5th, the worshippers eat only once, and on the 7th, they fast entirely, abstaining even from the use of water. The worship is performed at night, once at every watch; and is accompanied with singing, dancing, music and feasting. Those who have a permanent image of the god in their possession, worship that; and such as have none, make one for the occasion.

The benefits accruing from the performance of the worship of Sib on this night, are, deliverance from hell and admittance into Sib's heaven (for every principal god has a heaven of his own). This heaven, the Sri Bhágabat says, is 16,000 miles from the earth, on Mount Kailas. The god resides with his wife Parbati, in a palace of gold, adorned with jewels of all kinds, and surrounded with forests, gardens, trees with all kinds of fruits, and flowers of every fragrance. The kalpa tree grows here, from which a person may obtain not only every kind of fruit, but all other things he may desire. There is also a flower named parijatá, whose fragrance is most sweet, and extends 200 miles in all directions. The inhabitants of this heaven are Sib's sons Kartik and Ganesh, and those of his disciples who have attained beatitude. The time is spent in festivities, sensual enjoyments, and abominations of all kinds.

To prove the transcendency of the merit of celebrating Sibrátri, the Hindoos relate the following story, taken from the Puranas:—"A hunter of very low caste, and addicted to every kind of sin and wickedness, was once on this night overtaken by the darkness in a forest, before he could reach his dwelling; and to protect himself from the wild beasts, ascended a wood-apple tree (bel), whose leaf is always used in the worship of Sib. Underneath was a stone linga, the emblem of the god. During the night, the hunter happened by accident to strike off with his foot one of the leaves, which fell on the linga below. In the morning he proceeded home, and lived many years afterwards, one of the greatest miscreants ever seen in the country. On his death, the servants of Yama (the Hindoo Pluto), took immediate possession of his soul, as being the lawful property of their infernal master. When leading it along to the lower regions, they were met by a number of Sib's delegates, who laid claim to the prize as belonging to their lord. Not being able to agree, a scuffle ensued, in which Yama's servants having had the disadvantage, the victorious party conveyed the soul to Sib's heaven, where it was admitted to all the privileges and enjoyments of the place. Yama, having heard of the loss of a subject whom he had fully reckoned upon, proceeded to Sib, and angrily inquired into the reasons of the injustice done to him. Sib granted that the hunter had, during all his life, been a most reprobate character, and so far, certainly, had become liable to the punishment of hell; but added, that once, on Sib-rátri, he having dropt a leaf of the wood-apple tree on the linga, this act, though unconsciously performed, was yet so deserving, that all his sins had been removed, and that besides, such a transcendent degree of religious merit had been acquired, that in consequence he had become entitled to all the bliss of heaven. Yama acknowledged the propriety and justice of Sib's decision, and retired to his own dominions."

### THE DURGA PUJA.

*Government offices shut for about ten days in October.*

The Durgá Puja is celebrated in honor of the great goddess Bhagabati, the wife of Sib, who is here called Durga, on account of her having destroyed a terrible giant named Durga, who had subdued the three worlds, and compelled the very gods to worship him. She also destroyed another famous giant named Mahisha, who likewise overcame the gods in war, and reduced them to such a state of indigence that they were wandering about the earth like common beggars. The wars and exploits of this goddess are described at length in a book called Chandi, which is in great repute among the natives, and read by them more, perhaps, than any other of their writings.

The Durga festival, which was instituted by king Surat, was originally held in the spring; but Rama having in the Treta Yug celebrated it in autumn, it has ever since continued to be kept at the latter season of the year.

The image of the goddess is usually made of clay, in the shape of a female with ten arms. In one of her right hands is a spear, with which she is piercing the giant Mahisha; with one of the left, she holds the tail of a serpent and the hair of the giant, whose breast the serpent is biting. Her other hands are all filled with different instruments of war. Against her right leg leans a lion, and against her left, the above giant. Her sons Kartik and Ganesh, with several goddesses, are often placed by the side of the image.

The festival, commences about the 6th day of October, and lasts till the 16th.

On the 6th, a ceremony called bodhan (awakening) is performed, for the purpose of awaking the goddess, who, as well as the other inhabitants of the celestial regions, are supposed to be asleep since the festival called Sayan Ekadashi.

On the 7th, in the morning, the ceremony called sankalpa (vowing) takes place. The officiating priest offers to the goddess—represented on this occasion by a pan of water—flowers, fruits, sweetmeats, &c., pronouncing divers formulas, and makes a solemn promise that on the succeeding days, such a person will perform the worship of Durga.

8. The ceremony of Pranpratishtha, or giving of life to the idol, follows. This is done by the priest repeating several incantations, and touching the eyes, forehead, cheeks and breast of the image with his two forefingers,

whilst, at the same time, he utters this prayer,—"Let the soul of Durga long continue in happiness in this image." The image having now become a proper object of worship, quantities of fruits, sweetmeats, rice, wearing apparel, &c., are presented to it, and crowds of people come to pay their adoration at the shrine, and to admire the tinsel and gaudy ornaments with which the goddess is adorned.

The 9th is the day appointed for the bloody sacrifices. It is a most revolting sight. The beheading of the bleating victims,—the blood flowing on every side,—the frantic dances of the worshippers besmeared with gore,—the horrid din of the tom-toms and the deafening shouts of the multitude, make the spectator fancy that he is in the company of demons rather than of human beings. Buffaloes, goats and sheep are the only animals offered in sacrifice on these occasions. The head alone is presented to the goddess, with some of the blood put upon a plantain leaf. The bodies of the sheep and goats are used for food by the worshippers, and those of the buffaloes are given to the shoemakers and other persons of low caste, who deem the flesh of these animals a great dainty. The Hindoos, who are worshippers of Vishnu, not being permitted by the rules of their sect to shed blood, offer as substitutes for living animals, pumpkins and sugar canes, which are cut in two with the sacrificial knife before the goddess.

On the 10th, the Bisarjan, or casting the image into the river, takes place. The priest first dismisses the goddess with these words,—"O goddess, I have to the best of my ability worshipped thee; now go to thy residence, leaving this blessing, that thou wilt return next year." After this, the image is taken out and placed on a bamboo stage, and carried on men's shoulders to the river, where it is put into a boat filled with people, who, after rowing for a while up and down, and exhibiting the most disgusting gestures, let down the idol with all its tinsel and decorations into the stream. The people then return home to partake of an inebriating beverage made with hemp leaves; and thus the festival closes with scenes, in too many instances, of the most shameful intoxication.

Immense sums are expended at this púja; and many natives who but too often are deaf to the most pressing calls of charity, will squander thousands and tens of thousands of rupees on this occasion alone.

Few Europeans are aware of the excesses of all kinds committed, especially at night, during this festival, of which the singing of the most obscene songs and the performing of the most indecent dances, form only a part. It certainly is an imperative duty on every Christian to discountenance, to the utmost of his power, idolatry and all the revelries and demoralizing practices to which it gives rise. But, alas! what a matter for regret is it, that instead of doing this, many even among the most respectable and influential Europeans, by their attendance at the nautches given at this time, do actually *sanction* idolatry, and contribute in a great measure to the continuance of all the abominations connected with the Durga Puja; for it is well known that several of the most enlightened natives would long ago have ceased celebrating it, were it not that their vanity is flattered by the presence of the distinguished guests who honor them with their company.

### *Baruni*—April 4.

This is a bathing festival, and takes place on the 13th day of the decrease of the moon, being this year the 4th of April. When it falls on a Saturday, and the star Sota Bhissa* is then on the meridian, it is called Maha Baruni; and again, if the star Shuba Jug is in conjunction with Sota Bhissa, it is called Maha Maha Baruni.

The benefits of bathing in the Ganges, or other sacred places at the Baruni, are equal to those resulting from bathing in that river at the time of 100 sun eclipses; the fruits of bathing at the Maha Baruni equal to those of bathing at a million of sun eclipses; and those of bathing at the Maha Maha Baruni are so great, that three millions of generations of the ancestors of the bather are saved from hell by this single act of piety of their progeny.

At these bathing festivals, the natives from the remotest parts of Bengal and Orissa proceed to the Ganges to perform their ablutions. Tribeni, six miles above Chinsurah, is especially resorted to by immense crowds; that place being held very sacred on account of the junction of three rivers, and called for that reason by the natives the "little Prayag."

### *Sri Rám Nabami*—April 16.

Is held on the 9th day of the increase of the moon of Bysack, or the 16th of April, in honor of Rama, who on this day became incarnate, to destroy the giant Rabana, who had stolen his beautiful wife, Sita, and carried her to his kingdom of Lanka, or Ceylon. The history of this god, who is an incarnation of Vishnu, his wars, and his final victory over Rabana, with the aid of an army of monkeys, form the subject of the celebrated epic poem called the Ramayana.

A very strict fast is kept at this period. On the day

* Aquarius.

before the festival, the worshippers eat only once. On the day itself, they touch no food whatever, and abstain even from the use of water. Every Hindoo, who breaks this fast, is threatened in the shástras with the hell, Kumbi Pak, whose chief punishment consists in being whirled about on a spit in eternal fire. Multitudes of clay images of Rama are made on this occasion, and worshipped much in the usual manner, with offerings of sweetmeats, fruits, wearing apparel, golden ornaments, &c., which are appropriated by the officiating priest. The image of Rama is painted green. He is represented as sitting on a throne, or on Hunuman, the monkey, his faithful auxiliary in all his wars, with a crown on his head. He holds in one hand a bow, in another an arrow, and has a bundle of arrows slung on his back.

At military stations, the Hindoo sipahis are fond of getting up rude theatrical representations of Ramas war with Rabana, when the principal characters, including monkeys, are personified. The Madras sipahis go to great extremes on such occasions.

### *Jagaddhatri Puja*—November 8, 9.

Jagaddhatri, (the nurse or mother of the world,) is another form of Durga; she is represented as a yellow woman, dressed in red, and sitting on a lion. At this time is a very popular festival held in her honor, when bloody sacrifices are offered, and large sums expended in illuminations, dances, songs, feasting the brahmuns, &c. Much indecent mirth takes place, and numbers of men dance naked before the image, deeming that highly meritorious and pleasing to the deity! The benefits expected from this worship, are the four things usually promised in the Hindoo shástras by the gods to their votaries; viz., the fruit of meritorious actions,—riches, —the gratification of every desire,—and future happiness.

### *Kartik Puja*—November 14, 15.

Kartik is the son of Sib and Durga, and the god of war. He is represented as a handsome young man riding on a peacock, holding in his right hand an arrow, and in his left a bow. A clay image of this god is worshipped on the 14th at night, once at every watch; and the following day it is thrown into the river. No bloody sacrifices are offered. Married persons desirous of offspring are among the principal worshippers of Kartik, whose power is believed to be unlimited in confering that boon. The beauty of Kartik is quite proverbial among the Hindoos, who, when they wish to describe a handsome man or boy, generally say, "He is Kartik personified."

The most interesting feature in the ceremonies connected with the Kartik Puja, is the illuminating of the temples and large buildings with rows and festoons of small lamps, which really present a very pretty appearance.

### *Churuck Puja.*

The Hindoos ascribe the origin of the swinging festival, as it is called, to the austerities of a certain ancient raja. This individual was desirous of an interview with Seeb. He accordingly had recourse to the various modes of self-torture usually practised at this festival, when Seeb made his appearance and gratified all his wishes.

In the month of March, a leading votary of Seeb begins for a fortnight before the festival to cook his rice in a particular kind of earthen pot. The other Sunnyasees, or worshippers of Seeb, begins to do so on the first day of the festival. They fast till evening of this day, when they burn the wood of a wild plum tree in a hole of the earth, and suspend themselves over the fire, with their heads downward and their feet upward. A sort of scaffold is erected for this purpose.

On the second day of the festival, some climb date trees and repose their naked bodies on the thorny boughs; others throw themselves down on long, thorny bushes, collected for the purpose; run over hot ashes, &c., &c.

On the third day they erect scaffolds and spread sharp knives and pointed instruments on or in bags of straw, and cast themselves down upon them from a height of ten to twenty feet.

On the fourth day, some bore their hands and tongues with iron rods, swords and knives; others stick themselves over with pins; others make an incision in the skin under their arms, and passing ropes through them, which are held by others, dance to and fro; at night they practice other similar austerities.

On the fifth and last day, is the swinging ceremony, when hooks are thrust through the integuments of the back, and in Orissa both men and women are swung by them from a horizontal beam fixed on a perpendicular one, amidst crowds of gazers, men, women and children.

The next day they go from house to house with the hooks sticking in their backs, capering and grinning like so many infernals, to collect contributions from all who will give.

The chief actors in this piece of cruelty and foolery, are the lowest caste Hindoos, who are often employed by rich Baboos. The festival is, we trust, on the wane.

In some places magistrates have forbidden it to be observed in cities.

Besides these are numerous bathing festivals; a fair held near Cuttack, on the sands of the Mahanuddee; the Hooly or red powder festival, in honor of Krishnoo; with others of inferior note.

Among the most prominent features of Hindooism in Orissa, an observer could not fail to be struck with the vast, never ceasing crowds of pilgrims flocking to and from Jugernath. It would, at times, appear as though half the world were going on pilgrimage. Many of the pilgrims which pass through Orissa have come a journey of hundreds of miles, in some cases perhaps not less than a thousand. On, and on, and on they go, men, women and children; many on foot, others on horses, camels, elephants, and in vehicles of all descriptions.

Apart from what may be termed the regular worshippers of the idols, an observer would be constrained to notice great numbers of devotees, in all sorts of dress and undress; many besmeared with ashes, and large masses of sunburnt hair wrapped around their heads. Some having an arm erect and stiff, with nails longer than eagles' claws; some sitting on a tiger skin, performing their devotions; some seated beside a fire with the burning sun over head; others plying their trade of begging, singing songs and beating cymbals; and all presenting such a variety of grotesque and disgusting appearances as time would fail me to describe.

The daily worship of the Oriyas generally consists of repeating the name of his chosen guardian deity; in going to the river or tank to bathe, where he repeats some formula, pours out water from his hand to the sun or his ancestors, perhaps takes home a brass lota of water, and pours out a portion of it as he goes at the

root of some sacred tree or over his idol. At dusk, the wife usually places a lighted wick before the door, or in some convenient place, to scare away the evil spirits. Occasionally a Hindoo may be seen reading some portion of a poorana or book relating to the gods. These are the most obvious daily ceremonies; some, more devout than others, will pause at the temple, make a prostration before the idol, offer a short prayer and go home. Some will salute the image with clapping of hands, snapping the fingers, making a rumbling noise with a finger in the mouth or beating the cheeks, then make an obeisance and pass on. A few add repeating the name of their god on a rosary.

On occasion of some annual festival or gathering, the Oriyas may be seen dressed in their best; the women going in groups, dressed frequently in blue, orange, or crimson silk dresses, while others adhere to their usually clean and becoming white costume,—the men generally dressed in white, and carrying their little brothers or sons on their head or shoulders, and their sisters or daughters astride on their hips. Thus they issue in groups from their scattered villages, and thread their way through rice fields and jungle to the place of meeting. The people never present a more interesting or picturesque appearance than on such occasions.

Assembled at the place where the festival is held, the first business usually is to bathe; then a visit is paid to the temple where the offering is made; the females often receive a red mark where the hair is parted on the forehead, and the men make their prostrations, and perhaps prefer their request to the idol. On these occasions often have I seen mothers bowing down the head of the child, and teaching it to clasp its infant hands in adoration of the image; and often, too, have I felt the wish that Christian mothers generally were as assiduous in teaching their offspring to bow the infant knee and lisp the infant prayer to our Father in heaven.

After these ceremonies have been attended to, the people seem to have nothing more to do than employ themselves much as people do in an English fair. They walk about among the shops or goods exposed for sale; listen to the music of some wandering company; attend a sort of theatrical exhibition; make their purchases, and towards evening wend their way home.

In the dark places of the earth are the habitations of cruelty. When the Orissa missionaries entered the land, the suttee fire was blazing to consume the widow with the corpse of her husband. Infanticide was practised in various places, and other abominations were prevalent, which, we trust, have passed away forever. The Khund sacrifices still continue; the devotees still occasionally are crushed beneath the wheels of the car of Jugernath; the Churruck poojah is still rife and rampant; and many an obscene nightly revel is held all over Orissa. Large companies of Oriyas, under the profession of sutsung, or fellowship with the true, meet at night oblivious of the distinction of caste, to eat, dance, sing and commit all uncleanness with greediness; and there, by day and by night, more secretly or more publicly, idolatry may be seen influencing all ranks, prostrating all minds, deluding the hopes and depraving the morals of the whole nation. It is impossible to describe minutely how it enters into all the ramifications of society; controls all the private, domestic and public interests of life, and while endlessly diversified in character, and seemingly at war with itself in many essential points, yet still preserving, from age to age, a marvellous identity and an unimpaired vigor.

II. Perplexed and bewildered with the foregoing manifestations of Hindooism, and utterly unable to reconcile the various discordant systems and practices he is daily called to witness, the inquirer into the Hindoo system would turn to the sacred books and thence endeavor to learn what Hindooism, as sanctioned by the so called divinely inspired shastras, really is. But here a serious difficulty meets him at the outset. He finds, to his dismay, that there is no one single volume reverenced alike by all, and to which all may appeal; but, instead of this, there is an inconceivable multitude of books, some of them written only in Sanscrit, and to be interpreted only by the brahmuns; and others, translated, or compiled indeed in the vernacular dialect, yet still so numerous and bulky, that the longest life would scarcely suffice to allow of reading them through. We will attempt giving the reader some idea of the character and extent of the Hindoo shastras, as they are commonly styled.

### 1. *Veds.*

First of all in point of antiquity and authority are the Veds. These are the most ancient compilations in India, some say in the world. It is probable that they were first collected and arranged by a sage called Byasa, A. M., 2700. That is about the period of the foundation of the Assyrian Empire, the time when the Judges ruled in Israel. Originally the Veds were three, but subsequently a fourth was added. They are styled, Rig, Sama, Yajur and Atharva. These venerable works refer to the patriarchal form of religion observed among the ancestors of the brahmuns, and consist, for the most part, of hymns, prayers and precepts. They are chiefly addressed to the elements, and thus favor idolatry, although their fundamental principle is,

"There is but one God without a second." This one God is the supreme Spirit, pervading all things, from whom all proceed, and in whom all must at length be absorbed.

A few things still are current among all Hindoos which are traceable to the Veds. Such as the divisions of time,—the system of caste,—the ceremonies referring to marriage,—the shraddha or funeral feast, with rites addressed to the manes of progenitors, and the rules for brahmunical observances.

## 2. *Historical Poems.*

Next in point of antiquity to the Veds are the two great poems entitled the Mahabhárat and Ramayuna. The former consists of 100,000 couplets referring to the ancient kings and celebrated characters of ancient days. It treats especially of the wars between the solar and lunar races of Hindoo sovereigns. The Ramayuna is chiefly occupied with accounts of Rama, a king of Ayodhya or Oude, and the conqueror of Ceylon; it contains 24,000 verses, mostly couplets.

These works are the sole depositories of whatever historical knowledge the Hindoos possess. This is extremely meagre, puerile, and in every respect unsatisfactory. They probably led to hero worship, and are still reverenced as divine compositions by all orthodox Hindoos.

The Mahabhárat contains a sort of episode entitled the Bhagabut Geeta. This is an address by Krishnoo to Arjoon on the battle field, and furnishes a singular, yet full account of the mythologico philosophical Pantheism of the brahmuns, and of the mystic theology of Hindoos generally.

### 3. *Philosophical Works.*

Next in order perhaps we should place the six durshunas, or philosophical works of the metaphysical Hindoos. These six works emanated from as many schools of philosophy; four of which are reputed orthodox and two atheistic. They correspond very nearly to similar schools among the ancient Greeks. These works are 1. The Mimansa. 2. The Vedant, compiled by Jamuni, about 200 years before Christ. This is the most popular advocate of Hindoo theism. 3. Niaya. 4. Patunjala. These four are reckoned orthodox. 5. Sankhya. 6. Baiséshika. The two latter are hetorodox.

Next to these may be reckoned the OOPANISHUDS or theological appendages to the Veds. The OOPAVEDS, treating of music, medicine, war, mechanical arts, &c. The VEDANGAS, treating of grammar, prosody, astrology, geography, arithmetic and details of religious ceremonies. The OOPANGAS, treating of history, logic, moral philosophy and jurisprudence. All these, however, subserve the purposes of Hindooism.

### 4. *The Pooranas.*

These gigantic mythological poems are eighteen in number, containing 400,000 verses or 1,600,000 lines. Each poem should consist of five parts, relating to original and secondary creation; chronology; the genealogy of gods and men; the reigns of the manus or presiding sages; the history of kings, with a vast variety of legendary tales. They are evidently, in their present state, the work of leaders of opposing sects, written to uphold some favorite god or mode of worship. To me they appear to be a compilation of all the tales and legends known to the writers; and where not of Hindoo origin, they have been altered so as to accord with Hindoo ideas. These are the great modern authorities for all kinds of idol worship and ceremonies.

Professor Wilson says some of these pooranas were written A. D., 700 to 800; while others are not more than 200 years old, if so much. The most modern are the Bhagabut and Brahmuniya poorans.

After the regular pooranas come the OOPA PURANAS, or inferior pooranas; and a vast variety of poems which would only bewilder the reader to particularize.

### 5. *The Tuntras.*

These are works written chiefly for the purpose of upholding the worship of the female deities, and are authorities for all that is most revolting and abominable in Hindooism. They are divided into two classes, orthodox and heterodox, or the right and left hand systems. The latter is the most popular division, and finds its votaries among the debauched Baboos of Calcutta; though, alas, they are not wholly confined to that city. A modification of this system may be recognized in the Sutsung party spread over many parts of Orissa.

### 6. *The Vernacular, or Pancrit works.*

All the above works were written in Sanscrit, though many of them now exist in translations; but besides these, there are numerous original works written in the vernacular languages, and exercising a vast local influence. Such works abound in all parts of India. Every sect has its own books, written by its own votaries. Those within my sphere of knowledge which are most popular, are, the works of Kubeer, in Hindee, or those works ascribed to him—the works relating to Choitunya, in Bengali—a work in Teloogoo, by Vemana—the Shreemot Bhagabota, and other works in Oriya, not excepting a little work called Anunta Goyi, by an Oriya reformer. All the above works, and many others, have great influence in Orissa.

Here, then, is a very brief enumeration of the authorities to which an inquirer after accurate information respecting Hindooism must have recourse. It is no wonder that mere tyros in Hindoo mythology, in haste to give their opinion, commit such glaring mistakes, and darken counsel by words without knowledge. Very seldom do we read a work on India that does not abound with misrepresentations of Hindooism, confounding system with system, and mistaking one god or set of gods for another. Possibly the reader may detect some inaccuracies in this brief sketch, though he certainly will find nothing essentially erroneous.

It is not to be supposed that the Hindoos generally, are conversant with these multifarious works. Perhaps not a man exists who has read the greater half of them. Each class has its favorite works, which he deems orthodox, and looks with contempt on the rest; or at least as being nothing to him. The great body of the people read very little, and that little with less of discrimination or intelligent inquiry. The most are satisfied with a few poems, or songs, a meagre collection of slokas, or wise sayings and couplets, and a small collection of tales and fables.

This hasty survey of Hindooism may lead us to remark in conclusion, that Hindooism, so far from being one unchangeable system, has from age to age undergone great and radical modifications.

1. There was the ancient system of Pantheism inculcated in the vedas.

2. This system corrupted and confounded with he-

ro worship, especially that of Rama, Krishnu, Hunuman, &c.

3. Then came the age of philosophical speculation, giving rise to Buddhism, and various mystical opinions.

4. These gave rise to the modern systems of idolatry, with the various pooranas and their abominations. Those in favor of Siva, or Mahadaiv, were advocated by Sunker Acharjya 700 or 800 years after Christ; and those in favor of Vishnoo, by Ramanuja, A. D., 1200; while that especially in favor of Jugernath, was advocated by Bullabha, about A. D., 1600.

5. The Tuntras, or systems in favor of Shakti, or female deities, most likely sprang up also about the latter period.

6. We have now arrived at an age when Hindooism has become with the multitude a mere confusion of all systems which in former ages have been kept separate. A corrupting mass of all evil and of all error.

III. Our view of Hindooism as actually seen in Orissa, will be far from complete, without a brief enumeration of the leading religious principles, and a succinct account of the actual moral convictions of the existing population of the land. These we shall classify under three heads, viz:—their views of the existence and character of Deity—the being and destiny of man—the means of securing future happiness.

1. The existence and character of Deity.

The highest Hindoo authority declares there is one God. This being is spoken of in the neuter gender, without parts or passions, infinitely removed from the apprehension of man. No temple is dedicated to his honor—no worship is ever offered to his name. He exists for the Hindoo as but a mere abstraction. We have nothing to do with him, nor he with us.

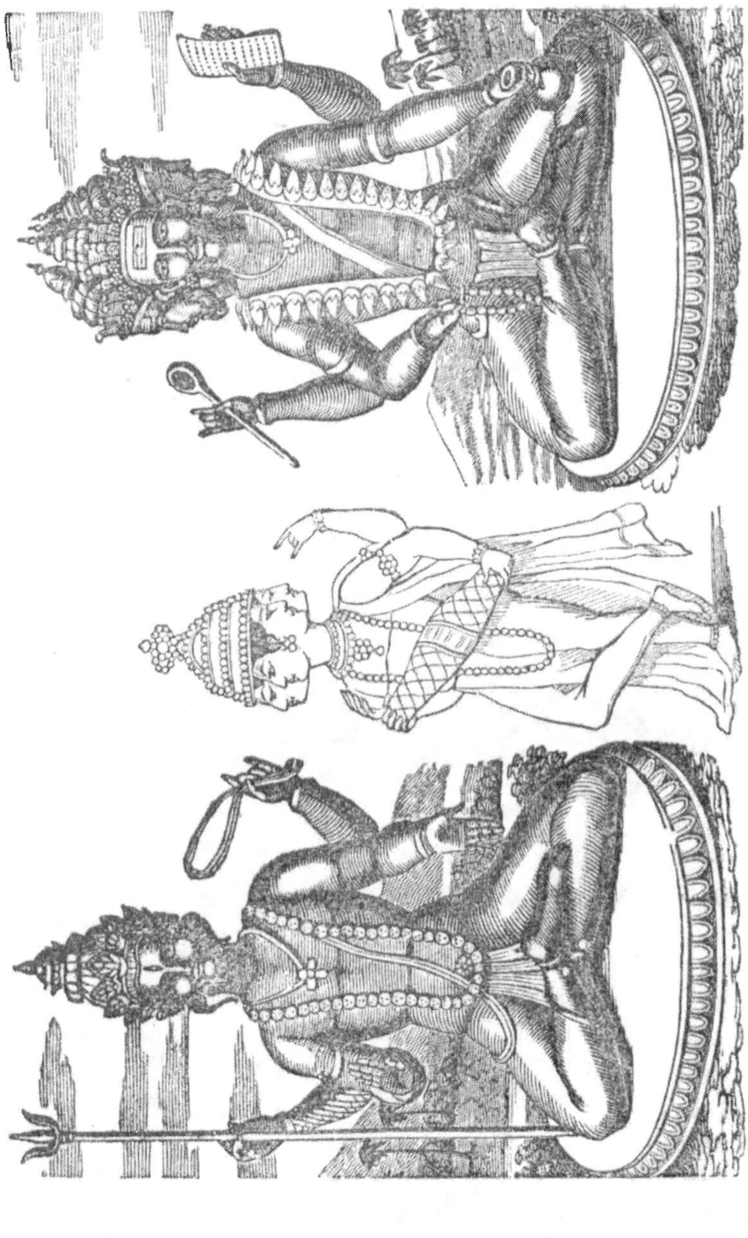

The Pooranas identify this one Brahma with some special divinity. The Vaishnavas with some form of Vishnoo. The Saivas with some form of Seeva. While the worshippers of the female deities in like manner contend the divine energy is specially manifested only through them. There are different degrees of divinity contended for in connection with different gods, men, animals, and even inanimate objects.

The Pauranicks generally are both pantheists and materialists. They excuse all the abominable deeds of their gods, by calling them the *lila*, or sport of the gods, and therefore what would be sin in us, is not so in them.

The work of creation, preservation, and destruction, is ascribed to the Hindoo triad, Brahmá, Vishnoo, and Seeva, or to their endless incarnations or manifestations. And to these three and their energies, may be reduced the whole rabble of Hindoo gods. Now while these are the orthodox views of a Hindoo, and those which in argument he would seek to defend, it is at once a remarkable and cheering fact, that he really holds views of God in perfect antagonism with his written creed; and when developed, utterly subversive of his pantheistic notions. In familiar and serious converse, the Oriya constantly recognizes a moral governor of the world, feels his responsibility and his guilt, and sends up his aspirations to him for protection, pardon, and redress. His views are obscure, and he would be unable to give any intelligent account of his convictions; but they are in him, to be appealed to and pleaded with, by the missionary of the cross.

2. In relation to the being and destiny of man, there is a similar distinction to be made between the Hindoo's creed, and the positive existence of first moral principles, in his very constitution. According to his creed, univer-

sally professed, and pertinaciously maintained, the Oriya calls his soul a portion of the divine essence—an emanation from God. He believes in endless transmigrations through every form of animal and vegetable life. When he dies, he speaks of passing into some other body; and after innumerable births and deaths, he hopes to be absorbed into Brahma at the last.

He ascribes all the good or evil he shares in this world, to his conduct in a former birth; and that previous conduct must infallibly control all his future existence. This is his view of fate. It arises out of his own good or evil deeds, where, or when, or how performed, he neither knows or wishes to understand. While these are his avowed sentiments, which he never, even for a moment seems to question, he yet, like all other fatalists, constantly acts as though no such creed existed. He trembles in view of his moral delinquencies, he fears the judgment to come, and seems quite prepared to admit the reasonings and appeals of the missionary, based on a totally different system of doctrines.

3. Out of these general views of God and man, spring the actual efforts put forth by the Hindoo, in order to better his eternal destiny.

It is the ascetic alone who seeks direct absorption into Brahma; and very few even of this class, aspire to this final beatitude of the Hindoo—self-annihilation. The majority of the people hope, by various gifts and offerings, penances and pilgrimages—the worship of the gods, and reverence of their spiritual guide—to obtain some more favorable station in another birth; or, peradventure, an indefinite period of happiness in some one of the fabled heavens of the gods. It matters little what peculiar modification of these general views the Hindoo adopts, he will find some favorite teacher or shaster to support his hopes and confirm his opinions.

Yet here, again, amidst the wild vagaries of the Hindoo mind, truth and conscience exert an influence favorable to the work of the missionary. The fears of hell and hopes of heaven, apart from all Hindoo perversions, are often seen working mightily in the poor heathen's soul. There are convictions which Hindooism cannot silence—hopes which Hindooism does not satisfy—fears it will not quell. One grand defect characterizes not only Hindooism, but every system of false religion, in every age and place, viz:—that while such systems seek to quell the fears of a guilty conscience, they fail to wean the heart from those sins which bring it under condemnation. And herein appears the divine excellence and superiority of the gospel, as adapted to the actual nature and necessities of man. The following extract from a speech of Dr. Eli Smith, of the Syrian Mission, is an almost verbatim statement of the writer's frequently expressed views on this point. "I am not aware that any plan of religion, from the classic fables of Greece and Rome, to the complicated mythology of India, and the simple dreamings of the American savage—has ever been wanting in vivid delineations of future punishment. And yet, far have all such religions been from preventing vice, and promoting virtue. The reason is, they contrive to relieve the conscience from fear, by ceremonies which release not the heart from sin. The natural man has two opposing principles within him: a wicked heart, enticing him to sin, and conscience, by holding up the consequences, warning him against it. It is only true religion reconciles the two, by changing the heart, till it speaks out in a holy life the same voice as conscience. All other systems of religion, are, in fact, contrivances of the (depraved) heart for its own indulgence; they leave the heart undisturbed, and aim at silencing conscience. This they accomplish by presenting certain ceremonies as a compromise for sin, and persuading conscience they are an effectual prevention of punishment."

The foregoing remarks have reference to the great mass of the population of Orissa; but we must not forget, that, while these are the largest body, there are several sections of the inhabitants of our field of labor, not to be confounded with these orthodox votaries of Hindooism.

Next to this largest class, may be mentioned the various tribes of aborigines, whether on the plains, or among the hills. The most numerous section of these aborigines on the plains, mingling with the general population under the sway of the East India Company's government, are the whole body of Pariahs. They are not called by this name in Orissa, unless in some case it be applied to them in the southern extremity of the province, though they are doubtless substantially the same class of people. With us they are called Doms, Bowries, Chiriamar, Mehetars, &c., &c. They are all comprehended under the designation of chandala, or outcasts, cut off from all intercourse with the regular Hindoo castes, deemed of all things most impure, and doomed to the most servile and degraded of employments. They have various distinctions among themselves, to which they tenaciously adhere, and by following the same mode of life, from generation to generation, some have raised themselves a step higher than their fellows in the social ladder. Hence some are bearers, others fishermen, others fowlers, others basket-makers, while others again are content to do the lowest work of scavengers and sweepers.

These poor, degraded beings have been benefitted considerably by the British rule in India; they enjoy a freedom from oppression, a liberty of action, and an undisturbed possession of property such as their ancestors never knew, and, in consequence, are fast rising in the social scale. Neglected and oppressed as they have been, from time immemorial, it is no wonder that they have sunk into the lowest depths of ignorance and immorality, or that they have become excessively suspicious of their fellow-men and addicted to the meanest vices. And yet I have often been struck with their quickness of apprehension, readiness to receive the leading principles of truth and righteousness, and their susceptibility of grateful impressions. They have many redeeming features visible through their deep degradation, mental, moral and social. As Hindooism does not acknowledge them as being within its pale, so they, while necessarily influenced by the prevailing superstition, hold comparatively light by its authority. They however call themeslves Hindoos.

Other and larger sections of the same aboriginal stock inhabit the hills and jungles of Orissa. I am of opinion that all the various classes of Coles, Khunds, Santals, Saburas, Bhomijas, &c., &c., are in fact but so many different sections of the same great family who originally peopled India. Driven by their brahmun conquerors from the plains, they have found a refuge amidst the inaccessible fastnesses of the hills, and there, from age to age, have maintained a sort of rude independence, or nominal subjection to the Gurjat princes and Zemindars. The notions of religion entertained by these tribes are wild and incoherent in the extreme, but generally of a gloomy and terrific character. The Khunds, it is well known, are extensively addicted to human sacrifices; some tribes of them to infanticide, and all, Khunds, Coles and others, to excessive intoxication, with its concomitant evils.

They have, however, certain redeeming qualities, such as freedom from the excessive mendacity and duplicity of the Hindoo, and according to their means they are hospitable and generous.

These outcasts from the general family of India well merit the attention of the Christian missionary. The very genius of the gospel bids him condescend to men of low estate, while their number, their political condition, their freedom from shackles which bind the orthodox Hindoo, their evident capacity for improvement, the bearing their conversion must have upon the evangelization of the whole people of the land, point them out as a class of the general population of Orissa, which deserve our serious attention and the employment of the best efforts we can make for their conversion.

The Mahomedans are another important portion of the inhabitants of Orissa. They are supposed to constitute a seventh* part of the Honorable Company's subjects in the Mogul-bundi, or best cultivated parts of Orissa. The original Mussulman population of the province are descendants of the first Affghan invaders of India. They are commonly called Patháns, and were long a turbulent and troublesome race. It cannot be said that they are perfectly satisfied with their position in the land even now, but generally they have settled down as an integral portion of the population. They have increased their numbers, not only by natural increase, but by accessions from other tribes of Mahomedans and occasional conversions from among the Hindoos. Many of them are farmers, but most of them seek employment as soldiers, police officers and servants to Europeans.

* Perhaps a tenth is nearer the truth.

These professed followers of the false prophet in Orissa are a hard-mouthed, contemptuous, ignorant race. They are the Catholics of the East; bigotted, proud, intolerant, inaccessible. They will occasionally side with the missionary in pleading for the authority of God and in deprecating idolatry, but sneer at the doctrines of Christ and any application of our exhortations to themselves. They need no Saviour. They can listen to no authority save that of Mahomet, and often gnash their teeth with rage at our mission.

Still Mahomedans have submitted to the gospel, and at most mission stations a few are found numbered with the disciples of Christ crucified. We have hitherto done very little for them beyond the publication of one or two tracts specially addressed to them, and an occasional appeal to them when found among our auditors. We must not, however, overlook them when estimating our responsibilities in connection with the evangelization of Orissa.

A fourth portion of the inhabitants of the land who claim our sympathy and share in our labors, is the class denominated East Indians or country born. These are the descendants of the Portuguese, Dutch, French or English residents in India, and native Hindoo or Mahomedan females. They are not numerous in Orissa; but from the midway position between natives and Europeans, which they occupy, their neglected condition, the fact that so many have been savingly benefited by missionary labor, and finally that several of them have rendered useful service in the various departments of missionary labor, they cannot but be regarded as an interesting portion of our charge. Hitherto the East Indians have occupied far too low a place in the scale of society. They have too generally been down-trodden by Europeans and spurned by the natives. The consequence is, that they have become isolated from all, dispossessed of self-respect, jealous of all parties, and too often exceedingly low and immoral in their habits. A brightening day is now dawning upon them. Many have risen in the esteem of themselves and others. They now occupy a more elevated place in society, have become intelligent, moral and respectable members of the community; and, if they are not wanting to themselves, their course will now be onward and upward till they attain their proper sphere and influence. The children of this class have always shared in our educational efforts as well as in our more direct ministerial labors.

Lastly, our own countrymen demand and have a share in our missionary exertions. I am a debtor, saith the apostle, both to the Gentile and the Jew, to the wise and unto the unwise. And in this sentiment we have ever sympathized. Many a son and daughter, too, have left Christian England neglectful of the gospel there so extensively proclaimed, to be brought to a saving knowledge of the truth by the missionary in some out-station in India. To these happy results we may hereafter again recur. Meantime we content ourselves with noticing this class as a section of the residents in the land for whom we care. Perhaps at our various stations, inclusive of Midnapore and Berhampore, upwards of a hundred and fifty of these may be found. They include commissioners, judges, collectors, military officers of all grades and their assistants, of various standing and employment. The same individuals seldom remain more than three to five years in the province.

Here, then, brethren, we would say to the supporters of the Orissa Mission, is the lot of our inheritance; the field of labor assigned us by Providence, and ceded to us by the common consent of the Christian church. We stand pledged to seek the salvation of these varied tribes, and to them all we have the fullest freedom of access; we mean so far as political freedom and absence of all ecclesiastical obstructions are concerned. Whatever may be said of China, Orissa is fully open to evangelical labors.

We have remarked in reference to the Oriya Hindoos, that beneath the workings of their mythological, pantheistic creed, there is an under current of intuitive convictions, of first principles, betokening the existence of a divine control still exercised in the heart and conscience. We add that similar statements may be made of all the other sections of the human family in Orissa. Neither the blasting influence of heathenism,—of Brahmunism,—of Mahomedan intolerance or of European exclusiveness, have been able to silence altogether the voice of God in the soul of man,—there is still there a something which answers to the call of truth and right,—a fulcrum on which to place the gospel lever and overturn the whole moral being of the man. It is to this the missionary must make his appeal; it is the only real door of hope in this valley of sin and death. Most cordially and joyfully does the writer, in reference to this point, adopt the language of one whom he feels to be a whole-hearted fellow-laborer in this work,* and whose book, he regrets, he had not the opportunity of perusing before his own was written, and he applies the quotation to the whole of the abovenamed population of Orissa.

"We would vindicate, in the most absolute sense, the entire comprehensibility of the gospel by the most untutored Indian. The gospel is adapted to the Hindoo, not as he was or might be, *but as he is.* We would disclaim every demand for a preparatory process as neces-

* Rev. W. Clarkson, missionary in Western India.

sary to the comprehension of the gospel. We say, with emphasis, that the gospel in the hands of the evangelist 'apt to teach,' ready to explain it by suitable illustration, and consequently able to touch the springs of conscience, is alone effectual to the end of conversion. We ask for education, but not to prepare a way for the gospel; we believe that the gospel makes a way for itself. We say, with confidence, that the aboriginal of India's mountains and forests, who never saw a written character, is fully competent to understand the fundamental truths of the gospel. If the evangelist will assume pedantic forms of instruction, or clothe the gospel in the rigidities of theological systems, he will find among the Hindoos no intelligent audience, nor be rewarded by seeing converted souls. If he will use their own imagery; borrow their own illustrations; think, as far as may be, *their* thoughts, and speak *their* words, and make them all the vehicle of communicating those simple truths in the belief of which is eternal life; he will find that the gospel is indeed the power of God, both to convince the understanding and impress the heart. If he do so, he will find that the Hindoos can understand his message; and if they do not believe it, it is because they will not." I add, in the name of my colleagues and myself, that our experience in Orissa corroborates the accuracy of the foregoing testimony.

## CHAPTER V.

Commencement of the Orissa Mission—The night of toil—Modes of missionary labor.

Upwards of forty years ago, that distinguished friend of India, Dr. Buchanan, when on his visit to the Syrian churches of the Peninsula, travelled through Orissa. He paused at Pooree, to witness the annual carnival at Jugernath, and there penned those graphic statements respecting this gigantic outrage upon all that is dear to God and man, which have ever since made thousands of Christian hearts mourn over the connection of Britain with these abominations. Sad and sick at heart, the doctor turned away from these scenes of pollution and wretchedness, and pitched his tent on the retired banks of the Chilka. There, on the 24th June, 1806, he penned the following note : — "I felt my mind relieved and happy when I had passed beyond the confines of Jugernath. I certainly was not prepared for the scene ; but no one can know what it is, who has not seen it. From an eminence on the pleasant banks of the Chilka Lake, (where no human bones are seen,) I had a view of the lofty tower of Jugernath, far remote; and while I viewed it, its abominations came to mind. It was on the morning of the Sabbath. Ruminating long on the wide and extended empire of Moloch in the heathen world, I cherished in my thoughts the design of some Christian institution, which, being fostered by Britain, my native country, might gradually undermine this baneful idolatry, and put out the memory of it forever."

About ten years after Buchanan had penned these

lines, a society was formed among the General Baptists of England, which, under the direction of an all-wise Providence, was to be honored as the harbinger of that blessed consummation which Buchanan so ardently desired. The above-named body of Christians had ever considered the commission of our Lord, "Go—preach the gospel to every creature," as the grand charter of their distinctive principles. They believed that the provision made for human redemption was commensurate with the command to preach the gospel; and hence they could not hold themselves guiltless while making no effort to publish that gospel beyond the limits of their native land. Stimulated to the work, and guided in their efforts, by the zeal and wisdom of their venerated secretary, Rev. J. G. Pike, a society to send the gospel to some heathen country was organized among them, A. D. 1816. Just when this infant "institution" was preparing to send forth its first missionaries, the late Mr. Ward, of Serampore, undertook to be their guide and helper in their untried enterprise. In company, therefore, with this excellent servant of Christ, Messrs. Bampton and Peggs embarked for India; and after consultation with the senior brethren at Serampore, Orissa was selected as the site of their missionary labors.

On Feb. 12th, 1822, our esteemed brethren landed on the coast of Orissa. They soon proceeded to Cuttack, and immediately commenced operations in this capital of the province. In less than two years, Mr. Bampton removed to Pooree, and fixed his station within sight of the mighty Jugernath. These brethren were subsequently joined by Messrs. Lacey, Sutton, and other missionaries sent out from England; and other stations, both in the southern and northern extremities of the province, were formed. This was for the Orissa missionaries the night of toil. For six wearying years they labored on, "hoping against hope." The work itself was disheartening, but more disheartening still the general opinion of the futility of their labors.

Mr. Peggs, after four years service, worn down by bodily and mental afflictions, returned to his native land. There he long sustained his claim to be one of India's best benefactors, and closed his faithful course in January last, while pastor of the General Baptist Church at Burton-on-Trent, England. Mr. Bampton labored on with extraordinary perseverance and self-denial, till, at the end of his sixth year, he was honored to admit by baptism the first Hindoo into the church of Christ in Orissa. Others, however, had for twelve months previous been inquirers at Cuttack, from among whom Gunga Dhor, a high caste brahmun, was baptized by Mr. Lacey, March 23d, 1828.

Soon after the baptism of our first convert, Mr. Bampton's health began to fail; and in two years more consumption had run its course, and dismissed his pious spirit to the heavenly rest. He lies interred by the side of Charlotte Sutton, on the dreary sands of Pooree; but his example, and the memory of his virtues, are embalmed in the hearts of his surviving colleagues. Thus, as in the case of Abraham of old, our first possession in the promised land was a burying-place for our dead.

Fifteen years ago, a society was formed in a kindred branch of the Baptist Church in America, and its first missionaries were appointed to labor in connection with the General Baptist missionaries in Orissa. Messrs. Noyes and Phillips, the first missionaries of this new society, were first directed to Sumbhulpore; but the insalubrity of the climate obliged them to withdraw, not, however, until one beloved sister and two children had died, and the survivors had become greatly debilitated by sickness. They have since formed stations at Balasore, Jellasore, and Midnapore, and have had consigned to them the whole of the northern portion of Orissa.

The following pages have reference to the labor of both these societies, for they are, though supported by different denominations and from different countries, in point of fact, but one mission, laboring in the same field, pursuing similar plans, and aiming to effect one grand object — the conversion of Orissa to the faith of Christ. It is hoped that this brief outline will be sufficient to conduct the reader clearly and intelligibly through the subsequent pages of this book.

The following is a list of all the missionaries who have been engaged in the field, with the date of their embarkation.

| | Embarked. | Left, or died. |
|---|---|---|
| Rev. W. Bampton, | June, 1821. | *1830. |
| Mrs. Eliza Bampton, | " | 1832. |
| Rev. J. Peggs, | " | *1825. |
| Mrs. Eliza Peggs, | " | 1825. |
| Rev. C. Lacey, | June, 1823. | |
| Mrs. Ann Lacey, | " | |
| Rev. A. Sutton, | August, 1824. | |
| Mrs. C. Sutton, | " | *1825. |
| Rev. J. Cropper, | February, 1828. | *1828. |
| Mrs. Eliza Sutton, joined, | June, 1826. | |
| Mr. W. Brown, | 1831. | 1837. |
| Mrs. Mary Brown, | " | " |
| Rev. J. Goadby, | 1833. | " |
| Mrs. Anne Goadby, | " | *1834. |
| Rev. J. Brooks, | 1834. | 1845. |
| Mrs. S. Brooks, | " | " |
| Mrs. Julia Goadly joined, | " | 1837. |

* Those thus marked have died.

| | Embarked. | Left, or died. |
|---|---|---|
| Rev. Eli Noyes, | 1835. | 1842. |
| Mrs. C. Noyes, | " | " |
| Rev. J. Phillips, | 1835. | |
| Mrs. M. Phillips. | " | *1838. |
| Rev. J. Stubbins, | 1836. | |
| Mrs. Anne Stubbins, | " | *1837. |
| Miss E. Kirkman (Mrs. Stubbins,) | 1837. | |
| Rev. H. Wilkinson, | 1838. | |
| Mrs. C. Wilkinson, | " | |
| Mrs. Mary Ann Phillips, | 1839. | *1840. |
| Rev. O. Bachelor, | 1840. | |
| Mrs. C. Bachelor, | " | *1845. |
| Miss H. Cummings, (Mrs. P.) | " | |
| Rev. T. Grant, | 1841. | *1843. |
| Mrs. E. Grant, | " | " |
| Miss Derry, (Mrs. Buckley,) | " | |
| Mr. William Brooks, | " | |
| Mrs. E. Brooks, | " | |
| Rev. J. Buckley, | 1844. | |
| Rev. W. Millar, | 1845. | |
| Rev. W. Bailey, | " | |
| Miss Collins, | " | |
| Rev. J. Dow, | 1844. | 1848. |
| Mrs. Dow, | " | " |
| Miss Merril, (Mrs. Bachelor,) | 1847. | |
| Mrs. Millar, | 1848. | |
| Mrs. Bailey, | " | |
| Rev. Mr. Cooley and Mrs. Cooley, | 1849. | |

When the Orissa missionaries commenced their labors, one dark, unbroken night of sin and sorrow overspread the land, and the darkness had been growing darker and denser for ages. All appeared so dark and discouraging, that it seemed to say, Your prayers cannot pierce this gloom, nor your labors open an avenue sufficient to let down a ray of heaven's light on this idolatrous province.

Yes, and thus it continued for nearly seven long years. How fearfully long they seemed, none but ourselves and those who have been similarly circumstanced, can possibly tell. Of all the various temples which covered the land, not one was devoted to the worship of the living God. Of all the endless acts of worship daily performed, not one was offered to Him who alone is worthy. Not one prayer was addressed really to God ; not one voice was raised in praise to Him. Of all the myriads thronging the pilgrims' route, not one was a pilgrim in the ways of Zion. Idolatry, and idolatry only met the eye, and assailed the ear, and grieved the heart. The only exception to this general heathenism was the almost equally debased system of Mahomed. Thus it had been from remotest ages, and thus it still continued to be. There was no relief to the picture; no ray of light shining athwart the gloom profound; no hope or indication of better days was known or wished. It was the region of darkness and the shadow of death, without any morning, and where the light was as darkness.

We have already directed attention to some of the most prominent features in the idolatry of Orissa, and described the general gloom which overspread the land. When the gospel first dawned upon Orissa, of no place under heaven, perhaps, could it with more propriety be said, "The people which sat in darkness saw great light; and to them which sat in the region and shadow of death light is sprung up."

Ere, however, we could make known from our own lips the everlasting gospel of the grace of God to sinful men, in this heathen country, the strange language must be learned ; and month after month, if not year after year, be spent in silent, depressing study. Our first missionaries had few helps to the acquisition of the Oriya, and obtained their first acquaintance with it through the medium of Bengallee: a process which vitiated all their subsequent attainments. This difficulty is now to a great extent obviated. Oriya grammars and dictionaries have been provided, and a variety of elementary works to facilitate the young missionary's progress have been printed.

While thus engaged in studying the language, our brethren made various attempts to benefit the people, and also to preach the gospel to those who understood the English language. A brief enumeration of the means employed, both then, and during the subsequent history, is all that we deem necessary. For a fuller detail the writer refers to his narrative of the mission, published in 1833, and to the periodical works of the Society.

When our brethren reached Cuttack, in 1822, there was no kind of public Christian worship. The Sabbath was well nigh confounded with the other days of the week, and so completely had professing Christians allowed themselves to live without God in the world, that the natives supposed that the Pheringees* were destitute of all religion. Many and striking were the remarks made to this effect in the earlier days of the mission. The Orissa missionaries immediately commenced an English service, and it has been continued ever since. At first we had preaching in one or other of the resident missionaries' dwellings; but on Nov. 6, 1826, a small chapel was opened and dedicated for divine worship. The chapel was nearly destroyed by a flood some few years afterwards, and rebuilt at the expense of the Cuttack community; but in 1838, in consequence of increased attendance, it was pulled down and greatly en-

* Probably a corruption of Franks.

larged. The brethren, Messrs. Lacey and Sutton, who raised the contributions for and officiated at the opening of the first chapel, were spared to perform the same duties for the enlarged house. Many instances of good might be noted in connection with this service, and one missionary and his wife, now laboring in a distant field, were here brought to a knowledge of the truth. The church book shows a goodly list of persons, European and East Indian, who have been baptized and added to the church at Cuttack. Other chapels at Midnapore, Balasore and Berhampore have since been erected for occasional English worship.

Since the erection of the first chapel, a chaplain has been occasionally stationed at Cuttack, which has led to a diminution of interest in these services, while the increased number of native converts has seemed to justify the missionaries in a comparative neglect of the English and East Indian part of the community. The result has been unfavorable to the religious and moral habits of the latter class especially. They are left as sheep without a shepherd, and there is reason to fear will, if entirely thus left, sink beyond recovery.

The Cuttack chapel stands on a piece of ground where once an idol's temple stood, thus furnishing a sort of earnest that one day the temples of the land, now dedicated to idol gods, shall give place to the temples of the living God, and throughout all the land the true worshippers shall worship Him who is a Spirit in spirit and in truth. The following extract from the Society's reports may be here suitably introduced.

"The chapel at Cuttack has been enlarged to more than double its former size. Its present dimensions are fifty feet long by thirty wide, with a verandah ten feet broad on the sides and front. This enlargement was rendered necessary by the increase of Europeans at the station; by the additions made to the native church, and by the increase almost every month of the native congregation. This rendered the former chapel inconveniently small, especially on those Sabbaths when the Lord's Supper was administered. Mr. Sutton collected for the object about seven hundred rupees, which he transferred to the hands of Mr. Lacey, who had much of the superintendence of the work. A circular was sent to the Christian residents in Cuttack and the vicinity, which soon raised about five hundred rupees more. To this, subsequent additions were made, and the whole expense amounting to one thousand four hundred and twenty rupees, has been defrayed. Above an acre has been added to the chapel ground. A tank has been opened in the centre of this ground for use on baptismal occasions. This tank is about one hundred feet wide. With the soil taken from the tank, the ground in the old chapel yard has been improved, and the whole of the ground enclosed with an embankment to prevent the ingress of the flood in the rainy season. The whole of the ground which has been enclosed, is planted round with cocoa-nut trees of five years' growth, which add much to the appearance of the place, and will hereafter add to the usefulness of the addition. The cocoa-nut plant being the exclusive perquisite of the sacerdotal class, and being usually planted around the temples of the land, their appearance around this Christian sanctuary produces a favorable impression on the natives.

"The chapel was re-opened on Lord's day, August 19. Mr. Sutton preached in the morning from 1 Cor. 3:9. In the afternoon the native congregation assembled at four o'clock, and Mr. Lacey preached on Isa.

54 : 11. A goodly company of natives, all clean and orderly, were present, and many were in tears.

"Mr. Lacey preached again at seven in the evening from Isa. 54 : 2, 3. The attendance was again good, the attention serious, and the whole a day of much holy pleasure.

"Mr Lacey adds :—

"'I find it is now just twelve years since the chapel was first opened. I laid the foundation stone in May, 1826, and brother Sutton gave an address. On November 5th of that year, I delivered the first sermon, and brother Sutton preached in the evening. We have been spared through twelve eventful years, in an Indian climate, and are now permitted together to re-open the chapel after an enlargement to more than twice its former size. This is what is seldom seen in India. We were then without a single native convert, and yesterday the coldest heart must have been warmed, to have beheld our native Christian congregation.'"

In connection with English preaching, the brethren early instituted a Sabbath school and then an English day school, to which at length was added a boarding department for a number of poor and destitute children in English habits. These were truly benevolent efforts, and for more than thirteen years did the English school afford the means of instruction to many who must otherwise have remained in total ignorance. The average attendance, in the boys' department, was from 60 to 100 daily. In the girls', the number was much less. The boys' school has since been merged in one established by Government, and the girls' is still continued on a small scale by a few benevolent residents at the station.

While the Orissa missionaries thus sought to benefit any they could reach, through the medium of their own tongue, they were earnestly intent on the acquisition of the Oriya language, and instructing the people through that medium. They considered themselves as sent to the Oriyas. Hence, so soon as it was practicable, they established a number of native schools both for boys and girls.

Those for the former were kept up for a number of years at considerable expense, but in the unanimous opinion of the brethren, the results did not warrant a continuance of the system. A number of children were thus taught to read, a knowledge of the elements of Christianity was to some extent diffused, and a sort of focus in the towns and villages thus supplied for the missionary to secure the attention of the people to his addresses when visiting the schools. But it is not known that a single convert was ever gained from this source. One of the schoolmasters, however, embraced the gospel, and his conversion is in part to be ascribed to his being obliged to read the gospels as a schoolmaster. While the writer is of opinion that a system of such native schools is not to be recommended, he thinks that in special cases, and in the establishment of new stations, one or two such schools may be established with advantage. That is, they may serve as a convenient introduction of a mission.

The girls in these schools, it was soon ascertained, were either training for prostitutes, and a knowledge of reading would enable them to acquire their filthy songs, or else they were poor, low caste children, whose presence, not for the purpose of learning, but show, was hired by the schoolmaster. They were of short continuance. It is now pretty generally conceded, that nothing of importance can be accomplished in heathen Hindoo female education, until the more general education of the males, and a considerable improvement in the morals and domestic economy of the people generally.

While the school system for native heathen children was thus gradually abandoned, a growing interest was felt in the education of our converts' children, and an asylum for such and any others whom we could have entirely under our control, was established at Cuttack in the year 1836. Others have since been established at Berhampore, Balasore and Jellasore. We shall refer, hereafter, to these truly interesting appendages to our missionary operations.

While the scattered condition of our converts at first rendered it necessary that these children should be brought together and boarded as well as educated, yet, as they increased and began to form themselves into villages, the village school became a desirable appendage. Accordingly several schools have thus been formed, both in Cuttack and in country stations. The supplies for the boarding school are thus limited, but this is a result we anticipated and desired. There will still be enough of orphan and destitute children to keep up a considerable boarding establishment for both sexes.

From the elementary schools thus established, has the necessity for a Normal school, or as it was first called, a preparatory school, arisen. Some of the lads in these elementary schools, who manifest superior aptitude for study, have been received into the asylum as boarders, and pass through a course of two or three years study of a superior character to what is enjoyed in the elementary schools. They are especially taught to read the Scriptures,—a brief work on geography and natural philosophy,—grammar,—the elements of Sanscrit grammar and the Amara Cosha, or Sanscrit dictionary, with similar studies. It is hoped some of these lads will become our future schoolmasters. And, finally, a Theological Institution has recently been established for the training of native ministers, to which reference may be made hereafter.

In connection with these efforts to train the young in the religion of the Bible, the brethren early commenced the preparation and distribution of tracts. With very few exceptions, this department of labor has devolved upon the writer, and he has now before him a list of about fifty tracts. Most of these have been collected and reprinted in three volumes, while the materials for a fourth volume are at hand.

In connection with these tracts, which are of a purely evangelical character, several larger religious works and elementary school books have been prepared. Of the former, we may instance part of Doddridge's Rise and Progress, Pilgrim's Progress, Barth's Church History, and extracts from Baxter's Call; of the latter, Elements of Geography, Astronomy and Natural History; Reflections on the works of God; A Companion to the Bible; Peep of Day and Line upon Line; Sketches of Orissian and Indian History; Dictionaries, Grammar and Vocabulary; Arithmetic, &c., &c.

To these may be added the whole Bible translated into Oriya, and a collection of hymns for public and private worship. This brief enumeration may suffice to show that considerable progress has been made in the preparation of elementary works needed in the work of instruction.

All the above, however important, and however essential as part of our general operations, are yet to be esteemed subordinate to the preaching of the everlasting gospel to the people in their own language and in their own towns and villages. He who stops short of this, cannot be justly designated a missionary to the heathen. Many indeed do stop short of this, and may be more honored or applauded by the worldly wise in India as elsewhere; and strong are the temptations to earn this meed of praise at this cheap rate. For while of all the servants of Christ, an itinerant preacher of the gospel most resembles his Lord and most fully acts out his great and last command, yet he is also in a heathen land called to the exercise of the most self-denial and to the endurance of most severe labor and reproach. The missionaries in Orissa have ever been characterized as itinerant preachers of the gospel. True, they have done much less in this department than they should and might have done, and it is hoped much less than they will hereafter accomplish; still, this has ever been esteemed by them their chief work, and they have labored in it more than most of their fellow-missionaries in other parts of the field. For a detail of their labors and itineracies, the reader is referred to the Narrative of the Orissa Mission and the periodical publications of the Societies in England and America. We shall in this chapter merely enumerate the chief places of preaching and talking to the people in Orissa.

1. The bazárs, public places of resort, and vicinity of temples, &c. The missionaries early commenced this kind of labor, and for many years, regularly as the evening came, they sallied forth to preach and teach the things concerning the kingdom of God. It is still the practice of the missionaries, as a body, though perhaps it is not so zealously prosecuted as in years past. Opposers of missions were loud in their expressions of alarm lest such discussions should lead to rebellion and all manner of evil; those fears have long since subsided,

and the only objection that now remains, is its supposed undignified character. Doubtless it ill accords with the notions and feelings of the votaries of pleasure and fashion, it does so in England and America; but our standard of taste and propriety in such matters must be the example of the Divine Missionary and his apostles. What was not unworthy of the Son of God, cannot be deemed too low for the observance of his humble followers. And there is this fact moreover to be considered, that in India our work and circumstances compare very closely with those of the apostles.

2. Native schools and chapels were, to some extent, made use of as preaching stations in the early days of the mission, and are extensively employed by many missionaries in other parts of the field. While our system of schools continued, these were very favorable preaching places, especially for young missionaries, and as such may be still, to some extent, recommended. We never succeeded very well with native chapels,—perhaps a chief reason was, we began them before we had sufficient knowledge of the language to conduct the service efficiently. It is at least now deserving of consideration whether an evening service, by candle light, in an open-fronted chapel, might not be attempted with fair promise of success, especially in our city and town stations.

3. Native markets. These are important places for the missionary to attend. They are found on certain days in most parts of the province, and draw together the people from an infinitude of small villages and hamlets which the missionary could hardly visit in detail. Here, beneath some shady tree or wall, the missionary may stand and preach for hours to a large congregation. Its only drawback is the noise of the market.

4. Heathen festivals. These are held in connection

with some idol's temple or sacred spot for bathing at a great many places in Orissa. There is also a number of large festivals annually celebrated at Pooree, besides the great car festival. The Orissa missionaries have been in the habit of attending many of these, and have found them, next to markets, the most important preaching opportunities which the province affords.

5. In addition to these special journeys to particular places, we have been in the habit of taking long journeys in the cold season for the purpose of travelling from village to village, and preaching the gospel in every village throughout extensive districts. In this way the seed of the kingdom has been scattered broadcast nearly over the whole land. A specimen of these journeyings and preachings may be hereafter afforded.

6. Finally, we have regular Sabbath and week day services in our chapels for the Christian native community. On these occasions, both the native preachers and English or American missionaries officiate, and the services are conducted in the same order as is usual in English.

The above is a brief enumeration of the principal means employed to spread the gospel in Orissa. It will be seen that the missionaries had every thing to do, from the elementary school book and the little tract, to the preparation of grammars and dictionaries and the translation of the word of God. They had not one native Christian to help them, nor for years was there any hope of their gaining a single convert. All was dark, dreary and discouraging. But the blessing came at last. God's truth, wherever faithfully and perseveringly proclaimed, is all powerful, and it is only because we do not fully trust it, that it ever appears not mighty to save. The instances of success yet enjoyed, may be regarded as mere corruscations of that greater body of light which is breaking forth all over the land. Our eyes may seem to fail with longing for the bright rising of the sun of righteousness; but so certainly as day succeeds the dawn, will the glorious day of gospel light irradiate these lands. The bright glancings of the coming morning already tinge the mountain tops, and how cheeringly will the song yet be sung in Orissa,—" Arise, shine, for thy light is come, and the glory of the Lord is risen upon thee," " Amen."

## CHAPTER VI.

Pooree as a missionary station; notices of the place—Native account of the temple and its idol—Pilgrimages—Car festival—Pilgrim tax, &c.

So soon as the pioneers of the Orissa mission felt themselves settled in the province, they began to contemplate the formation of a second station. As the great temple of Jugernath gave eclat to the mission, it is not surprising that they sought to establish one of their posts in its immediate vicinity. Mr. Bampton was the pioneer devoted to this arduous enterprise, and he was just the man to carry the war into the very citadel of Satan's empire. "He was a good man, and full of the Holy Ghost and of faith." Prudently did he commence, and zealously did he prosecute his self-denying labors at this station, till he finished his course, after nine years of extraordinary toil and patient endurance. In 1825, he was joined by the writer, and his beloved companion, who soon found an early grave on the barren sands of Pooree. The station was reöccupied by the writer after Mr. Bampton's death, and maintained till the year 1833, when ill health drove him from the field. Since that period, no missionary has fixed his abode at Pooree, but several have paid it an occasional visit, while at the recurrence of the car festival it has been visited nearly every year by several European and native brethren.

The district has been lately reöccupied by Messrs. Millar and Bailey; but these young brethren have, in accordance with the advice of Conference, fixed their place of abode at Pipplee, a large village on the high road, nearly midway from Pooree and Cuttack. This district has hitherto yielded but little actual fruit, but the prospects are now far more cheering than they have ever been. These brethren include Pooree in their field of labor, and purpose spending several months of the year at that station.

Those who preach the gospel at this emporium of idolatry, have especial need to observe the direction of the apostle, "in meekness instructing those who oppose themselves, if God peradventure will give them repentance to the acknowledging of the truth; and that they may recover themselves out of the snare of the devil, who are taken captive by him at his will." Often have the brethren there had fellowship with that apostle, when he speaks of having, "after the manner of men, fought with beasts at Ephesus." As Demetrius, and the workmen of like occupation, fearing for their gainful craft, surrounded the preacher, and shouted out for the space of two hours, "Great is Diana of the Ephesians!" so have we often been assailed for even a longer period, day after day, by the pundas and priests, who fatten on the spoils of Pooree; and amidst the deafening shout of "Victory to Jugernath! victory to Jugernath!" have been fain to preach the gospel amidst much contention.

Those days of toil and sad depression can never be erased from the writer's mind. Often has he taken his solitary way along the desolate beach at Pooree, dropping scalding tears over the deep depravity of the people, or, prostrate before God in his study, has mourned over his own unprofitableness and unfitness for his high office. Such days of heart-searching and humility probably fall to the lot of few, though every missionary in the field doubtless knows, more or less, what the above words imply.

No native of Pooree has been baptized, but there have been a few from the neighborhood, and several of our converts have spoken of deriving benefit from our labors at the Ruth Jattra, or car festival. Several instances, too, have been noticed of converts who have been added to churches in far distant stations, referring to our tracts or missionary efforts there.

A document has just come to hand from two missionaries of the London Missionary Society, who visited Orissa at the last car festival, which, while it confirms the statements put forth from time to time by the Orissa missionaries, furnishes an interesting view of the growing vigor with which idolatry is being assailed in that hard-fought field.

"In the month of June, 1849, a band of nine European missionaries and ten native assistants visited Pooree, about three hundred miles from Calcutta, where the festival is held, in order to preach to the multitudes of pilgrims. Pooree is regarded by the Hindoos as peculiarly holy, and contains about thirty thousand inhabitants, but a large part of the houses are for the accommodation of travellers. Within the town, enclosed by a wall twenty feet high, are more than fifty temples, of which that of Jugernath is the chief.

"The zeal with which the worship of Jugernath is maintained, is easily explained. There are some six hundred and forty officers of the temple, four hundred families of cooks, one hundred and twenty dancing-girls, and three thousand priests, all of whom are supported by the fees and contributions of the pilgrims, and by the sale of holy food, for which they receive about eight times as much as it costs. It is regarded as sinful for pilgrims to eat any other food, and this monopoly is very gainful. The great wealth thus amassed furnishes a powerful mo-

FESTIVAL OF JUGGERNAUT.

tive to deceive the people with all sorts of lying wonders. Some of them acknowledge that they care nothing for Jugernath, but are only engaged in his service as a matter of speculation. Besides the fees and perquisites which they receive lawfully, there are immense offerings made continually to the idol—food, clothing, money, jewels, &c., which are of course appropriated by the idol's retinue. Agents are sent out, with the most villanous fabrications concerning the greatness of Jugernath, to attract pilgrims.

"There are twelve festivals observed at Pooree, each of which is attended by thousands; but the principal, or *car* festival, occurs in June or July, just at the time of the greatest heat, and at the setting in of the rains. Three cars, for Jugernath, and his brother and sister, are erected outside of the temple. The car of Jugernath is forty-five feet high, resting on sixteen wheels, each seven feet in diameter. The idols are hideous wooden blocks having a rude resemblance to human heads set on pedestals. They are placed on their cars, and at a given signal the vehicles advance a few yards at a time, the priests at each pause coming forward to recite addresses and songs. They are thus drawn to the temple of Gundicha, about a mile distant.

"In the present case, on the 22d of June, the main street, the roofs and verandahs of houses, and every other accessible point of observation, were crowded at an early hour with dense masses of human beings. The cars were not finished, and before they could be got in readiness the day wore away. A terrible storm came on, and men and women, one hundred thousand in number, without any adequate protection from the tempest, stood for hours waiting for the appearance of the idol. It came at last, and was hoisted to its place, (but not till its mouth had fallen out and disappeared,) and the pilgrims, having gratified their curiosity, went away. The next day the cars could not move, owing to the heavy rain. Thousands of spectators were assembled, and to these the missionaries pointed out the helplessness of the idol, as shown by the accident to its grim countenance,—not without apparent effect on the minds of many.

"During the progress of the festival, the missionaries and their native assistants divided themselves into three or four bands, each collecting an assembly of seven or eight hundred persons in the street, and preached on such topics as seemed suitable. When the pilgrims set out on their return, they distributed tracts and books among them, which were received with gratitude. They computed that in all, one hundred and fifty thousand pilgrims had been present, and judging from past experience, the dissemination of Christian truth among the multitude will not fail to produce its desired effect in some cases. Many have heretofore embraced the gospel from only hearing it at such places of resort, the Holy Spirit working through the truth.

"It is computed that several thousands perish annually in consequence of the hardships of the pilgrimage, and thousands are led to the commission of sins against both soul and body, in these legalized orgies."

### *Notices of Pooree.*

The site where the town of Pooree now stands, was, it is affirmed, in former ages under the sand. A great part of it was overrun with forest trees and jungle ; here gods and sages chose their abode, and practised their austerities.

The Hindoos are fond of believing that a temple was built on the spot where the present temple now stands, by

Maharaja Indradummun; but, as I have already observed, it is their common practice to mix up with the ancient sovereigns of India those of the provinces, inducing all sorts of anachronisms. It is not impossible, that a raja of the same name may have reigned in Orissa, but of this we have no record. The present temple was built by Anung Bhim Deb, A. D., 1198.

We have so frequently described the temple, that we refrain from lengthened statements on the present occasion. We will, however, present a short extract from Lieut. Lawrie, respecting the temple enclosure, and a part of a lengthened description of this enclosure, from a native poem, translated by my fellow-laborer, Rev. Charles Lacey, of Cuttack. The former writes—

"Taking a telescopic view of the temple, from an elevation one and a half miles north-east of the town, we behold the Bara Dewal, or great temple, nearly 190 feet high, towering majestically above the dark and gloomy landscape below. The entire height of the tower from the ground is about 210 feet." It resembles, says Stirling, a phial with the stopper inserted; but Lawrie compares it to "an old-fashioned pepper-box, multilateral, and of nearly equal diameter until approaching the top. The remainder of the box is very similar to the upper portion of the tower of Orissa."

"The stone wall, enclosing the Bara Dewal and the edifices connected with it, is about thirty feet high. The area forms nearly a square, or rectangular, 660 feet by 650. Within this area are upwards of 100 temples, apparently from 70 to 80 feet high, dedicated to the principal deities of the Hindoo Pantheon. The singh Dwar, or principal entrance, is flanked by huge griffins, and a little in front of it stands a beautiful column of black marble, of an architecture between the Doric and Corinthian."

We now proceed to the account, by the native writer, and which is sold to people visiting the temple.

### *A Description of the Sacred Enclosure at Pooroossuttom.*

North of the ocean lies the divine inheritance of Hurree. In that inheritance is the mystic conch, or shell, of Vishnoo, which winds to the distance of twelve and a half miles from the centre. The navel of this shell forms the centre of the divine inheritance, and on it stands the divinely celebrated Blue mountain, to the name of which listen with reverence. Sebo is unable to comprehend its glory, and therefore how feeble are the efforts of mortals. The very name of this mountain causes the hearts of men to rejoice; and well it may, since to listen to a recital of its glories at once destroys the guilt of ten millions of births. Put aside, therefore, all stubbornness of heart, cultivate devotedness of mind, and in a timely manner put your trust in Sree-Krishnoo. Do this, and you shall obtain deliverance, shall obtain supreme felicity, and finally be admitted into the temple of the supreme Hurree.

Observe, then, that at the chief entrance, you have in the first place a sight of Patita pàbun.* Then on the twenty-two steps, which conduct you into the interior, you see Kasi biswanath,† who, not being permitted to proceed further, stands in the posture of meditation, on the full godhead of the place. Next you come to the Bhogamundab, or hall of food, where the holy food is collected; seeing which, all guilt is taken away. Here, bow your head down to the floor. When you have seen the god Ajanunath, whose hands reach to his calves, pass on till you come to Bighnaswer, or he who destroys difficulties. You now arrive at the divine Banyan tree, in which Mungala or Doorga, is incarnate. At the root of this tree dwell Krishnoo and Rhoodra

* A form of Vishnoo, signifying, He who is steps for lost souls to ascend from misery.

† A form of Seeb, or Mahadab.

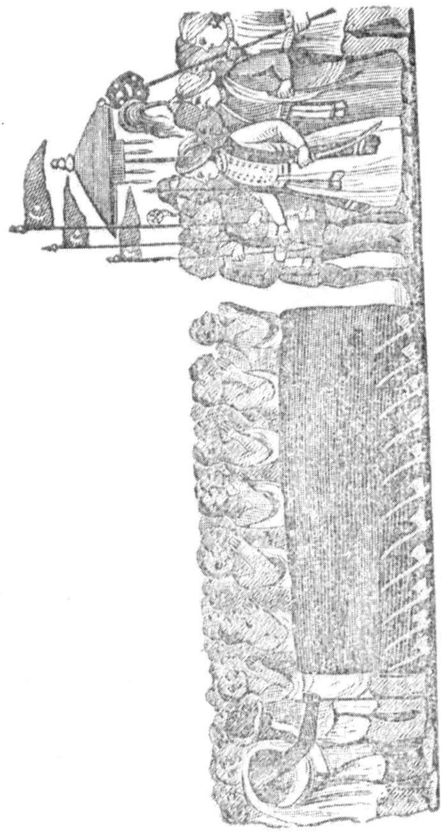

or Mahadab. Walk round these two or three times. Under this tree also you see Anunta sayuna,* or the eternal sleeper, on his serpent with seven mouths. From this place look upwards, and you may see the Chockra † of Vishnoo, on the very point of the temple's pinnacles. Meditate on it. After seeing the Khetrapall, you depart and come to Nursingnath.‡ Your next sight is the sacred Hall of Deliverance,§ where holy brahmuns constantly sit, disposing of all matters connected with religion from the sacred books. Then you come to the Rhoenekund or trough of Rhoene, in which is the wonderful crow with four arms, who obtained divine worship and immortality by performing austerities. In the water of Rhoeni-Kund, you perceive the shadow of the Chokra on the summit of the temple, which wonder has now been worshipped for ages. Next, there is Bimalákee. Victory to her! She is the proprietress of the holy inheritance of Hurree, and listens to the cries of all. In the hall of this goddess, is great Doorga, destroying the pride of the demon Moyésá. Also, here you see the forms of Nunda, Josoda,‖ Krishnoo, and his companions, standing all about. Here is Surruswottee,¶ Nillamáhádab,** and Bhadákáliká.†† The goddess Surruswottee must be particularly regarded, for she is inclined to mercy. Victory to thee, O Lockshmee! the bestower of the fourfold good, holiness, riches, happiness, and salvation! Thou also givest supreme bliss. In the hall of the divine Lockshmee, you must sit down for a few minutes, and repeat your Máhámuntra.‡‡ Arising from that, you worship Honuman,§§ and

* A form of Vishnoo, sleeping on the serpent, which is an emblem of eternity.

† A mace, an emblem of power.

‡ A terrific form of Vishnoo, half lion and half man, in which he destroyed the demon Heronakya.

§ Hall of the Hindoo Sanhedrim.

‖ The reputed parents of Krishnoo.

¶ Daughter of Brumha, the Creator.

** A form of Vishnoo.

†† A form of Doorga.

‡‡ A string of names, as follows: Hurree, Ram, Krishnoo; Hurree, Ram, Krishoo. Krishnoo, Krishnoo, Hurree, Krishnoo, Krishnoo, Hurree, Ram, ram, hurree, Ram, ram, hurree.

§§ A deified monkey.

then prefer your requests to him. Then you proceed to the Feet-washing trough,* into which run the streams of the sacred Ganges, the Jumna, and the Surruswottee rivers. Dip the tip of your finger in this, and take the drop on your tongue, and thereby you will destroy boundless guilt. With the little that remains on your finger, mark your forehead, and if the agent of justice sees you, instead of punishing, he will praise you!

From this trough you may see the sun rising, in his morning beauty, to the eastward. In the eastern corner, also, you may have a sight of Pátáléswar, or the god of the infernal regions, in the deep and dark well. In the northerly corner is Doorga, called Setala, accompanied by Máhádab. Then, near the golden well, there is the northern goddess, a form of Doorga and Sebo, with her attendants, devils, witches and spectres. Mounted on two elephants, there are the two brothers, Jugernath and Bolabhudra, with their foot-marks imprinted on the stones. Seeing which, you must think you are bathing in the five rivers, or tirths, i. e. Gungá, Jumuná, Surruswotte, Godábery, and Sáradu. Here is the immortal Bur tree, called the tree of honey and curds, at the foot of which are the foot-marks of Vishnoo, his chockra and podma. These are all in the hall of the great Lockshmee. While you meditate on these rivers, and as it were bathe in them, remember, that even the very fear of death is destroyed. Next, and near at hand, is the great Choitan, a sight of whom destroys the guilt even of the murder of Brumha. But let me tell you, ere I proceed, that, putting all worldliness from your minds, and thinking on the feet of your spiritual guide, you should perigrinate the sacred enclosure four times.

Now you pass to the Jagamohun, or the place which fascinates the world. Here you see the two brothers arrayed in military uniform, with their weapons of war, mounted on their war-horses. They are returning from Kánchekábaree; they were thirsty, and asked drink of a milkmaid, who refused to give them. Here you perceive Jugernáth is pledging his Botchàorring with her, for a drink of her sour milk. See how she holds out her hands, to

* A trough of dirty water, filled from the washing of the idols, &c.

receive the ring. Sebo, and he with four faces, (Brumhá,) are standing near with their hands joined, in act of adoration.

Now, you come to the pillar of Gorurà, the bird and vehicle of Vishnoo. Here, for sixteen times, you must throw yourself down on the ground, on your face, with your hands stretched out forward, and make your devotions to Jugernath in a spirit of devoted love. Then turn to the two door-keepers, Joya, and Bejoya, and with joined hands touching your forehead, humbly solicit permission to enter the divine presence. This done, enter the Chundun-urgully, or place of the presence, earnestly looking on *the face*. There, on a pillar of blue emerald, in a golden shrine, is Bhogwan! They sit on a throne of diamonds, even the four forms, that is, Bulabhudra, Jugernath, Subhadra, and Sudursun. Victory to Subudrah! Victory to Subudrah, the beautiful maid! Victory to Balabhudra! and Victory to Jugernath!

There is much more, in a similar strain.

Pilgrimages to reputed holy places, such as the confluence of rivers, hot springs, or other natural phenomena, as also to celebrated idols or the tombs of saints, have ever been popular in India. But perhaps no pilgrimage was ever so extensively practised and so generally famed, as that of the pilgrimage to Jugernath. By what fortuitous concurrence of circumstances that ugly idol became so celebrated, it is difficult to imagine; but, beyond a doubt, the example and influence of Choitunya, the Bengali reformer, had a very considerable share in rendering the worship of Jugernath popular. The continuance of that popularity is doubtless in a great measure to be ascribed to the interested zeal of priests and rulers who have fattened on the spoil. All governments, native and foreign, have regarded Jugernath as fair game, and have employed their power and prestige to render attractive the pilgrimage and increase the revenue from this polluted source.

The location of the Orissa missionaries being the site of this celebrated temple, they have been brought into direct collision with Government support of idolatry in India. And as one of the most offensive features of that connection has been the abominations of Jugernath, they have been from the first obliged to take part against it. It must not however be hence inferred that the Orissa missionaries are the adversaries of the Honorable Company's rule in India. So far from this being the case, I may safely reiterate the assertion made in our first Indian report, that the Government have no more attached friends than they. In this view it is to them a matter of sincere satisfaction that many of the servants of the Honorable Company's Government in India have expressed similar views on this subject to those of the Orissa missionaries, though differing widely from them in many other views and opinions.

Mr. Peggs, formerly of the Orissa Mission, has furnished so long a list of testimonies bearing on this point in his pamphlet on the pilgrim tax, that it is unnecessary for the writer to say a word more on the subject. The writer has watched the progress of the controversy relating to the pilgrim tax from the beginning, and often taken part in it. Few things have occasioned him more surprise than the rash statements made and believed by succeeding Government functionaries in relation thereto. And yet materials for the formation of a correct opinion on the case were always accessible, that is, with a little research and willingness to be instructed.

In the office of the Commissioner at Cuttack was deposited a book, in manuscript, containing a full history of the connection of Government with the shrine, and there it continued till within the last five years. The writer has, at twenty years distance, twice read that

book, and has always found it to agree with those Government regulations and minutes of Governor Generals which have seen the light. Particularly does it agree with the printed documents furnished by the home authorities in 1846. Instead of going back to the earlier periods of the Company's sway in Orissa, writers on the tax have usually begun with the regulations of 1805, and hence have stopped short of necessary data.

When the British troops entered the province in 1803, Lord Wellesly enjoined on Col. Campbell to pay all respect to the brahmuns,—to assure them their personal property would be held inviolate,—to preserve the sanctity of the temple, and tell them they would have to pay no tribute or revenue beyond what they paid to the Mahratta Government. Nor was he to disturb the existing system of collections at the pagoda. But he was to be careful not to contract with the brahmuns any engagements which might limit the power of the British Govment to make such arrangements with respect to the shrine as might hereafter be deemed advisable.

The same spirit pervades all the correspondence, but no pledge is any where given to endow the temple; on the contrary, it is every where supposed that the temple would be a source of emolument to the Government far beyond all expenses incurred for its management. It is quite evident that the temple of Jugernath was ever regarded by our predecessors in the Government, whether they were the native Oriya sovereigns, the Mahrattas or the Mussulmans, as a legitimate source of revenue, not as a burden on the state. They made certain allowances for the support of the temple and its services out of the proceeds of the pilgrim fees and donations frequently specified. It was thus that the British Government took the shrine under its charge, expecting to make large sums of money thereby, out of which they would have to keep up the establishment. The manner in which they agreed to do this is fully detailed in the aforenamed manuscript, as well as the schemes and plans proposed and adopted for the increase of the revenue from this source.

*Here, then, was a pledge involved, viz.* :—while Government took the whole proceeds of the temple, they were bound to pay the expenses of it, and these expenses were, after much duplicity and chicanery on the part of the pundas, compounded for at the rate of 55,000 rupees per annum. It was a fair bona fide business transaction,—a bargain between the Government and the temple authorities. What was objectionable in it arose from the contrariety of the whole matter to the law and spirit of Christianity. It was encouraging unutterable abominations, and making money from all that was hateful to God and injurious to man.

The natives constantly urged the Government connection, as a proof of the divinity of Jugernath, and pointed to the gaudy cars, the active Government officers, and Government badges on their servants, as indisputable proof that Government honored the idol.

When, therefore, the voice of Christianity was heard, and Government desired to withdraw from its connection with the idol, the plain, simple course was to throw back all the revenues and perquisites of the temple (so far as they were legitimate,) to the hereditary guardians of the shrine, and stand clear of all connection with it, as in the case of other temples. From this obvious course, however, they were diverted by the representations of the then collector of the tax at Jugernath supported by the then acting Commissioner. It was at their instance Lord Auckland encumbered the settlement of the matter with a grant which is now contested. The above gentleman contended there was a pledge to support the idol, which is now proved to be incorrect, and this error embarrassed the otherwise obvious and easy mode of settling the question. Such, too, is the expressed opinion of the Revenue Board. They say:—

"We have endeavored to examine the question of 'pledge or no pledge' abstractedly and apart from all religious considerations, and we have no hesitation in declaring that we cannot find that the Government have ever bound themselves by any pledge, conditional or unconditional, not to discontinue the allowance paid to the temple. On the contrary, it is the conviction of the Board the Government payment might fairly and honestly have stopped simultaneously with the abolition of the pilgrim tax."

Lord Auckland acted in opposition to the advice of his council when he proposed his final measure on this subject, and did so in the face of at least three considerations which should have deterred him from his most injudicious arrangement.

1st. The advisers of it were men who had either prejudged the case,* or were far too interested to deserve implicit control over his views in opposition to those of his council.

2d. The priests themselves offered to relieve Government from their contribution on being allowed to collect the usual fee for admission to the temple.

3d. He was under no necessity thus to adopt a plan which would, without relieving Government of the odium of its connection with idolatry, embarrass all further attempts to settle the question finally; at least, not until

* See controversy in the Englishmen for 1838.

he had referred the whole case to the Court of Directors for their approval.

I should say that from these considerations as well as from the fact that further investigation proves that the ground of the aforementioned gentlemen's advice was unsound,—namely that there was no pledge,—Government is quite justified in rescinding that plan and adopting the alternative proposed by the priests themselves, taking care that the fee so collected shall not be demanded on the authority of Government, but on the ground of the right the proprietors of the temple possess, to make such regulations respecting it as they please.

The Orissa missionaries have, from time to time, felt called upon to report progress in this matter, and to utter their protest against the connection of the British Government with the idolatries of India; they do so not as political demagogues, but as Englishmen, jealous for the honor of their country, and as Christian philanthropists who daily are called to mourn over the injurious effects of that connection. They ask neither for patronage of themselves or any other religious professors in India; but they do ask of Government to carry out their own professed rule of action, viz., to govern India with impartiality. The line of conduct they advocate is indicated by that ascribed to a certain heroine of other days.

> "Favors to none, to all she smiles extends,
> Oft she rejects but never once offends."

While we deprecate the government patronage of Jugernath, we as loudly exclaim against all injustice toward his votaries. Let the donations and endowments afforded him, not by governments, but his worshippers, be held sacred to him, and so say we of Mahomedanism and of Christianity; but let there be no partial support, by the State, of any class even of Christians.

Such substantially were the views of those worthy men, who, until their dying hour, so strenuously and so consistently opposed this connection of Britain with idolatry in India,—Messrs. Poynder and Peggs. They lived not to see the desire of their hearts fully accomplished, but they lived long enough to see that their work would not be in vain,—that this unnatural upholding of heathenism by Christian men must come to an end. That it was now a mere question of time.

The editor of the Friend of India has ever been a staunch opponent of the grant to Jugernath, though he has sometimes, very inconsistently as we think, objected to the Orissa missionaries taking the stand they have done in opposition to it. We cannot refrain from inserting lengthened extracts from important articles on this subject which give a fair view of the state of the question when the author left India.

### *Government connection with Idolatry.*

We publish, with some feelings of regret, the resolution of the Missionary Conference at Cuttack relative to the connection of Government with the shrine of Jugernath.

" *Resolved*, That as a very general opinion is prevalent that the Government of India have abandoned their connection with the temple of Jugernath, we deem it obligatory on us, as a Missionary Conference assembled in the province of Orissa, to state that such is not the case.

" It is indeed true that Government have restored certain lands to the proprietors of the temple and abolished the pilgrim tax, they have moreover ceased to receive the presents and other emoluments connected with the idol, and thus far they have done well; but the Government do still in fact, though in another form, contribute more largely than before to the support of the idol, inasmuch as they have not only relinquished the lands and other emoluments of the temple, from which they formerly received a revenue, but have added an annual donation of 35,000 rupees, while they allow the proprietors of the temple to receive all presents and levy any contributions they please on the pilgrims; so that a much larger source of revenue than ever is now open to the raja and other interested parties.

"We do therefore consider the continuation of this yearly grant to Jugernath as most anti-christian in itself, and an act of partiality towards the idol which is inconsistent with the neutral position the Government profess to sustain towards all systems of religion in India.

"We further agree that this resolution be sent for insertion in the *Friend of India* and *Calcutta Christian Observer*.

"*Cuttack*, *Nov.* 22, 1845."

Our old fashioned notions lead us to think it scarcely compatible with the object or the position of missionary associations in this country thus to step forward and gratuitously pass a vote of censure on the conduct of Government. We are afraid it is likely to do more disservice to the missionary cause, than benefit to the object in view. This battle must be fought in England and not in India; and the present movement can scarcely fail to create irritation, but will not promote success. If any repugnance still lurks among any of the influential members of Government to cut the shrine adrift, we must trust for its removal to the same authoritative interference from home, to which we are indebted for the previous triumphs of this cause. After what we have so often written on this matter, we shall not be suspected of any lukewarmness. We believe Lord Auckland committed a fatal error when he listened to the advice of the functionaries in Orissa, rather than to that of his council, and disobeyed the orders of the directors by giving the sanction of Government to a donation which was "not in the original bond." He has thereby inflicted a degree of embarrassment on the Court of Directors which is sharply felt. The desire to meet the wishes of the religious public at home and the claims of duty, is, in this instance, encountered by the anxiety not to weaken the hands of Government by openly disallowing what has been openly sanctioned by the highest delegated authority in India. But the directors have not lost sight of the matter; they have been steadily pressing it on the local authorities, and have insisted either on their pointing out the treaties or engagements under which it has been deemed indispensable to sanction this donation, or to indicate the mode in which the connection may be dissolved. The subject is still under discussion, and though a flapper from Exeter Hall would perhaps not be redundant, yet we could wish it had not been manufactured at a Missionary Conference, and openly announced to the world.

There is one assertion in the resolutions which we cannot but believe to have been inadvertently adopted. We allude to that in which it is stated that the proprietors of the temple are permitted to "levy contributions." It may not be easy to distinguish, at the shrine of Jugernath, between a free will offering and a "forced benevolence." The object of the pilgrim is generally to give as little as possible; that of the priest to obtain the last possible farthing. But it is contrary to law to *levy the slightest contribution*. Until we have done with this degrading and polluting connection, which arose conjointly from an indifference to Christianity and the love of money, it is necessary to keep this fact prominently in view, that every priest at every other temple in India is permitted to levy whatever contributions he pleases, and to establish his own scale of fees, according to the supposed value of the spiritual advantages of his shrine. But the priests at Jugernath were positively forbidden, by a distinct regulation, to demand any of those fees which they had previously been in the habit of demanding, because Government had resolved to take on itself to provide for the expenses of the temple out of the proceeds of the pilgrim tax. So long, therefore, as Government continues to furnish funds for the expenditure of the shrine, the priests cannot morally or legally exact a single contribution, and if these exactions have been winked at by the local authorities, they have laid themselves open to censure. The priests have no right to demand contributions of the pilgrims while they receive an equivalent from the State. Almost every one appears to think that the wisest and most equitable plan which Government could adopt in the dilemma in which they have been involved by Lord Auckland's most injudicious donation, is at once to repeal the law which forbids to priests to levy *fees* from pilgrims, and having thus restored to them their ancient and strictly legitimate sources of revenue, and placed the temple on the same footing on which every other shrine stands, to withdraw the donation at once.

Again, on a final review of the whole question, the Friend of June 25th, 1846, remarks :—

We have recently received a copy of the correspondence between the Court of Directors and the Government of India and Bengal, regarding the connection of the British Government with the various idolatrous shrines in India, and more especially with that of Jugernath. We are thus enabled to review this vexatious question, with the aid of all the information which the researches of the Bengal Government have brought to light; and we must intreat the attention, and we fear also, the patience, of the reader, for a few moments.

The main question at issue is, whether Lord Auckland was borne out in affirming, that " our promise of the allowance for the support of the temple was distinct and unconditional." It is not denied, that within a very short period after taking possession of the country, the British Government, in its anxiety to conciliate the people, by leaving every thing in the *status ante bellum*, found itself identified with the shrine; but it is impossible to discover any pledge whatsoever in our early proceedings, or indeed in any proceedings at all, except those of Lord Auckland.

We are enabled to trace, from the earliest period, not only of our own administration in Orissa, but of that of the Hindoo rulers who preceded us, a close and inseparable connection between the tax on pilgrims, and the public donation from the state. That donation was invariably a portion of the produce of the pilgrim tax. The Mahrattas are reported to have realized from it a sum varying from two lakhs and a half to five lakhs a year, and the sum which they expended on the temple, in the year 1800–1, was 20,393 Rs.; in 1801–2, 21,498 Rs., and in the year preceding our conquest, 18,432 Rs. Thus the temple of Jugernath has, from the time when it was wrested from the Mahomedans in 1755, been made to support itself. Not only has it received no independent assistance from the revenues of Government, but it has contributed largely to swell them—in the days of the Mahrattas, to the extent of several lakhs of rupees a year; and under our own administration, by an amount varying from half a lakh to a lakh of rupees annually. Of this fact, the priests of the temple were fully aware. They knew that they had no claim on the resources of Government separate from the revenues which the temple was enabled to contribute to them. They felt that, when in our total ignorance of the circumstances of the case, and in the excess of our uncalculating generosity, we intermitted the pilgrim tax, on first occupying Pooree, but were disposed to continue the donation which the Mahrattas had paid, their own interests were placed in jeopardy. They dreaded lest, when we found that the donation had been paid out of the tax, we should eventually discontinue it, on the ground that the funds which supplied it had ceased to exist. Hence their anxiety that the tax should be reïmposed; for although they knew that it must tend to diminish the number of pilgrims, they hoped, that as long as it was collected, it would be a security for that portion of it which fell to their share. The tax was accordingly reëstablished, and a proportion of it, varying from one-fourth to one-third, was made over to the support of Jugernath.

The advocates for our continued connection with Jugernath, place great reliance on an expression in Regulation XII. of 1805, which refers to the continuance of pensions of a religious character, and declares that nothing therein contained should be "construed to authorize the resumption of the established donation for the support of Jugernath." This has been interpreted as an irrevocable pledge to grant this donation in perpetuity. But this is a forced construction, which neither the plain meaning of the terms, nor the analogy of our legislation will justify.

We admit, that there was an established donation; that it was as old as the rise of the Mahratta power in Cuttack, and that our Government determined to continue it; but we contend that it was inseparable from the fund which supplied it; that the very first sum ever paid by our Government—called the customary advance—was authorized in the same despatch in which the establishment of the tax to provide means for paying it in future, was sanctioned; and that as long as our Government prevented the priests exacting their usual dues of the pilgrims, and forbade them to sell the spiritual benefits of the temple at their own price, and drew all fees and taxes into its own exchequer, it was bound by a higher than a legislative obligation to devote a portion of these revenues to the maintenance of the temple, and that any attempt to evade this obligation would have justly subjected Government to censure.

Thirty years after, the attention of the public in England was drawn to the subject, and the identification of the British Government with the idolatrous institutions of India, roused the indignation of the nation, and the public voice demanded that the support thus ministered to superstition by the British authorities, which gave it an adventitious vigor and eclat, and injuriously affected every effort to introduce the truths of the gospel, should cease. The subject was pressed on the consideration of the local authorities in 1838, when Lord Auckland, the Governor General, was at Simlah, separated from the members of his council. The object of the Court of Directors was to separate the Government of India, absolutely and forever, from all connection with the shrines of idolatry. The members of council advised that the pilgrim tax, and the donation which had been paid out of it, should cease; that all the estates belonging to the temple should be restored to the raja of Khoorda, to whom the temple belonged, and that the entire management of the shrine should be made over to him, as its hereditary guardian; and that the priests should be at liberty to collect from the pilgrims those fees and dues which had been prohibited by our laws. Unfortunately for his own credit, and for the best interests of the country, Lord Auckland turned a deaf ear on the advice of his council, and opened his mind to the views of the local authorities. . . .

The conduct of Lord Auckland on this occasion is inexplicable. He could not have been ignorant, that it was the grand object of the Court of Directors, and of the Whig Government, of which he himself had been a member, to withdraw from all connection with the shrines of idolatry in the East, to withhold from them that eclat which they derived from being supported by, and identified with Government. To secure this object, the Court of Directors were ready to make the most substantial pecuniary sacrifices, and to relinquish the pilgrim tax at Jugernath, at Gyah, and at Allahabad. The execution of their wishes was entrusted to his Lordship, and he was bound to keep this object sacredly in view, in whatever arrangement he made. He had no vocation at all to interfere in the matter of these shrines, but in order to give effect to their wishes. That there was some little difficulty in the case, will be fully admitted. The opinion of the Cuttack commissioner was entitled to some weight: and he advised that the donation should be perpetuated on grounds which, having already gone over, we need not recur to. But his Lordship must have been fully aware that such a settlement of the question would be directly opposed to the intentions of the court, and to the universal wish of all who took an interest in the question in England; that it would place this difficult question in a more complicated position than ever; that it would substitute for an obligation, the existence of which was controverted, a new and direct obligation, and render it more difficult than ever for Government to withdraw from the connection. The advice of his council was in direct opposition to that of the Cuttack commissioner. In these circumstances, it was incontestibly Lord Auckland's duty to have suspended his decision, and referred the matter back to the Court of Directors, sending them at the same time the opposite opinions he had received from Cuttack and Calcutta. The subject had been under consideration for years; there was no necessity for haste; and the overland mail would have brought the resolution of the court in six months. But, instead of adopting this obvious and equitable course, his Lordship affirmed, that which it is impossible to substantiate, that, "on taking forcible possession of Cuttack, we conciliated submission, by binding ourselves to the accustomed maintenance of the temples of the country." He pronounced that our promise of the allowance for the support of the temple was "distinct and unconditional,'' and at once pledged the Government of India to the annual grant of a donation of 36,000 Rs.

The reader will kindly bear in mind, that under the Mahratta Government, the priesthood at Jugernath were permitted to levy a fee from the pilgrims in addition to their free-will offerings. These fees are styled in our own regulations, their *usual dues*, and the priests at the shrine were distinctly forbidden to collect them at the time when the British Government determined to take the entire receipts of the temple into its own hands, and to provide for the whole of the expenditure out of this fund. From the papers now published by order of Parliament, the public is for the first time informed, that when the question of severing the State from the shrine was under discussion, the priests of the temple *expressed their willingness to release the Government from their pecuniary obligation to support the temple, provided they were allowed* "*to collect the contributions.*" Nothing, therefore, would have been easier than to have dissolved this connection to the entire satisfaction of those with whom alone we had ever made any stipulations, and without the slightest imputation on our national faith. It was only necessary to repeal all the laws by which we had assumed the collection of the tax, and forbidden the priests to demand their usual dues; to divest ourselves of all farther concern in the management of the shrine, and restore it to its natural guardians, with directions to provide for its support out of the contributions of the faithful. But this golden opportunity was lost. Lord Auckland overruled this reasonable proposal of the priests, by declaring that our engagements were made with the *Hindoo public!* which, if it had any meaning, must have referred to all those who came on pilgrimage to the shrine from the various provinces of India. But the idea is altogether preposterous. If we ever gave any pledge at all, it was to the influential conclave at Pooree, whom we were anxious to conciliate at the period of the conquest. We never wasted a thought on the people of Bengal and Bahar and the Deccan. This assumption, made with the view of escaping from the increased obligation which the consent of the priesthood laid on Government of withdrawing altogether from the support of the shrine, only serves to demonstrate the total absence of any substantial ground for continuing our connection with it.

When those in England who had taken an interest in dissevering the Government of India from the temples of idolatry, found how dismally their hopes had been frustrated by Lord Auckland's settlement, they knocked loud at the door of the India House, and insisted upon a full explanation of this transaction. The directors, urged by this pressure from without, which, however unpleasant, is yet irresistible, wrote out, time after time, to the local authorities to request the production of the *specific grounds* on which it was stated in Lord Auckland's minute of the 17th of November, 1838, that "our promise of the allowance for the support of the temple was distinct and unconditional." This requisition brought the subject anew under the consideration of the Governments of India and Bengal, and the minutes recorded by its members, shewed that in their opinion the settlement was open to the most serious objections; and that at the time when Lord Auckland fixed on the British Government the continuous support of this shrine, our connection might have been dissolved with ease and honor. The sentiments contained in Sir Herbert Maddock's minute, may be considered as embodying the views of all the members of Government regarding this most unfortunate arrangement.

"At that period, during the government of Lord Auckland, when the abolition of the pilgrim tax was the point urged upon the Government of India by the Court of Directors, it might have been easy to abolish the tax as an impost from which the Government derived an income, and to separate the Government from all concern with the temple, and this might then have been effected even without restoring the Satais Huzree Mehal, or its revenues to the raja of Khoorda and the priests of the temple, for he and they would have been ready enough to close their connection with the Government, if they had been allowed to collect the tax on their own account; and this would have been the simplest course to adopt, both because there could have been no objection on the score of offence to religion in the tax being continued, provided the British Government had no concern in the collection and derived no pecuniary benefit from it, and because the probability then was and now is that whatever is saved to the pilgrims in the remission of the tax is exacted from them in some other shape, over which the Government cannot and ought not to have any control.

"That opportunity was lost, because, as it appears from his minutes, Lord Auckland thought it the duty of Government to protect the Hindoo votaries from the exactions to which they might have been subjected if the levying of the tax had been left uncontrolled in the hands of the Pundahs and others interested in it as a source of income to themselves. I do not suppose that the abolition of the tax was likely to diminish to the people the expense of their pilgrimage, and whether it was likely to have that effect or not, the matter was one that might have been left to be settled between the parties interested in it. For whether the temple has its resources increased by an annual donation from Government or not, we may feel perfectly assured that its priests will so manage their affairs as to extract, whether it be in the shape of tax at the barriers, or in the shape of fees at the gates and in the interior of the temple, the whole of the little store that the pilgrim has brought with him."

The position, therefore, in which Lord Auckland has placed the matter, is this,—the estates of the temple have been restored to the priests; the scope for extortionate gains has been indefinitely enlarged by the abolition of the pilgrim tax, which brings pilgrims in greater numbers, and with more money, to the presence of the idol; and in addition to these revenues, which are greater than the *curia* of Jugernath have enjoyed since we took possession of the country, they have the donation of 36,000 rupees a year paid regularly from our treasury. They have the same opportunity as before of magnifying the dignity and consequence of the idol to its votaries, by representing it as directly supported and encouraged by the liberality of the British Government, and they are now enabled to reap a larger harvest than ever from this—to us most degrading—representation. It would scarcely have been possible to devise any plan by which the mischief which the Court of Directors were so anxious to avoid, could have been more effectually perpetuated.

The question is, what course we are now to pursue, after the mischief has been done, and the monthly donation granted, and a kind of obligation imposed on us to continue it? Lord Ellenborough cuts the gordian knot at once. Although his lordship considers that we had incurred the obligation to support the temple, he adds: "If we think it wrong, now we have deprived ourselves of the revenue we derived from the pilgrims, to continue to perform the obligation we were understood to have incurred, of supporting the temple, it would be better to allow the receipt of a moderate tax, to be paid to the priests for the sole purpose of defraying the charges to which we are liable, the disbursements of the sum being left in their hands as well as its receipt." Mr. Bird is of the same opinion. He proposes that the prohibition to collect fees, which was reënacted in 1840, should be repealed; and that the ministers of the temple should be authorized to levy from the pilgrims such religious fees as may be consistent with former usage, and that all lands originally belonging to the temple, which upon inquiry may be found to have been improperly resumed or alienated, be restored, or, if restoration be impossible, that other lands of equal extent and value be assigned in their stead. Mr. Millet proposes a compensation for the temple revenues resumed by Government, and is willing to effect the adjustment by a transfer of land. Sir Herbert Maddock, in a minute, written nearly three months after his former minute, from which our previous extracts have been drawn, opposes the views both of Lord Ellenborough, Mr. Bird, and Mr. Millet. With his lordship, he agrees in considering an assignment of land objectionable, as a mere expedient for seeming to withdraw our patronage, while virtually we continue the same extent of support as before. He is thus opposed to the proposal of Mr. Millet, of effecting the adjustment by a transfer of land; and the argument on this point appears conclusive. To give support in money and support in land are equivalent, and however we may succeed in deceiving ourselves into the notion of a difference, the natives of India would universally understand that it was the same patronage of the rulers of the country, under another form. To the proposal of Lord Ellenborough and Mr. Bird, that the priests should be at liberty to demand contributions from the pilgrims—

which they could afford with greater ease since the abolition of the tax—Sir Herbert objects, that although this settlement of the question might have been effected before Lord Auckland's Act in 1840, and although Government might have been relieved from all further payments in support of the endowment by permitting the priests to levy certain fixed fees on pilgrims as an equivalent for the established donation of Government, and this might have been effected without any legislative enactment, merely by the Government ceasing to collect the tax and authorizing the superintendent and priests to collect such fees as had been collected under former dynasties, yet it is unadvisable and impolitic after the passing of that Act. This argument disposes at once of the supposed *pledge* on which Lord Auckland's settlement was based. If we were bound by any enactment, or any distinct engagement, to make this donation, we could not by any possibility have escaped from it without infamy. But Sir Herbert has put the question on the right basis; that of popularity with the priests and with the people; and it is on this ground alone that it requires to be dealt with. His objection to the measure of leaving the priests to draw the support of the temple from the "contributions" of the faithful, is "that it would offer no advantage to the people; and that while it left them to the almost uncontrolled exactions of the brahmins, must convey to their minds the idea that the Government, in withdrawing the support which it had hitherto afforded to the priests, and in revoking the boon accorded to the people by Act X. 1840, has, for the first time, exhibited a total disregard of the interests of both parties." But we venture to think, that any such feeling of dissatisfaction would be short-lived, except in our own minds, which require as much to be looked after as the minds of the people, because we are so apt in this matter to mistake our own prejudices for those of the people. It is certain, that the *actual* position of the pilgrims would not be injured by any such arrangement. The only parties who would really suffer are the priests; and to them the arrangement would undoubtedly be any thing but palatable. When they were told that the monthly donation of the British Government was to cease, and that in its stead they were to be left at liberty to collect those fees which had been customary under former dynasties, but which were now legally interdicted; they would at once perceive the extent of their loss; they would feel, that though they had not collected their *usual dues*, they had never allowed the pilgrim to escape with a pice; that this arrangement would at once cut off 3000 rupees a month, paid in cash, and give them in its stead—the privilege of collecting funds which they had long been in the habit of exacting. But it is worthy the consideration of the Directors of the East India Company, and of the people of England, whether a feeling of dissatisfaction which can have no foundation but in a constant and habitual breach of the law, is entitled to much consideration; and whether it is upon such grounds that the British Government is to submit to the degradation of perpetually paying 3000 rupees a month towards the support of this idol.

It is not to be supposed that the question will be allowed to remain in its present position. Some steps *must* be taken by the Directors in whose hands it now is, to complete the separation of Government from all connection with the shrine. The earnest attention which the subject has received from the principal members of Government in India, has placed it in a much clearer light than before, and made the path of duty more clear than ever. Our plainest and safest course is, to restore to the temple any revenues which have been alienated; to repeal the enactment which forbids the priests to demand their *usual dues*, and allow them to collect from the pilgrims the contributions which were "customary under former dynasties;" and then to withdraw from all connection with the shrine, and leave it, like *every other* shrine at this Presidency, to be supported by the zeal and liberality of devotees, and managed by its own conclave.

It will be seen from the above statements that we have now a new difficulty to overcome arising out of a pledge really given. A new opponent of the pledge has lately entered the field, Lieut. Lawrie, already noticed. He makes extensive use of a plan suggested by a Hindoo writer in the collector's office at Pooree, for relieving

Government from its own imposed obligation. To that work all parties interested in this question are referred.

The foregoing remarks about the tax were written before the writer left India, and, of course, before he had seen Lieut. Lawrie's book and the head clerk's proposal for levying upon the Muthdharis, or hereditary holders of the revenues of religious establishments at Pooree, the allowance to Jugernath at present granted by Government. The writer does not clearly understand the justice of this proposal, nor can he perceive that there is any necessity for such a course. It may be perfectly right and honest, but he is not in circumstances to express his approbation of such a measure. He fears there is both fraud and bad policy involved in this matter.

The last peg on which the friends of the tax have hung their plea, is that of compensation for the Sayer duties, viz., poll tax, &c. The writer sees no force in this plea. Such duties were levied by the raja as governor, not as superintendent of Jugernath; and with his deposition the right devolved on the Company's Government to abolish or modify them as they judged right, without any reference to the temple or its officers.

If the Government will but throw back the original endowments of the temple, and allow the priests to receive, as in other temples, the voluntary offerings of the worshippers of Jugernath, they will do all that justice requires. The tax was levied for the Government, and not for the priests, and when Government chooses to relinquish it, the priests, so far from having cause of complaint, have ground for rejoicing, inasmuch as this measure leaves so much larger a fund on which they can and will practice their arts of extortion.

If the Muthdharis, as the head clerk insinuates, defraud the temple by embezzlement of what should be poured into its treasury, let the rulers of the temple have their redress in the civil courts. Jugernath has a right to the endowments of his votaries, and by their regard for him let him be supported or fall.

At the same time, while Government ought not to *sanction* any levying of a tax either within or without the temple, it has no right to forbid the pilgrim giving, or the priests receiving, any fee they may mutually agree upon. This arrangement may be abused, but, then, this is an evil which must be met in the courts of justice, as in other cases of fraud. Government must hold the balance equally betwixt man and man. There can be no doubt that the acknowledged endowments of the temple, with the sale of mahaprasad, or holy food, and the fees or offerings of worshippers, will constitute an ample revenue for the support of the idol and the shrine, and for the maintenance of all their officers in a style of luxury equal to their brethrĕn in any part of India; until, as the writer devoutly hopes, Christianity shall sap the foundation of this and every similar idolatrous establishment, and "From the rising to the setting sun, the name of the Lord shall be great among the Gentiles, and in every place incense and a pure offering shall be offered unto his name; for my name shall be great among the heathen, saith the Lord of hosts."

## CHAPTER VII.

Feelings towards first converts—Early hopes—Old Gooroo and his disciples — Names of first converts — Reflections — An account of Rama Chundra—Erun and his son, Erebon.

Those alone who have labored in a mission from its commencement, and are privileged to welcome into the fold of Christ the first converts from heathenism, can fully appreciate the above title. Succeeding laborers may enter the field and rejoice over larger accessions, made by their ministry to the church of Christ, but they can never sustain precisely the same relationship to the converts, nor enter fully into those emotions, at the first accessions to the flock, which filled the heart of pioneer missionaries. The writer has been sometimes pained by the apparently entire absence of interest which some missionaries and Christians have evinced for the native converts, and has often thought that on this point there has been a defect in missionary preparation. While it is true, that none can experience precisely the same feelings, as the first missionaries, for the converts from heathenism, still, it assuredly is both desirable and practicable for young missionaries to make some near approximation towards an acquaintance with those feelings, and so to an understanding of that sort of sympathy which their senior fellow-laborers and the native converts expect to receive from them.

Several of our most interesting and prosperous missions have had to endure long patience ere they were cheered by the addition of a single convert. It was so with the Baptist Mission to Bengal, with the Missions to

Burmah and Ceylon; it was so, in a remarkable degree, with respect to the Missions to Greenland and the South Seas, and it was so with respect to the mission to which these pages refer.

A preceding paper describes the night of toil through which we passed, and details the means generally employed by us for the evangelization of the province. Long did we use those means with so little apparent success that we were, in the estimation of our countrymen, a company of enthusiasts and fanatics to expect that we should ever make converts in this peculiar province of Satan's empire. Often have we insensibly been led, in our accounts of this period of the mission, to refer to the phenomena of the early dawn. After long watching, we first discern a faint ray of light in the eastern horizon; but soon the gathering mists obscure that faint indication of the coming day, and denser gloom appears to have gathered over the heavens; anon, however, a brighter tint is seen, infallible signs of the early morning appear, the reflected rays now gild the mountain tops, and the bright orb of day appears to scatter every cloud of doubt and pour increasing glory o'er the land. It was even so with us in relation to the progress of our work. Now and then an apparently sincere inquirer excited our expectations and sustained our hopes; but soon, alas, some sinister motive became too apparent, or where there seemed to be perfect sincerity, there were yet wanting moral courage and faith to brave the losses and crosses of first breaking the bonds of caste and endure the wrath of offended relatives. It may not be inappropriate here to notice one of these cases as a specimen of several others, which, for a time, helped the missionaries to believe that their efforts would be eventually crowned with success.

In two or three of our early missionary journals, there are notices of one of those weary wanderers after rest that exist in India, and who spend their days in travelling far and wide in search of that peace which the gospel alone can give.

"A Hindoo introduced himself to us this evening, as we were addressing the people in the great road, near Jugernath's temple. He listened with great attention, and on some one opposing, he came forward, with his hands respectfully joined, and with watery eyes exclaimed, 'This is the truth.' At first we thought him deranged, but his pertinent replies and serious manner convinced us that we were mistaken, and that what we thought insanity, was anxiety for his soul's welfare. We subsequently learned that he had been anxious about salvation for some time,—that he had been on pilgrimage to Saugur Island, to Brindabun, in Northern India, and Seetabund Rameswar, or the straits leading from Southern India to Ceylon, but found no cure for the sting of sin. He now expressed himself convinced that his course was nearly run, that he was a sinner and so unfit to die, that he had in vain sought relief by worshipping the Hindoo gods and in his attendance on the most celebrated devotees. He, a short time ago, first heard the gospel, but had feared, as we were Sahibs, to open his mind to us, but that being much concerned he had ventured to do so now. We rejoiced in what we heard,—encouraged him to persevere, and for a time he appeared very hopeful. Indeed, on seeing the Lord's Supper administered, he begged hard to be allowed to partake." He continued an inquirer for some time, but at length, for some reason or other, he disappeared, and never was outwardly numbered with the flock of Christ.

We have had many similar cases since. Perhaps the following instance, mentioned by Mr. Lacey, may explain some of them. The narrative shows the bitter opposition and persecution that some Hindoos have to endure when they would walk in the way of life.

The case of another man from the village of Khundittar gives me much hope and anxiety. About a month ago he left his house and family and came over and joined himself to our people here, observing that he could no longer sustain the apprehension he had of his sinfulness and danger, and wished to be instructed respecting Jesus Christ the Saviour, and profess his name. He remained a night and part of the next day. About noon his friends discovered him, and came in a band and forcibly carried him away. He was in the chapel reading the New Testament at the time. Our people remonstrated with them, but to no purpose; he was carried off and confined in his house. His friends, under the instigation of the brahmuns, administered the juice of the duttoora* seed and other deleterious drugs, which in three days reduced the poor man to a state of idiocy. He generally now says just what his people tell him to say, but when we go to see him, he recognizes us and wishes to join us, calling us his Christian brethren. I went last evening and demanded to see and converse with him, but his friends would not allow him to come out of his house. They have married his two infant daughters, that in case he should make his escape, they may be disposed of to their husbands. I have been acquainted with him for years; he is very intelligent. Moreover, all our people confirm the statement that he has always been, and was when he joined them, perfectly sane. The people are in the habit of administering poison to their friends to prevent them from becoming Christians, or rather to destroy their responsibility, and have an excuse for confining them. Several of our converts have been so served.

I am informed that before he finally came out to join the Christians, his people, in order to divert his mind from thoughts

---

* Thorn apple.

of Christianity, took him to Jajepoor and several other places; caused him to hear the bhagabot and other books read, as well as adopted other methods which they thought likely to have that effect, but in vain, and, as a last resource, they confined him to his house, and began to administer deleterious drugs to him, and it was secretly and in the night that he made his escape. They all testify to the man's great anxiety about the salvation of his soul, and that he had no hope but in Jesus Christ.

This case evinces the importance and necessity of having a European missionary at this station. I believe that many of our Khundittar converts would have been lost had it not providentially occurred that they came out either when I was here, or by appointment to meet them at the time; and had a European been here, the people could not, they would not, have attempted to carry off Rogusaho. Do send a man especially for Khundittar. Let him come with directions to settle here and no where else. The people require the presence of a European constantly, while the neighborhood presents a large and most interesting field of labor.

### *The old Gooroo and his Disciples.*

Oft disappointed by instances similar to the foregoing, the Orissa missionaries still labored on hoping against hope. At length a brighter scene dawned on their delighted eyes, and hopes were raised which issued not in disappointment. An old Gooroo, or spiritual guide to a number of devoted disciples, was the instrument, in the hands of God, of introducing us to our first converts at Cuttack.

Although the details of this event have appeared before, yet from their connection with the progress of the gospel in Orissa, a brief outline deserves a place in the present chapter, and for various reasons the writer prefers transcribing an account already drawn up by himself and presented to the public in India.

Sundradas was in early life a warrior under the Athgura raja, one of the hill chieftains in Orissa. If ever he had been taught to read, he soon lost the ability to do so. He was naturally a shrewd observer of men and things, and possessed a large share of what is called mother wit. He soon felt his superiority, though himself unlearned, to his rustic associates, and assumed the character, first of a devotee and then of a spiritual guide. He knew how to make use of the learning of others, and early enlisted into his service several of his disciples well versed in the writings of Khubeer, Choitanya, and especially of an Oriya reformer in his own vicinity, who lashed the vices of the age most unmercifully. The old man picked up a number of striking predictions respecting the speedy dawn of the golden age. Piety and peace were to pervade the earth; discord and falsehood and violence and fraud were to disappear; the cattle were to go and return from pasture without a shepherd or keeper; the fields were to need no hedges or embankments; the people were to be clothed in silk and scarlet, and all were to live happy in the bonds of fraternal affection. In this reformation he was to have a conspicuous share, and the Sahibs, who had just conquered Orissa, were to consult him as their spiritual guide. Our first acquaintance with him he artfully represented as the commencement of this his spiritual reign.

At this period he taught his disciples to abstain from certain kinds of food, to bathe at certain hours, to live as brethren, regardless of the strict observance of caste; and especially to unite in the burnt-offering of clarified butter, which he carried to a great extent. He also promoted night-revels, under the name of sut-sung, or communion with the true.

The following account of the old Gooroo is from one

of his disciples, Rama-Chundra, whose memoir is given hereafter.

Soon after this period I had an interview with Sundra-baba-jee, and he gave me much instruction about the worship of Spirit. Moreover Doitaree-niak, Gunga-dhor sorengee, Gunga-mahantee, Jugernath-potaniak, Gunda-dhur-beswal, Krupasindoo-saho, Rhadoo-das, Soodurson-rowte, Ram-kristnoo-das, Puramaser-mol, Puraswa-maha-patra, Kartike-suil, and many others, very closely connected themselves with him. "The commandments," he said, "which I shall give you, you must not disobey them." He then commanded us to bathe twice a day; offer water to the sun; eat on the second hour of the day; indulge our bodies with food and ease, doing little labor; and whatever we desired at any time, that eat. But he forbade to use warm drink, and tobacco, fish, flesh, and oil. He commanded us to eat unwashed rice, and to sanctify the place of eating with ashes. He told us to remain much under the influence of opium and other soothing drugs; to eat early in the morning; not to destroy beasts, animals, fish, or birds, or any thing that has life; not to cut down trees or shrubs, but to consider all things that have life as ourselves, and as one spirit; for that in all substances, and throughout all forms of materiality, Narayun dwells incarnate.

He forbade us to lie or steal, or commit adultery; to be angry, hypocritical, envious, or hateful. We were also commanded to lay aside idol worship, pilgrimages, offerings, fastings, distinguishing marks, sacred thread and mala. "All things," said he, "are full of God; worship him. For hatred return not hatred, for persecution persecute not; for blows give not blows; spend no one's wealth, and borrow money of no one. Love your enemies as well as your friends. Love your wives and children as your own souls. Reverence your parents. Take no one's goods on trust. Give not false witness, and cheat or defraud no one. Without distinction, salute all men; look upon aged people with the same respect as you do your parents, and if the poor and needy beg of you, give to them; and if not able to do that, speak to them with kindness and respect." In this manner he gave us much instruction. Teaching he said, "This world will be destroyed, but they that, hoping in God, keep his commandments, will be preserved. The true religion will be proclaimed, and falsehood will disappear."

He moreover uttered many other prophecies, and said, "My birth into this world is divine, though that is known to no one. I shall become the ruler and judge of all nations; Hindoos, Mussulmans, and Pheringees; and all other classes of men will regard me; both male and female will reverence me; for Boladab, in the form of light, has entered into me. I shall destroy the load of sin which has accumulated in the world. There shall be no more war, or noise, or disagreement, or malice, or adultery, or theft, or lying, or disease, or sorrow, or pain, in the world any more. Wild beasts, as tigers and bears, venomous reptiles, as serpents; as well as all other vicious or injurious animals, shall bear no more malice towards man: and the herds of cattle, without a keeper, shall return to their homes, without destroying the cornfields of others. The clouds, knowing their proper season, shall give timely rain; and the earth shall produce its full and proper fruits. Into the hearts of mankind shall the Holy Spirit be placed; and male and female, clothed in silk and satin, shall worship the Lord and sing his praises with joy. One loving the other, all shall know the Lord."

Thus did he deliver to us many prophecies; and our hearts, believing his words, greatly rejoiced; and whatever he commanded us to do we carefully performed. We bathed in the morning, ate unwashed rice, left off using flesh, fish, paun, smoke, and oil. Lies, and theft, and adultery, we dreaded in our minds; and we avoided the company of liars and malicious persons. We laid aside the worship of the mala, the sandal marks, and the poita; and the idols that were in our houses, leaving their worship, we tied them up to the roofs of our houses. We plucked up the tulsee tree, left off pilgrimages, sacrifices, and ancestorial shradda; and no longer worshipped cows, or brahmuns. We no longer eat prusad, nor sung obscene songs to the sound of the khunjuree. We avoided the society of those who were litigious and quarrelsome; and loving all men, we worshipped spirit. Thus we were obedient to Sundra-baba-jee.

About the year 1825, the gospel first began to penetrate the dark region where the old Gooroo and his disciples resided. Some of these disciples, in their visits to Cuttack, obtained various tracts, which they eagerly read, and communicated to the Gooroo. Among others, was a small catechism containing the ten commandments, with the elements of Christian truth. This peculiarly interested the old teacher, and he resolved to adopt the decalogue as his standard of morals. His disciples had already passed through a preparatory course, which fitted them at once to unite with their Gooroo. But it is said, "the entrance in of thy word giveth light, it giveth understanding unto the simple," and so the old man found out when it was too late. His approval of our tracts encouraged his disciples to read them, and they soon grew beyond the narrow limits within which he sought to confine them.

In October, 1826, while we were at worship on the Sabbath, a deputation arrived from the old Gooroo to ask our advice in a novel and interesting affair. It appears that he had appointed several of his leading disciples to promulgate his favorite Das-agya, or ten commandments, in the neighboring villages, and also to collect ghee for a large burnt-offering. In the execution of their commission they got into trouble, were severely beaten and grievously abused, and now they wished for advice how to proceed in seeking redress for this outrage.

Our conversation with these men was so interesting and surprising, it revealed such an extensive acquaintance with our books, and especially the gospels, united with so much correctness and apparent sincerity, that it drew forth alternate smiles and tears. At length my senior colleague united with me in the determination to pay a visit to the old Gooroo, and talk the matter over fully. Accordingly, next morning we set out upon our attractive journey. That day can never be obliterated from our memory. It was to us as the first dawn of the sun of righteousness upon this region and shadow of death. How did our hearts burn within us by the way! and how did our aspirations rise to heaven: "Lord, send now prosperity!"

Our first interview with the Gooroo was to us interesting and affecting. He had prepared for our reception by spreading cloths under a wide-spreading banian-tree, and as soon as we arrived, hastened to greet us. He appeared to be about fifty years of age, rather below the middle stature, and somewhat corpulent. He was not besmeared with ashes, as is usual; but wore a chain round his waist, to which was attached a shred of cloth. This was his only dress. His complexion was fair for a Hindoo, and his countenance mild and prepossessing. A smile played about his lips, and vivacity sparkled in his eyes. He at once saluted us by prostrating himself at our feet, while we in return raised him up and shook him by the hand. Our preliminaries adjusted, we proceeded to business, and soon branched off to a general discussion respecting Christianity. The old man, though still bewildered in the mazes of mysticism and heathenism, yet possessed many correct views and made many striking remarks. He illustrated the folly of distinctions in caste by pointing, first, to the sun, then to clothes of various castes spread out to dry! These, he said, would be defiled by touching each other, but the sun dried them all! He illustrated the death of Christ by supposing the case of a criminal condemned to die, for whom another offered himself as a substitute. Referring to the New Testament, he said to his disciples, "My children, there is truth, and there is great truth. There are gifts of rice, of clothing, and of wisdom. This is wisdom, the highest gift—rice decays, clothing perishes, but wisdom never dies. Take this, my children, and let it be your guide; all the silver and gold in the world cannot purchase this." He said many more things that gave us pleasure; and would have eaten or done any thing else with us, involving a loss of caste, but this we forbore for that time.

Such was the old Gooroo. This interview, and many others, greatly excited our hopes respecting him; but he never embraced the gospel. Many of those we saw that day have since been added to the flock of the Saviour, as the first fruits to Christ in Orissa. But the old teacher grew more and more averse to our mission. He indeed gave himself forth as an incarnation of Jesus Christ, and tried thus to retain his spiritual power. He even appointed twelve apostles, after the example of Christ. But he persecuted those who left him—gradually grew more mystical, and died without any distinct creed of any sort, excepting this: that he told his attendant disciples that he who made him, had sent for him; and desired that his body might be buried in his house. There it rests, and is worshipped by a few attached, but very ignorant disciples. His spirit has received its sentence from Him who judgeth right.

We cannot here present a detailed account of the several disciples of the old Gooroo, who sooner or later embraced Christianity. Such details are furnished in the publications of the General Baptist Missionary Society; but the names of several of these first converts shall be briefly mentioned, and a more lengthened account of one or two leading disciples be appended to this chapter.

Gunga-dhor-suringa, a brahmun of respectable character and family, was the first of the old Gooroo's disciples who avowed Christ. He was baptized in the Ma-

hanuddee river, March 23, 1823. The conflict was long and painful ere he could renounce his caste, his family, and as for a time it appeared, his attached wife, with all worldly honors and prospects, to be the first to leap the fence of Hindooism, and avow his faith in despised, villified Christianity. But he was just the man for leadership. Bold, ardent, sanguine, the very Peter of our band, resembling the great apostle to the circumcision, in both his excellencies and imperfections. Gunga obeyed the voice of truth within him, and in the spirit of a martyr risked the loss of all things for Christ. His family at once and forever renounced him, all excepting his wife, who, after a short wavering, cleaved to her husband. She subsequently embraced the gospel, and recently died in the faith of Christ. Gunga at length became an efficient preacher of the gospel, and so he still continues.

Next came Rama-Chundra, son of the last Mahratta governor of the fort at Cuttack, when it was taken by the English. He is and has ever been a man of sterling character, and is now assistant pastor at Cuttack, not officially recognized, but really discharging its duties.

Soon followed others, as Doitaree-Naik, Radhoo-das, Kurun-sahoo, Krupa-sindoo, Bamadeb, Balaram, Kineeparee, Hurreeparee, Trilochun, and others, with their wives, various relatives and connections.

While this work was going on at Cuttack, our zealous and ever-honored brother, Mr. Bampton, was instrumental in the conversion of Erun, a respectable individual at Barhampore, in the district of Ganjam. He indeed was the first baptized, though not the first converted in our mission. Other conversions followed, and we trust that the series will never be interrupted, till Christ shall reign over all the earth, and all be blessed in him.

Of these converts we may remark, that they were won

from the common mass of heathens solely by our efforts. There were no intermediate steps by which their conversion to Christianity was facilitated, or which in any mind can justify a suspicion that they did not act under the pure influence of their own convictions. We have heard and read of persons in India and elsewhere being brought to embrace Christianity, at least in profession, from their connection in some way with professed Christians, from embarrassed circumstances, from loss of caste, or from some other mixed or unworthy motives. But no suspicion of this sort attaches to these Orissa converts. The gospel found them in a retired part of the country, deeply immersed in heathen practices, intently pursuing their Hindoo system, and unconnected in any way with European influence, literature, or patronage. They, in the usual way of distribution, received first a tract or two, then the gospel; then, though not at all contemplated originally, sought the guidance of the living teacher of Christianity, and finally, constrained by the power of divine truth, abandoned their idols, their caste, their standing in society, their livelihood, and all their hopes as Hindoos, to become the followers of Christ.

2. We may remark, that these first converts were all men of good caste, and regular members of the Hindoo community,—and this remark indeed applies to the majority of our converts since. They had much to lose in this respect, and some of them felt this very keenly. In the south of India, the Christian converts generally are poor, and a kind of outcasts from the great Hindoo family, or rather were never included in it. And though as deeply immersed in idolatry as any, had not the same scorn and contumely to endure, by becoming Christians. Yea, it must have been, in the eyes of the Hindoos themselves, an advancement in their status in many respects.

It is not meant by these remarks to imply that the soul of the lowest pariah is not of infinite value, and, abstractedly considered, as much an object of desire as the salvation of the soul of the most learned brahmun. But it is meant hereby to show that the gospel, in the case of these conversions, exerted its own peculiar power, without any adventitious aid, and against the full force of Hindoo prejudice and opposition. This is a consideration of some importance to those who go forth making aggressive warfare upon Satan's empire in India, without human patronage, without any preparatory helps, and thus face the full power and influence of Hindooism.

3. Again ; it is pleasing to observe, that these converts have all held on their way without a single instance of final apostacy. For a view of the moral transformation effected in them by the gospel of Christ, we refer to another section, but the remark is of importance in the present reflections. There have been stumbles and falls in several instances; but there has also been, so far as man can judge, genuine repentance involving real reformation. Their renunciation of heathenism is decided and complete, their reception of the gospel is earnest and sincere, their outward observance of Christian duties exemplary, their living, and in several cases, their dying, testimony to the truth of the gospel, eminently satisfactory; and we may still say of them, as did St. Paul of his Corinthian converts, "Ye are our epistles, written in the heart, known and read of all men; forasmuch as ye are manifestly declared to be the epistle of Christ, ministered by us, written not with ink, but with the spirit of the living God, not in tables of stone, but in fleshly tables of the heart."

4. These circumstances gave a tone and character to our first efforts, which have been of considerable impor-

tance to our mission. The converts were such as Hindoos themselves could not puff at, or treat with contempt. The Calcutta baboos and others have been fond of casting reproach on Christian exertions, by saying that none but a few poor, ignorant people had embraced the gospel. Now this is not true as a general statement of any mission I am acquainted with; but it is especially untrue in Orissa. The people who have embraced the gospel there, are at least equal to their neighbors in intelligence and respectability. They are, some of them, brahmuns, astrologers, school-masters, writers or accountants, as well as farmers and husbandmen. They were not despised as ignorant or mean, by their fellow Hindoos, their neighbors and friends. They were a fair sample of the whole community. And their having cheerfully suffered loss for Christ, and gained no advantage such as was slanderously reported was to be the price of their conversion, has stopped the mouth of multitudes. It has placed the gospel before them as a claimant for their faith and reception of it, on the ground of its own intrinsic worth. This is a point I deem of supreme importance. I dread whatever interferes with the integrity of this principle. It is not to strengthen the power of truth, but to weaken it, when converts are unduly petted or rewarded, or improved in their temporal circumstances by any means apart from that gain which godliness insures. This is to substitute human motives for divine, and earthly considerations in the place of heavenly and eternal. In these respects we have reason to rejoice in the character of our first conversions.

5. The gospel thus acquired a status and a character of permanency which has continued to tell upon our work ever since. It was of great importance that the Oriyas should learn from our first converts what was the

nature of the change in their position, in their civil, social and spiritual character, which the gospel would effect. This would be a sort of precedent to which succeeding inquirers and converts would readily refer. And so, it has been. Would that the standard were never lowered! Great vigilance and discretion are needful here. We must take heed that we do not, on the one hand, demand what apostles did not require; and, on the other, beware of confounding the natural and spiritual man. There is, and must be seen to be, a difference, radical, vital and vast, between a real and a merely nominal Christian. Our first converts often refer to the care and caution exercised in their own case, when we meet to consider of the reception of candidates for baptism now.

Again, from these converts were gradually evolved the elements of the visible church. Some became able preachers of the word, others deacons, others schoolmasters, and assistants in various ways. Then came the marriage union, the family altar, the Christian village, the rural chapel, the village school and all the outward manifestations of the gospel having taken root in the land, with the promise of its continuance and increase.

And the leaven still operates. There appears to have been a special vitality and power in the first moment, which can be referred to no other than a divine influence. Perhaps when the secrets of all hearts shall be revealed, and when He who seeth in secret shall reward openly, this first movement of the Spirit of God upon the chaos of darkness and confusion in Orissa will be traced up to the piety and prayers and labors of some unrecognized individual now. At least from the manner in which this and most of our seasons of refreshing and instances of conversion have been brought about, there is little room for individual glorying. No one can say, "This work was mine and to me be the glory." May we and all missionaries of the cross ever feel that to God is due all the praise, and cherish rather a habit of reflecting soberly upon our deficiences, our errors, our unbelief, and our other numberless causes for humiliation, that so we may, one and all, ever and devoutly say, "Not unto us, not unto us, but unto thy name give glory."

We will now give a somewhat detailed account of the conversion of Rama, chiefly furnished by himself, in order to illustrate the early struggles of our first converts. The translation is by Mr. Lacey.

*Conversion of Rama Chundra Jachuck.*

The second convert baptized at Cuttack was Rama Chundra Jachuck. His grandfather, Lucksmajee Jachuck, was Mahratta governor of the fort at Cuttack, not long before the capture of the fort by the English in 1803. Rama's father was named Hoebutra Jachuck, and is represented by his son as at one time possessed of considerable wealth. Rama lost his mother when he was about two and a half years old, and when he was about five years of age, the English conquered Orissa. The family then removed to the village of Bhoyerpoor, when his father also died.

Rama was sent to school at the age of twelve years, and must have made very respectable proficiency in the ordinary school learning of Orissa. By the time he was fifteen years of age, he acquired the pernicious habit of chewing opium and other intoxicating drugs, and soon after became excessively depraved and immoral. At this time his religion consisted in the worship of the gods venerated in the family, and the occasional repetition of the name of his chosen deity.

At eighteen years of age he was married, and supported himself and family by farming the abovenamed village, and occasionally disposing of valuable articles, as swords, daggers, &c., left him by his father. He now assumed the sacred thread, worshipped the family idols with punctilious regularity, became a sort of devotee, heard the shastras daily, went on pilgrimage, and, to use his own language, desired very earnestly to discover the true knowledge of God. He associated with various religionists, joined their midnight revels, ate opium, &c., and, he adds, "notwithstanding my zeal in religion, I became very immoral and spent my days in sinful practices, my heart sometimes surfeited in these things, but I then knew no better way."

When he was about twenty-seven years of age his family consisted of four children, but he soon lost two of them, leaving a son and daughter, who grew up to maturity. The death of his children with an epidemic, probably the cholera, in his village, produced considerable anxiety in his mind respecting futurity. He now became connected with the old Gooroo, to whom reference has been made, and was thus brought into the way by which Providence led him to an acquaintance with Christianity. Sundra-baba-jee, he says, now became my spiritual father and I became his spiritual son, and in this relation I had great love for him and venerated him much; he had also great affection for me.

Soon after this, the Padree sahibs, viz., the missionaries, came into the country and distributed the holy book. We obtained the New Testament, the Ten Commandments, (a tract so called,) the Jewel Mine of Salvation, and other books. Sabbath after Sabbath came we together in the evening, and by the light of a lamp, fed with clarified butter, we read these books and the Bhagabut, (a history of Krishnoo,) and united in singing holy hymns. The meaning of these books Sundra-das explained to us; but sometimes when we could not understand, he chastised us as a schoolmaster does his pupils. Thus we remained as children under a teacher.

Whether the old Gooroo perceived that the Christian books were making his pupils wiser than their teacher, or from some other cause, the old man abandoned many of his spiritual views of God and relapsed into gross idolatry and its attendant abominations. He became addicted to indecent practices with his female disciples, which involved him in a quarrel with their husbands, and, finally, occasioned his expulsion from his hermitage. In the meantime Rama, with some other leading disciples, visited Cuttack and became acquainted with the missionaries. He says in his own account of himself, "Day after day the good name of Sundra-das diminished, for on account of his evil deeds our hearts did not love him. For a year I served him with sincerity, but afterwards, seeing his wickedness, I lost my regard for him. I served him in word, but in my mind I sat in judgment upon his deeds. When sacrifices were made and gifts were presented, though the shouts of the joyful multitude rent the air, we were sorrowful in our heart. The sins of former years all appeared before our mind and seemed augmented a thousand fold. He had turned away many from the worship of Spirit.

"It was now my evil heart lusted after all kinds of sin and wickedness, and works I had never committed to them did my wicked heart incline. Thus I had in my mind a sense of indescribable sin. At the same time my soul despised the idols. One mind said, 'These things man has made, they are not God.' In order to test them, I threw unclean things upon them,—I trod on them,—some I burned,—others I broke to pieces, and others I threw away. I forsook the worship of sun, moon, stars, fire, water, brahmuns and devotees. I also disregarded the various shastras and pooranas. To this mind my other mind said, 'What, are you turned against these? to a certainty you will fall into hell. No one will endure you, for your forefathers worshipped these.' Hence my soul was filled with sorrow and alarmed with apprehension; and I became baptized in the sea of distress. My body also now became emaciated with fevers, cough, and eruptions; and I had no desire after food, drink, &c., and I had no certainty of life. My soul cried continually, 'O Lord, O Lord!' My mind said to my mind, 'You have trespassed against gods, brahmuns and devotees, and all that is holy; and, therefore, guilt oppresses you, therefore disease has seized you, and you will to a certainty die and fall into hell. This birth of yours, is passed in vain!' Thus speaking, my mind exclaimed, 'Ah! ah!' and I wept. I got a little better, and as I lay in my house I thought in my soul, 'Who can tell but that the merciful God, who made all things, will save me?' But, again, the other mind said, 'That God will never save you, for he hates sin, and does not hear the words of sinners.' This body is full of evil desires and base propensities, and in the twinkling of an eye I was filled full of evil thoughts. When I cried out, 'O Lord,' and began to be serious and thoughtful, then I ran into sinful thoughts, my desires after God were scattered, and my desires after sin prevailed, and in what way soever I attempted to improve my heart, I could not be steady and successful. I read and informed my mind from the holy book, the bhagabot, and other books that are original and excellent; but my soul would not obey. One mind said, 'I will commit sin,' another said, 'I will hope in God, and work the works of righteousness,' thus in my body did two minds war, and I could not steadily preserve my resolution. And now I had no desire to rise from the place where I sat, and in the time of eating my food, my imagination represented many unclean things before me. I had no desire to arise from sleep. Towards wife, or children, or house, and the like, I had no desire; and cut off from all, I laid me down in my apartment. Lying there my mind said, 'Flee to other countries; otherwise hang yourself; otherwise plunging in water, drown yourself; otherwise stab yourself with some weapon and die; otherwise eat poison and die; otherwise go into the jungle and be devoured of tigers, bears, or serpents, and die; otherwise let yourself be bound in iron fetters.' My heart was distracted, and this mind again said, 'O soul, quickly quit this body! in such an unclean body why longer remain?' 'O that I had never been born!' I cried, or, 'Why died I not in my mother's womb?' or, 'Why grew I up in the world?' or, 'Why read I the Scriptures?'—'How have I sinned!'—'I am guilty before God!'—'I shall sometime fall into the torments of hell!'—'Had I died in ignorance, I had had no guilt; how shall I endure the torments of eternal fire? Knowing, knowing, I have committed sin, and there is no hope or help for me! Had I never been born, then should I not have had conscience.' Thus, mind cursed mind, saying, 'Formerly you had no such guilt, you had not such an unclean heart, you loved to read and hear the Geeta and Bhagabot very much; how has your heart become thus evil? Your birth is in vain,—you have sinned against your spiritual guide, and against brahmuns, and against holy devotees, and against gods, and against holy places, and against the practice of offering gifts, oblations, and sacrifices; and against sun, moon, water, wind, fire, and Sundera-baba-jee; and against Shree-Ram-Krestnoo, with the ten incarnations. These you have not worshipped.' Hence my soul became oppressed with fear. My spiritual guide gave me a name to meditate upon, but I have not meditated on it; I have been untrue to that covenant. Then, again, my mind said, 'They against whom you have sinned, they can forgive your transgression;' and again I thought I would worship these things. But against these things my soul rose up, for I saw clearly that as these incarnations are themselves sinful, I cannot be saved from sin by worshipping them. 'What,' said I, 'can a sinner save a sinner?' 'What, can a blind (man) lead a blind?' 'What, trusting in that which is false, can I obtain truth?' So I was hopeless of being delivered by them.

"Just at this period, I resolved to read the 'Good news,' away from home; and my soul labored hard in this and said, 'By trusting in this Saviour thou mayest be delivered.'

"Soon after this, Gunga-dhor went with the Padree-sahib to Calcutta, and in a little time he from thence returned; when Padree-sahib and myself and Sundera-baba-jee, had much conversation about religion. Then the Padree-sahib rose up and went to Cuttack, and we all departed to our houses. My soul said, 'Trusting in this Saviour, I can be saved.' I met Gunga-dhor in the way, and we had much conversation. I said, 'Stay yet a little while, and I will accompany you, for truly this Lord is Truth; we will together devote ourselves to this Lord.' 'No!' he said, 'I am determined to go and be baptized; you can make your mind steady, and then follow me.' At this time I went to the house of a brother in Dekanal; that brother died before I was born, but the sister-in-law and his other dependents said, 'Come, O brother, and marry the wife of your brother,* and you shall have this house, and these bullocks, and cows, and this money, and all these goods.' I said, 'In all these there is no use; for riches, money, kingdoms, and such like, will last but for a short period, and in eternity they will not serve me.' Coming from that place, in the way I heard that Gunga-dhor-suringee had been baptized into the house of the Sahib, and my mind said, 'Gunga-dhor has done well.' When I arrived at my house I heard much abuse, and many lies spoken of Gunga-dhor.

* The Mahrattas marry several wives.

My family now forbade me to read the Holy Book, saying, 'Reading this book Gunga-dhor has gone and has given his caste into the house of the Sahib, and if you read it, you will do the same.' Others said, 'As many as have associated with Sundera-das, will run into the house of the Sahibs.' Thus I heard much blasphemy, and received much abuse; and thence became ashamed and refrained from reading the Holy Book. Soon after, I had several interviews with Gunga-dhor, and about my salvation to me he said a few words. I said, 'The Lord has given you strength and drawn you into his way, and when he shall give me strength, I will profess Him, but I will not do so because you persuade me.' He, therefore, now left me, and I went home and secretly, in my own apartment, read the 'New Testament,' the 'Essence of the Bible,' the 'Ten Commandments,' and the Nistar-rotnakar. Now I had great experience in my soul, and compared the Bhagabot, the Geeta, the Prophecy, and others of the books of this country. In this employment I spent night and day for some time; and from examination, I found that the Holy Book exhibited one God to my faith and love, but that this country's books exhibited many. Also I perceived that they command me to observe a great many things, and pursue many ways; therefore my mind cast off all regard for them. My soul said, 'One God! and if I contemplate Him, I shall find Him.' One day, (it was Lord's day,) as I was bathing, I tore off my small necklace from my neck, and said, 'O soul, art thou this day baptized into Christ Jesus?" From this day, in secret, closing the door of my apartment, I prayed unto the Lord, saying, 'Thou God of heaven and earth, I will bless thy name a thousand times, for whereas I was in the valley of death, thou hast opened unto me the path of life; I was overwhelmed in guilt, but thou hast manifested a means of holiness; that holiness is our Lord Jesus Christ; taking his name, I confess my sins, and do thou forgive all my iniquities. Moreover giving the Holy Spirit, sanctify my soul.' Thus did I pray unto the Lord.

"How shall I openly profess Jesus Christ, and so become his disciple? for the Lord suffered death for my transgressions! I will be baptized in water in his name! Unto sin, I will be buried in water; and will rise again unto the Lord, and will tell of the good tidings of him to every body! Thus I meditated and resolved, as I remained in my apartment. Now I spoke the word of God to several persons, and the promises of God imparted strength to my soul. Gunga-dhor called at my house, and I entertained him with eating and drinking; the next day he went to Thangee, and in the evening returned to my house. The next day also he remained, and took refreshment with me. I said in my heart, 'This is Saturday, and to-morrow is Lord's day; I will arise and go to Cuttack, and will be baptized in the name of the Lord.' Thus resolving, I informed my wife that I was going to be baptized in the name of the Lord. Hearing this they (the family) began to weep, and cried out, 'Ah! ah!' and became filled with distress. Many people of the village came together to dissuade me, but I could not regard their words: so I left my house. As when a corpse is carried out for burial, the people follow weeping and wailing, so did they all follow me. Sodanunda, my son, threw himself down at my feet many times, and would not release me, saying, 'Indeed, if you will go to Cuttack, then, tying a rope round my neck, I will hang myself; or, plunging in water I will die.' I said, 'If you will destroy yourself, what can I do! I must go to Cuttack and profess the Lord; from this day I am dead towards these people, and towards all, and towards thee. If thou wilt be the Lord's, then I will be thine.' Thus speaking, I repeated to them the following verses, viz:

"My father and my mother who?
And who my wife and child?
Illusions strong surround me here,
In this delusive world.

Follow, my soul, the certain light,
Which Jesus to thee gives;
The soul that firmly follows Him,
With him for ever lives."

"Thus speaking, I departed towards Koojebur; and there I had an interview with Sundera-baba-jee; I said to him, 'Until this day I have walked with thee, but now I have discovered thy designs and motives, and works. Thou, and such as thou art, are taken in the snare of Satan; and being filled with delusion from him, ye all seek your own praise and glory; but remember that in the last day there shall, to such, be great distress. The people are lovers of themselves, are covetous and proud, and full of bitterness and blasphemy, are abusers of parents, are ungrateful, unholy, selfish, without pity, murderers, liars, and accusers of each other. They are hard-hearted, of unsubdued lusts, despisers of holy men, unbelieving, conceited, and swelled with haughtiness, lovers of pleasure more than lovers of God, idolators, deceivers of others, and deniers of truth. From all such turn away, for being filled with sin, they err in many ways. They are always learning, but are not able to come to know the truth. They, entering into their houses, have turned aside ignorant women.' And I said 'Thou art such a false Christ,* who, speaking wonderful words, hast led us astray; now, by the grace of God, I have obtained to know the gospel. What! is not Jesus Christ, the Son of God, who died for sinners, now in heaven? Whosoever shall believe on His name, will obtain the Holy Spirit, and finally he shall reconcile him to God, and cause him to enjoy eternal life! These words saying, I leave your communion, and go to be baptized in the name of the Lord.' Thus, I came away from him, and I had an interview with the Padree Lacey. I spoke the words of my heart before him, and then said, 'I beg to be baptized in the name of the Lord.' He replied, 'Stay a few days, and when I am satisfied with the state of your mind, I will baptize you.' This hearing, I took leave, and came to my house in Cuttack, and there I remained praying in a sorrowful heart, and said, 'O Lord, let me profess thy name soon.' In a little while Lacey Padree and Gunga-dhor came to see me, and asked for the state of my mind; and then he prayed with me. Thinking in his mind, he said, 'I will baptize you to-morrow,' and then he departed. This evening I ate dry food, and then went to rest. In the morning my brothers and friends arrived, and much they dissuaded me, but I heard not their words at all. At four o'clock in the afternoon we went to the side of the river, and the Christian brethren all came together. Many people collected, and the brethren sang hymns of praise to God. Lacey

---

* Sunderadas gave himself out to be Jesus Christ, and that, as he was once incarnate in Judea, so he was now become so in Orissa. He, in accordance with this character, chose twelve of his principal disciples to represent the twelve apostles.

Sahib delivered instructions from the Holy Book, and then took me with him into the water, and baptized me in the name of the Father, and Son, and Holy Spirit. Arising from the water, I stood on the bank, and said to the people, 'Buried I was to sin, but have arisen to the Lord. Do you believe on the Lord, and you will obtain deliverance.' They then blasphemed, and said, 'Your caste is lost, your line is sunk; now you may eat bones, and pig; and drink liquors. You are become a slave in the house of a Sahib. In this land your father ruled, but born into their line you have now introduced disorder therein; your face we will not look upon! O that you had died! it would then have been well! You have let fall all our Hindoo race! Cursed be thy life! Why did not you beg your bread, or clean out privies rather than do this?' Thus, cursing, they gave much abuse.

"Thence I went to the house of Padree Sahib. He lovingly put two cloths upon me and Gunga-dhor; they were both alike. In the evening, in the house of worship, all the brethren uniting, we sung hymns of praise, and besides there was preaching and prayer. All the believing brethren and sisters according to the commandment of the Lord, the evening feast in remembrance of the Lord's death he (the minister) caused us to eat. It was bread and wine; the bread for his flesh, and the wine for his blood. These we did partake of. After a blessing we all departed to our houses. Next day the tenant of my house in Boxe-bazar, rose up against me, and put me out, saying, 'You are become a pariah, and why do you stay in the house I occupy?' So I came to my house at Bhoyerpoor. Here no one would let me in, and I stayed in the open shed next to the street. Many of my relations and neighbors persuaded my wife and children not to unite with me, but to leave me. I spoke to my family with sincerity, and my enemies all fled, but my wife and children remained with me, though they would not yet come near me. One day and night I fasted in the open shed. The next day I applied to and reasoned with them. They had now fasted for three days. I continued to reason with them as before baptism, and to explain to them the way of holiness, and in a little time they became reconciled to me. From that day, reading the Holy Book and praying, I have continued, and from village to village I proclaim the good news of the Saviour.

"I cry, saying, 'Hear all mankind,
The way of Salvation is come.
For my own and for your sins,
The Son of God did die.
His name is Jesus Christ,
He bore the curse for man.
But he triumphed over death,
And now sits at God's right hand.
Whosoever believeth on him,
Eternal deliverance will get.
From hell he will surely escape,
And in heaven will joyfully sit.'
This hearing the people all,
Declare it a cursed word.
They cry out, 'Thou art a devil,
And hast done a very bad work.
Ah! are you alive, and not dead!'
They also used impudent words.
'Go you! your face we see not!
Otherwise you we will beat.'
Some said, 'Worse than a sweeper,*
Flesh eater, and drinker of liquors.
Himself having drank liquors,
Comes to teach us wisdom!
Who has sunk his own descent,
And has entered Pheringee's house;
Eats flesh of pigs and cows,
And also who murders fowls;
Who will eat all sorts of flesh,
Of so low and filthy caste!'
Some said, 'You eat leavings,
And while alive are dead.'
But some said, 'He is right,
This he does to get rupees.'
Again some said, 'Thou cursed,
Much more vile than dung.
Who can'st not be addressed in words,
Nor yet be seen with eyes!'
Others made sport and play,
As each felt disposed.
Prostitutes, robbers, and thieves
Uttered all their curse;
Crying, 'Kill him! kill him!
That destructive demon!
Who after death in hell,
On a pig a tick will be.
Or else a dirty maggot,
Or else a stinking bug.
Put dung into his face!
Put dung upon his head!'
Others dust and cow-dung threw;
And in sport clapped their hands.
Some pulled off my robes,
Creating great sport.
Lifting up a high hand,
Some struck me on the head.
Some who knew me, cried,
'A good man's son is he,
But now becoming poor,
For bread his honor sold.'
And in many other ways,
Abuse and shame they gave.
All hearing, Rama-chundra,
Rejoiced in the Lord;
And God's word declaring,
This persecution bore,
And with his wife and babes,
With God's grace he remains."

"Thus I remained in Bhoyerpoor for a year and a half, but six months from the beginning was received by the Padree to be a 'Proclaimer of the Good-news;' I receive seven rupees per month to provide food. On this I live, and daily proclaim the word of God. Afterwards I removed to Cuttack, and lived in my old house. Then my wife turned to the Lord, and we are united in one heart; and taking our children with us, we daily live praising God. O all my holy brethren and sisters in the Lord, my crown and my rejoicing; to you all, Rama-chandra sends thousand thousand loving salutations. Thus has the Lord changed my heart, and separated me from this world, and has gathered me into his fold. That I may remain in that fold, faithful unto the end, in your times of daily prayer, pray daily for us to God. And to God our Father, and the Lord Jesus Christ, be glory and power for ever and ever. Amen."

* A person who removes filth and does the lowest work.

### *Brief Notices of Erun.*

We have, as yet, no detailed account of the history of this venerable Christian brother, but as the earliest baptized convert in our mission, and especially as the only known case of native conversion arising out of the labors of our honored brother, Bampton, I feel reluctant to omit a few items respecting him. A fuller account will, in all probability, be some day furnished.

Erun is a Telinga, of the weaver caste, and professedly of the Jungum sect. A class of Seevà's worshippers, distinguished by wearing the emblem of Seevà in a silver case suspended round the neck. Erun is fond of mentioning some striking particulars of his father, which is, according to his representation, the closest approximation to the case of Cornelius, or to a seeking after God, if haply he may find him, by a Hindoo, that has ever come under the writer's knowledge. He has, however, never been able to satisfy himself whence the old man derived his peculiar views. It is not impossible he may have received some light from the Europeans or their descendants, who, at one time, resided in considerable numbers at Ganjam.

Erun states that his father lived to be about 105 years of age, that "His eye was not dim, nor his natural force abated." It was his daily practice to ascend a loft over his workshop, for retirement, and there pray to the God who is here and there and every where and sees all things. He enjoined upon his son never to lift up his hands to his head in adoration of an idol, though he allowed him to wear the outward symbols of idolatry; and thus he continued till his death. Erun is now upwards of eighty years of age. He first heard the gospel from the lips of Mr. Bampton, about the summer of 1827, in the streets of Berhampore. And the writer has heard him say that when he heard Mr. B. describe the character and attributes of the Eternal God, he involuntarily exclaimed, that is true, that is true, that is just what my father used to tell me. He at once offered to accompany the missionary, and, in consequence of some remarks by Mr. B., took off and broke in pieces his emblem of Seevà with the case. This conduct brought upon him considerable trouble from his heathen neighbors; but he persevered in seeking further instruction from the missionary, and gradually breaking through many difficulties he at length publicly renounced idolatry and took upon himself the yoke of Christ. He was baptized by Mr. Bampton on the 25th of December, 1827.

Erun, at the time of his baptism, had two wives. His elder wife left his house and went to reside with her friends six weeks before his baptism, but the younger one remained, though with great reluctance, and in a dogged determination neither to eat with him, or of any thing he had touched, or do the least thing for him. The elder one at length took a considerable portion of his property and decamped, which had some tendency to reconcile the other to stay with her husband, which she has done ever since, but has proved a miserable, wicked idolator, corrupting the morals of her children and piercing the old man through with many sorrows. The voluntary and determined departure of the old wife, though she abstracted an undue share of moveable property, yet saved both Erun and ourselves much trouble. We have had to deal with but one other case of polygamy in the mission; in this case, the man for years lived with both wives and had a family by each. A preacher once proposed taking a second wife; but we told him that however the Scriptures might tolerate the retaining of two wives, married according to heathen law, yet we could sanction the *contracting* of no such marriage; and that in the case of ministers it was plain they should be the husband of one wife. Here the matter has rested in our mission ever since.

Erun has held on his way as an upright, honorable man, having a good report of them that are without. But he has never attained to any very clear views of evangelical truth. We insert an extract from a communication of one of the Berhampore brethren, containing the last information respecting this worthy old Christian, and a brief account of the conversion of his only son. This once profligate young man is now a student in the Oriya Mission Academy.

"*Erun and his Prayer*.

"Of Erun, now so advanced in years, some interesting statements are made by Mr. Bailey.

"'During the last twenty years, you have heard much, from various parties, about our old friend Erun. He is certainly an extraordinary man; how he has managed to live so long amid so much wickedness, and, at the same time, maintain his standing as a Christian, I am at a loss to know. Surely, in this case, we have abundant evidence that God is able to preserve his people from sin under the most trying circumstances. 'The Lord knoweth how to deliver the godly out of temptations,' 'My grace is sufficient for thee.' The old man knows very little, comparatively speaking. But he knows that the idols of the heathen are all false, and that Jesus Christ is the only Saviour for sinners. I have had many interesting conversations with him, and have always felt satisfied, in my own mind, that he is a Christian. Come what may, you invariably find the old man cheerful and happy. He often refers to brother Bampton, and of the great joy he felt when first he heard the gospel from Bampton; tell him that he will meet with Bampton in heaven, and he is enraptured with the idea. The old man is very much respected by his heathen neighbors, and they, without exception, will bear testimony to the integrity of his character. Sometimes he accompanies us to the bazaar, and now and then he addresses the people; his tale is always the same, nevertheless, he delivers it with great earnestness. 'The gods are all false, I would set my feet upon them and smash them to pieces; Christ is the only Saviour for sinners, come to Christ and he will save you.' A short time ago, brother Stubbins preached a sermon in our chapel upon repentance, and in the application some cautionary remarks were given upon the liability of deceiving ourselves upon this momentous subject. Just before brother Stubbins sat down, old Erun rose much affected with the sermon, and as the tears rolled down his cheeks, he said, that during his Christian course, he had had many fears lest he should have deceived himself after all; the remarks he made, from a full heart, were well timed, and produced a good impression upon the congregation. He frequently comes to our house and takes a cup of tea with us, but before he eats or drinks, he always asks a blessing.

"Curiosity led me to converse with the old man upon the subject of prayer. I said I should like to know how he prayed. I will give you an honest translation, and then you will be able to judge for yourself.

" 'O Lord God, thou art the creator of all, thou art the giver of life; how true, how holy, how merciful art thou! Thou art a Spirit, thou art almighty, thou art an exceedingly holy Father. I am sinful and depraved, put far away my wickedness. Thy wisdom is boundless, I cannot comprehend it. At this time I worship at thy footstool, I worship at thy footstool. The Lord Jesus Christ, being merciful, became our surety, and shed his own blood; how shall I discharge the debt under which I am laid? (i. e., for the Saviour's kindness.) When thou wast crucified, the earth quaked, the rocks were rent, the heavens trembled, the sun was darkened. By thy command, O Lord, the Lord Jesus Christ arose from the grave, angels bore witness; and after remaining forty days upon the earth, he ascended to heaven; but in the last day he will come again, when the angel of the Lord will blow the trumpet, then all people will arise; at that day he will set all believers on his right hand, but all unbelievers on the left. To all believers he will give immortal bodies, he will give them glory, he will take them to the holy city, the walls of which are garnished with precious stones. O Lord, how true, how holy, how merciful art thou; I am not able to understand thy character. I worship at thy feet; O Lord quickly accomplish thy will, destroy all the gods. Give my brethren wisdom, and save them; save my first brother and his wife (brother and sister Stubbins); save my second brother and his wife (brother and sister Buckley); save my third brother and his wife (brother and sister Bailey). Save my four brethren and their wives (native preachers and their wives); save my brother and my sister, save my wife, save my adopted son, save my daughters, save my own son, save his wife, save all my friends and relations. This blessing I will always ask. Save all thy servants, save thy church. O Lord, save me. I worship at thy feet, I worship at thy feet; with my eyes closed I pray to thee.' "

### " *Conversion of Erebon.*

" An encouraging instance of the converting grace of God has been witnessed in Erebon, the son of Erun, the first convert baptised in Orissa. When his father became a Christian his mother continued a heathen, and trained up her son in all the hideousness of idolatry, while she instigated him to pursue the most loathsome practices. His conduct was so wicked and disgusting, that scarcely any thing could exceed the hopelessness of the missionaries respecting him. His vices sunk him almost to the grave ; and his wretchedness led him to attempt self-murder, but he was mercifully rescued from death. Supremely miserable in the course to which his wicked mother had trained him, he resolved on becoming an ascetic, and spending his days in the jungle. He left home for this purpose, but was pursued and brought back to his friends. Referring to this period, in a conversation with Mr. Buckley, he stated that he had attended to his heathenish observances, had presented his offerings to his gods, but found no solid peace and rest : nothing but weariness and trouble. He mentioned this several times. In fact, the wretched youth was seeking for something which heathenism could not give. He then, as another expedient, determined to renounce society to go and live in the forest ; and he prepared himself for his intended new course of life by abstaining for a week from food, excepting a little fruit. While in this state some of the native preachers met with him, and in effect said, 'Come with us, and we will do thee good.' Balajee prayed with him, and while earnestly offering supplication for the young man, the native brother, overcome by his feelings, burst into tears, and was for a time unable to proceed. How softening is the influence of Christianity! Who that has beheld the perfect indifference, the fiend-like apathy of the Hindoos to the temporal and spiritual miseries of others, would expect to witness a Hindoo's voice stopped with weeping because he was praying for an ungodly and wicked young man? How different the heathen and the Christian! Two beings from two opposite worlds could scarcely differ more, than, in such a case, the man differs from his former self. This circumstance made a deep impression on Erebon's mind. Enlightened by the Eternal Spirit, he saw how sinful he had been. He mentioned in particular, how often he had grieved his father and despised his authority ; but he hoped, by the grace of God, he should do so no more. At length he determined to be one with the disciples of the Lord. 'Come what may,' he said, 'let reproach, or tribulation, or persecution be my lot, this people shall be my people, their God shall be my God, I will live and die with them.' After referring to his vile and disgusting character, Mr. Stubbins adds :—'Imagine, then, what were my feelings last Saturday afternoon, when, in the presence of a thousand spectators, young and old, rich and poor, male and female, I led him down into the water and baptized him in the name of the Father, Son, and Holy Ghost. And then, again, on the following day, when he was received into the church of Christ, you will better imagine my feelings than I can describe them. As we surrounded the table of the Lord, there sat the venerable father, some eighty-four years of age, and here the once wicked son, but still the child of many prayers, rejoicing together in Christ.' "

Kartika.

## CHAPTER VIII.

Conflict between Hindooism and Christianity—Conversion of Seebo Saho—Lukhein-das—Two women—Damudar and Somnath—Govinda-Sarthi—Reflections.

The great Redeemer, when informing his disciples what would be the effect of their ministry, said unto them, "Think not that I am come to send peace on earth: I come not to send peace, but a sword. For I am come to set a man at variance against his father, and the daughter against her mother, and the daughter-in-law against her mother-in-law. And a man's foes shall be they of his own household." See Math. 10: 32–39.

And on another occasion he said, in reference to the losses and crosses involved in a profession of his name. "There is no man that hath left house, or brethren, or sister," &c. Mark 10: 29, 30.

These are portions of the word of God, which missionaries and their converts better understand, than most of those who live and labor in Christian lands. Everywhere the "carnal mind is enmity against God," and when any individual becomes renewed in the spirit of his mind, there must be a contrariety between him and his former friends or companions, and there must inward, if not outward opposition, be felt towards him. Two cannot walk together except they be agreed. But in the case of conversion from heathenism, and especially from Hindooism, there is a complete breaking up of ties and relationships; family, civil and religious. The individual becomes an outcast from Hindoo society, whose touch is pollution, whose name a curse. According to Hindoo laws, he is at once separated from his race, his wife, his children, and his property; and this law *still operates to a great extent* under a Christian government in British India. There has been an attempt at alleviating the rigor of this law, by Lord William Bentinck, but there are those who execute the law, who will not or cannot understand its intended bearings, and whose rule of interpretation is all but unmitigated Hindooism. Hindoo officers too often rule in the courts, and too often sway the decisions of their Christian superiors.

This section is intended to illustrate the difficulties which oppose the profession of Christianity in India, by actual cases which have occurred within the writer's experience. They will refer to trials and obstacles arising out of the above-named family, civil, and religious relationships of the Hindoo in Orissa. A case from another part of the field may be added, to show that the difficulties are common to Indian missions.

### *Account of Seebo Saho.*

This devoted brother was a native of Arada, a village situated on the southern bank of the Khursua river, within the domain of the raja of Mudhpoor. He was of the Boisa caste, and his ancestors had engaged in merchandise for several preceding generations. To this occupation Seebo added the practice of medicine and farming. The family were in good circumstances, and much respected as people of sterling character.

Seebo was of a studious, contemplative turn of mind, and very early addressed himself to the study of the shastras, and plunged into all the intricacies of Hindooism. His history, furnished by himself, presents a singular, yet extremely painfully interesting detail of fruitless efforts to find rest to the anxious spirit in the mazes of Hindoo speculation.

> "In vain would boasting reason find
> The way to happiness and God,
> Her weak directions leave the mind
> Bewildered in a thorny road."

Diligently did he read and carefully transcribe whatever he thought interesting or instructive in the various books within his reach. He treasured up an immense store of Hindoo stories, allegories, muntras, spiritual nostrums, and fanatical prescriptions for the attainment of beatitude. He spent much time and money in the service of deceiving brahmuns, boishnobs, and pretenders to magical means of rendering visible the invisible God. He submitted to various penances and painful attempts at mental abstraction. One of his spiritual guides directed him to seat himself upon a mat made of kusa grass or a tiger's skin, with his face toward the east, his feet crossed in a particular manner, his right hand on the left shoulder, and his left grasping his great toe; and thus, with undiverted gaze, his sight was to be directed to the end of his nose, while he mentally repeated his incantation. He was informed, that after a few days of silent abstraction, he would see the supreme spirit, in the form of a white swan, hovering over his nose. In this contemplation of the divine light, he was assured was complete emancipation from the bondage of material existence. Many similar practices he had recommended to him, for all of which a fee was exacted, until his soul was completely bewildered.

Seebo was married, at the age of twenty-seven years, to a girl of ten years, and took up his abode with the rest of the family. Shortly after this circumstance, his elder brother died, and devolved upon him the care of the whole family, consisting of his aged mother, his brother's widow and children, besides younger brethren. These he supported by diligent attention to business, though he did not abandon his religious speculations. Gradually, however, his mind opened to the absurdities of idolatry, and his faith in idols became much shaken. He now became the prey of a different class of deceivers, under the guise of reformers, and travelled through another wearying round of observances. He says, "These disappointments did me much injury, for now, in a fit of hopelessness, I abandoned myself to all kinds of wickedness. These my evil practices strengthened day by day ; I despised all mankind, but thought most highly of myself. Afterwards, I became the subject of mental grief and burning anxiety.

"I continued in this state of mind for some time, when I obtained a blessing of a new and satisfactory kind; it was a copy of the gospel, by Mark. A person engaged in trade had received this from some padree at Balasore, and when I first saw it, it was much injured by rain and bad usage. He gave this book to me, but on account of its wet and torn condition, I could not get much information from it. I showed my book to many pundits, but they could or would not help me to understand it. Some said, this is not a proper book for you to read, tear it up and use it for wrapping up medicine. I however stored it up as a treasure, and resolved to master the book myself in private."

He afterwards fell into the hands of another teacher, of a more candid spirit; but in vain did he ask of him how "the soul might obtain deliverance from sin and death." This teacher is again referred to in the memoir of Lukhyan-das.

Seebo at length visited Pooree at the car festival, but

was coming away dejected and oppressed, when he saw some of our missionary body distributing tracts. So, tightly binding his cloth round his loins, he forced his way through the crowd and asked for a book. He obtained the gospel of Luke, and the jewel mine of salvation. This was the beginning of days to Seebo. He read his book daily, and often many times a day, till he had become acquainted with the sufferings of Christ, and understood that he suffered and bled for the sins of mankind.

He gradually obtained other tracts, and portions of scripture, and with several friends spent much time in comparing them with the Hindoo shastras. He also explained his book to his brothers, who for a time listened very favorably to his new views. A storm, however, was soon raised against him, and he was accused of sinning against the gods of his ancestors, and abandoning the instructions of his gooroo, or spiritual guide. Seebo however maintained his ground, defended his new sentiments, and gradually gained courage to avow his regard for Christianity.

"When (he proceeds,) the people heard me declare my sentiments, they maintained that I uttered blasphemy, and that it was criminal to look upon my face, inasmuch as I had forsaken the Bhagabot and had received forbidden shastras. I could only answer these accusations by saying, No, brethren, you err, I am convinced that the gospel is a revelation from the very mouth of the Deity; otherwise some fault might have been discovered in its pages. Hence I receive it as the revelation of God. Don't indulge in inconsiderate opposition, but use your understanding, and judge. Some of the people, hearing my remonstrances, became more calm, but still maintained that God had not confined all mankind to one book, but had given a diversity of revelations, as best pleased Him. Nevertheless, said they, we believe many will now regard those books, and finally they will prevail. I now obtained another addition to my stock of books, i. e., the gospel by Matthew. This book I also read with diligence, and I obtained so much light and strength from it, that I entirely renounced idolatry. This very much exasperated the inhabitants of my native village, and they abused me for not attending to the rites of my deceased ancestors.

Seebo here gives a long, interesting account of the discussions had with his neighbors; of various kinds of persecution; and finally, of the raja, under whom he lived, giving orders to secretly cut him off.

He then proceeds.

After this conversation, each departed to his home, and my own mind was in a very agitated state.

I often, in the silence of my own house, meditated upon God, and directed my prayers to Him, saying, O Lord God, thou heavenly Father, thou hast formed the world; thou dost preserve, and thou wilt destroy it. Thou, O Lord, knowest the mind, the thoughts, and the power of all. O Lord, I am a great sinner; I am unequalled in transgression. I have done thee displeasure often, and in many places, and there are no limits to my iniquity. I am fit only for hell. O Father, thou art alone the Saviour of the destitute, thou hast sent thy Son Jesus Christ to save the poor and the helpless. He has shed his precious blood to save perishing sinners from eternal hell. Trusting in the name of that Saviour, I earnestly pray that thou wilt forgive my sins. With a steady hope I entreat this blessing of thee. O Lord, besides thee I have no friend, and I have set my mind firmly to trust in Jesus Christ. Some, to please the wicked, are ready to lift up their hands to smite me; O Lord, save me from these. I have none but thee to help me. O hear my prayer. As to those who persecute me, place thy Holy Spirit in their hearts, that believing in Jesus Christ, they may be filled with the praise of Thy name. O Lord, accept these my prayers, for the sake of Jesus Christ.

On the night of this day I said to my wife: O my beloved wife, He who created you and me, is God. He has loved the world, and in mercy has sent the gospel to us. In the gospel it is written, that the Lord became incarnate for us; and that for us he died, that he might bear the punishment due to our sins. By this substitution pardon is offered to us. So far as the body is concerned, he died; but on the third day he rose, the conqueror of death. For forty days he was seen by his disciples, after which he ascended into heaven. Now it is necessary that men should believe on him, for henceforth unbelief will be visited with punishment. On this account, I have believed on Christ.—She answered, You can use your own pleasure, I do not forbid you. We are violently persecuted about Christ, and cannot worship him. I replied, that those who persecute us are ignorant, and consequently their opinions are not to be regarded as a rule.

In answer to these entreaties, she replied, I am an ignorant and stupid woman, and know nothing about religion; do as you think best. I had many such opportunities of conversing with my wife, and she always said: Do as you please; I have no power. This undecisive answer gave me both pleasure and pain.

After much time spent in the delusive hope of persuading my wife, I once more went to the house of my friend the weaver, and there read the book called the "Immortal History of Jesus Christ," and was greatly affected by the following passage in the thirty-first chapter:

> "The darkness foul of sin the people love,
> And their devotions by their works they prove."

The people lost in error, love darkness and hate the light; how dreadful a state!

Thinking this over in my mind, I was greatly agitated, yea, almost to distraction. I said to Lukhein-das, Dear brother, hear what this book says. I then read the passage. After this, I said, I will flee from among this people, I will go to Cuttack; I will seek the advice of the minister—will ask him to admit me to the Christian community. What he says shall be my law; I will adopt him as my guide; here, I find, I shall never enjoy rest and peace. While we were thus talking, a person, a fisherman, came up and said to me, Brother, what are you thinking about! already the raja's people are in quest of you; and should they find you in the dark, they are determined to murder you. This information I state upon authority—the people are bound together to accomplish their purpose. I advise you not to go to the minister, but to yield to the wishes of your friends and your people; for should the raja's people kill you, I dare say that Jesus Christ will preserve you! I told him, You know my mind; I am not afraid of what man can do unto me; I have God and Jesus Christ the Saviour, and the Holy Spirit the Comforter, to help and support me; and I have no fear. What I have long desired is now near at hand; I shall soon assume the profession of the Lord Jesus. Had not my enemies threatened me, I probably never should have left this place. O how God produces entire devotedness to himself! Blessed, blessed be God! now is the time to enter the way of life; now will I endeavor to enter thereon. I may seek such another opportunity in vain, should I neglect.

Thus speaking, I said to Lukhein-das, Now, even in the dawn of to-morrow morning, will I depart hence. Here I see nothing but horrid darkness. Lukhein-das said, To-morrow morning, brother, we will depart; I too am afraid of remaining in this place. Darkness every where prevails, not one appears willing to receive the gospel; many are bitterly opposed to it, and persecute us for our attachment to it. We must forsake friends, caste, relations, companions, and all, for the sake of Jesus. We have none here like-minded with us; and, therefore, come, brother, and let us away.

Some of my friends said to me, What will your wife and family do, if you go? I replied to them, that I did not worship my wife and children; besides, Christ says, that for his sake, whatever we may lose, we shall receive an hundred-fold increase. Jesus Christ does not mean that we shall have an hundred wives, this would not do; or hundreds of children, we could not get rice for them; but that he will take care that losses for his sake shall be more than made up even in this life, so that we need not be depressed. I believe this promise shall be accomplished.—They attempted to destroy my resolution by various arguments, as that I was head of my family—that I held the farm in my own name—that the family owed money, and had money owing it in my name, and as all writings were in my name, and would become invalid by my loss of caste, I should ruin the family. None of these things moved me.

Then said Lukhein, Call and speak to your brothers, or they will be concerned to know what has become of you. In consequence of this advice, I determined to go to my house. I found my family had all retired to rest. I took a little rice which I found in the cooking vessel, and retired to my mat also, but was too anxious to admit of sleep. I lifted up my heart to God in prayer, and said, O Lord help me! Thou hast made me and all men: O be with me in this hour of trial! Thus by turns I lay in anxious meditation and earnest prayer. Towards morning I arose, and finding that the night had passed far away, I awoke my youngest brother, and told him all I felt, and what I intended to do. He is a kind brother, and himself has some thoughts about Christianity; but he was not prepared for such a disclosure as that I made to him. He earnestly dissuaded me from my purpose, and also from reading the New Testament. I seriously asked him, whether to save our own souls was not a work of the greatest consequence, and a work to be attended to, without consulting rajas, and brothers, and caste mates? He admitted it was, but argued the opposition which it involved to the customs and religion of the country. After some conversation of this description, I again mentioned my determination to join the Christians, though I should be intercepted on my way by the raja's people. I asked him to bring me some money for my expenses. Thus enjoining the greatest secresy on him, I departed from my house, and found my way to the house of Lukhein-das. I awoke this friend from his sleep, and while it was still dark, we departed towards Cuttack. Some friends and associates lived at Nursinghpoor, and we called upon them on our way. At this place we found our friends ready to accompany us; but after some talk we advised them to remain till we returned.

After some difficulty Seebo and his companions found out our residence. Mr. Lacey was at that time living with the writer, so that we were both together when they obtained their first interview. It was a very interesting occasion, one of those we can never forget. Our new inquirers had made extraordinary progress in scriptural knowledge, and were quite prepared to profess Christ in baptism. After several days' intercourse, they were sent back to their village accompanied by Rama Chundra, who, after making suitable inquiries on the spot, was instructed to return and consult with us as to the propriety of administering the ordinance there or at Cuttack. Seebo proceeds :—

When we returned to our village, the people were very much exasperated against us, and had, in my absence, persuaded my brothers against me, so that they would scarcely admit me into my house. Brother Rama Chundra saw and had much talk with all those who wished to believe in Christ, and he was pleased, and soon returned to Cuttack to give his report. He soon came back again, bringing word that the minister would come to see us in a few days. Until the time of his arrival we were very anxious, and the people persecuted us; but when he arrived we were encouraged. Lukhein-das went to see the Padree, at the bazar of Jogusingh, about two miles from my house, and he engaged to come to my place and see me also. I engaged to go and see him. I could not get away to see him, for my brothers forcibly prevented me; and seeing and fearing the storm, some of those who had promised to worship Jesus Christ turned against me. In the afternoon the Padree came to my place, and they sung a hymn before my house; but I was very much afraid, and could not say much to him. As they returned from preaching, they again called at my house, and we had much conversation. I felt my resolution return, and lost all my fear.

The next day Lukhein-das went to the tent of the minister, and they there agreed to baptize us on the following day, in the afternoon. About four o'clock of that day the Padree arrived at my door to accompany me to the river and baptize us, and I came out of my house for that purpose. When I rose on my feet to go, my next youngest brother got up and stood in the path and said, Where are you going? I said, I am going to follow

Jesus Christ. He said you may follow Jesus Christ in your house, you shall not go away. He then took his cloth and twisted it round my arm and held me fast by it. I remonstrated with him and tried to comfort them, but they were strong in grief and would not hear. The minister and native Christians stood some way off, waiting for me, and inch after inch I pulled forward towards the river. Now my wife, with the other women of my house, ran out and cried, and tore their hair, and tore their clothes, and fell down at my feet. My wife seized me by my cloth, and I let it go in her hand. They laid my little daughter at my feet, and asked if I could leave my child. Their grief was very great, and it was a great trial to me. I remonstrated against their using such means, but it was of no use. I stood and told them that I must give up all for Christ, and that I was determined to be baptized. They now dragged me to the house of my spiritual guide, and he tried to dissuade me, and when he did not prevail, he cursed me. Then the steward of the raja came up to us in his tonjhon, and was very angry with me, and threatened to punish me. After some time they urged me to sign over all my family property to my brothers, and make myself responsible for all our debts; and I was willing to do this to satisfy all, but when I consulted the Padree about it, he advised me not to do so, and so I refused. Then they said they would carry me to the deputy collector, who was at some distance from my house, and they said they would abide by his decision. I said I would go to him, but would not promise to abide by his decision, as no one could be my judge in religion. However, we went towards the deputy's tent. They had now been pulling me about for some hours, and the Padree stood at a little distance, waiting the result. At length, through the coming up of a police officer, I obtained my release. The minister now descended to the river, and I and Lukhein-das and brother Sanantana followed him. Before we had got down into the water, they again ran up and seized me; but when the officer returned, they again set me at liberty. Now we went into the water, and the Padree baptized us in the name of the Father, and Son, and Holy Ghost. The people all crowded round us in the water to hear the celebrated mantra (incantation) which had such power, and all listened with silent attention. When we had been baptized, the people all ran off, except some who loved us, and they accompanied us to the minister's tent. We sung some holy hymns on the way, and were filled with joy.

That night I remained at the tent, and next morning went to my house to my wife and family, but I was shut out. I tried to persuade them to let me in, but they would not, and my wife and child would not receive me. They told me I was dead, and they should be purified from me. After in vain attempting to get possession of my house, property and family, I was advised to petition the Commissioner. I however petitioned the magistrate first, who refused to give me my property or family, and threw my petition on the floor. Then I appealed to the Commissioner, and he upheld the magistrate's decision. Now I was made very sorrowful. Thus I remained some time, till the Padrees wrote to the Commissioner upon the subject. Then the Commissioner said, "If Seebo will present a petition to that effect, I will reconsider his case." This I did, and the case was reversed, while an order was given to the daroga of Jajipoor to deliver my wife and child to me. The Padree went with me to Khandittar, to be present when the daroga came. My wife wept, and was very unwilling to come, but she must go before the magistrate to say in court that she would not accompany me. The people therefore put her out, and she came away to the large road. When she got to the large road, she said she had lost caste, and could not return to her house, though she should refuse to accompany me; and so she did not wish to go to Cuttack, but agreed to receive and go with me. Then a writing was drawn up before witnesses that the woman had of her own accord consented to accompany her husband, which was despatched to Cuttack, and my wife and child remained with me.

Having recovered my family, I renounced my property in favor of my brothers, for they would have been ruined by a division of it. They became humbled and asked me for this, and so I did not attempt to recover my property.

After I was baptized I went to live at Cuttack, and my wife in a little time became reconciled and happy. I soon was called upon to preach the gospel, but the people every where were very bitter against me. I went about to the markets with the Padrees and we spoke to many people and distributed many books. My mind is now satisfied, and my anxieties are gone, only I long to see the people turn to the one God through Jesus Christ. They are wandering and stumbling in darkness, and are servants of Satan.

"In darkness I wandered, oppressed with care,
And was brought by my fear to the verge of despair,
From Gooroo to Gooroo, I changed my faith,
But none could unto me, discover the Truth.
Then on me his pity, the Saviour bestowed,
And sent me his gospel which leadeth to God;
And now though I've lost all my friends and my caste,
Yet I know I shall gain my salvation at last."

This is the history of Seebo Saho.

### *Lukhein-das.*

Intimately blended with the account of Seebo Saho is the following brief memoir of Lukhein-das. It was, for the most part, written by himself, and translated after his death by Mr. Stubbins. It presents a pitiable view of the state of an immortal mind led captive by the horrid delusions of Hindooism. Lukhein, when a Hindoo, possessed the spirit of a demon. He was a wandering byraggee, and his curses were most bitter against those who displeased him. Some instances occurred in which it was believed persons died through the fear and dread excited by his curses. But under the influence of the gospel he sat at Jesus' feet clothed and in his right mind. He preached the gospel, and after a short course died of the cholera. It is trusted that he has now for some years been, what he ever will be, a saint in light. This short history contains almost a volume of awful representations respecting the dreadful darkness and delusions by which the unhappy millions of India are beguiled.

SECTION 1.—*Lukhein's early history and horrible delusions.*—I was the younger of two brothers, and when I was fourteen years of age, my father, Loknath Das died. About this time I began to read various shastras, and also to study the two principal ways to bliss, viz. :—the way by meditation and the way by works; and when any holy men, such as Pundits, Brahmuns and Boishnobs came into the neighborhood, I delighted to sit with them, to obtain sights of their gods, and, like a thief in the night, to steal out and join them. I ate with my companions various intoxicating and stupefying drugs, thus I became quarrelsome, tumultuous and insolent; insolent to my mother, insolent to my neighbors, sometimes loving, but often insolent to those with whom I sat. Sometimes I went to see Jugernath, and sometimes visited holy places, &c., &c. In this way, creating great confusion, I wandered about. What sin was, of that I never thought. I then began to steal, commit fornication, and covet the wives and property of others. Thus committing sin, I began to be troubled and afraid, and sometimes felt anxious to know how sin could be pardoned; but the Bhagabot says, that "No one can commit so many sins that Krishna's name cannot destroy." Again, another book says, "Eating a piece of food offered to Jugernath, the size of a grain of sand, even the sin of killing a brahmun is destroyed; how, then, can any other sin remain?" I, therefore, dried some of this holy food, and put it into a basket, and after bathing, ate a morsel, made also the sacred marks on my forehead and various parts of the body, turned round the rosary, closing the eyes, repeated my prayers, counted how many times I had repeated the names of the gods; poured water on the roots of the toolsi tree and made obeisance, put a little of the earth from the toolsi roots on my forehead, took a little of the water I had poured on the tree and sprinkled my head, letting a drop fall into my mouth; offered water to the sun and made obeisance, worshipped Radha, Krishna and Mahadeb. The water in which the various gods lave, and utensils had been washed, I drank and applied to my head. I also made obeisance to brahmuns, gooroos, boishnobs, &c., and at night assembled with all castes in sut sung, when passages from the shastras were read and explained. Should the question then be asked, "Ha, brother, how will the soul be saved?" Some replied, by serving gooroos; some replied, by repeating the name the gooroo gave at initiation; some said there are many names, the essence is every thing, as it is written in the shastras. Others said, God is in all things; this one spirit pervades all, therefore it is not proper to be opposed to any, but to look upon all things as God, and consider them as a part of yourself,—thus has said the supreme sea of mercy; and, again, in the black age the saviour of men will descend and dwell in the bodies of ascetics. In this way, remaining in my home until twenty-two years of age, I worshipped gooroos and brahmuns, received instructions at the feet of devotees, and attending to fastings, pilgrimages, worship of the gods, &c., &c.

At this time a certain Abadhut, (one of the most rigid of the class of ascetics,) whose name was Madhu Das Handia, came into my neighborhood. I daily went to worship at his feet, and to receive instruction from him.

The devotees who were with Handia said, "Let us take Lukhein Das with us and teach him the mysteries of pilgrimage; the rope, too, we will give him." They also said to me, "O Lukhein Das, absconding from thy house, come with us to-night, for here we will no longer remain." Hearing this, I returned to my mother and said, I have some business to attend to in a certain place, I must go and do it, you need not therefore seek for me. Thus saying, I departed from my house, and fleeing from the village, I came to a grove near Narasingapore, where I conealed myself in a tree; because, as the devotees were leaving, many people came to receive from them their blessing, and I was afraid lest I should be seen. About four o'clock in the morning, when all the people had left, I descended from the tree and came to the matt. As soon as I entered it, I worshipped at the feet of Handia and the other devotees, and received the dust from their feet, when Handia, with great joy and affection, loudly vociferating Hurre Bol! offered sacrifices and incense on the fire. After that, we did eat of ripe plantains, and the five productions of the cow, (viz., dung, urine, milk, curds and butter,) mixed with treacle. We also ate opium, gunja and other intoxicating drugs, and binding our wallets on our backs, we made ready to depart. Some baboos came up at this time, made obeisance and departed. Then Handi, calling upon Hurri, arose; Balaji and Sadhu Charana called upon Nar-singha (one of the incarnations of Vishnoo,) and taking up a provision bag, arose; Jhata Das and Bhagaban Das, calling upon the mighty Hanuman, (the monkey god) took up their drinking vessels and arose; and Bama Das taking up his cudgel, by which even demons are conquered, arose. Thus arising, we departed, travelling as far as Gopalpore, where we forcibly entered into the houses of the cow-keepers, and taking away their curds, milk, rice, went outside the village and feasted ourselves. Thence we went to another place. Here, thinking of my mother and my brother, and remembering all my former friends, I became exceedingly troubled and wept much. In this way, in many villages and jungles, we wandered about, and at length stopped in Rantila, where is a cave, in which we remained three months.

Here Handia gave me the rope, and taught me to sit in various postures, to retain my breath, to diminish my quantity of food, &c. He also taught me a number of incantations, how to put marks on different parts of the body, and what god dwells in each part; (the Hindoos have an idea that different parts of the body are the seats of different gods,) and how I must worship each. He told me also what I must daily perform; that I must watch at night, and not allow myself to go to sleep, must eat little, never clean my teeth, nor bathe nor wash myself, must drink my own water and eat my own dung; becoming perfect in these practices, I should be an abadhut. Such was the instruction Handia gave me.

Departing from Ranchipore we came to Bhobaneswer, and visited holy places, gods, &c. Thence to Pooree and saw Jugernath, and all the rest of the gods and shrines; the devotees and the holy men, &c.

After remaining there for a few days, we went to Gogal mountain, and halted in the matt of an abadhut named Hari. From that place Handia went to a matt at Nursingpore. Then I remained a short time with an abadhut named Jalandra, who seemed much attached to me.

§ 2. *Wanders about—Receives a Christian tract—Perplexities, Deliverance from a tiger, &c.*—When I descended from the mountain, and wandered about in the villages, I ate and drank in any body's house, whether high or low caste; Hindoos or Mussulmans. Wherever songs were being sung, the bhagabot or other books were being read, or sut sung was being performed, thither I went. I afterwards entered the matt of my old gooroo, Handia. He was very pleased to see me, and inquired why I had left Gogal matt. I told him of the old gooroo's adultery and other sins. Hearing this, he became troubled in his mind. I then remained about three years in Nursingapore matt, and afterwards set out with Brinda-ban Das, to go to the holy place, Brinda-ban; but when I had been to Calcutta, and had bathed in the Ganges, I resolved not to go thither, and so returned to Nursingapore. Thence I went to Jakardi, where I remained: there I received a holy book, called the Jewel Mine of Salvation. Seebo Saho also gave me the Ten Commandments; these I sketched over and could not forbear saying, these contain good words, I will read these carefully, they are full of excellent instruction. I one day read the Ten Commandments in the hearing of Madhu Das; he said, "These are the books of the demons, go not astray with these." Others said, they destroy people's castes. Others said, in the four ages of the world our religion and practices have existed, we will follow them. In this way, all united to despise the holy book. I said, why do you, not understanding, revile. To which they replied, understand it yourself, we do not wish to have any thing to do with it.

Hearing this, his gooroo said, you are become an enemy to gooroos; begone from my presence; go and worship your Jesus Christ; you have read the books of the Sahibs, go and be a Sahib. But my god is great, see my disciples, god dwells in all things, and at will assumes various forms; if on him you meditate with a steady mind, you will safely pass over the sea of life. Behold! Lukhein-das, I am now an old man; over my head eighty years have rolled. I have kept company with many devotees, visited many shrines, performed many vows, offered many sacrifices, studied many austerities, served many gooroos, experienced much fatigue, promoted the welfare of many by my blessing, and the misery of many by my curse; and dost *thou* now come to teach *me* wisdom? That can never be, go your way, and learn from Seebo Sahó, and let him be your gooroo, or be you his. All present said this was just.

I was grieved in my mind and said, I will worship my new Lord, I will be a disciple of Jesus Christ, you Jugernath, Radhu, Krishna, Rama, Gobinda, Kesabe, Doitari, Mahadeb, Chundi, Chamudi, Boirab, Gunesh, Kalee,—and all you three hundred and thirty millions of gods; you ten incarnations of Vishnoo, with the other forty-two incarnations; you gooroos, brahmuns, devotees; you stones, wood, rivers, muntras, juntras, your bades and badantes; you songs bhagabot, ramayun; you holy places, Kasi, Brundabun, Dwarica, &c.; Gunga bathing, Jugernath darsana, Brumha gyna,—all these are decitful and vain, in them is no salvation for the soul. Hearing this, they all said with one mind, let us attend to our worship, and not hear his words. They then attended to their devotions, saying, that the name of Rama is a destroyer of, and a barrier to all sin,—that the first syllable, Rá, puts sin out of its dwelling, (the heart) and the final mă is the bolt that fastens the door to prevent its reëntrance. The supreme one holds the bullock and plough, and ploughs continually, while Hurri, Ram, Krishnoo, are the seeds which they sow. Handia then said, this is the way we worship, how does Lukhein-das worship, let us hear. I said, mine is very different from that. I then said, the God of heaven, who is the King of kings and Lord of lords, and God of all men, even he, is the true gooroo and the Saviour of sinners. Here the old man interrupted and ordered me to fetch some gunja.

After this, I wandered about several months, and at length came to Tabaculi, to Baba Jee's matt, where I found many devotees; I remained for some time and read the Holy Book: seeing this, they inquired what book are you reading? what is its name? I replied, this is the Holy Book. If that, said they, be the Holy Book, what are ours? I said hear what this book is; as God is pure and sinless, without spot, so is this book, and those are cleansed from sin who follow its instructions. It is written in this book, "That God so loved the world, that he gave his only begotten Son, that whosoever believeth on him shall not perish, but have everlasting life." (Then follows the substance of Luke's gospel.) Whoever receives these truths, will obtain salvation, but whoever rejects them will dwell through endless ages in hell. Behold, ye holy men, and men of all castes present; behold and meditate on this book, and seek that ye may find. One man said, all that Lukhein-das has said is evidently true, for when at Pooree one day, I heard a Sahib in the large street preaching much about Jesus Christ; but the Pundahs so much opposed, and made such a disturbance, that I could not clearly understand; still I know that the book Lukhein has, is the book of the Sahib's religion. Some inquired what is the Sahib's caste? Others said, they are of the race of demons. Others, that in this black age, Vishnoo has taken a white body, and they are, therefore, incarnations of Vishnoo. To me they appeared as gods. In this way there was a great division among them.

Thence I started for Mungurapoor, and passing through a dense jungle, where no houses were, night overtook me, but the Lord evidently preserved me, for about midnight a large tiger came and crouched himself down just opposite me by the side of the smothered embers of a fire, which I had lighted for my protection, but I had gone to sleep and neglected it. I knocked my stick among the embers and he started back, but soon returned with an indignant growl; again I knocked with my stick, and again he retired, but again returned, wagging his tail, and looking at me with increased fury; I thought now I must die, and prayed to Jesus Christ to preserve me. Again I dashed my stick backwards and forwards, and set up a most hideous yell, at which he became alarmed and marched off, when I ascended a tree, where I remained for the rest of the night. In the morning I prosecuted my journey, and arrived at Jharda Khand, in the district of Pagurdi. Here the people all clothe themselves with leaves and worship the god of the jungle; of the shastras they know nothing. I got some gunja from them and left, returning to the matt of Handia. He kindly asked how I was, and receiving my worship, bestowed upon me his blessing.

He afterwards said, You are following the instructions of demons, depart from my presence. I said, It is not good to dwell with such deceivers as you are! You have deceived me! Behold a Baba Jee, (a term of respect applied to devotees,) what excellencies are to be found in you! The signs of a devotee are freedom from lust, anger, envy, &c. What are your signs? but to eat out of vessels of the impurest kind, never to clean your teeth, never to wash your dirty, stinking cloth, nor bathe your filthy body, to eat gunja till you are drunk, to blink your eyes like an owl, and abuse like a madman, and place your hopes on the things of others! Yes, Handia, you put ashes on you like a devoted saint, but live in forbidden practices! You go to the ground where the dead have been burnt and pick up the refuse of wood, and carry away the vessels which have been used in burning the body; you put the ashes of the dead upon your head, and mat your hair; eat gunja at night and fast at day dawn! At night you hear a little of the shastras, burn incense, and foolishly talk with the foolish, and call yourself a god among them,—blessing those who give you any thing, but cursing those who refuse, saying, incense burns black, he will die. Doing these things you still call yourself a holy man! Hearing this, he ordered me to depart, saying, I will not again behold your face. Hence I came to Madabil.

In that village was one Kesari Das, in whose house I remained. Here I saw Seebo Saho, and a brahmun who was skilled in the wisdom of the shastras. Seebo asked me what wisdom Handia had taught me. I replied, I have had many gooroos, and have associated with many devotees, but have not ascertained how salvation can be obtained. I have adopted the abadhut's rope,—smeared myself with ashes,—eaten in every one's house,—have eaten from the vessels of all castes,—have rejected all idea of caste,—have visited holy places and worshipped gooroos,—have been in hard fastings, watchings, fears, sorrows, afflictions, and distresses often, but have found no salvation. Seebo then said, There is a supreme wisdom, which, if you are able to obtain, all your desires will be gratified.

Here the hopes of the "weary wanderer after rest" were excited only to be disappointed, for he was directed to Hal Dhar Panda, who, after considerable expense and preparation, gave him certain magical lines to study, by which he was to obtain every blessing. Having done this, the various castes enjoyed an abundant feast,—putting the food into each other's mouths, and otherwise conducting themselves most disgustingly.

§ 3. *Seebo and Lukhein-das wander about together—Grow in gospel knowledge, and are at length baptized.*—Departing thence, I and Seebo wandered about to several villages, attending to the worship which had been lately prescribed; we also read the holy book, and when people inquired of us how they could obtain salvation, we said, Behold, in this word it is written, that to save sinners Jesus Christ became incarnate.

One day we came to a house where a great contention arose in consequence of Seebo Saho's declaring that the religion of Jesus Christ was the only true religion. I told him the people would revile; but, never mind, said he, if I die, be it so; why should we again turn to the worship of Vishnoo. Our spite against the gods daily increased, and we declared that in all this world there is no Saviour but the Lord Jesus Christ. On one occasion a boishnob inquired who was the Saviour; I said, Behold, O Baba Jee, you worship wood and stones, you wear necklaces and marks, you perform pilgrimages and penances, you offer many sacrifices, but in none of these can you obtain salvation; you have recourse to various means, but all are useless; your nature is sinful, and sinful are your works. I then told him of the true sacrifice. In this way making known the gospel, enduring persecution, we daily read the holy book. Some heard in love, and some reviled.

At this time we received a tract, called the Life of Christ, and read "the multitude delight in darkness." This darkness, said Seebo, is sin, at the thought of which we both wept. I then said to him, Brother, what is your mind? behold those who neglect this book can never obtain salvation, but must be partakers of God's wrath. Behold, O brother, Jesus Christ gave his life for sinners, he delivered himself up to be a sacrifice. Thinking on these things, my mind has become distressed. Behold, O brother, we are great sinners! In this sinful world, from our birth until now, how much have we strayed—how many sins committed, how many times reviled our parents, and who shall number our thefts, adulteries, &c. How many, both gods and men, have we worshipped, and how many vain works performed. Remembering these, together we wept and lamented, and charged our souls to beware of sin, and to regard the holy book. I said, O brother, I will no longer worship these gods nor holy men, I will no more go on pilgrimage or remain a boishnob, but, putting my trust in Christ, will obey his commands. Several heard this, and said, we also will trust in him. But others said, Seize him, beat him, then this boishnob will flee away, and Seebo will remain quietly at home; their assembly too will be broken up, and every one will be afraid to go near them. We will so rebuke them, that no one will read these books for fifty rupees. Seebo then said, I also believe in the Lord, and whether people revile, or whatever they do, whether I live or die, I only desire to be the Lord's.

Having thus resolved, we together prayed—O Lord Jesus Christ, we desire to come to thee, but know not the way; O Lord Jesus, show us the way; and we will walk in it. Having thus prayed, Seebo returned to his house, when the supreme gooroo arrived. Seeing him, Seebo bowed not, at which the gooroo grumblingly inquired, Ha, Doctor, (Seebo was a sort of native doctor,) why do you not worship me? Seebo said, it is not right to worship such as you; we have one Gooroo whom we know, but such as you are no longer our gooroos. He asked me afterwards, whom I and Seebo worshipped. I said, like you we once worshipped many gods, but now we only worship the Lord Jesus Christ. Hearing this, he became very enraged, and seizing a large stick, ran upon Seebo to beat him, saying, By my withering and destructive curse, you shall become dust: (meaning that he would die.) He then made a great disturbance among the people of the village, and departed.

At this time an order from the raja came, saying, that as he had heard that we had read the Padre Sahib's books, the people were to beat us, and drive us away, wherever we might sit, and all who consorted with us. Seebo then said, Ha Baba Jee, if we should stay here, the raja will cause us to be taken and beaten, and what else he will do we know not. I replied, Who is he, and what can he do? Clearly he may afflict our bodies, but he he can never hurt our souls. He alone who is King of kings and Lord of lords, can punish souls: why should we fear a mortal, though he be a raja? Rather let us fear Him who is able to seat us in heaven, or to sink us to hell. I then said, O Seebo, and my beloved companions, I will depart from this place early to-morrow morning. Seebo said, if you profess this religion, I will profess it too ; and being your companion, whatever befalls you, shall befall me. I then said, whoever wishes to believe in Jesus Christ, let him go with me to-morrow ; but all fearing the raja, each one departed in his own way. Seebo said, I will go : call for me at my house in the morning, and if I live, you shall then know what I will do. After all had departed, I resolved in my own mind, that if none would go with me, I would go alone ; thus resolving, I prayed to the Lord, and fell asleep.

Rising early, I again remembered the Lord ; put my things together, and left those with whom I had been staying. Many wept, and many followed me : Seebo came out of his house to meet me, and again we were followed by many, who wept and lamented bitterly. A Sankari said, O Baba Jee, and O brother Seebo, if you wish to go, do, and understand all about this religion ; I also believe in Jesus Christ, and in all that is written in this book. He then wept, and gave us a little money for the road expenses ; coming with us a little way, Sanantani wept much and said, through the mercy of the Lord you are walking in his way, I shall eagerly watch your return from Cuttack.

On the way we talked together much about religion. That night we remained hungry and slept in a hut. At Bhoyerpore we inquired for the Christians, but the people reviling, said, we know nothing about them. Thus we went along, till we arrived at Chowdry bazaar. With a little fear and a little shame, we asked some people where the Padre Sahibs lived. But they, reviling, said, Why do you inquire for them? One day, knowing not whither to go, we went and seated ourselves at the foot of a Kadamba tree, against Padre Sutton's house ; at this time a painter came out of the house ; I called to him, saying, Ha, brother, I wish to ask your something—come here. When he came I asked him whose house it was ; he replied, it is the Padre Sahib's. I asked him if he would introduce us to the Sahib, as we had something to say to him. He said, come along, fear nothing. As soon as we reached the door, Lacey Sahib's Mem (Mrs. Lacey) asked us to come in and sit down.

Then Lacey and Sutton Sahibs, with Rama-Chundra, Krupa Sindhu, and Doitaree, came to us; Lacey Sahib inquired whence and for what we had come. I said, my house is at Olassa, in Madhupore; this is my companion. We have received and read your books—the Jewel Mine of Salvation—a Gospel—the Ten Commandments, and various other books, I have read for several years; during which time, I have been opposed and persecuted by all castes; but my wish still was to leave them. The raja and his people have opposed us; but let them oppose; our wish is to live according to this religion, therefore have we come. Do, my dear Sahib, tell us how we may obtain salvation. Lacey Sahib then gave much instruction concerning time and eternity, body and soul, sin and holiness; the birth, miracles, death, resurrection, and ascension of Christ. Sutton Sahib also gave much instruction, and after him Rama-Chundra, and Doitaree.

He was subsequently baptized with Seebo and Sanantana, as already mentioned; and from that day forward went on his way rejoicing.

The next case to which I would refer, is that of two women, a mother and daughter, but both married women, who were led to embrace the gospel. This was a very uncommon occurrence. Probably there are few similar instances as yet recorded in the history of Indian missions. For both these women heard the gospel, believed in Christ, and were baptized, in opposition to their Hindoo husbands. But their conduct involved them in all but a martyr's sacrifices.

Komalee and her mother Daunee, with their husbands, lived in the neighborhood of the old gooroo, and were for a time numbered among his disciples. It is to his mode of worshipping God she refers in the following memoir, dictated by herself; but she at length, like most of the old man's disciples, obtained too much scriptural knowledge to be held in his snares, and finally desired to become a Christian. She thus proceeds:

The God who created me, him in my heart I feared, and forsook the idolatrous customs of men. My soul I devoted to the worship of God, and my body I devoted to my husband. My husband also adopted the same kind of worship. We now passed a little time, in one heart and in one mind worshipping God, and attending to the business of life. Some time after this, my dear boy died, and caused great distress to my family and myself. My friends said to me; "Women have no business to worship God; you have been worshipping, and therefore this is come upon you; your son is dead." My father and husband joined in these expressions, and reproachingly said, "Let your God give me my child back." In answer I said, "Very good; if because I worshipped Him, God has taken my child, then it is well, let the child go." From henceforth my husband renounced the worship of God, and took to the idols. He also commanded me to leave off God's worship, and worship idols, urging that if sons were to be taken, there was no good in worshipping God. I said, "If our son died, did he not die for himself? with the cause of his death what have I to do? I must worship God for my own salvation." He then said, "If you will not leave off this worship, then I will make you." I asked him, "How will you make me?" He replied, "Tying a noose in a rope, I will kill you." I said to him, "Very well, what you are able to do, that do." In a little time, as he said so he did, for he tied me with a rope and beat me much. This I bore, and Sunderadass exclaimed, "Ah! ah! in the cause of devotion to bear all this! This woman will find her way to heaven; she has been greatly tried." Thus I remained, convinced of the folly and sin of idolatry, and having nothing to do with the customs of my neighbors. I saw that the world was false and vain. I was weak and persecuted, and what I endured for many days, that no one knows. Like as a man when under the care of a police officer, is narrowly watched, so did they watch me. I much desired to be baptized and profess the Lord. At length I opened my mind to my mother, and told her I was determined to be baptized. In her I found a friend, for she also thought of the true worship. She however with me observed the strictest silence. My mother was the messenger of information for me, and in particular did she talk with

Sundradas about my resolution. Then he sent Mongraj, one of his disciples, to settle my mind, and then return to him. He came and tried to comfort me, but I said, "When the Lord comforts me I shall be comforted, now there is no alternative." This determination of mine was talked of by him, and all the village got to know what was my resolution, and my relations more than ever tried to prevent me. My father and husband went to Sundradas, and said to him, "It is through your vile instructions that the honor of our families is gone, for our wives meditate running into the house of the Pheringees." Our husbands were unchanging in their anger towards us, for they suffered persecution and shame on our account.

We sometimes talked to them, and said, "Behold, how vain is man, how vain and uncertain the life of sinners; soon they die, and then having no hope they perish forever! Behold, the God that made them, Him have they forsaken, and the stream of time carries them to hell, their spirits go to hell. O they have no hope! This is a world of sin and guilt, and to remain in its customs, either for us or for you, is not and will not be well. Besides, this is the time of mercy, the day of salvation; and now, if you will listen to the voice of God you may obtain this grace and be saved. His voice of warning is going out to all, commanding us to flee from the coming wrath. Come then, and let us flee, husbands and wives, parents and children, let us flee together—flee from sin, and take refuge in the Lord." Thus we entreated them with many words, but they would not hear.

Unsuccessful with our husbands, we considered how we might secure our own salvation. About this time the brethren Gunga-Dhor and Doitaree, heard by some means that our minds were impressed with the importance of our eternal salvation, and they were deputed to see us, if possible. They came over to our house, and through an interview with Sundradas, we saw them and heard words from them, while they also heard something about our experience. Hearing what we said, Gunga-Dhor rejoiced and was filled with gratitude. To him I said, "O brother, how can we escape? this at present we see not; O brethren, devise some means by which we may be delivered from our bondage and misery, that we may obey the Lord and be joined to his people." Then Gunga-Dhor said, "If your minds are firmly fixed on serving the Lord, be not afraid, for the Padree will come, and we will come, and will devise some means by which you may come and be baptized." Thus speaking, the two brethren departed, and we again remained for some time. At length, the Padree Sahib and the Schoolmaster Sahib, with the brothers and sisters from Cuttack, came to a place about half a mile from our village called Ungoderee, to the house of a Christian brother named Korunasaho. They arrived at his house about nine o'clock in the forenoon. My mother went to Ungoderee earlier in the morning, and when they arrived brought me word: hearing this, my mind was filled with joy, while my heart leaped with pleasure to think of going to the Christians, and following the Lord's commandments. We informed those who were living in the house with us, that now we were going, when they lifted up their voice and mourned and wept aloud. I had a daughter, and her I committed to their care till the father came home. Having done this and made some other arrangements, we came out of our house, leaving all but the little child of ten months old, which I was nursing, him I took with me. On the road we passed by some of our neighbors, who were our inveterate enemies; they were at work among their crops of rice; they saw us, and stood to look at us. Then said I in my mind, Now it will be well for me to die, for they will sieze us and carry us back. Thus were we exercised in our hearts, and we lifted up our prayers to God, and said, From this danger, O Lord, do thou deliver us! and the men stooped down to their work, and took no further notice. Then we proceeded on our way, and soon arrived at the place. After we had entered the house, we saw the Padree, and made our salutation, and then we sat together on the floor, and were questioned about the state of our minds. The Padree said, "Why are ye come?" and then we told him that we had discovered that we were guilty sinners; that neither our own works or our idols could save us; that Christ died for us, and we trusted in him, and were come to take his mark upon us. While we were talking, my husband and others of our village arrived, and called out, Dooie (justice) Padree Sahib! Dooie company! After a while they were invited into the house to talk with us, and they said, "Why are ye come here?" We said, "We are come here that we may save our souls." They said, "Your souls cannot be saved here!" We replied, "We are sinners and trust in Jesus Christ, and are come that we may assume a profession of his name." They said, "Show us your Lord." We answered, "Our Lord is invisible, and not as wood, or stone, or earth, or water, or flesh; he is a Spirit, and so cannot be seen." Then they gave us much abuse, and took Lacey Sahib to witness. Lacey Sahib said to them, "I will not forcibly baptize them; talk to them and persuade them, and if they consent take them away." Some confusion occurred when we went out to be baptized, after which a neighbor said to my husband, "Come, let us return home; these women have gone over to the barbarians, their honor is gone, and we can have no more connection with them. Come, let us depart hence; I will not witness such disgrace." Thus speaking they departed, and we were baptized.

After the baptism of these two females, the husbands, at the instigation of some of the enemies of our mission, brought the case into court, to be tried by our old opponent, the collector of the Pilgrim tax at Pooree. He ordered the women to be stripped of their ornaments, with most of their clothes, and deprived them of every particle of their property; the child was forcibly taken, in open court, from the mother's arms, and given to its father, and an attempt made to implicate the missionaries and native preachers in a misdemeanor. The husbands actually performed the funeral rites for their wives, as though they were dead, and then married others. They however acted more under the influence of others than their own judgments, as they long afterwards called occasionally to see their old partners.

The magistrate subsequently bound several preachers, in the penalty of fifty rupees, not to baptize a Hindoo married woman without her husband's consent, and sent a public letter to our missionary brethren, enjoining on them the observance of the same rule. The full details of these proceedings are published in the Society reports. These will verify every part of the foregoing statements.

It devolved on the writer of this book, at the express injunction of the Society at home, to bring this whole matter before the Governor-General in council. The documents were first forwarded to his private secretary, who stated that the bond exacted from our native preachers was illegal, and that we should meet with no practical obstruction in a proper prosecution of our work. At his instance the matter was hushed, and we have proceeded quietly on our way.

### *Govinda.*

Apart from those trials which man has inflicted and which man may remove, the Hindoo convert must endure much, arising out of the antagonistical relationships of heathenism and Christianity. The Hindoo is often strongly attached to family connections, and feels deeply the rending asunder those ties which bind him to home and kindred. We do indeed meet with much that seems not well to agree with this assertion, but as we have elsewhere stated that the Hindoo conscience may be reached, notwithstanding the blighting, hardening effects of Hindooism, so we may prove that despite the tendency of the system to induce the negative of natural affection, yet still nature will ofttimes speak out, and show she dwells in black and white the same. We shall adduce two cases, omitting those of Damudar and Somnath, illustrative of this class of trials, which the young convert must encounter. Mr. Lacey writes :—

" A case of conversion of singular interest connected with this station, is that of Govinda. In the course of last summer a respectable young man, attended by two servants, arrived at Berhampore as an inquirer about Christianity. He came from a village upwards of thirty miles off, secluded in the midst of jungle, near the Goomsur hills, and was the son of a very wealthy Hindoo. Ten years before, some of his friends had visited Gunga Saugor, and returning, one of them received a tract, 'The True Refuge,' at Balasore. This man carried the tract home and laid it in a box, and there it lay for more than eight years. About the end of that time, Govinda was at his friend's house. His eye fell upon the tract, and he inquired, 'What is that?' his friend replied, 'A Sahib's book, will you read it?' and saying this, put it into his hand. The tract appears to have lost two of its leaves, but Govinda took it and read it. A new kind of light began to enter his mind. In reading, he did not at first feel its influence, but afterwards felt somewhat annoyed that the objects of his trust and adoration were so exposed and set aside. He read on and on; the tract commended itself to his understanding; the Holy Spirit opened his heart to receive its truths. His confidence in idolatrous refuges was shaken, and his trust was transferred to Christ, the true Refuge. In this state of mind he obtained some other tracts, especially the prophecies of Isaiah, given to a man at Munda Mari. His friends, however, began to take alarm, and expended large sums of money in ceremonies to cast the evil spirit out of him. They violently opposed him. 'What! can you become an outcast? Can you forsake the religion of your forefathers? Can you bring your father with sorrow to the grave?' He replied, 'In serving the gods of the heathen, I have no pleasure, I cannot obtain salvation from these false refuges, and will therefore go to Berhampore,' where he hoped to learn more about the gospel. His father entreated him on no account to lose caste, and wished him to swear by the Maha Prasad, or food offered to Jugernath, and other idols, that he would not renounce caste. This he refused to do, saying, 'That what they called holy food, was, of all things, most unclean, and that he should not feel any oath made by that, at all binding.' His father then wanted him to take some other oath, but this also he declined, declaring that he would not lay himself under any obligation whatever. At Berhampore both the European and native brethren had much conversation with him, and he appeared to have received a degree of light and knowledge which was perfectly amazing. He received a good supply of books and left on the following morning, telling the people in the bazaar, as he passed through, that he should go and see whether his wife and friends were willing to become Christians with him. If so, well; if not, he should come out and leave them. The brethren heard no more of him for some weeks, when a servant came with a native letter requesting more books, which were sent at his request. He rapidly grew in knowledge, gave up his bad habits, and desired to be baptized. He said, 'I feel as if I could endure any thing for the sake of Christ; I feel as if I could suffer martyrdom for his name; I will never forsake the religion of Jesus.' Mr. Stubbins thinking it important that he should confess Christ in Bagara, his native place, proposed that the brethren should return with him thither. As they journeyed, they were met at the bottom of the Goomsur hills by his father and a party of his friends. Neither by threats nor promises could his father prevail on him to renounce Christ, but he persuaded him to defer his baptism. It was, says a missionary, truly an affecting scene to witness the tearful pleadings of his aged father. Govinda was his only son. Every promise was made to him, that if he would return he might follow Christ and do as he pleased,—that no control should be exercised on him. Govinda at length determined to go with his father, as his doing so would assuage the poor old man's grief. The father now probably supposed that he had gained his point; but as Govinda had lost caste by eating with Christians, his father and friends were anxious that he should go on a pilgrimage to the Ganges or Jugernath to regain it. He objected, telling them that there were but two castes in the world, the godly and the ungodly, and to the former he would cleave till death. He also assured his friends again and again, that the visit they proposed was of no use. 'Jesus Christ was his shrine; he wanted no other, and would have no other.' At length he so far yielded to his father's wishes as to agree to take a journey, and in company with four attendants or priests, set out, furnished with plenty of money. He went forward to Cuttack, and soon made out the residence of the missionaries. Mr. Buckley observes, "I was much struck with his extensive and accurate knowledge of divine truth, as were all our friends. I never met with one so advanced as he in Christian knowledge and experience at the commencement of his course. A considerable inheritance is likely to be alienated from him; but when this was referred to in conversation, he instantly quoted our Lord's words:—'If God so clothe the grass of the field, which to-day is, and to-morrow is cast into the oven, shall he not much more clothe you!' He had no doubt that the God whom he served would take care of him." After seeing the missionaries, he told his attendants that he had accomplished his pilgrimage, and should go no further; that at Cuttack he should bathe and terminate his wanderings. They took the alarm, reasoned, persuaded, remonstrated, but all to no purpose. Violence, which in other places they might, and most likely would have offered, they dared not offer there. He inquired what money they would want for their journey, presented them with some, and bade them farewell, not, however, without entreating them to forsake their refuge of lies, and to trust in Christ. A young brahmun, who was a family priest, was much affected, and wept loudly as he came away. On the next Lord's day Govinda was baptized by Mr. Buckley, and then sat down at the table of the Lord. A female convert was baptized with him."

We will next select an instance from the records of the Berhampore station; it refers to Sarthi, a convert baptized in 1846. The narrative is furnished by three of the brethren there stationed.

### *Sarthi.*

The case of Sarthi Marana is one of peculiar excitement and interest. He is about twenty-four years of age, and is by trade a carpenter and blacksmith, and a very superior workman, especially in the latter branch. For some years he has manifested great concern about his soul, and used frequently to come down for religious conversation,—attend public worship, &c., and on many of these occasions brought with him a number of his own caste people, who also seemed favorably disposed toward Christianity. He is naturally timid, hence the difficulty to him, of coming out, was very great; besides which he had an aged widowed mother living with him, to whom he was much attached. On the morning of the 2d instant, however, he came to my house to bring some work home, when I seriously urged the question, "How long haltest thou between two opinions?" exhorting him by every consideration, if he believed Christianity was true, to avow fearlessly that belief; and the eternal God would strengthen him to do so if he sought his aid, &c. He left me and went over to the native Christians, and after much conversation with them he said, "Why should I longer delay, I know not how soon I may die; I believe that Jesus Christ alone can save me, and henceforth I will serve him and him only;" he then broke caste by bathing and eating with the Christians. Soon after, I had all our delighted band, with Sarthi, bold now as a lion, at my house, to declare all that had been done. I had a great deal of most interesting conversation with him, and at the close supplicated the divine blessing to rest upon him, and that strength might be given him to endure, with Christian magnanimity, the trials that awaited him when his friends should know of what he had done in bringing down at once, in their estimation at least, seven generations of his ancestors from the thrones of bliss on which they have been seated in all their heavenly enjoyments, shutting them into the deepest pit of perdition, and cutting off all hope from his descendants to the latest period of time! It is truly no wonder that the Hindoos should oppose conversions to Christianity, when they consider them in this fearful aspect. I encouraged him to go for his tools, &c., with some of the brethren in the afternoon, but to go trusting in heavenly strength,—and to go expecting opposition,—to go therefore from a throne of grace. Accordingly they started off rather early, when it was too hot for us safely to go, but I wished them, in case of disturbance, to send for us immediately. His house was not more than half a mile from ours. After they had been gone about an hour, a messenger arrived in breathless haste, saying they had seized Sarthi and dragged him into his house, and there they had fastened him up; that the mob was about to fall on the native Christians, and what would be the end? &c.; but all was spoken in such broken sentences, owing to the agitated, breathless state of the man, that I could scarcely make out any thing of the real state of things,—however myself, brethren Buckley and Bailey were soon on the spot, and found the brethren singing at the top of their voices in the midst of a dense, confused crowd, but Sarthi was shut up in his house near. I stopped the singing, and commenced as loud as I could, "Talk they of binding the Christian? as well might they talk of binding the sun in the firmament,"—"Talk they of putting out the candle the Lord himself has lighted, as well might they attempt to extinguish the light of all the hosts of heaven," &c. I spoke till quite exhausted, and was truly amazed at the death-like silence of the people. Damudar next began, and at the top of his strong sonorous voice exposed their system of caste; but he had not said many words, before there was a tremendous rush to the opposite side of the road; the fact was, Sarthi had broken asunder his bands, and forced his way through a crowd, infuriated as incarnate devils. O I shall never forget the scene! some were dragging his hands, some his hair, some his clothes, some pushing, some screaming, some were cursing, his mother beating her head upon the ground,—his sister tearing her hair, beating her naked breasts, and wailing in agony. All was done that could be, to force him back to his house; we all went to his assistance, and amidst many hard blows, and kicks and curses, succeeded in getting him to a stone on the other side of the road; here he sat with the sweat streaming down him, smeared over with dust, mud, &c., his hair hanging down, (the Hindoos tie up their hair behind as females do in England,) his body trembling, his eyes as though they would start from their sockets, and himself ready to die of fatigue. Opposite to him stood his sister, just raised up from a bed of charcoal dust, ashes, and filth,—the upper part of her body bare, her hair dishevelled, her face writhing, and expressing language words would fail to do. One would have thought she had violently forced her way from the pit of perdition, and had come to exhibit the infamy and torture to which the lost are subject; others were forcing along the mother, in all her sad dejection, from a pond where she had been to drown herself. She was presently brought and placed at the feet of her only son, and that son worse than dead! This aggravated the affecting character of the scene,—

here she sat beating her withered breasts saying, "O my son! O you wretch! was it for this you hung on these? for this I fed you? for this I carried you on these old worn sides? &c. O Sarthi, you wretch! what have you done!—what have you done! how have you brought down your father and ancestors from heaven to hell! and how have you opened the flaming pit for me and all after me! You wretch!—you wretch! what shall I do!" And again she wept and writhed, and knocked her head upon the stone, and stretched herself on the ground, and rubbed her streaming eyes on his feet. He chucked her lightly under the chin and gently tapped her shoulders saying, "Mother, why do you thus? why should I go with you to hell? come with me to heaven,—come with me and I will feed you,—I will work for you,—I will give my life for yours,—come with me, I cannot go with you to hell,—come with me to heaven,—come with me to Jesus Christ,—come with me to heaven," &c. Having rested ourselves a little, as well as the crowding mob would let us, for we were almost, as the American said, drowned in our own perspiration, we were anxious to get Sarthi off, his mother having left him with sobs and tears and bitter wailings and curses; but we saw we should have difficulty. Sarthi got up to go with us, but the crowd rushed on him, seized his hair and hands and cloth, and dashed him to the ground; first one dragged him along by his hair, and then another; and then another, through mud, over stones, broken bricks and tile; I really feared they would have killed him. Their object was to get him into the house again; but he determined not to go, and we determined, if possible, he should not go, for the probability is, if he had, he would have been killed. It was a dreadful struggle; we were pulling him one way, and his people another; some saying, kill him! kill him! kill them all! we shall only be fined a little, kill them! kill them!! Some brahmuns now came up and encouraged the people in their violence; Balajee lay sprawling on the ground,—some kicking and some dragging him. Soon a regular battery of stones, bricks, mud, iron cinders, &c., opened upon us, and what the end would be, we were at a loss to conceive. Amidst the fire of the enemy, we succeeded in getting Sarthi off to some distance, but the people came upon us again, and again they dragged him back, and several of us received severe bruises; however, after all, we managed to get him away. Brother Buckley fortunately managed to get away, to be ready to take Sarthi home when he should be liberated, just as the extreme violence commenced, so that he escaped. Brother Bailey had a very narrow escape,—a large stone passed before him, which must have seriously injured his head, had it hit him; as it was, he only got pretty well speckled with mud. I came in for rather a worse portion. After having the breath squeezed out of me, or thereabouts, some one gave me a severe stroke on the leg with a stick, and shortly after this, a large iron cinder came on my back with a tremendous thump and nearly knocked me down; however it was not a time "*to feel if one was hurt*," as a good, dear friend (now in heaven) said he was doing when thrown from his horse. The native brethren, servants, and in fact all our people who were there, were hurt more or less; I suffered a good deal for nearly a fortnight from the blow I received on my back.

When we got Sarthi fairly out of the way, brother Buckley conducted him home, and dressed his wounds and bruises—Bailey and I returned to the scene to hunt up Balajee, who had remained behind; we found him quietly talking to the people; I again spoke, and was listened to with considerable attention to the close; but when we left, they gave us some more mud and a regular Hurre Bol! When we got home, I went over to brother Buckley's, and found Sarthi there rejoicing in the Lord, and being rubbed with embrocation by some of the brethren. Seeing that all was right there, I returned, to have my own wounds attended to, and get off my speckled and saturated, should-be white clothes; then in came five or six of the native brethren to have their wounds examined. I mixed a plentiful quantity of hartshorn and laudanum, and it was truly amusing to see the wry faces and hear the peculiarly expressive Ohs! and ba's! and exclamations, "keree katuchi!" (how it cuts!) &c. All this almost over, brother and sister Buckley came to spend the evening with us; together we rejoiced, sang, and praised God: feeling sure the devil would never be able to extinguish the candle that had that day been lighted in Bha Pore. The delightful, but eventful day was closed by singing, "Watchman! tell us of the night!" &c., and by brother Buckley offering a most appropriate prayer.

Of the spirit exhibited by the Christian Hindoos after Sarthi had been rescued from his enemies, some interesting particulars are related by Mr. Buckley.

I, with three of our preaching brethren, and others, accompanied Sarthi to our house, and surely our hearts burned within us as we talked by the way. One of our native brethren broke the silence by saying, "Be of good cheer, brother, heaven will make amends for all." Another responded, "Remember Christ's words, 'Ye shall be hated by all men for my sake, but he that endureth to the end shall be saved—fear not them that can kill the body.'" A third said, "Do we not see that Satan is the prince of this world?" Again it was said, "Brother, be of good cheer, think of the exceeding great reward in heaven." Thus did we encourage our friend, by telling him of the precious promises made to those who suffer for righteousness sake; and by directing him to the final recompense. At length we reached our house, and after so much excitement and violence, were glad to sit down quietly under our own verandah. Mrs. Buckley soon heard of the outrage, and came to see if any evil had befallen her husband. Mrs. Stubbins soon after joined us, and while we told them of all things that had happened, they dressed the bruises of those who had been injured by the affray. While this was being done, one of our people said, Brother Sarthi! the Lord has delivered you this day from the power of Satan: let us bless his name. Another remarked, how suitable was the prayer, "Father, forgive them, for they know not what they do," for the perpetrators of the outrage. While we were thus employed, others came up, one limping, another pointing to his bruises, brother Stubbins bending his back, and bearing in his body the marks of the Lord Jesus; brother Bailey's soul was all on fire, and I believe he regretted, that he had not been knocked down and well pommelled in the affray. For myself I was thankful that I had escaped unhurt. The schoolmaster, Bhobananunda, (i. e. the joy of the world,) came in, pencil and paper in hand, smiling, and saying that he had stayed in the thickest of the stones, and had written down the names of the ringleaders; "This day (said he,) we have had the honor of suffering for Christ." I never saw them all so happy as they were on this occasion. It occurred to me, that it was after a violent persecution that it was said, "The disciples were filled with joy, and with the Holy Ghost." No one ever suffered for Christ without feeling that His precious truth was worth suffering for. The steadiness, the firmness and joy of our new brother were very pleasing; I could not but pray that his future course might to the end be marked by the same holy devotedness to the Lord; but it is much easier to make a noble confession for Christ once, than to convey a spirit of martyrdom into every duty of every day, for many years. Still, all things are possible to him that believeth.

We reluctantly omit the account of Sarthi's baptism, and attempts to obtain his wife. In this he failed; she positively refusing, before the magistrate, to live with him any longer.

Various attempts have been made to obtain some modification of the Hindoo laws, which have so oppressive a bearing on all who, from any cause, renounce caste. Lord William Bentinck caused an act to be passed during his administration with this view, but it was always evaded by the courts. An act has, however, just been issued in the Calcutta council chamber, which appears likely to bring the wished-for relief. We cannot forbear inserting it in this place.

"On the 11th of April, 1850, a law was passed, the most material clause of which is in these words: — 'So much of any law or usage, now in force within the territories subject to the government of the East India Company, as inflicts on any person forfeiture of rights or property, or may be held in any way to impair or affect any right of inheritance, by reason of his or her renouncing, or having been excluded from the communion of any religion, or being deprived of caste, shall cease to be enforced as law in the courts of the East India Company, and in the courts established by royal charter within the said territories.' "

I shall close this chapter with an appropriate extract from the report of the London Missionary Society for 1847:

" It is well known that, up to a recent period, the loss of caste, in India, was followed by *the loss of property;* and this fact, of course, has operated as a powerful impediment to the progress of Christianity, especially among the more respectable classes of the Hindoos. Many instances, however, have occurred, in which native converts have forsaken houses and lands for Christ's sake, and the gospel's; but in none has the sacrifice been followed by a greater amount of steadfastness, and self-denial, than in the character of the late Naraput-Singh, who was faithful unto death, and has at length received the crown of life.

" He was received into the Christian church, by Dr. Carey, seven-and-thirty years ago. By embracing Christianity, he was deprived, by the Hindoo law, of property to the amount of £800 per annum; and, instead of affluence, he lived contentedly upon the limited salary of a native preacher till he died."

"Our departed brother," observes Mr. Kennedy, "never expressed regret for what he had done. He knew that he had chosen a better portion than this world could give. We do not remember to have once heard him boast of the sacrifice he had made, and claim on that account the admiration of his brethren. He had good talents for speaking, and he was ever ready to exercise them, in proclaiming the gospel to his countrymen. He had some failings of character which we had reason to regret; but he was honest in the cause of God. He had a firm trust in Jesus, as the only Saviour, and earnestly wished the conversion of his countrymen. Two evenings before his death, he was asked, if he now regretted the steps which in youth he had taken, of joining the people of God ; and he replied, with all the energy he possessed, 'No—no ! Never, never !' We have the fullest confidence that he has entered into the joy of Heaven."

The concluding observation is applicable to the whole of this chapter. "Such (say the directors,) are the triumphs of the glorious gospel, in India, over pride and self-righteousness, ignorance and pollution. More *decisive* they could not be; and that they have not been more *numerous*, cannot awaken surprise, and surely ought not to awaken or excite dismay, much less dissatisfaction."

## CHAPTER IX.

The training of youth in Hindooism and Christianity.—Sources of supply for the asylums.—Deaths of various Hindoo pupils.

An interesting department of missionary operations is the education of youth. We have already adverted very briefly to this subject in our fifth chapter; but it is hoped that a more extended notice of the demoralizing influence of idolatry on the young, and our attempts at Christian education, will not be unacceptable to the reader. The remarks which follow are the substance of an address delivered to several Sabbath schools, both in England and America.

To train up a child in the way he should go, is a duty inculcated by divine authority, but it is one that is very inadequately appreciated by the majority of even religious people. The observations and statements here presented, may perhaps show its importance by contrast, that is, by first giving some account of the early pernicious influence of heathen customs, and then directing attention to our attempts at introducing Christian education.

We must begin at the beginning of our account of the pernicious influences of heathenism on the youthful mind, and briefly trace it up to early manhood.

1. Idolatry in Orissa anticipates the very birth of the child, and at three stated periods before the infant sees the light, are certain prescribed ceremonies punctiliously observed. We have enough of superstition in relation to this subject lingering in many a nook and corner of

our own land, to preclude the necessity for any details here. Those who are curious may consult Mr. Ward's book on the Hindoos, and similar publications.

2. At the moment of birth, ghee, that is, clarified butter, should be put into the mouth of the child with a golden spoon. Other rites follow, and its nativity is cast by a professed astrologer. The aspect of the heavens, especially the conjunction of the planets, are carefully noted, and from these the future life of the child is predicted. All this is recorded, and the account carefully preserved.

3. Then follow a series of ceremonies at certain fixed periods; such as giving the child a name at ten or eleven days old—if a boy, it is usually the name of some god or devotee; taking it out, in order to look at the moon as its ancestor; and so on. At six or eight months, or when the child has cut his teeth, he is to be fed with rice milk, accompanied by certain ceremonies; and at two years old his hair is shaved off, except the sacred lock at the top, called churá.

4. At a later period, if of the higher classes, the boy is invested with the sacred thread, when a long round of idolatrous ceremonies is performed. Then comes giving the muntra, or sacred name or sentence, by the family gooroo; and finally marriage, at a very early age, especially in the case of girls. All these occasions are rendered interesting and imposing to all concerned, by abundance of feasting, music, and other festivities. Where there is no sacred awe of the Deity worshipped, there can be little moral restraint, so that whatever ministers to the pleasure, or pride, or ostentation of the parties, consistently with Hindooism, is, if possible, freely indulged.

If sent to school, the books they read are stuffed full

of immoral stories relating to the gods. From the primer to the most elaborate classic, works on grammar, prosody, law and logic, all are surcharged with licentiousness.

5. But it is at the various festivals and gatherings of idolators, we see the influence of heathenism in its most attractive light. How often have we, on these occasions, had recalled to our minds the graphic language of Isaiah, "Lift up thine eyes round about and see : all these gather themselves together, they come to thee; thy sons shall come from far, and thy daughters shall be nursed at thy side." It is then from every point of the compass, from the numberless scattered villages, the sons and daughters of Hindooism pour forth in successive streams, dressed out in their gayest attire ; the men generally in white, and the women in groups, dressed in white with broad borders of blue, orange, or red, with here and there one in crimson, blue or yellow silk. The fathers and elder brothers carry the little boys upon their shoulders, and the girls astride upon the hip, and thus they "flow together," all tending to the great gathering-place.

And there you may see many a father teaching his child to join the palms of his hands, and lift them in adoration of the idol, and many a mother bowing down her infant daughter's head before some filthy emblem of Siva or image of Krishnu. Others, a few years older, come toddling along with hands full of offerings, which they lay before the idol, and bow themselves prostrate on the earth. Men and women, fathers and mothers, boys and girls, people of both sexes and all ages zealously engage in the idolatrous service, and contribute, without shame, to the performance of the most puerile rites. Mothers teach their daughters to make some of the most filthy images of the mud of rivers, and initiate them into practices the most corrupting in their moral tendency.

At the last Seebratri, or night festival, in honor of Seeb, which I attended, I saw a number of mothers and step-mothers teaching their young married daughters to perform a certain pooja, with a view to secure becoming mothers. This pooja consisted of sitting opposite the temple with lighted lamps on the head, shoulders, wrists, hands, perhaps knees and upturned feet, and thus remaining unmoved most, if not all the night, meditating on the idol, using various incantations, and attending to the midnight songs and revels in honor of the god.

However otherwise respectable and interesting these females may really be, it is plain such exposure and such scenes must pollute the mind and render it familiar with every lascivious gesture, word and deed.

6. From the general corruption of manners has arisen that curse of idolatrous nations, very early marriages. That interesting period of female life, in which the girl passes into the state of womanhood, and becomes fitted for the discharge of those duties, which, in the course of Providence, may be expected to devolve upon her, is unknown in India. She is scarcely a girl before she is a wife, a mother, and perhaps a widow. In Orissa she is often betrothed in mere infancy, without any power of her own to choose or refuse, and before she enters her teens has been married and conducted to her husband's house for life.

According to that vile libel on woman so sedulously inculcated by heathen wisdom,—a female must always be dependent first on her parents, next on her husband, and when he dies, she should burn on his funeral pile and accompany him to the other world. Thank God for the abolition of Suttees.

Hence female schools in India are thronged with young wives and betrothed girls, and not unfrequently now by young widows. But among the higher classes, and indeed all classes but the very lowest, the female is never taught either to read or write; but she is taught a thousand things connected with debasing and polluting idolatries.

7. The demoralizing influence of idolatry is remarkably and most painfully apparent in the young men and youths of India. More interesting lads there cannot be, nor scholars of more hopeful promise. I believe every one who has had to do with the tuition of Hindoo youth will give this testimony; and up to a certain age it is impossible not to feel a strong affection for them. But no sooner do they border on manhood than they become extremely foppish, vain, dissipated and stupid. Their precocious intellect seems to have received a sudden check, and they become quite different beings. Nor when the character of Hindooism in its gods, its books, its festivals, and its influence is considered, can this be matter of surprise.

It is painful to add, that to heathen licentiousness, duplicity and chicanery, Europeans are fast introducing habits of intoxication. Hitherto this vice has been confined to a few of the very lowest classes of society, but it is now fast spreading through the highest. In Calcutta the evil is dreadful, and it will not be long before it overspreads the whole land.

8. It is thus that the young Hindoo, as soon as he is born, opens his eyes upon idolatrous ceremonies,—he grows up surrounded with idolatrous influences,—the rites and ceremonies of heathenism mingle in all the events and occurrences of life, they extend their ramifications every where, into every thing,—his food,—his dress,—his ablutions,—his sleeping,—his sneezing,—when he walks out and when he sits down,—when he

engages in any enterprise and when any affliction overtakes him. At all times, in every thing, he is taught to regard the gods; to dread their malignant influences; to propitiate their respective dispositions; and to adore above all their servants, the priests. He is full of fancies and fears about evil eyes, witchcraft, lucky and unlucky days, ghosts, goblins, devils and falling stars, so that he is always hunting after charms, incantations and specifics.

Oh it is wretched to be trained up without God, and the prey of every infernal delusion. "Fear ye not their fear, neither be ye afraid, saith the Lord; but sanctify the Lord God in your hearts, and let him be your fear and your dread." "Blessed are the people who have the Lord for their God; yea, blessed are they whose God is the Lord."

If the Christian fathers and mothers I now address were, on their dying beds, compelled to leave their children in the hands of such idolators, to be thus trained up for evil, yea, must I not say *for hell*, what would be your feelings? How would it embitter your last moments! How earnestly and anxiously would you look around for some means of rescuing your beloved ones from a fate so terrible. But is the case altered because these children are not yours? because they are the sons and daughters of our fellow-subjects in Orissa. O think, it is not one or two, but a million at least of young immortal beings, who, at this moment, are training up in all the abominations of Hindooism, without God and without hope,—a million of these young immortals within the boundaries of that field, which we have undertaken, as a denomination, to cultivate for Christ! Have you ever realized this fact,—have you, when we have been pleading for the support of our schools, endeavored to picture to yourselves this state of things, or have you thought us unnecessarily pressing in our object and unreasonable in our requests? Surely you will think so no longer.

II. We come now to a little oasis in the desert of Hindooism, a little verdant spot in the moral wastes of Orissa,—the establishment of our asylums for native children. Oh happy day for Orissa when we shall see, as in happy England, or, in relation to this matter, happier New England, a thousand Sabbath schools established in the land, and the majority of its interesting youth flock to these sacred institutions; when as upon you this day the preacher may look around, and while narrating to them the happy change the gospel has made in their present and future prospects, he shall stimulate them to send the gospel into the yet wilder regions that stretch far away beyond them. Well, for these days we wait, these days we or our successors shall surely see; meantime we have to narrate the beginning of these days, the early glimpses of the dawn of that blessed morning which is thus to enlighten all the land.

1. Let me briefly notice the origin of our asylums. Those who have attended to the history of our mission will remember that a number of day schools were established at its very commencement. They were, however, taught by heathen masters, for no others could be got; and too often, when our back was turned, heathen books were substituted for those we introduced. And at all times an idolatrous influence was successfully exerted at home in counteracting what little of Christianity was taught at school. These schools, therefore, were continued so long only as we could do no better. We could not be satisfied to send the children of our Christian converts to them, and thus play back again, as it were, into the hands of Satan. But we concluded, that while at-

tending to such schools, we were much more bound to give our native converts' children the best education in our power.

Our converts then were few and scattered through distant villages, so that our first step necessarily was to bring them together in a suitable boarding establishment. Being encouraged by a few friends on the spot, we determined therefore to establish an asylum for both boys and girls, in which we would collect and educate, entirely under Christian influence, not only the few children of our native converts, but all of a suitable age whom we could get entirely under our control. The blighting influence of caste makes it difficult thus to obtain any Hindoo children, but Providence most astonishingly prospered our way; so that besides the children obtained from our native converts, a much larger number was supplied from other sources, to which we shall briefly advert.

1. The first considerable addition made to our asylums was occasioned by famine. Three successive years was the earth as iron beneath our feet and the heavens brass over our head. It was then the improvident Hindoo, dependent on his rice alone for sustenance, and having scarcely any other resource, was gradually reduced to the lowest pitch of wretchedness. You have heard of the late sad effects of the failure of the potato crops in Ireland, and may thus judge of the very similar results of famine in Orissa.

Many parents sold their children for a scanty pittance,—many were abandoned by these famine stricken fathers and mothers,—and many wandered far apart, in hopes of obtaining the means of subsistence, never to meet again. We purchased several of these children, or rather gave their parents a trifle and engaged to keep their famishing little ones. Several other children were picked up near hospitals and places where food was distributed, and a few, of their own accord, presented themselves at our doors and begged to be taken in. Of these poor children, many were too far exhausted to recover; some, when the famine had passed away, fled from the asylum and returned to their vagrant life, and others remained to the salvation, we trust, of both body and soul. Many affecting details might here be entered into, but space will not suffice.

2. Another source of supply for our asylums was the Pooree and Cuttack pilgrim hospitals.

Many hapless children are annually left to perish at the great car festival of Jugernath, or on the road to that high place of idolatry. Their parents or friends are struck down perhaps by the cholera or some other direful disease, and the children are left unprovided for. Doubtless, in many cases, they are intentionally left behind by their wretched parents. Some of these children find their way to the large hospital or asylums at Pooree, and thus come under the notice of the doctor. If he be a benevolent man, he may befriend these and send them to our asylums. Such was Dr. Cumberland, at Pooree, and Dr. Minto, at Cuttack. These gentlemen have sent several children to our schools and contributed generously for their support. Several others have, to a greater or less extent, imitated this good example.

3. The Meriah pooja, or Khund sacrifice, has also been made to contribute its portion towards filling up our schools. The details of this murderous rite have been in various ways presented to you, and I must not enter upon them. Suffice it to observe, that year by year hundreds of children are kidnapped from their native villages and sold to these wild Khund tribes, who

fatten them for the slaughter, and then on the day of sacrifice cut the livid flesh piecemeal from their victim to deposit in their turmerick fields. This rite the British Government are endeavoring to suppress, and many of the rescued victims have been placed in our asylums.

The author intended to give a detailed account of the Khunds, and of the benevolent efforts now making by Government for the extermination of the cruel Meriah Pooja, but his book is already becoming too large, and he must forego his intention. He cannot, however, exclude a condensed account, published in the Friend of India in 1841. Within the last three years nearly 800 victims have been rescued by Government agents from this atrocious sacrifice, many of whom have been placed in our mission schools at Cuttack, Berhampore and Balasore. All honor be to the Government for this benevolent work.

The Khunds inhabit the district of Goomsoor, in the vicinity of Jugernath's temple, in Orissa, and are remarkable for the prevalence of human sacrifices among them. In 1837, Capt. Millar rescued several males and females, some of whom were to have been sacrified in a few days. In 1838, Capt. Campbell, assistant to the collector of Ganjam, rescued more than a hundred while on a tour in the Khund country. It is hoped the sacrifice will soon be either wholly suppressed or entirely changed in its character, animals being substituted for human beings.

Meriah Pooja, or human sacrifice, takes place once in a year, in one or other of the confederate Mootas in succession. The victims are stolen from the low country, or are brought from some other distant part, and sold to those Mootas where the sacrifices are performed. If children, they are kept until they attain a proper age. This cruel ceremony is thus performed. When the appointed day arrives, the Khunds assemble from all parts of the country, dressed in their finery, some with bear skins thrown over their shoulders, others with the tails of peacocks flowing behind them, and the long winding feather of the jungle cock waving on their heads. Thus decked out, they dance, leap and rejoice, beating drums and playing on an instrument not unlike in sound to the Highland pipe. Soon after noon, the jani, or presiding priest, with the aid of his assistants, fastens the unfortunate victim to a strong post which has been firmly fixed into the ground, and there standing erect, he suffers the cruel torture of having his flesh cut from his bones in small pieces by the knives of the savage crowd, who rush on him and contend with each other for a portion.

Great value is attached to the first morsel cut from the victim's body, for it is supposed to possess greater virtues, and a proportionate eagerness is evinced to obtain it; but considerable danger to the person of the operator attends the feat, for it happens also that equal virtues are attributed to the flesh of the lucky holder of the first slice. To guard against so disagreeable an appropriation, a village will generally depute one of its number to endeavor to secure the much desired object, and they acordingly arm him with a knife, (mereri,) tie cloths round him, and holding on by the ends, at the appointed signal, rush with three or four hundred others at the miserable sacrifice; when, if their man should be successful in his aim, they exert their utmost efforts to drag him from the crowd (so few being able to approach the wretched object at once). Should he escape unhurt, the whole turn their faces to their homes, for, in order to secure its full efficacy, they must deposit in their fields, before the day has gone, the charm they have so cruelly won! The intent of this human sacrifice is to propitiate Ceres.

In Guddapoor, another and equally cruel sacrifice frequently precedes the one already described. A trench, seven feet long, is dug, in which a human being is suspended alive by the neck and heels, fastened with ropes to stakes firmly fixed at each end of the excavation, so that to prevent strangulation, he is obliged to support himself with his hands over each side of his grave.

The presiding priest, after going through some ceremonies in honor of the goddess Manekseri, takes an axe and inflicts six cuts, at equal distances from the back of the neck to the heels, repeating the number, one, two, &c., and at the seventh decapitates him,—the body falls into the pit and is covered with earth, when the hellish orgies, first described, are enacted. Women are sacrificed as well as men. Since the arrival of the troops in the Khund country, a female found her way into the Collector's camp at Pattingia, with fetters on her legs. She had escaped during the confusion of an attack on the Wulsa, or hiding place of the people who had charge of her, by our men, and related that she had been sold by her brother to a mootikoo of one of the Pattingia Mootas', for the purpose of being sacrificed ! ! I need not say that she was instantly released, and that she abjured all further connection with her people, and was sent to the asylum at Cuttack.

The form of invocation of the Khund goddess forms an infernal hymn, of which the following is a specimen.

"Hail, mother, hail! hail goddess Bhobanee!
Lo! we present a sacrifice to thee;
Partake thereof, and let it pleasure give,
And, in return, let us thy grace receive.
With music's various sounds, on festive day
Lo! thee we worship, and thy rites obey.
Hail all ye gods who in the mountain dwell,
In the wild jungle, or the lonely dell;
Come all, together come, with one accord,
And take the sacrifice we have prepared:
In all the fields, and all the plots we sow,
O let a rich and plenteous harvest grow;
O all ye gods and goddesses give ear,
And be propitious to our earnest prayer.
Behold a youth for sacrifice decreed,
Blooming with tender flesh, and flushed with blood;
No sire, no matron says, This youth is mine,
His flesh, his blood, his life, his all, are thine;
Without the pale of sacred wedlock thrown,
We took and fed him for thy right alone.
Now, lo! with rites from all pollution free,
We offer him, O Bhobanee, to thee:
Taste now this offering, satisfy thy heart,
And bid us joyful to our homes depart;
Taste now this offering, and propitious be,
And let us each, marks of thy favor see.

This extract was repeated from memory, by Abraham, a Khund boy, in the school at Cuttack, to Mr. Lacey, who, of course, translated it; he was then a great fat boy, and would soon have been sacrified, had he not been rescued by the English officers. He well remembers, and relates, how he was stolen from his mother. She was then a widow. They had laid down to sleep for the night, when the men entered the hut, and, beating the mother and children, placed poor Abraham over their shoulders, blindfolded him, and carried him off. His death is referred to at the close of this chapter.

4. These, then, added to our native converts' children, are the sources of supply for our asylums, and such are the children destined in Providence to receive the first Christian education in Orissa. It may, however, be proper to remark, that as our Christian community increases, our converts settle in villages where the native chapel, school house, and all the regular means of instruction in righteousness follow in succession. Thus we have Choga, Khundittar, Christianpoor, &c. And in each of these is a Christian day school already established. Our supply from this source therefore for our asylums, will, very happily, be diminished, but it will be to open another means of training our youth in Christian habits. Let us, however, notice a little more particularly the asylums which we have had under our care.

5. Our school was opened, May 3, 1836, with six boys and three girls; but since that period more than 100 of each sex have, for a longer or shorter period, found an asylum under our care. All our schools have lately had a considerable increase.

As the majority of these lads must labor either in cultivating the soil or some kind of handicraft, our chief object is to teach them to read understandingly their Bible, hymn book, and such other works as are in circulation, —such as Bunyan's Pilgrim, a part of Doddridge's Rise and Progress and Baxter's Call, three volumes of tracts, Outlines of General and Church History, Elements of Geography and Astronomy, &c. To which we add writing and ciphering.

Some of these manifest superior aptitude for learning, and promise to make future schoolmasters and catechists. From these a higher class is selected, and is now called our Normal School.

And from these, again, some of the baptized youths have been admitted into the theological department.

Our object for the girls, is, while giving them a plain education, such as is mentioned for the first school of boys, to which we add knitting, sewing and spinning, is to render them sensible, modest, industrious and pious young women; fitted to be helpmeets to their husbands in the humble sphere which Providence has assigned them. Hence we avoid all merely European ornamental branches, which can be of no use to them in after life.

We deem it to be a matter of first rate importance, to avoid whatever might raise them above the sphere in which they must move, and those economical habits without which they cannot subsist.

6. To wean these young converts from idolatry, and train them up for God, is, of course, our grand object. As it respects the former, I think we have been all but universally successful; but to change the heart belongs to a higher power. The means of grace, however, are regularly enjoyed. In the morning they have prayer in each department of the asylum, and in the evening all meet in the school chapel. On Sabbath mornings a lecture is addressed to them especially, and afterwards a Sabbath school is held. They also share in more private efforts, and in all the public general means of grace.

Nor has the divine blessing been withheld. Upwards of fifty souls, we trust, have been born again, and admitted to the church by baptism, from our asylum at Cuttack; while of several others, who have not thus been added to the church, though we can give no statistical account, we yet cherish a good hope.

It may not be uninteresting to insert a few extracts from the Society's report in relation to the conversion of some of these pupils. During the absence of Mr. and Mrs. Sutton, at Calcutta, Mr. and Mrs. Lacey took the charge of these Institutions. Referring to these, he observes:

"Few things are of equal interest with many of the dear children in our school. Saved from death by protracted starvation; saved from prostitution worse than death; they are here provided with the blessings of food, clothing, and habitation, and are taught the knowledge of God, which has made many of them wise unto salvation. How altered are their circumstances now, as they listen, (which they often do with eyes glistening with tears of gratitude,) to what the Lord has done for them. Could our friends of the destitute Hindoo children attend with me only on one occasion of the domestic worship of these rescued and now happy children, they would feel a glow of pleasure which would amply repay the pains and expense they incur in supporting this school."

Makunda, supported by friends at Chesham, is one of them. He is described as a clever youth, capable of learning any thing that can be taught him in his own language. He dates his first serious impressions from a sermon on the text, "My little children, of whom I travail again in birth till Christ be formed in you." He was baptized in December. As a pupil he stands in the first class, and to all he can learn in Oriya has added the study of the Sanscrit grammar. This is a very difficult language, but he bids fair to make as good progress as any student we have. There is no deficiency in talent, but he will need great grace to keep him humble and docile. If he be kept by the power and grace of God, he will, in all probability, be a man of some importance in the history of Christianity in Orissa.

Solomon was saved from butchery among the Khunds. He was always an obedient, well-behaved youth, and quite a favorite with Mrs. Sutton, but had no decidedly religious impressions till the revival commenced. When asked what first seriously impressed his mind, he said it was the abridgement of Baxter's Call, (in Oriya of course,) and especially the perpetually recurring words, "turn or die;" and then his impressions were deepened by other means of grace. O let the unconverted in England or America remember that this sentiment is as applicable to them as to the poor heathen victim rescued from the murderous Khunds, whoever they are, whether rich or poor, learned or ignorant, young or old, they must turn or die. Solomon died at Calcutta; his age was supposed to be sixteen.

Abraham might be about seventeen years of age. He, too, was saved from the heathen butcher's knife. Of him Mr. Sutton writes:—"He was the most rude and unpromising of all the Khund lads, averse to the restraints of the school, and loved to steal away whenever he found an opportunity, to fish, hunt squirrels, shoot birds with a bow and pellet, at which he was very dexterous, &c. In fine, he gave us much trouble, and we feared we should never be able to make any thing of him. Still there were occasions when his mind was tender, and he applied steadily to his book, though it seemed very hard for him. At length I sent him out with brother Lacey, hoping he would manage him better, while his country excursions would gratify Abraham's taste; but brother Lacey could do nothing with him. He came back to the school, but ran away two or three times. As a last resource, I asked the commissioner to take him as a chuprassee or servant of any kind, but he could find no opening for him. At this last failure, Abraham again started, expecting to find his way by some Sumbhulpore boat to his native village, and return to his old habits. It was long before we could trace him, and indeed all seemed inclined to let him go. We however, and especially Mrs. Sutton, yearned over poor Abraham, and could not give him up. We thought of these boats, and despatched a messenger to see if he were there. There poor Abraham was, on his way with a heavy heart up the river, and directly his eye caught the Christian superintendent; he said he thought of Christ the good Shepherd, seeking after the lost sheep until he found it. He resolved to return. This was on Saturday, and I saw him not till the next day in the children's chapel. Without knowing aught of his feelings, I preached from 'Ye were as sheep going astray, but,' &c. The awakening had commenced the previous Sabbath, but this morning's sermon produced a marked effect. I could see the big tear from Abraham's eye, as he hid his face behind his book, drop, drop, drop, till he could refrain no longer, and went out. The next evening, when several of the serious boys came to converse with me, Abraham was among them. This was our first interview, and the poor lad threw his rough arms round my neck, and sobbed out, 'I was as a sheep going astray, but now return to the shepherd and bishop of my soul.' I think my wife and I felt something as angels feel when a sinner repents."

From this time Abraham continued an inquirer, and subsequently a candidate. On his arrival at Calcutta, contrary to all his former habits, he took his testament, which latterly he had learned to read pretty well, and spreading his mat near the gateway (which he watched, as is the custom in Calcutta,) there for hours he continued reading. He continued this course in perfect health till the day of his death. Mr. Sutton, when referring to some candidates that were baptized, adds, "Two are, I trust, in heaven, whom we expected to baptize here." Solomon and Abraham were these two. Were not these brands plucked from the burning? First rescued from the Khunds, and then from the power of Satan, that more savage foe of God and man. Abraham died of the cholera.

Others baptized from the male department, are *Dasiya*, son of a Christian at Choga, supported by friends at Portsea. "He is young," writes Mr. Lacey, "and small of stature, but his Christian experience is scriptural and satisfactory." He is of the agricultural class. *Rutna*, the son of Roguburdas, the person who gave up his large idol hunooman when he became a Christian. Rutna is very young, but exhibited a ripeness of Christian experience which made it impossible to debar him from baptism and the fellowship of the church. *Jacob*, who was rescued from the murderous Khunds, is another of these converts.

The accounts of youthful female converts are not less interesting.

*Gundie* is an orphan girl. She was brought by her parents in the time of a severe famine, to be disposed of, as best they could, which of course would have been to a house of ill-fame in the city. Providential mercy brought her within the reach of Cuttack asylum, where her soul and body have both been saved. Gundie gratefully acknowledges her obligations to God, for her preservation from sin and misery, for her comforts and her hopes. She is stated to be a very superior girl. Her attention is always good, and her information considerable and correct; her Christian experience is clear and satisfactory. Her feelings are ardent, when she speaks of what Christ has done for her. Her lips readily utter the grateful sense that she has of redeeming mercy, while accompanied with tears of gratitude and love. *Phoola*, (or a flower,) is a very pretty girl, but her amiable and now pious disposition is her chief ornament. She is of the brahmunical caste, and is the betrothed wife of Somnath, the young Brahmun preacher. She was obtained from her parents on the demand of her betrothed husband, enforced by an intimation of legal proceedings. She is about fifteen, and has been in the school a little more than a year. Besides these, among the baptized, are *Nilu*, the daughter of a Khunditta Christain. *Chalee*, rescued from starvation by serjeant Ball, an old friend of the missionaries, and deacon of one of the churches. *Dabika* is an orphan, rescued from vice. Mr. Sutton observes, "Tears of gratitude will flow, while I record the name of this brand plucked out of the fire; the last of three rescued from infamy and wretchedness, and now all three members of the church of Christ, intelligent, affectionate, good and obedient girls." Who that knows the Saviour's grace or even the feelings of humanity, can contemplate this circumstance, without lively emotions of delight and gratitude? and without feeling attachment to the cause of missions strengthened many fold? Three orphan sisters, children of heathen parents, saved from the vices of idolatry, and the miseries and pollution of harlots, brought to love and follow Jesus, and inspired with the hope of dwelling with him in ceaseless purity and joy, are an ample recompense for many tears, and toil, and much expenditure; and a rich answer for many prayers.

The last on this interesting list for the present Report, is *Cassia,* for a short time a member of the church below, now, it is trusted, gone to that above. Her death will be noticed further on.

7. Of those who have left the institution, some eight or ten are employed in connection with the printing office, several have been brought up as house servants, one has learned to be a dirjee, or tailor and milliner combined, as is the custom in India; some are employed as writers, and several are farmers. To these those may be added, who are now studying for the ministry, and several who have entered on the work. Hitherto, nearly all have been provided for as soon as they were of an age suitable to be thrown on their own resources.

All the girls who have married, and they amount to about thirty in number, have been married to native Christians, and several to native preachers. Of course, some are in better circumstances than others; but, with very few exceptions, all are doing well, and are living testimonies to the value of the institution.

I have been hoping to establish a village with the young people rescued from the murderous Khunds, and the Commissioner has promised me land for this purpose. But circumstances have hindered, hitherto, the accomplishment of my design.

8. There is no portion of our late beloved charge, which occupies a more sacred place in our fondest affections, than those who have died happily in Christ, and now mingle with the blessed in heaven. Often have we grieved to see our children die, and contemplated the

ruin of our hopes respecting them, and the service they might render to the church on earth. But now, we cannot but rejoice that so precious a portion of our treasure is in heaven—safe from all the storms of life—safe from all the evil influences of that idolatrous land—safe from all fear of being lost forever. Yes, they are where we wished them to be, where we too hope to go ; though we fain would have kept them longer here.

We will affix to this chapter a few slight notices of the death of a few of our dear pupils of both sexes, as specimens of many others.

9. I have thus far spoken chiefly of our own institution at Cuttack ; but, happily, ours, though the first, is not now the only one in Orissa.

A few years after our school was established, Mr. Stubbins removed to Berhampore, where a number of rescued Meriah children were made over to his care. These formed the nucleus of another school, which, under Mr. and Mrs. Stubbins, Mr. and Mrs. Wilkinson, and Mr. and Mrs. Buckley, has flourished in two divisions—for boys and girls—to the present time. Of these, many interesting notices have been presented from time to time.

Our American friends at the north have also established two other schools, at Balasore and Jellesore, of a similar description. In the latter, a number of Santal children have been received, which it is hoped will open the way for the entrance of the gospel into a new tract of country, among a hitherto unnoticed tribe of mountaineers. It is pleasing thus to observe the dawn of a new day gilding the mountain-tops of long—long benighted Orissa.

## *Deaths of young Hindoo Christians.*

The records of our mission in Orissa show that the language of the poet is as applicable to India as to England or America.

> "Flowers have their time to fade,
> And leaves to wither at the north wind's breath,
> And stars to set,—
> But all, thou hast all seasons for thine own, O death!"

We have found it so, and among those of our beloved ones, who have been gathered into the heavenly garner, many have died young. I shall here insert a brief notice of several. Nor shall I confine the instances to those who have been actually admitted by baptism to the church on earth, for there are several to whom this privilege was not afforded, who are, nevertheless, admitted through the grace of Jesus to the general assembly and church of the first born in heaven.

### *Poonee.*

Among our earliest losses by death was little Poonee. She was the daughter of an Oriya brahmun, and was placed by her father in our asylum along with her brother on occasion of his embracing Christianity. This man had a kind of temple of his own, in which was a large image of Hunooman, the monkey god, fabled to be an incarnation of Seeb. This great stone image, of a deep red color, was made over to us when the father embraced the gospel. He had then no proper wife, and the children were placed under our care. Poonee was a very interesting, intelligent child, then about six years of age. In the school record it is stated of her that she was very steady and womanly in her habits, the most ready at getting her lessons of any one in her class, and seemed to understand the way of salvation. She was seized, about two years after entering the school, with the most malignant kind of small-pox, which gradually accomplished its work, till it removed her, we trust, to heaven. During her illness, she was observed to be much engaged in prayer, and her manner of prayer struck the superintendents as peculiarly serious and devout. I saw her often, though from the dreadful effects of her disease, very near approach was not deemed advisable. She always appeared especially amiable, patient, and most lamb-like in all her words and conduct. The night before she died, she prayed much, especially for her father, who was then manifesting an unstable disposition. All were interested in her and loved her. A few minutes before she died, she put her hands over her sightless eyes and prayed, saying, "O Lord, into thy hands I commit my spirit," and then gently letting her hands fall, she expired.

We hope she was saved in Christ. From her foster mother we afterwards learned she was concerned about her soul, said she knew she was a great sinner, and prayed to know how she might believe in Christ.

Among those who died of the same disease may be mentioned Eliza, daughter of Bunnamali, one of the Khundittar converts. She was about seven years of age, and we are not without hope that she is one also whom the Saviour has taken to himself. She conversed much with the converted girls, Poddee and Dabikee. She prayed much, especially during the last few weeks of her illness, that her sins might be forgiven her, and seemed to commit herself into the hands of Christ.

These are mentioned as specimens of little girls rescued from the very midst of heathenism,—brought under Christian influence for a brief period,—and then removed, we trust, to swell the multitude of the redeemed in glory. "Even so, Father, for so it seemed good in thy sight."

I will now mention an instance or two of older girls, who have been baptized and received into the church previously to their removal to the church above.

### *Cassee.*

Cassee was the daughter of Balaram Jachuck, one of the Bhoyerpoor converts, and half brother to Rama Chundra, our native preacher. Cassee was placed in the school at its commencement, and was always a pleasing, though not a decidedly serious child. It was of this little girl that the following anecdote was related.

"Her father, on one occasion, heard some one apparently talking in a low voice in one of his out-buildings; attracted by the sound, he listened, and soon perceived that it was his little daughter, Cassee, teaching her still younger sister to pray. Let children who pray not, mark this. Let professedly Christian parents, who do not teach their children to pray, mark this. A little Hindoo girl, just emerged with her parents from the gloom of heathenism, felt it to be a Christian duty to pray. And now attend to her prayer which she taught her sister. 'Oh! Heavenly Father, I am a great sinner; pardon my sin. Pour thy Holy Spirit into my heart for Jesus' sake. Amen.' Her father related this with pleasure to Mr. John Goadby, and, surely, it may convey instruction to many in Christian lands to record it here."

Cassee however, after this did not grow in religion as we fondly hoped. Indeed for a long time she became seemingly indifferent, if not averse to it. We feared for her exceedingly when we saw one after another, her juniors in the school, seriously impressed and following Christ, and she as unpromising as ever. God, however, at length had mercy upon Cassee. Her impressions became deep and strong, and but a few weeks before she was suddenly called away, she openly professed her attachment to Christ and was baptized. That day she for the first and last time sat down to the Lord's Supper; before another month had passed, she drank of the new wine in the Saviour's kingdom. She continued quite well till that day three weeks, when the text at the chapel was, "I am a stranger with thee, and a sojourner, as all my fathers were." Cassee heard the discourse, and on her way home was attacked with fever, which on the following Tuesday evening terminated fatally. She was conscious of her approaching end, though no one else thought her likely to die at that time. She had had similar attacks before, which yielded to the usual remedies. But so true it is

"No medicine, though it often cure,
Will always baulk the tomb."

She was very desirous I should not leave her, which duty obliged me to do for a time, but as she felt she was dying, I was sent for. She was talking, when I arrived, to her young companions of the Lord she loved, and of the heaven to which she was going, to the delight and astonishment of all. When, on seeing me, she threw her arms around my neck, gave me a most significant look, as if she would speak, but could not, then joined her hands and lifted them reverently to her forehead; her head then sank upon my shoulder and she gently expired. All felt hers was a happy death. Her memory is to us as ointment poured forth, and we think of her with unmingled pleasure and thankfulness.

> " Long do they live, nor die too soon,
> Who live till life's great work is done."

*Kustooree.*

Miss Derry, now Mrs. Buckley, mentions the death of this young female at Berhampore. She was one of the victims rescued from the murderous Khunds, and for two years was placed in the Cuttack asylum. She subsequently returned to Mr. Stubbins's care at Berhampore. She was one of the first baptized from among these rescued victims, and, we trust, was thus saved body and soul. While on a visit to Ganjam, she caught the fever peculiar to that place. When visited by her kind superintendent, she said, in answer to some religious remark, " I love the Lord and know he will not leave me." " I am a great sinner, but Christ died to save such." She could not then converse much, but requested Miss D. to pray for her. This was on Monday; on Wednesday about midnight she expired. The girls in the school said they spent the former part of the night with Kustooree in singing hymns and talking about heaven. A short time before she breathed her last, she said, " Come, sing hallelujah, I am now going home." " Thus," adds Miss D., " I trust she not only obtained a great temporal, but an eternal deliverance also. I doubt not her happy spirit now beholds the King in his beauty, and unites in the song of the redeemed."

Mrs. Stubbins mentions the death of a very pleasing little girl in their asylum of about eight or nine years of age. When she knew that she was dying, she appeared perfectly composed, and said to her weeping school-fellows clustering around her, " Children, why do you weep for me? I am going to the Lord."

These are our witnesses before the throne, and we trust will be our joy and crown of rejoicing forever.

I will now select a few instances of the deaths of our male scholars, though, as in the case of the females, they can be but few.

*Senjama.*

This is one of those for whom we sorrow not as those respecting whom there is no hope. Senjama, with a little brother, and a sister who has since fallen asleep in Jesus, was rescued from the influence, we cannot say care, of a drunken, immoral father. They were all interesting children, and I apprehend had been much indebted to their mother, who had lately died. Senjama grew up a steady lad, became one of the best compositors in the printing office, and appeared very anxious, though he made no profession of religion till a few months before his death. A disease of the eyes gradually increased till he became quite blind, and, at length, an attack of diarrhœa brought him to the grave. His name had been for some time on the list of candidates for baptism, and he was received by the church at the very hour, perhaps the very minute, in which he was received to the church above.

I had the following conversation with him the day on which he died. It was noted down on my return to the house from visiting him. After some previous conversation, in the Oriya language of course, I inquired, Well, my boy, is your mind fixed on Christ? He answered, Yes. I have no hope but in Christ. He is the only Saviour. After a pause, he added, I should like to have received the sign of discipleship (baptism) before I go away. But in this I shall sustain no loss. I wish my brothers and sisters should know my desire. I replied, it was well this was in your heart, that is much better than a mere (indifferent) attention to the outward rite. (*S.*) Yes. So far as that is concerned, there is neither good nor evil in it; but I should like to make this profession. (*Self.*) You may be taken soon, Senjama; are you aware of this? (*S.*) Yes. I cannot say how soon,—it may be to-day, suddenly; or it may be a day or two hence. I should like to see mamma (Mrs. Sutton). (*Self.*) In yon happy world there is no darkness, all is light. (*S.*) Yes, all light, all joy; here there is no joy for me, it is a dark, dark place; but there, ah!—Here he turned to an aged relative, sitting by and weeping, and said to her, weep not for me, má, weep not for me, let no one weep for me. You will not live long here, má. I am going fast home, you will soon follow me. (The old lady is a Christian.) She could only sob in reply. I again said, yes, Senjama, thus we go home, one by one, it matters not who goes first; but to reach that happy home is the great concern. (*S.*) Ah! yes, that is all, that is all. I much wish to see mamma. I left him and sent Mrs. Sutton to see him. In the evening he was suddenly taken worse, and while I was at the chapel attending a church meeting, he died. Mr. Lacey returned with me to see him, but when we entered his house we found he had expired. He had just completed his sixteenth year. I may add that in the above conversation there was a character, a depth of feeling, and a brightening up of the intellect which afforded unusual interest. We indulge the hope that his reception to the church on earth was but the emblem of his reception to the church in heaven.

### *David.*

David, or Dáood, was another of the lads who had been sold in his childhood to the barbarous Khunds, and rescued by the humane interference of the British Government. If Abraham was very unpromising, Daood was the most degraded of them all. He was so sullen in temper, so lazy, and so dirty in his habits, that he more resembled one of the diseased pariah dogs, we see lying in the ashes in Indian villages, than a human being. Mrs. Sutton remarks of him — "It appeared as if he would be fit for nothing but to sweep the school-houses, and in our own mind we had devoted him to this office. But, about three years ago, he changed of a sudden. He became serious, took to his books, and without half the pains formerly bestowed upon him, quickly learned to read. He surprised us all by his attention and intelligence. And when he came to read with the Scripture class, we found he had, by his voluntary efforts, not only overtaken, but outran those who were much in advance of him. It was indeed most gratifying to perceive how well he understood and how much he enjoyed reading the blessed word of truth. With this expansion of the intellect, there was a desire manifested to be employed in the printing-office. His wish was complied with; and as a sore had broken out in his foot, a place was assigned him, where he could sit and work. He continued to dwell in this office till his disease appeared to be the leprosy, and he was removed to the hospital. A few weeks ago, as he seemed to be very uncomfortrble there, and wished to be removed, we had him taken to the house, and put under the care of a native convert and his wife. It soon appeared that he was incurable, and all that could be done for him was to give him food, nursing, and make his outward circumstances as comfortable as possible. [Some time previously to this appearance of disease, David, and three others, were admitted to the church of Christ, by baptism, and ever after walked consistently with his profession.]

"A few evenings ago," continues Mrs. S., "I walked over, with Mr. S., to see him. I cannot distinctly recall his expressions, in relation to the state of his mind, but the purport was, that he felt himself to be a poor, helpless sinner, and that Christ was all his hope for salvation. His testament and hymn book were his constant companions for a long time past. Often has he been found reading them; and Mr. S., when he went to see him while he was dying, found them close by him, as if one of his last acts, while strength remained, was to read. We feel satisfaction in the thought that he has gone safe to heaven."

I can add, that, several times, when walking away from this deeply-afflicted youth in his little cabin, I have felt my heart full of admiration at the wonder-working power of the gospel, and its unutterable value to fallen men. David appeared to me as another Lazarus; though outwardly most wretched, yet, in fact an heir of glory, whom angels would bear away to everlasting rest. Blessed be God for the gospel of Christ.

[Many of the above facts were noticed in our journals, &c., in the order of their occurrence, and hence to some readers will not be new; but the author could not wholly omit, in this more permanent record, (as he hopes) all reference to these beloved ones. The statements have, however, been so much abridged as to rob them of much of their interest.]

We append a few depositions, taken in the magistrate's office, from the lips of some of the rescued Khund victims. They are specimens of many others, all from the same neighborhood.

*Deposition of Mania, daughter of Shukoo Mullick, aged ten years, inhabitant of Jebun Ganda, Duspullah.*

A year ago, my mother's brother, Soojun Mullick, sold me to Mangolee Naik Khund of Mouza Boori Gola, Duspullah, who employed me in fetching wood. I overheard the villagers a short time ago talking about killing me. I was covered with turmeric as a preparatory rite. They sent for the priest Junga Gooroo to kill me, and he came,—but I was spared, why, I know not. I wish to be sent to my grandfather and grandmother, who live in Jebun Gunda Duspullah. I do not know what has become of my father and mother.

*Jumna*, aged five years, does not know the name of her father or mother, but accidentally in her way to Pooree from Duspullah, saw her mother, who lives with a Massulman in Sirdapore, near Khoorda. *Sunari*, aged seven years, has no relative that she knows of in the world. Her father and mother she knows are dead. *Lutchma*, aged nine years, does not know who are his father and mother. *Duloo*, aged ten years, knows nothing about her parents.

*Deposition of Susta, son of Baleea Naik (inhabitant of Burreegocha Kh. Boad,) aged about twelve years.*

About three years ago, Rotna Pana, of Putka in Boad, sold me, for I know not what sum, to Sugaib Mullick Khund. He had previously brought my mother to live with him. I went with her—he then kidnapped me. I was employed in fetching wood. Last October, the paiks of the village in which I was, went to call the priest to sacrifice me, but the priest would not attend. He told them to wait until all the Government servants had left the killah, and then he would sacrifice me. There was no other meriah in the village but myself. Upon the occasion of sending for the priest, I first knew of the human sacrifices. My mother is still alive. The man who sold me, I have heard since my release, has died. I beg to be sent to my mother, who is in Ulut in Boad.

*Deposition of Sustaee, daughter of Jolee Mullick, (inhabitant of Bargoo Pajoo, Kh. Duspullah, aged about eighteen years.)*

About six years ago, as I was in the jungle searching for mangoes, my step-father's brother, Mongoloo Mullick, took me up in his arms, and carried me to Bouria Path village, and sold me for eighteen rupees to Sutre Mullick, who kept me for a "meriah" in his house. I made my escape a short time ago, and was running away with one Gonoo Mullick, when a man in charge of some buffaloes named Ram Gooroo, knowing me to be a "meriah," seized me, and restored me to my former owner, who put me in irons to prevent my escape again. In last Phalgoon, I knew that I was destined to be a victim. I was employed by my owner in all household matters, and also in planting rice in the fields. I do not know whether there were any other victims sacrificed. My father and mother are still alive in Sattekund Boad. I desire to go to them. I have never been married.

*Deposition of Subdee, son of Chemma Naik, aged fifteen years, inhabitant of Reggera Kh. Duspullah.*

About five years ago, my father and mother went to Patka in Boad, for the purpose of getting mangoes, as it was a time of scarcity; they took me with them; and when in the jungle at that place, Peenka Panoo, of that village, took me away and sold me to Gobur Naik, who employed me in fetching wood. Two months ago I was covered with turmeric, and then I heard from the villagers that I was intended for a "meriah." The villagers sent for one Ruthee Gooroo, a priest, but he refused to come, as the Government's servants were in the killah, and had forbidden the custom.

## The following incident occurred in the Cuttack school.

On the arrival of the children from Mr. Stubbins, a very unexpected and pleasing incident occurred. The children under his care were rescued by gentlemen under the Madras Presidency, while those placed under ours were rescued by the civil and military officers of the Bengal Establishment, and from different parts of the Khund country. On the arrival of the children at the compound, one of our boys almost immediately claimed one of the new girls as his sister. In a day or two another discovery was made. In the latter case, the girl would often stand, for a long time, behind a window, looking through at her brother seated in the verandah, learning to be a tailor. Her brother's name has been changed, but she says she remembers his being sold, she thinks by her father, and taken away before she was. Here is another black page in the history of heathenism. The striking similarity of features, and the consistent accounts of the children, leave no doubt of relationship. Of course they, as well as ourselves, were highly delighted with this singular meeting.

The following anecdote shows how infernal is the religion of India.

A man, having a wife and two children, was by some means or other kidnapped by the Khunds, and was preparing for sacrifice. His wife hearing of the detention of her husband, immediately repaired to the place of his confinement, but she found that she could only obtain the deliverance of her husband by giving up her two children to be sacrificed instead of their father. With these hard terms she at length complied. This happened during the period of the Company's troops being in the country. The woman being where the Collector was, told him her tale of woe, but without any expectation of his interference. He, however, humanely sent some officers to the village in which the children were confined, took them away, and delivered them to their parents, now again united. The Collector, whilst in the hills, related this circumstance to the friend from whom it has been received.

# CHAPTER X.

Hindoo females, and female missionary labors—Case of single females—Results of attempts to benefit the females of Orissa, &c.

The real influence of woman in the formation of the moral character, and consequently in the general elevation of mankind, is but just beginning to be understood. The page of history is indeed thickly bestrewed with examples of illustrious mothers who have trained their children to noble deeds, but there has been no distinct general recognition of her appropriate place in the social economy: of her irrisistible influence in training the youthful mind. We venture the assertion that it is only Christianity, and indeed, Protestant Christianity, which assigns to her her proper position, and places her where God intended she should be placed, viz.: by the side of her husband; not as his slave but his helpmeet, not as his toy but his equal self, his firmest friend, his most endeared coadjutor; his bosom companion, the partner of his joys, sorrows, responsibilities, and cares; and especially as the watchful guardian and faithful trainer of his children.

Savage man has in all ages treated woman as his slave. He has thought himself called to the pursuits of war and the chase, to council and conflict, while to the wife he has assigned the drudgery of the house and the farm; to build and keep the one and toil on the other. It is so to this day in nearly all Africa, the wilds of America, the islands of the sea, among the lower classes of Asia, in short, wherever Christian influence is not felt. And deeply is woman depraved in China and in India. In both cases they are kept in entire ignorance of even the elements of such learning as is commonly taught the other sex in both these populous countries. It is only in a few cases that woman is ever taught there. Not a school, I believe, exists for the tuition of females, apart from missionary establishments, throughout either land. A few Zemindars and rajas are known to teach their wives to write and keep accounts, because they must in some cases thus guard their own interests; and a few abandoned females are taught to read and sing the abominable songs about the Hindoo gods in prosecution of their hateful trade. But none are taught with a view to the cultivation of their minds or the elevation of their moral characters. The Hindoos believe the effect of learning to woman must be just the reverse.

The old Europeans were not a whit more advanced than their brethren in New Zealand or Madagascar. Woman was by them treated as the slave and drudge of the man.

In a more advanced stage of society, where man has emerged from barbarism, amassed wealth, collected around him the pomp and parade of life, woman is in many cases made his toy. She is kept, guarded and secluded, in the haven or seraglio, encouraged to waste her existence in decorating her person, and tricking herself out with those meretricious ornaments which may please her capricious lord and master. Such is now the case with the higher and wealthier classes of the Mahomedans, Hindoos and Chinese; and very little better, substantially better, is the lot of multitudes of women in some countries of Europe.

In the age of chivalry woman, especially when invested with youth, rank and beauty, was made man's idol. The old romances are full of absurd illustrations of this remark which we cannot here stop to adduce. But Christianity, we repeat, is the only system that places her in her true position and invests her with her right influences.

While either sex may say, in relation to the gospel,

> "O what return can mortals give
> For such immeasurable grace!"

most emphatically may woman acknowledge her obligations to that gospel. Let Christian women contrast their own happy lot, hard as it may often seem, with the lot of their sisters in China and in India, and they will say that especial obligation rests on them to attempt the mental and moral elevation of their wretched, degraded sisterhood in those vast lands. Many have felt these obligations, and have been foremost in our missionary enterprise. They are generally our best and most faithful collectors, our most constant attendants at the monthly concert, our most self-denying contributors, and many of them our most zealous fellow-laborers in the foreign field.

In the early stage of the missionary enterprise, at least in Orissa, the sphere of female missionary agency was very limited. Still, our sisters in the mission rendered good service in the superintendence of our day schools, and when opportunity offered, in the tuition of East Indian girls. This, with occasional visits to the few families of poor Christians at our large stations, was nearly all that they could do in direct missionary labor. One of our sisters deserves especial mention for the intrepidity with which she accompanied her husband on horseback, on long missionary journies. Often has she started with the tent and baggage long before day light, to pursue her solitary route through wild jungles and over the narrow ridge of paddy fields, while her husband has gone in another direction in search of villages, markets and other places at which to preach, ere he returned to his tent for breakfast. Our sister Bampton will be long remembered by her early colleagues with respect and affection, for her self-denial and devotion in this work. This kind of service is rendered somewhat smoother now than it was then, yet it, under the most favored circumstances, involves much real hard labor, and calls for the exercise of much Christian zeal.

Another field of labor open to our sisters, is the native Christian families and those who have given up caste and connected themselves more or less with Christians. Among these there is much work to be done, many lessons to be inculcated, much assistance, which they alone can render, to be imparted, prayer meetings and bible classes to be held, and much training in the right ways of God needed.

Nor need the visits of our sisters in the missions to be confined altogether to these. It is quite possible, under suitable circumstances, for them to gain access to many heathen families, and converse with the female members of such families. Some of our sisters have done this, and with prudent management, this department of Christian effort might be indefinitely enlarged. It is not, however, a field which promises a very abundant harvest until the male sex become more willing to embrace Christianity.

I have pleasure in making a few extracts from the communications of some of our sisters in reference to these departments of female missionary labor.

Mrs. Lacey in writing to a female friend, in 1834, has given an encouraging account respecting the opportunities now offered for female exertion:

"There never was such a hopeful field of labor for a

missionary's wife as now among the native female Christians and their children. The women are all learning to read as well as the children, and some of each read and understand the New Testament very well indeed. One of the female scholars is about fifty years of age, and she is nearly ready to be put into the Testament class."

In the earlier days of the mission both Mrs. Lacey and Mrs. Sutton performed long missionary journeys with their husbands, and often engaged in conversation with groups of heathen females. Other duties have of late years kept them more at home.

Mrs. Stubbins's letters contain various facts connected with these benevolent labors. We insert the following as specimens:

"It is nearly six years since I accompanied my beloved husband on a missionary tour. It was commenced at this place, Conchin, and we hope to visit nearly if not all the same places we then saw. This evening Soorja being tired with her long walk, I left her to rest in her tent while I went into the village and had rather an interesting opportunity with three families in different parts of the village; I was surprised to find how distinctly they remembered my former visit. The first inquiry was, 'where is the baby you then brought with you?' alluding to Harriet, then an infant; this gave me an opportunity of explaining why we left our friends to reside in this country, and that the salvation of their souls is a matter of far greater importance than the dearest earthly ties. If there be one way of reaching the heart of a Hindoo female more than another, it is to appeal to her feelings as a mother; I have sometimes witnessed the starting tear when, in an answer to their inquiries, I have mentioned that we have left all our relatives and two dear children in England, in order that we might instruct them in the way of life. Had a long conversation with each party, on the folly of idolatry, and the adaptation of the gospel to their sinful state; they seemed interested.

Jan. 3d.—On this sacred day, while thousands in our native land are listening to thrilling addresses, or surrounding the table of our Lord, we are in the very midst of an immense large market, surrounded by thousands of idolators; still we feel happy in the thought that it is the will of Christ that we should be where we are, and doing what we are. This morning Soorja accompanied me into the village, and had a pleasing opportunity with a number of women; one of the party spoke of Mrs. Buckley's visit last year; I inquired if they remembered her instruction; for some time silence prevailed, at length one of the women said, 'She told us we ought to worship the one true God.' Being pleased with this mark of attention, we addressed our conversation to her; she observed, 'We are ignorant, but if you will teach us we will listen to you;' she explained much that we said to others, and on leaving pointed out her dwelling that we might visit her in the evening.

Jan. 4th.—Last evening a number of women from the market came round the tent and occupied most of our time, so that we were not able to visit the woman who had excited our interest, till this morning. She spoke of her gods and all her false hopes; Soorja observed, 'formerly I trusted in these things, but now I see the folly and feel that they are entirely unable to save me.' The poor woman inquired by what means she had been enlightened, and what was her present mode of life. In answer to my inquiries as to what benefit she had derived from fasting, bathing before sunrise in the coldest weather, she gave me a graphic description of the children, her husband scolding, and her own temper ruffled: at the same time acknowledged that her nature was as sinful as before. Her next inquiry was 'How must I worship the true God?' It is very difficult for a Hindoo to understand the nature of prayer; with them it consists in simply repeating the names of their gods. After trying to explain in as simple a manner as possible the nature of prayer, I repeated a simple one several times over. Another woman who had listened attentively took up several sentiments as if anxious to make them her own; though we stayed nearly an hour their attention did not seem to flag. There were eight or nine present, but the two referred to, appeared more especially interested."

**Mrs. Stubbins, after referring to their wearying movements from place to place, for nearly four months, and their arrival at Midnapore, furnishes some information of her exertions there, for the poor benighted daughters of India, that should excite much pity for those perishing millions, and that shows the importance of female efforts among them.**

From the character of the place, I entered upon my work with considerable depression of spirits, but am thankful that in no place which I have continued to visit for a length of time, have I met with a more cordial reception. There are, I apprehend, near a hundred Oriya houses in different parts of the town; to these I principally confine my visits. Not unfrequently, however, we are joined by the Bengalee women, who learn from their Oriya neighbors the substance of the conversation. The Oriyas, though generally living in small communities, are also a good deal scattered amongst the Bengalees; hence when I suppose I have found out all the houses in a neighborhood, I am, in one way or another, introduced to new ones. A few weeks ago, a woman whom I have frequently visited, said, "Come early tomorrow evening and I will conduct you to a woman who wishes to see you, and who wept much last night on hearing a tract read. I have since had several pleasing opportunities with the woman alluded to. After spending half an hour the other evening with several women who affirmed that by worshipping Rama, &c., sin would go; a person standing by, asked if I would not go a little farther into the town, as several Oriyas had sent messages saying they wished to see me. After passing one door, with a promise to call another day, I was about to take my seat in the verandah of a good looking house, when a respectable, but rather elderly female, of the Karana caste, accosted me by saying, "Do come to my house, which is close by, for I have long wished to converse with you, but hitherto have had no opportunity." This led to a conversation which occupied the remainder of the evening, nor would she allow me to depart without promising to renew my visit.

Of efforts among the heathen females in the vicinity of Berhampore, this estimable friend states:—

While the early part of the morning is chiefly devoted to the Christians, the evenings are spent in visiting heathen women in Berhampore and the surrounding neighborhood. In this employment I feel an abiding interest, and though it may afford less *present* fruit than some others, I feel it is not on that account *less important.* I gain ready access to hundreds who are willing, and even in some instances pleased, to hear the gospel. Many, it is believed, understand it sufficiently to enable them to receive or reject it; they commonly acknowledge themselves sinners, and as it regards their own system, quite hopeless. In these visits I am occasionally accompanied by one or more of our Christian females, whose presence appears to have a good effect.

Mrs. Wilkinson, writes,—

The other day I had a pleasing conversation with the wife of Denabundoo. I shall give it nearly *literal*, as any improvement or embellishment I might attempt, would be but a poor substitute for its own native simplicity. She came, as she frequently does, for religious conversation, told me how anxious she was to be baptized and to unite with the other Christians at the table of the Lord. I asked her some questions relative to the state of her feelings formerly, and wherein they now differed. I said, " How did you feel when your husband began to inquire about Christianity?" She replied, " When my husband first came to the Sahib's house, to teach the children, my mind was very easy about myself and him too,—but he had not been there long, before he began to bring home strange books, which he used to spend many hours reading. I asked why he did so? He replied, " These are true, come sit down and listen." But I became very angry, and refused to listen. Then he said, " These are not like our shastras, they are devoured by these as by fire." I said, " What! will you lose your good name, and forsake your brethren, sisters, friends and relations, to live with the Sahib?—I dare say you will." Then my mind for many days was sorrowful, so I sent a messenger from the brahmuns' street, where we lived, to a distant street, where my husband's brother lived, saying, "Go tell them the thing that has come to pass in our house; bid them all come quickly and talk to my husband, perhaps he will mind them." So they all came and we mourned one with another, as the Hindoo people do when a death has happened in the family. I was so unhappy that for three days I cried and could not cook our food. While we were all weeping, my husband smiled and said, "If you will all listen, I will make known to you some of the truths I read here." So he read and explained to us the Nestar Rutna, (Jewel Mine of Salvation, a tract so called,) while he was reading, my mind began to change; I thought, who can tell but these are true. When my husband went to live among the Christians, I and my children were taken to the house of my husband's brother. While there, I thought if my husband is right, we are all wrong, and resolved to go to him as soon as I could; when I heard that he was coming for us my heart was joyful, and now since I have lived here, I have learned to walk the good way with my husband. Formerly, though sunk in sin, I was not unhappy on account of it; now I have much sorrow of heart because I am a sinner, but trust in the Lord Jesus for salvation. On my expressing a hope that she would pray for her children, and endeavor to train them as a Christian mother should do, and not as she did in the times of her ignorance,—she said, "I do pray for them, and try to teach them what is right,"—and added,—"Yesterday, my little boy (six years old) went to the next house, and while the woman was gone to the well for water, he brought away some tamarinds. I was grieved, and said that is very naughty, you must go return them and beg to be forgiven. He obeyed me and did so." This very simple anecdote may possess little interest where almost every mother would have done the same, but when contrasted with the manner in which heathen females treat the faults and sins of their children, it gave me a pleasure which I cannot describe.

Another, and an altogether unexceptionable sphere of female labor, is the schools. Some of our first sisters in the mission sighed in vain for the privilege of training the youthful daughters of Orissa in the paths of piety; but now there is a wide and an effectual door opened unto them. Under the head of schools, lengthened statements respecting this department will be found. Mrs. Sutton, when entering upon her work in Orissa, thus contrasts the facilities for labor in Calcutta and Orissa.

I find that the natives here are vastly more prejudiced than those in Calcutta; indeed in the heart of Cuttack it is almost impossible to obtain girls of respectable character; you must be grieved indeed when you come to hear that those were of another stamp whom you collected together, and respecting whom you entertained such pleasing hopes. Sister Lacey, on discovering the deception, and the grievous motives that induced the girls to learn to read, broke up all the schools. Indeed their immorality rendered it necessary. But let us not be discouraged. I doubt not but a few years, with persevering efforts, will overcome the difficulties, great as they are; and notwithstanding what I have written, we have one which may be denominated a Girls' School, as there are in it eleven of our own sex and only seven boys. These, we hope, are all virtuous children: we have been very particular in trying to admit none but such, and banished two of whom we were somewhat suspicious. We also formed a school at Toolsapore in October. It consists of ten girls and about fifteen boys; their improvement is as good as can be expected, and I am much pleased with the prospects of the school. Every time I visit it, a number of women (some the mothers of the children) collect together in an adjoining yard to see me, and hear what I have to say to the children. When I first went, they seemed very shy; used to peep at me very slyly with their caparas half over their faces, and if I addressed myself to them, would run off, apparently half frightened out of their wits; but by degrees I gained their confidence, and we are now very familiar. The last time I visited the school, a mother of one of the girls took me into her house, and a most comfortless hovel it appeared, but I suppose was quite as good as the generality of the natives possess, for it had two rooms; one was all but empty, in which she said she sat and slept; in the other room was her god, Krishnoo, which she showed me without the least hesitation: here, also, she had a large chest and some jars, indeed it appears that the whole of her little property was deposited in the idol's room. Perhaps this was in order that it might be well protected!

It will be seen that in some of the above departments of female labor, it is only the missionary wife or widow who can be suitably employed. The state of Hindoo society, and the circumstances connected with missionary journeyings, would generally render it unsuitable work for single ladies; while in the schools and Christian villages they might with propriety and advantage be well engaged.

The question has often been proposed to the writer, as to the propriety of sending out single females to engage in missionary work, and he confesses it is one to which he finds it extremely difficult to give a satisfactory answer. It is next to impossible to furnish any reply to this question, which is applicable to all parts of the field, and to the ever varying circumstances of particular stations. In some cases, single sisters can render very acceptable aid in Indian Missions; in others, it would be felt that to send them out, was an intrusion and a hindrance. As a general rule, the writer is of opinion they should only be sent at the deliberate and decidedly expressed wish of the missionary with whom they are to reside, and in whose labors they are to share; or when some near relative or intimate friend wishes for any individual to assist them in their work. In such cases, a single sister may be welcomed with entire cordiality, and a happy, useful sphere of labor be opened up before her. But I use the words *deliberate and decided* wish, in reference to such brethren, as well as to others, because caution is necessary in this case. Such sudden and entire changes occur in missionary families, that it becomes those who invite out a single sister, to make suitable provision for her comfort and usefulness in case of a change in their own circumstances. Suppose, for instance, (what has occurred several times to the writer's knowledge,) they should be obliged to leave the station for another, or perhaps to leave the country as soon, or before the young lady arrives; will, in such cases, a missionary family at the station welcome her? or can she be elsewhere so accommodated that she will feel herself happy and useful? or will she have the mortification of feeling that she is an intruder and a burden? Let matters of this sort be carefully and suitably arranged, and provision made for her return, if necessary, and then I would say, let our single sisters be sent to India wherever there is a door of usefulness open to them. And I must, in justice, add, very few indeed have been sent out who have not done well, and fully justified the expectations of their friends.

For further remarks on this subject the writer directs attention to the publications of the Ladies' Society, established in London, for the Promotion of Female Education in the East,—a Society whose unostentatious and judicious exertions deserve a much larger meed of praise, and more generous support, than it has hitherto received.

The author is happy in being able to present the following extract of a letter from his esteemed fellow-laborer, Mrs. Wilkinson, to a friend in England, on the subject of this chapter. It is strikingly in accordance with his own views, as above presented.

On the subject of your inquiry, as to whether much can be done by English females here among the heathen women, there is a diversity of opinions among those who have labored for years in the country ; but this may arise from the difference which exists among the natives of different castes, or in different parts of the country,—or it may be from the want of proper views in the persons who attempted it; as very much depends on the suitability of the visitor for this work. An intelligent, judicious, *married* female, with ardent love for souls, an aptitude to see into the native character, and a good degree of *moral courage*, might, in my opinion, be very useful. In the present state of Hindoo society and morals, a *married* female has much more chance of doing them good than a single one, though the latter may have much more time at her command for the work. I cannot say how much good may be done by these visits, but much may be attempted; though the apparent success may be very little for years, it is clearly a duty to attempt to do something. When we consider that they cannot be spoken to by the missionaries or native preachers, they cannot come to hear the preaching, they cannot read, so that unless some females can be found that will go to their houses and make known to them the way of life, it is next to an impossibility they should ever become acquainted with it. For the females of our mission circle there are three distinct and important fields of labor; one is the charge of female orphan asylums. For this, doubtless, a sensible, energetic, unmarried female, acquainted with the best system of education at home, is most suitable, because she could devote herself entirely to her charge. But such a one should be placed in circumstances where she could have the counsel and guardianship of elder and more experienced members of the mission. Another important work is, attention to the female members of our churches and to the wives of inquirers; in almost every case their former habits have been the unrestrained indulgence of bad passions; and though when they enter the church, there may be satisfactory evidence of their conversion, they are but weak in the faith. Their moral sensibilities require to be cultivated, they do not discern the duties they owe to their families, and are very weak when exposed to temptation. Unless an amount of labor equal to the demand is bestowed on this department, we shall not see our female members established in the faith, or an ornament to our religion.

Finally, he would recommend to all interested, a nice little book by Mrs. Weitbrecht, of Burdwan, which, from a cursory perusal, he deems a judicious work.

We will now insert a few extracts, chiefly from letters written by Oriya females, illustrative of the beneficial results of our attempts at elevating the long-degraded daughters of Orissa. We would gladly enlarge this chapter, but time and space forbid. Other facts and illustrations will be found scattered throughout the book.

*Dukhee to Mr. Sutton.*

My beloved Papa,—You have twice asked me to write a letter to you, but I have nothing to write except I write about myself. First, my two brothers and I came to Cuttack (the family were weavers, and resided from fifteen to sixteen miles distant), after which my two sisters came also. My brother then sold me into a *very* bad house. He did this by the advice of my uncle. He then returned to my country and brought my mother. It was in consequence of the death of my father that all this affliction came upon us. After my mother's arrival, in a few days she died, and my brothers and sisters subsisted by begging. As for me, I fled, for the owner of the house gave me much affliction, and sought to destroy my body and soul. I fled to Chowleah Gunge (about two miles distant,) and there I wandered on the river's brink. From this place I was brought by "Kartick's father" (the superintendent of the boy's school). Subsequently we three sisters all met here together. When I came to the school I was foolish and ignorant, I knew nothing. But blessed, blessed be the Lord, he brought me from that way into his own way. Now it is well with me; and that I may continue in His way till death, is my constant prayer. Papa, you have loved me much, but now you are about to leave us, and go to Calcutta, our minds are very sorrowful, because you have given us much good instruction,—but when you are gone, who will thus instruct us? What more can I write? To you Dukhee writes this letter.

*Podee to Mr. Sutton.*

My beloved Papa, to you Podee desires to write this letter.

I am well. You have loved me much, and by the mercy of God, in this school I have acquired some knowledge. How much have you labored for our good! How much instruction to benefit our souls have you given! In that instruction my soul delights. You have taught us to serve God from our youth, that we may serve him for a long time; and that if we thus believe in the Lord, then he will save us from much evil. By this instruction I have been much benefitted. How much good advice do you give us from day to day. If I regard it, and walk according to it, then it will be for my good. My mind is at times steadfast towards the Lord, and at other times it is unsteadfast; then I pray, and it becomes steadfast again. O my beloved Papa, to you I send my loving salutation. What more can I write—forgive the faults in my writing. I am not able to write much. This note Podee writes to Papa.

Of Ekedi Mrs. Buckley writes:

Her natural disposition is forward, ardent, and fearless. She had been the subject of serious impressions for a considerable time, though the evidence of her having experienced a saving change was not till recently satisfactory. I had a very interesting conversation with her when she became a candidate; the manner in which she spoke of her state as a sinner in the sight of God—of her deep sorrow before God on account of her sins—of the Lord Jesus Christ being her only confidence—of her delight in reading the Scriptures and prayer—and of her desire to be baptized, because it was the Lord's command, was very pleasing. I think you will be interested in the following letter:

"Very dear Friend,—We are, through God's mercy, well. We have lately been to Gopalpore and seen the wonderful works of God in forming the great ocean. As I looked upon the foaming waves of the sea, I said, this is not man's work; only the one living and true God, who made the heaven and the earth, could make the great sea. Dear friend,—I received with great joy your kind letter and present: such tokens of affectionate regard towards me, brought tears of joy into my eyes. What was I, that God should have been so merciful to me, and given me such dear friends? I desire to praise him for his goodness. Thus far this year the Lord has preserved my life, but many around us have died (of cholera) without any knowledge of the true God, and of the way of salvation. In this respect, dear friend, we see the mercy of God to us. But still more is it manifested in His putting it into the hearts of his true people to love us, and care for us. I know that from the world I can find no true happiness—that here we have no abiding-place; I know that only heaven contains undecaying treasure: when that treasure is gained, none can take it from us. O! I earnestly desire to gain this treasure. I have resolved, by the grace of God, never to leave my room in the morning, without meditating on His goodness to me, and reading his holy word, and praying for his protecting grace. We generally go into school at half-past six o'clock, and remain till half-past eight; at nine o'clock we read the scriptures with Papa and Mamma, after which we knit or sew till half-past twelve. I have then a little time for reading the Scripture alone, and thinking of its meaning. At night I often review the day, and think of the different portions of the word of God I have read, and of what has been my conduct. In this my soul finds pleasure. I will tell you freely about my mind. I have for some time felt much on account of my sins, and I have some hope that my sins have been washed away by the blood of Christ, and that, unworthy as I am, the Lord Jesus loves me. I have committed my body and soul into the hands of the Lord Jesus Christ. How wonderful the love of Christ to sinners, that he should have come into this world and suffered so much to save them. How worthy to be had in everlasting remembrance! But what a mighty enemy we have to contend with,—who feared not to tempt the Creator, the Saviour of the world. But how much easier is it for him to tempt us and lead us into sin. Dear friend, ask for heavenly strength to be daily imparted to me, that I may not fall into the snares of the wicked one, but may be always watchful, trusting not in my own strength, but in the strength of Christ, that thus I may persevere in the way of holiness. Beloved friend, my mind goes toward you; I hope to meet you in heaven. Remember me in your prayers. I pray for you. Our dear teacher loves us much, and gives us much instruction; she has been very poorly, and is now much weaker. Pray for our dear teacher, and ask your friends to pray for her, that she may be spared to us for many years."

This interesting young disciple is one of those who were rescued from a horrible death among the Khunds. Mr. Stubbins observes, "Her heart's blood was to have been spilt in the murderous Meriah sacrifice; but now through grace divine, her heart has been washed in atoning blood."

Suba, another young disciple, addressed the following letter to a Christian friend in Leicestershire:

My dear Friend,—I send you a little chit (note) as a small token of my love. My love to you is not forgot. Probably in this world we shall not see each other, but in heaven we hope to meet. O! that will be a joyful meeting, for we shall be in the presence of the Lord Jesus, from sin and sorrow free. In my body I have many times been afflicted, but time after time the Lord has made me well. I often think in what way I can show my love to Christ. Remember me in your closet prayers, that I may be preserved from the snares of Satan, that I may be watchful, and walk with an upright mind in the way of the Lord. I have many dear relatives who are heathens; over them my mind often weeps and is in trouble; I have many times told them about Jesus, but they make light of my words, and prefer trusting in their idols of wood and stone, to the precious name of Christ, the true Saviour of the world. Unite with me in praying for my mother, my only brother, and all my other relatives, that they may be saved from hell and believe in the Lord Jesus Christ. A short time ago two of my relatives died in their heathen state: hearing of their death made me sorrowful. I found comfort in reading the word of God, and meditating on the mercy of God to me. At this time I read xiv. chapter of John, and was made joyful, believing that my dear Saviour had prepared a place for me in heaven. How beautiful those words of Christ, "Come unto me all ye that labor and are heavy laden, and I will give you rest." Pray for me, that I may increase in faith and love to Jesus.

Of two ignorant village inquirers Mr. Lacey writes:—

I much wish I could impart unto you the pleasure I now feel, and which has been excited by the account which two females have just given us of their Christian experience. While I listened to their simple and straight-forward account, and perceived the sacred feeling bursting from their eyes, my heart exclaimed, Blessed women! O how God chooses the weak things of this world to confound the wise! Here a poor woman, unable to read a word; a little while ago buried in all the darkness of idolatry; a woman despicable in the eyes of her fellow idolators, even below the level of the brute creation—can now say when asked about her knowledge of Christ,—"Sir, Christ is the Son of God; he descended from heaven to earth to save a sinful world—he appeared as a poor and helpless babe—he condescended to sleep where goats, and sheep, and oxen lay—he labored to instruct wayward sinners in the knowledge of salvation—but O! how he closed his earthly life! He was arraigned by wicked Jews at Pilate's bar, and there was he accused and vilified. Pilate pronounced him innocent, and his wife sent to him a message to say, 'Have thou nothing to do with that just man;' but the Jews cried out, 'His blood be on us and on our children.' He expired on the crossed wood for me! He took the bitter sponge with which they mocked his thirst, but declined the draught; and amidst inexpressible sorrow and pain, he poured out his life to God.

When I think of my Saviour, my heart is melted and drawn towards him in love. On Friday they laid him in his tomb; on Saturday there he lay; but on the Lord's day he arose glorious from the dead, for angels came and rolled away the stone which closed his grave. Mary with anxious heart sought her much-loved Lord, to embalm his sacred body; but she found him not there, but saw the place where her Lord lay. Retiring with tears she said to Jesus, who sat under the shade of the banyan, 'What hast thou done with my Lord?' When he said, 'Mary!' And then Jesus ascended up to God, and sitteth on his right hand, a Prince and a Saviour; and his servants are commanded to preach the gospel every where, for the salvation of the world. Sir, I remember the sermon you preached last year, when you visited us, about the jailor, who asked what he was to do to be saved;—my heart has known no quiet since that time; but Christ is my great Redeemer, and I have put my trust in him. I am the poor beggar at the rich man's door, who gladly picked up the crumbs, but who was carried to heaven into Abraham's bosom. I have been buried in ignorance and sin, but Christ can save me. He saved the dying thief who prayed by his side; he saw Zaccheus on the tree, and said to him, Come down, for to-day is salvation come to thine house. The laws of God, one by one, have I broken; and I am reduced to hopeless misery; but I have cast myself on the precious blood of Christ, and though they should destroy my life, I will not, no I will not renounce this the foundation of my hope! I know I have experienced some change, for what in my heathenish state I loved, I now hate; and God has enabled me to overcome my sinful propensities, and will still enable me. I know that baptism will not save me, but I wish to be baptized, that I may profess the Lord. God has, I see, been gracious to me; he has, like a good shepherd, brought me where there are good pastures and living waters, and I wish to resolve to spend my life in his service and to his glory."

These are some of the remarks this Christian convert made, while a flow of uncommon tenderness manifested itself in many tears of penitence and love; who could hear without exclaiming, "Blessed woman!" Her companion, though with a mind less stored with divine truth, exhibits much good feeling and apparent sincerity; so much so that we could not but exclaim, "Who can forbid water, that these should not be baptized!"

Another who has ended a short but honorable course, was an interesting young woman named Dootake. Mr. Sutton observes:—

The first day of the current year died Dootake, one of our first pupils. She was the daughter of Bamedab, our native preacher, and born, of course, when he was a heathen. She was placed in our school at its first establishment, when she was about ten years of age. When about seventeen she was baptized, and not long afterwards was married to Anunta, the son of good old Krupa, deacon. He died when with us in Calcutta in 1842, and thus early Dootake drank of the bitter cup of widowhood. When we returned to Cuttack she accompanied us, and not long after went with her father to Berhampore; there she became acquainted with Jugernath, our oldest student, and became his wife. Less than a month before her death she gave birth to a son, but was attacked by fever and gradually sunk till her spirit took its flight on the first day of the new year.

Thus rapidly did she pass through all the stages of human life—a daughter, sister, wife, widow, mother, a sinner saved by grace, a saint in glory! Such we fondly hope she is now. Her amiable conduct endeared her to us all, and her husband bears testimony that her piety did much to confirm his own. Her death was improved from Ruth 1: 16, and some of us thought there was much of the same character in both. What an eventful twenty years was the period allotted to our departed sister! What an impressive lesson too does this brief record teach to all. "Be ye also ready." Give your hearts to God. "Wilt thou not from this time cry unto me my Father, thou art the guide of my youth."

We add one specimen of another class. Inquiries have often been made respecting Mary, the Hindoo girl, who accompanied the author to America in 1833. She is now twenty-one years of age, and has long been an assistant in our female schools. Last year she was baptized and added to the church at Jellasore. She has had but one year of regular schooling, the rest of her education has been obtained in our family. The following extract is *verbatim* from her letter written to the author in reference to her baptism. The previous specimens were written in Oriya; this, of course, is in English. It, therefore, is a specimen of what may be done by ordinary training in that language by a Christian family.

A great change has indeed taken place in me. I have obtained fellowship with the people of God. I can now apply those beautiful lines of Montgomery, which I have ardently wished that I could adopt when witnessing accessions to the table of the Lord :—

" Lonely I no longer roam,
Like the wind, the cloud, the wave,
Where you dwell shall be my home,
Where you die shall be my grave," &c.

I have since enjoyed a peace of mind to which I was before a stranger, yet I have cause to lament that I make so little progress in my Christian course. I seem constantly to need something to stimulate and rouse me into action. * * * * When I contemplate qualities laudable and virtuous in others, I endeavor to aspire after the same. Excellence appears to me as placed upon a summit, whence I may behold it at a distance, but to which I may not attain. This reminds me of Tantalus, who, for the loathsome banquet he had prepared for the gods, was plunged in water up to his chin, with apples hanging to his lips, yet unable to stoop to the one, to satisfy his raging thirst, neither could he reach the other, to relieve the cravings of appetite," &c., &c.

We would gladly insert other specimens from the letters of Miss Collins, Mrs. Phillips, Mrs. Bachelor and other faithful laborers, but these extracts must suffice. How rich a recompense for Christian zeal and benevolent exertion do they disclose; and taken in connection with other results of our mission, indicated in other parts of this volume, how amply do they justify all the labor and self-denial and crushing trial the female missionary who would be faithful to her calling must encounter in idolatrous India.

# CHAPTER XI.

**Thoughts on raising up a native ministry—Oriya native preachers, students, &c.—Specimens of native preaching.**

It will be seen, from various parts of this volume, that it is the opinion of the writer, English, and, of course, American missionaries, should not usually become pastors of churches, but consider themselves rather as the successors of the apostles and primitive evangelists, whose office it is to found churches and set in order whatever is wanting in them, and having been successful in one place, endeavor to be so in another, leaving indigenous ministers to watch over the flock, while they should themselves take the general oversight of the whole.

We shall, in this section, endeavor to illustrate this idea, and notice it in connection with several collateral matters of practical importance. In doing so, I am happy to avail myself of several valuable suggestions and remarks by my esteemed friend and brother, Rev. G. Pearce, of Calcutta, and by Rev. Mr. Clarkson, of Western India.

First of all, then, we consider it a settled point, that Missionary Societies do not contemplate sending forth a succession of foreign missionaries, to take the oversight of churches in heathen countries, but expect that such churches shall be so trained and constituted, that they may gradually become independent of foreign aid, and in their turn assist in sending forth their quota of laborers to evangelize other districts or other countries. There is no other principle on which we could ever expect to see the whole world converted to Christ.

There may be infinite diversity as it respects the difficulties to be surmounted in planting the gospel among a heathen people, and they may differ as greatly as to their fitness for self-government and self-sustentation; still we adhere to the expectation that churches will grow in all that pertains to the Christian character and conduct. This diversity will have its influence on the supporters of missions, leading them, in some cases, to continue their fostering care a longer or shorter period, as circumstances dictate, yet they do not lose sight of their plan. Their wish and intention is to preach the gospel in other places also.

This, then, being a fundamental principle in modern missions, and, we may add, what is of more importance, of Christianity also, churches should, of course, be organized, constituted and trained in reference to it. Indigenous pastors, therefore, must be raised up and ordained to the work and missionaries be prepared to resign the pastorate to them. In the meantime perhaps the native minister may rank as an assistant pastor.

Now there are two sources whence the native ministry may be supplied. One from among the best qualified of the adult converts, as is the case in Christian countries among some denominations, where men of suitable talents leave their profession and at once enter upon the work of the ministry, or carry on both conjointly; the other source is young men of piety, who are trained and educated in theological institutions expressly for the ministry. We conceive both sources should be acknowledged, though we can reasonably hope but for a small portion of the ministerial body to be supplied from the first named source.

Schools of the prophets have been established in every age, and we do not now intend to attempt a justification of them. We shall take it for granted, that the necessity, or advantage, or propriety of such institutions will be admitted, and that whatever arguments are applicable in their behalf in Christian lands, apply with tenfold force in heathen countries. Our inquiry is as to the best mode of conducting them so as to render them most efficient.

Some of the Scottish brethren contend earnestly for an exclusively English education, and are exceedingly impatient of opposition to their views in this matter. Now the writer would yield all honor to the able and excellent men who conduct these educational establishments in India, but as a practical man, he cannot agree with them. In Calcutta and its neighborhood English may be made the general medium of imparting instruction, whether secular or religious, and great facilities exist for carrying out this mode of instruction, but in the country it is not so; and as it respects training for the ministry, the writer much questions whether even in Calcutta it be the best mode. He is fully convinced that it is not, in the country. First, because a very small number of the men qualified for native ministers could learn English sufficiently well to be instructed through that medium. Secondly, teaching through that medium would greatly retard the cultivation of a native theology, and a facility in conveying theological ideas in a native idiom; render inapplicable most of the figurative illustrations employed, and make their ministry stiff and foreign. And, thirdly, in many cases such a training would foster ideas at variance with the simplicity and economy required in a native ministry.

This last objection is one of grave importance, and applies not merely to an English education, but to every scheme of education that raises the men beyond the sphere in which they are required to move. I take it for granted that as the constitution of missions and the teachings of the New Testament require us to raise up a native ministry, so, on the other hand, we must not raise up such a ministry as native churches cannot support. This sentiment should be our pole star in all the course we pursue, and, if fully admitted, will supersede the necessity of much argumentation which might otherwise be deemed necessary. Now a good English education, such as is implied in making English the medium of training for the Christian ministry, would, I fear, elevate young natives generally far beyond the sphere of their rural countrymen, would foster desires for a mode of dress and living, and lead to expenses for books and various articles, which the majority of the churches already formed could never support. At the same time such young men would be qualified for secular employment, which would bring them ample means of indulging their English ideas and increasing their expenses. Our young men, therefore, in the present state of things, would probably prefer secular to ministerial employ, and our hopes would be disappointed. I believe that the history of every existent theological or educational establishment, where English has been taught, will show that this is no mere chimera.

Again, ministers should be ensamples to the flock, not lords over God's heritage. But is there not danger that an expensive mode of education would disqualify native students in this important particular,—whether they would not become so genteel and Anglicised as to feel not only much in advance of their flock, but fitted rather for another grade of existence, and their flocks feel that they were far enough from being one of themselves?

And yet once more. In the part of the field where it

has been the writer's lot to labor, a good missionary of Jesus Christ must endure much hardness. He must be able to walk many koss a day, and that too through jungles, swamps and roads extremely muddy, and when he reaches his resting place or journey's end, be content to cook his own dinner beneath some neighboring tree, and there spread his mat to sleep at night. Such habits as are cherished in Calcutta, or in institutions similar to those established there, are little fitted for this kind of work.

In educating a native ministry, therefore, we must keep in mind the present actual state of things, the work to be done, and the ability of native churches. It will be time enough to raise our ideas as the churches advance, taking care that while we supply a ministry always in advance of their hearers, as it respects general and especially theological knowledge, we do not so train the ministry as that it shall cease to be a native ministry in feeling, habits, and sympathy with their people.

Young missionaries especially, and all who labor chiefly in English, are apt to overvalue everything English. They can convey their ideas best in English, can appreciate anything said or done in an English manner, and always more or less Anglicise all they have to do. More experienced laborers among the people, while they see reason to estimate at little value most of such efforts, feel at the same time that they create many incidental difficulties, and widen the already wide breach which exists between the mass of the people and themselves. My own conviction is that the sooner we adopt an opposite course, and confine ourselves as much as possible to native usages the better. And that until we do this our way will never be plain and open for real intercourse with the people, or for a just appreciation of native mind and feeling.

While it is of great importance to train up the native ministry in hardy, economical habits, it is not unworthy of remark that economy in our educational establishments is of a kindred character. The less we anglicise our establishments the less we shall need English teachers, English accommodations, and much expensive English apparatus; and of course the more we shall be able to avail ourselves of native teachers, and of various facilities which the country affords both for boarding and educating young ministers.

The plan of building large, expensive colleges may be considerably modified. The salary of one European master saved, will pay for three or four natives, and natives are good teachers of what they know. So while we may have suitable and even splendid accommodations, by conforming to the native plan and languages, we shall be at comparatively little expense. We shall not accustom the students to habits greatly differing from those to which they have been accustomed, and thus, while making them more efficient as ministers, shall not greatly unfit them for returning to native secular employ if found disqualified for the ministry. From these remarks the leading ideas of the writer will sufficiently appear.

First, he would avoid all unnecessary extravagance in buildings, varying only from native customs where a change would be an improvement.

Secondly, while European energy and intelligence are essential to the general control of such institutions, yet native help and talent should be employed, whenever it can be done with efficiency, always keeping in view that we hope natives will at length manage their own institutions entirely.

Thirdly. He would teach through the medium of the vernaculars and sanscrit as a general rule, not rejecting English under special circumstances.

Fourthly. He would adhere to native habits, dress, and customs generally, so that the young minister may be one with his flock, and create no unnecessary prejudice against the gospel as a foreign religion.

Fifthly. He would ever bear in mind that we are to train a ministry which native churches should be taught to support. We must, therefore, avoid expensive habits which native churches cannot maintain, or encouraging expectations of emolument which cannot be realized.

The writer is happy in believing that a reaction of opinion on this important matter has set in, and he indulges the hope that we shall soon arrive at a general perception of sound principles and an adoption of corresponding conduct.

In the meantime let neither our missionary boards or our home churches so urge the employment of native preachers as to bear down the opinions of the missionaries themselves. It would be doing missionaries generally, cruel injustice to suppose they are not ready to employ all the native talent they have, as far and as fast as they can. It is not every mission that is favored with suitable native preachers. The very earnestness of the churches about this matter, has already occasioned a mischievous overpayment of very mediocre talent in the presidency of Bengal. The following remarks, by a late Calcutta missionary, in vindication of himself and brethren, though written long ago, still deserve serious consideration:—

"Native agents have been so eulogized for their great

adaptation to the work, and especially for the very low expense at which their labors may be obtained, that to send brethren from christendom, except one now and then for the purpose of superintendence, must be viewed as an absurd exhaustion of funds, and an unnecessary, if not a wanton, sacrifice of life. Hence I am ready to believe that much confusion and injurious suspense have been felt by many serious Christians upon this subject, and some who would willingly have offered themselves for foreign service have become embarrassed in their judgments and been repressed in their zeal.

"Of the desirableness of fully employing native piety and talent in diffusing the gospel in India, there can exist but one opinion. But how to render them most availing to the purposes which all desire, is a subject upon which a difference has obtained. The opinion of some of us has been that persons but newly awakened from heathen superstition, with little previous mental culture, considering the present state of mind and morals prevalent in the country, can be but partially competent to make known, defend, and exemplify the gospel; that to send them, soon after their conversion, to occupy remote stations, cut off from the succors derivable from Christian converse and pastoral superintendence, where they must meet alone the assaults and the sophisms of proud Mussulmans and subtle Pagans, and must make head against all the crime and pollution of all around them, can scarcely fail to become perilous to their faith and character. Thus much too, experience has sufficiently verified. The Calcutta missionaries have employed native brethren in making known the gospel in every possible instance; but it has been in close connection with themselves. They have conversed with them and worshipped with them daily; and have almost daily yoked themselves in the same identical labors. And until native converts be found of superior order to any we have seen, and the state of society in the East be much improved beyond what yet obtains, I humbly submit whether this be not the most satisfactory way of turning native agency to account in missionary work. We are far from meriting the reproach of lightly esteeming native converts; we think they can at present be employed as auxiliaries, and that so employed they are highly profitable; but to confide in them alone would be to insure disappointment."

The Orissa missionaries have not been unmindful of the important matter to which this chapter refers. No sooner were native converts given to us than we sought to employ them in enlightening their countrymen. All who seemed likely to make preachers, were carefully and gradually introduced into the work. They were taken out by the missionary in his itineracies; encouraged to speak as they were able of their own experience in Hindooism and Christianity; employed in distributing tracts; and taught to regard themselves as bound to employ their talents for the evangelization of their country. The result has been, that a noble band of native ministers have been trained up by the Orissa missionaries. Perhaps no Indian mission has more able or devoted native helpers. Some fifteen of these men have been, after long trial, solemnly ordained as evangelists, and a few appointed to the pastoral office. There are others still in training for the work, while a still younger class are being conducted through a regular system of theological instruction for the ministry. We are far from having reached perfection in this matter, but a hopeful beginning has been made.

Among all the members of the rising church of Christ

in Orissa, the eye of the Christian missionary can rest on no one so interesting or so dear to his heart as the native preacher. Looking at him through the medium of the sacrifices he has made, the obloquy he is called to endure, the position he nobly sustains among his gainsaying and reviling countrymen, and contrasting all with the noble end he seeks to accomplish, and the real effects of his labors, he approximates to a moral heroism surpassing all human standards of appreciation, and to honor, which not man, but angels and God alone can understand.

The relation of the native preacher to the missionary receives no unapt illustration from the constitution of the Honorable East India Company's army. There we see the Hindoo Sipahis officered by Europeans, and thus led on to the subjugation of their own country to a foreign power. And so, for some time to come, must the European missionary take the lead in the warfare on Satan's empire, and conduct the converted Hindoo to the conquest of his own people unto Immanuel's sceptre. With European skill, moral courage, and Christian principle to direct, the Hindoo native preacher becomes a valuable and efficient soldier of the cross.

The following native brethren have, in most cases after a number of years of probation varying from two to six years, been ordained as evangelists.

| | | |
|---|---|---|
| Gunga Dhor, | a Brahmun, at Cuttack. | |
| Ram Chundra, | Mahratta, | do. |
| Pooroosbotama, | Writer, | do. |
| Doytari, | Naik, | do. |
| Bamadeb, | Writer, | do. |
| Balajee, | Brahmun, | Berhampore. |
| Dinabundhoo, | Schoolmaster, | do. |
| Seebo Sahoo, | Boisya, | Cuttack. |

| | | |
|---|---|---|
| Seebo Naik, | Naik, | Cuttack. |
| Damudar, | Mahantee, | do. |
| Pursuaram, | Unknown, | Balasore. |
| Ram-das, | Brahmun, | do. |
| Bonamali, | Khundait, | Cuttack. |
| Pursua, | do. | do. |
| Somnath, | Brahmun, appointed, but died before ordination. | |
| Lukhein-das, | Byraggee, died before ordination. | |
| Bikhari, | Naik, suspended before ordination. | |
| Sarthi, | Iron smith, | Berhampore. |

Of the above-named ministers, Lukhein-das, Somnath, and Bonamali, have honorably finished their course. They died with their armor on, and their memories are loved and cherished.

Poorooshotama, Pursuaram, and Bikhari have disgraced their high calling, but are still connected with the Christian community, and, we hope, penitents.

Tama, Komboo, Ghunoo, Jugoo, and Makunda, are young ministers who have completed their studies in the mission academy, and are appointed to preach, but have not yet been ordained. There are several others, as Mahesh, Silas, &c , at Jellasore and Balasore, in a similar position.

Important testimony has been borne from time to time by all our missionaries, to the value and efficiency of our native ministers, and these testimonies have been supported by brethren of other denominations.

Messrs. Lacroix and Mullins, of the London Missionary Society, thus write : "In respect to the plan of vernacular preaching, and engaging in extensive itineracies, the providence of God has peculiarly favored this mission by raising up within it a large number of very superior native preachers. Several of these brethren are men of character as well as ability; are well read in the Hindoo shastres, can encounter the Brahmuns in the most determined manner; can expose their pretensions and deceptions, and successfully exhibit the inconsistencies of Hindooism in the clearest light."

The editors of the Calcutta Christian Observer bear the same honorable testimony. They observe—"The native preachers are men of character and standing among their own people; very active and faithful in the Lord's work, and possessed of superior mental endowments."

The writer had selected various specimens of preaching and addresses by our native preachers, but he is obliged to withhold their insertion. He merely appends to this chapter a few sentences, to illustrate the highly figurative style in which the Oriyas are in the habit of presenting their ideas.

Very pleasant are the recollections of the writer of his various journeys and labors in company with his native brethren; and long could he indulge in recording their various excellencies and characteristic traits.

In general, the native preacher presents an aspect of meekness, chastened affliction, yet patient courage, such as crosses and losses for Christ's sake can alone induce. He is accustomed to be slighted often by European Christians, and continually by his own countrymen. Yet his labors and experience in the gospel give him an inward consciousness of power with God and man. He has much of the heartfelt joy of simple faith, much experience of a kind Providence, much practical trust in God's gracious care and promise, and much solid conviction of the truth and superiority of Christianity, and the true dignity which his office as a preacher of it, confers upon him.

Dear, honored, though despised brethren! much do

you need and deserve the sympathy and prayers of the Christian church. I love to think of you, as patiently and perseveringly prosecuting your labor in the noisy market or bazar, or amidst the taunting blusterings of the annual festivals and Ruth Jattra. Happy shall I be to again accompany you in our wearying journeys, and stand by your side amidst the crowded assembly, or perchance be seated with you beneath the banian's shade.

## NATIVE MINISTERS.

*Many pleasing anecdotes display the ability of these valuable brethren.*

Gunga was with us, and spoke with great power. He has his faults, but there are noble traits in his character; and in the bazar, in his best moods, he is an extraordinary speaker. His powerful voice, energy of manner, and mastery of the language, command attention. I have seen them writhe and smile at his exposure of their delusions—writhe at the severity of the lash, smile at the cleverness with which it has been inflicted. On this occasion he described the love of Christ well. When speaking of sin, he paused in the midst of his discourse, and sat down, requesting them to instruct him: he had been endeavoring to enlighten them, and would be glad to learn a little from them. After waiting a little, and no one answering, with that sarcasm which is so natural to him, he said, "What! have you nothing to say? you, such great pundits—such distinguished brahmuns! —you, who are the teachers of the people, have you no reply to offer?—not able even to explain what sin is? I wait to hear what such oracles of wisdom have to say. What! not able to say a word!" He then rose with dignity, and poured forth torrents of eloquence on sin and salvation.

Bonamali does not assume any superiority over the people; he bears with their trifling and foolish objections, and "in meekness instructs those who oppose themselves." When they are obstreperous, he often with good effect attacks them with their own weapons, and overwhelms them by urging principles recognized in their own shastres. His preaching, too, is often marked by fervor and affectionate entreaty. Once he began by saying, "Suppose a person was going a journey on a dangerous, jungly road: another person, who is better acquainted with the way, in kindness attempts to dissuade him, telling him that there are tigers in that direction, and that if he venture to go, he will certainly be destroyed. But he slights the kindly warning—he determines to go. On the way the savage tiger seizes him: now, how he bewails his folly and madness in not listening to good advice! But it is too late; he is in the paws of the tiger, and at the point of death. So you are going on a dangerous path,—the end of it will be hell. Once," he said, "I went this way which you are still going; once I served brahmuns and gooroos, and worshipped idols, as you do. But I obtained the word of God; I heard the gospel of Jesus Christ; I forsook the dark and dangerous way on which, like you, I went. And now, my neighbors, my countrymen, my brethren, with hands joined, and in love, I do humbly beseech you not to go that way whose end will be so fearful, but to forsake your sins and flee to the Lord Jesus. If you regard the message, it will be well with you; if you despise it, you will be like the man who, for slighting good advice, was seized and devoured by the tiger."

Mr. Buckley writes:

I should not think it much to say, that our native preachers, as a body, labor as hard as any in India. For instance, in the cold season they rise at early dawn, visit one or more villages, which are often distant, and do not generally return till after ten o'clock. Much of their time during the heat of the day is occupied in teaching the things which concern the Lord Jesus Christ, to those whom curiosity brings to the tent. About three, P. M., they go out again, and do not return till towards seven, P. M. And this, it should be remembered, is not their occasional, but their regular work (the interval of a few days spent at home excepted) for weeks and months together. At markets and festivals their labors are still more severe, and their ordinary work at home is by no means light.

Among statements referring to individuals, the following are very pleasing. Mr. Buckley heard Denabundhoo preach on Satanic influence, from 1 Peter 5:8. The power, malice, and subtlety of the wicked one were impressively enlarged on, and aptly illustrated.

He especially dwelt on the thought that Satan had not so much concern about idolators as he has about believers. A Hindoo illustrates every thing, and he illustrated this by supposing the case of a gaoler, some of whose prisoners had made their escape, and he asked whether the gaoler would be more concerned about those prisoners that were safe in prison, or those that had escaped? No doubt his chief anxiety would be about those who had managed to escape. So Satan did not need to look so much after idolators, with whom he did as he pleased, as after Christians, who had been delivered from his dominion. Some important remarks were made on the manner in which the wicked one adapts his temptations to different dispositions. The sermon was well adapted to leave on the mind a deep impression of the magnitude of our danger from Satan's devices, and of the necessity for watchfulness and prayer.

At a time when his mind was depressed and discouraged, Mr. Lacey mentions the cheering influence that he felt from listening to a discourse by Rama Chundra.

Last Lord's day the chapel presented a very exhilarating sight, both in the forenoon and afternoon. In the morning Rama Chundra preached to a tolerable congregation, and I was interested in and delighted with the preacher and the sermon. He took for his text Philippians ii. 21, 22. He did not dwell long upon the commendation of Timothy's character, but took occasion to notice two things; first, that some Christians professed Christ for their own things—for their own advantage and honor; and secondly, that others professed Christ for his sake. He was very discriminating, and his sermon was calculated to be exceedingly useful. The extensive quotation of passages all over the New Testament appropriate to his purpose, evinced how extensively and how well he has read the word of God. I was greatly affected by such an instance of good, and felt my complaining disposition reproved. Our excellent brother Rama Chundra is a noble instance of firm and decided Christian character, and these qualities give him great influence and usefulness.

Denabundhoo thus met the old objection, often urged, that Christians worship a God whom they have not seen:—

Look at a man ill of fever. See how restless he is! how he shivers! anon he is burning hot! parched with thirst, he rolls from side to side, vainly trying to find an easy posture. Wife, children, friends and the physician stand near; the medicine is prepared and offered to him, but, no; the sick man says, Why should I take this medicine? I want to *see* the fever. Show me the fever, then I will take the medicine. He then appealed to them whether the man would not be likely to die, if he continued to insist on seeing the disease before he applied the remedy; and they unhesitatingly admitted that he would, and laughed at their own folly. In like manner it was of course shown that if they refused to receive the testimony of the true God, because they had not seen Him, they were doing it to their own destruction.

The same brother furnishes an affecting account of a discourse that he heard from Damudar.

At Athagurda I was exceedingly pleased and impressed with Damudar's address. He dwelt at some length on the day of judgment,—the two great divisions that would then be made of the human family, and the sentence that would be pronounced on each. He, then, with much affectionate earnestness proclaimed the gospel, and in closing said, "I do not stand before you as if I was any better than you are, by no means. I am one of your own people; I have been a greater sinner than any of you. I confess it before God with shame and sorrow. But by the grace of God I have received the truth: I have found the way of salvation, and now I make it known to you. Once, my brethren, I worshipped the gods which you worship. Thousands of times I have repeated their names in the way that you do. Thousands of times I have worshipped the brahmuns and gooroos as you do, but I now see the folly and sinfulness of this course, and having discovered the true way, I proclaim it to you. In love, my brethren, I do humbly entreat you, listen to the life-giving word." Such remarks, delivered as they were with great feeling and power, were likely to do much good. The impression was marked. This is the way in which the gospel should be preached. The delivery of a message of love should be eminently characterized by a spirit of love.

The objection was made, on one occasion, that it was absurd for us to expect, with our little band, to spread Christianity all over the land. Gunga instantly met the objector as follows:—

Oh, brother, listen. A few years ago, our whole land was in darkness; these brethren, living 15,000 miles over the sea, heard of our state and had compassion on us and came to help us. I was a poor, blind brahmun, groping my way I knew not whither, but I heard there was light in the house of the Padree Sahib, and I went there and lit my lamp. I have now brought my light into the bazar, and you may light your lamp from mine, others will light theirs from you, and others, again, from them; and so you see, my brother, how easily the light may spread all over the country.

Another objector urged that it was all very well for us to trust in Jesus Christ, but the Hindoo had other saviours, as Jugernath, Krishnoo, Kalee, &c., &c., they would trust in them and be saved. To this Seebo Naik replied:—

Oh, brother, you are quite mistaken. God has made certain things to answer certain purposes; thus he has made the sun to give us light and heat. Now supposing any one should say, I won't have the sun which God has given us, I will make a sun of my own. Could he do it, think you? Again, God has appointed food to nourish our bodies. Suppose any one should say, I won't eat rice, or food of such kinds, I will eat sand or stones. Would this sustain life, do you suppose? And just so God has appointed Jesus Christ to be our Saviour, and a man may just as reasonably attempt to make another sun, or supply a substitute for food, as to set up another Saviour. There is no other name given under heaven among men by which we must be saved.

Another objected he could not live if he became a Christian, for then he must cease to tell lies. To this a native brother replied, pointing to the birds singing over head in the branches, and asked, "Do these tell lies? and yet your Heavenly Father feedeth them. How much better are ye than the fowls?"

Illustrations of this kind might be multiplied indefinitely.

### *The Orissa Mission Academy.*

Respecting the Institution during the first year the tutor states:—

There have been eight young men pursuing their studies in the Institution during the year. Four of these are accepted as missionary students, and all of them are married; four others may be called probationary students; of these, one is married and lives close by. They have prosecuted the prescribed course of study with some interruption, occasioned by my absence. But have, nevertheless, continued some of the branches of study, as Sanscrit, elements of natural philosophy, &c., all the year under Shem, an assistant teacher, kindly supplied by our Calcutta brethren from the Intally Native Christian Institution.

I have had close employ in studying and preparing various lectures for delivery in Oriya. These, so far as we have gone, have been taken down by the students and subsequently reviewed. In this way we have gone through the first series on doctrinal theology, also a complete course on preaching, prayer, habits of study, &c., and we are now going on with another set on the constitution and government of the church of Christ. Preparation has been made to resume our doctrinal lectures, with an additional series of exercises on Scripture interpretation.

The following were the subjects of the Essays appointed to be written by the students.

| | | |
|---|---|---|
| 1. | The Nature and Attributes of God, | Jugernath. |
| 2. | On Idolatry, | Tama. |
| 3. | The Offices of the Sacred Trinity, | Komboo. |
| 4. | God's Moral Government, | Ghunoo. |
| 5. | Original and Fallen State of Man, | Makunda. |
| 6. | Man's Inability to Save Himself, | Jugoo. |
| 7. | Inspiration and Use of the Holy Scriptures, | Das. |
| 8. | Our Present State as a state of Probation, | Hurree. |

An account is furnished of the first examination of the students by Mr. Stubbins, of which we omit all but the concluding paragraph.

We cannot close our report of the first examination of our Institution, destined as we trust to render essential service to the cause of Christ in Orissa for many years to come, without expressing the pleasure and encouragement, which, on the whole, we feel in the progress of these interesting young men, and recording our earnest prayer to the Giver of all good, that they may come forth in due time, fitted effectually to make known the undying truths of the gospel to their fellow-countrymen, and to be pastors of churches gathered to Christ in this benighted province.

We also trust that all our beloved friends at home will remember this Institution in their prayers.

# CHAPTER XII.

Missionary stations—Stations needed in Orissa—Work of Missionaries.

The choice of missionary stations and the right distribution of the missionary force, is a matter of grave importance. Nor will it often be found that the plan adopted in one mission is precisely applicable to another. Respect must be had to the Episcopal aspect, location of great towns, statistical returns, means of communication, civil and religious condition of the people, and other matters viewed in connection with the numerical force, modes of labor, and talents for usefulness of the missionaries in any given field.

The writer once thought that the plan adopted by the American missionaries, in Jaffna Ceylon, furnished an excellent model for most missions. But he now thinks it too contracted, and not applicable to our extensive fields of labor on the vast Indian continent. Most missions have, however, gone to the other extreme, and scattered their missionaries over by far too extended a field. To this point we cannot now further allude. Our present remarks must be confined to the field of labor assigned to the Orissa missionaries.

There can be little doubt that the present civil divisions and civil stations in the province will be the sites of the chief missionary stations also. At these the missionary with his staff of assistants, will have his head-quarters and superintend his sphere of labor. There is need, however, for other stations in order to bring the whole field under cultivation. This has long been felt necessary by the civil authorities, for the right government of the province, as well as by ourselves in a missionary view. And doubtless other civil stations will soon be established.

We will first glance at the stations already occupied or acknowledged by us, and then point out other required subordinate divisions of the field. These are distinguished on the map by a circle drawn round the spot. A dotted circle indicates that such a station is not yet occupied.

Our missionary occupancy of Orissa in its widest extent, will not be complete until we have resident missionaries in at least five principal stations, viz.: Midnapore, Balasore, Cuttack, Berhampore, and Sumbhulpore. And each of these must be the centre of several subordinate stations, more or less widely scattered, according to circumstances. It may be necessary to offer a few remarks respecting each of these grand divisions of our field.

1. Cuttack. This is the most important city in Orissa proper, and the first station occupied by our mission. When our brethren Bampton and Peggs settled at Cuttack, in the beginning of 1822, the population was estimated at 40,000. It is now estimated at 70,000. The town is located between the forks of the Mahanuddi and Katjuri rivers, and is both the head civil and military station in the province. Here reside the commissioner, civil and sessions judge, magistrate, collector, and their subordinates. Here also is the head-quarters of the military force, consisting of one and sometimes two regiments of native infantry, officered by Europeans, with their accompaniment of artillery, and non-commissioned officers. Here also are the jails, hospitals, church establishment and the different courts of justice.

The town is well situated for traffic and a considerable

amount of business is carried on. At this station we have usually three resident agents of the mission, viz.: a missionary in charge of the native preaching department, which is and has been from the first, Mr. Lacey—a missionary in charge of the schools, asylums, translations, and tutor of the academy for training young ministers. This office belongs to Mr. Sutton, but is now in part occupied by Mr. Buckley—and the superintendent of the printing office, which is Mr. W. Brooks.

The English services and the administration of religious ordinances, are divided betwixt the two resident missionaries. It is quite evident that this force is small enough for this important post. At this station we have three meeting-houses; in the largest, which is the first erected, or rather on the spot where the first was erected, for it has three times been rebuilt, we have a general meeting of the native Christians twice a day, on ordinance Sabbaths, but on other Sabbaths in the afternoon only. An English service is also held here every Sabbath evening, for the benefit of the English and East Indian community.

A second meeting-house is on the mission premises, where the scholars in the schools and theological institutions assemble for daily worship, and where there is also a regular religious service on Sabbath mornings, and on Thursday evenings.

A third meeting-house is in Christianpore, a part of Cuttack inhabited by native Christians, where there is divine service on Sabbath morning and Thursday evenings.

On the mission premises are the boarding asylums for native children, numbering upwards of fifty of each sect, to which reference has been already made. Here also is located the academy or theological institution for training young native ministers, and the printing office with bindery attached.

In the village of Christianpore is a day school for the children of the native Christians in that part of Cuttack.

The number of native Christians and other communicants at this station was as last reported, 141 adults. The nominal Christians, or adherents to the Christian community, not united to the church, are about 250 individuals of all ages. Making altogether of professed Christians 400 persons.

In the neighborhood of Cuttack, about six miles to the north-west, is the village of Odoyapoor, or Chaga, where there is a pure native church of fifty communicants, and a considerable nominal Christian community who attend religious services. This station is under the pastoral charge of an Oriya minister.

The city of Cuttack is the capital of a district of the same name usually called Central Cuttack. The population under the immediate jurisdiction of the Hon. Company is considerably beyond a million; six-sevenths of whom are Oriyas, and the seventh part Mussulmans. If we include the southern division also, as we ought according to our present arrangement to do, we shall have a population of more than two millions, inclusive of the inhabitants of the tributary mehals or native rajas. While therefore Cuttack is to be regarded as the central station of this division of our field, we need four sub-stations east, west, north and south of it. Nor can we ever hope to bring the gospel to bear fully upon the people until this arrangement be effected.

The first, or northern sub-station, should be at or near Khunditara (or one ferry boat). This would include the populous Thannahs of Jajpoor, Urrackpoor and some of the native states. At Khunditara we have already the elements of a Christian church, and a settled Christian community. We only need the appointment of a missionary, with his native assistants, to occupy this very interesting field. Here he would have a population probably of 400,000 souls, among whom to labor, in a very beautiful, healthy and fertile part of the province.

The second, or eastern division, would include the Thanas of Pahrajpoor, Hurihurpoor, Teerun, Kindrapara, Mulloo and Patamunday, with an immense population of 500,000 or 600,000 souls. This district has long called aloud for a faithful, devoted missionary—Oh when shall one be sent? This is a specially important division, and has to some extent been several times visited by the Cuttack brethren and native assistants.

The third sub-station has been already fixed at Pipplee; this includes Pooree, or Jugernath, with Khurda and the whole civil southern division of Cuttack. Here is a population of 500,000 of the Company's subjects, irrespective of those under native rajas.

This division was the site of the labors of the indefatigable Bampton, and here the writer of these papers was first stationed. Within the grave-yard, on the sands of Pooree, lie the remains of Charlotte Sutton and William Bampton, the first two laborers who fell in the service of the Orissa mission.

It has been thought best to renew our labors in this division of the field at Pipplee, a village midway betwixt Cuttack and Pooree. Here for the present are located Messrs. Millar and Bailey, with their partners, and several native assistants. This station was formed in 1849, and already have some additions been made to the little flock of Christ in this place.

These brethren consider Pooree as a part of their field

and purpose spending a considerable portion of their time at that peculiarly trying but important place.

The fourth sub-station required to complete our plan of operations for our first grand division, should be located to the westward of Cuttack. A very eligible place presents itself in the newly acquired Banki rajuary. Here or at Kontiloo, on the pleasant banks of the Mahanuddee, within easy reach of Cuttack, a missionary might find a wide field of labor, though less thickly populated than the other divisions mentioned.

In point of interest and importance this field would rise superior to the others, in the estimation of many a laborer. It would include several of the independent rajuaries as well as a large number of the subjects of the Hon. Company, but above all, it would be the most eligible post whence to bring the gospel to bear on the Khunds of this portion of Orissa. Here ground has been promised for the location of the young people rescued from the Khunds, and for a school to which it may be hoped the Khunds might at length be induced to send their children. From this station the missionary might, at suitable seasons, extend his labors towards Sumbhulpoor, or to that populous place itself, until it can be made the centre of another circle of missionary stations. The country of the Ungool raja in this immediate vicinity, has just been annexed to the British dominions.

These divisions of our field the writer earnestly urges upon the attention of the friends of the Orissa Mission *in England*, and beseeches them to leave no means untried to secure a missionary for each of these important posts.

### *Second grand division, or Balasore.*

Balasore is the name of a city, and a zillah, or civil division of the province. The city early became known to Europeans, and when the writer first visited it in 1825, he saw there the remains of five European factories, viz., Dutch, Danish, French, Portuguese and English. There were also the ruins of a Catholic chapel and several ancient monuments of deceased Europeans in the grave-yard, or place which once was so called. The inhabitants of Balasore now number probably upwards of 15,000, and the population of the whole district we have estimated at 600,000, exclusive of those under native rajas and wild tribes.

Balasore was as early as 1814 for a short time occupied by Mr. Peters, an East Indian missionary, under the patronage of the Serampore brethren. "Early in January, 1826, Mr. and Mrs. Sutton commenced missionary labors at Balasore, and labored on with various encouraging circumstances until the weak state of the mission, induced by the illness and death of Messrs. Bampton and Cropper, obliged them to retire again to the southern parts of the province." The station was resumed by Mr. Goadby in the year 1835, but in 1838 he returned to England. Meantime Messrs. Noyes and Phillips, who had been sent out by the Free-will Baptists from America, and who had commenced a station at Sumbhulpoor, were driven from their post by sickness, and accepted the charge of the Balasore district as a more suitable location for their infant mission. To these brethren the whole of this interesting field has since been ceded by the General Baptist missionaries.

Mr. and Mrs. Noyes, after a few years of arduous and promising labor, were obliged by sickness to return to America in 1841. They were succeeded by Mr. Bachelor, who reports a church of fourteen communicants and a nominally Christian community, including children, of a hundred souls. There is at this station at the present time a new meeting-house being erected in place of one formerly built by Mr. Noyes. A boarding school for native girls is in operation, while a few lads are studying medicine under Mr. Bachelor.

Thirty-four miles north-east of Balasore is Jellasore Patna, a second station occupied by the Freewill Baptist brethren. Mr. Phillips commenced this station in 1840, and has occupied it with indefatigable diligence and devotedness ever since. He has a good meeting-house, a church of twenty communicants, a boarding school for native Oriya boys and another for Santals. This latter people deserve special notice, as a section of aborigines whose language brother P. has reduced to writing, and taught the people to read for the first time since they were a people.

Jellasore is a large village connected with Patna, or Jellasore Patna, a large native village and bazar. It is well situated for missionary operations,—the missionary at this station being able to itinerate eastward and northward to the boundaries of the country, where the pure Oriya language amalgamates with the Bengalee, and gradually is superseded by that tongue.

The brethren in this grand division of the field ought, as soon as possible, to establish at least one other station among the Oriya population southward of Balasore. Bhudruck would probably prove a suitable place. Besides these, they should have a couple of missionaries devoted to the Santals. There are other posts which might easily be suggested. Mr. Cooley, the third missionary, has not yet fixed upon his permanent station, but has spent part of his time at each of the preceding stations. Surely the large community of Freewill Baptists do not intend to leave these important fields of labor with only three missionaries.

### *Third grand division, or Midnapore.*

Midnapore is also the name of a city and a zillah, and is situated at the north and north-east extremity of Orissa. The population of the city is a mixed multitude of Oriyas, Bengalees and Mahomedans. The Bengalee language chiefly prevails. The district is extremely populous, and extends to the banks of the Hoogly river and to the sea-shore. To the north and east of Midnapore, Bengalee is almost entirely spoken, while to the south and south-east there is a mingling of both Oriya and Bengalee, until the former gradually prevails. A missionary stationed here should be able to speak both Bengalee and Oriya, but the former is by far the most important. The Bengalee is gradually superseding the Oriya in this division of country.

Midnapore has been frequently visited by the Orissa missionaries, and in 1836 Mr. John Brooks resolved on making it his permanent station. Here he built a chapel for English worship, but was able to accomplish very little in direct missionary labor among the natives. He left to commence a new mission in Calcutta in 1841, and the station was made over to the Freewill Baptist brethren. These brethren thus remark respecting Midnapore:—

"Midnapore, though a large and important station, is at this time without a missionary, it having been the residence of Mr. Dow, who was last year obliged to return to America. This very devoted laborer had toiled hard and assiduously, and had been more than ordinarily successful in qualifying himself for preaching the gospel to the heathen, when, by a very trying and mysterious Providence, he was called to relinquish his chosen field of labor; and the tens of thousands of idolators who throng the streets of that populous city have, for the present, been left destitute of any one to break to them the bread of life. This has been a severe trial, both to the missionary himself and also to his colleagues; and they cannot but hope and pray that other laborers may soon be found ready and willing to step in and occupy this important post."

It will be seen that the Midnapore division of our field is somewhat alienated by language from the other divisions of the Orissa missionary operations, and which circumstance appears to render the propriety of its being connected with the Orissa mission somewhat doubtful. A remark or two on this point, therefore, may not be deemed inappropriate. The writer then deems it, on the whole, essential to the completeness of the Orissa mission, that Midnapore should be occupied by Baptists who sympathize with their general operations. First, because the district is connected with Orissa by geographical position, governmental regulations, and a large admixture of the Oriya people and language. Second, because missionary operations there would do much toward connecting our efforts with Calcutta, where there is also a large Oriya population, and with which city it is both desirable and unavoidably necessary that we should maintain continual religious intercourse; and then, thirdly, the real union and completeness of our sphere of labor will be effected. There are large gatherings of people at Sangur and also above Hoogly, where the Oriya laborer would find occasional profitable employ.

In relation to the necessity of acquiring an additional language, viz., the Bengalee, it may be remarked that this additional labor will, more or less, fall upon all our missionaries. Those at Berhampore would find it an advantage to be able to speak Teloogoo; others, at the central and southern stations, might feel it needful to acquire the Khund; those at Pooree, the Hindoosthanee; and those at Balasore and Jellasore, the Santal; so that, after all, the laborers are pretty nearly equalized in this respect. There is this advantage, however, in favor of the Midnapore missionary,—that he will find abundance of books and tracts in the Bengalee language ready prepared to his hand.

It may be doubtful whether the Freewill Baptists should occupy Midnapore, and the writer thinks they should not until they are able to double their number of missionaries. Until this is done, he deems it more important to establish a station south of Balasore and pay more attention also to the Santals.

To occupy this whole district efficiently, we need a sub-station at Keerpoy, Hidjeleekontai, Tumlook, and Calcutta. Here is a fine field of labor for any section of the Baptist church not as yet enlisted in the great cause of foreign missions.

### *The fourth grand division, or Berhampore.*

This embraces the most southern extremities of Orissa and large portions of the Khund territory. It may be regarded as bounded by the limits of the Ganjam Collectorate.

Ganjam, the principal town in the district, was once a very important and flourishing European settlement; the native population, it is said, amounted to seventy thousand souls, and the port was frequented by shipping from all nations. It has, however, gradually declined in importance, and the prevalence of a well-known malignant fever has greatly reduced the population. The ruins of the fort and the remains of splendid European residences attest the former grandeur of the station; but it is now no longer the civil or military head-quarters of the Government. This honor is divided betwixt Berhampore and a village lying betwixt Berhampore and Ganjam, called Chattarpore.

The town of Berhampore chiefly belongs to a native raja ; and contains, as does the whole district, a mixed population of Teloogoos and Oriyas. The location is considered far more healthy than Ganjam, and afforded a place of refuge for the European residents, and many of the natives of the latter place, during the plague of 1814. Ever since that period, it has been more or less occupied by the civil servants of Government, and has been the head-quarters of the military force of the district.

The writer first visited Berhampore in 1825. It was subsequently visited by several other brethren; at length a few individuals were baptized, and finally it was occupied as a missionary station by Mr. Brown in 1836. It has since been efficiently maintained by brethren Stubbins, Wilkinson, Buckley, and Bailey. There is at this station a good place of worship, a native church of fifty communicants, asylums for native youth of both sexes, a thriving Christian village, and lately a large tract of land has been secured, on which to locate an agricultural community of Christians.

Berhampore demands several sub-stations. Besides two missionaries for Berhampore and Ganjam, it requires two for Goomsur and Aska. These would have an opportunity of seeking the evangelization of the Khunds in that neighborhood, or rather region. Other posts doubtless might be occupied with advantage.

### *Fifth grand division, or Sumbhulpoor.*

This is the name of a large, populous town, situated in the hill districts of Orissa. It lies in the dák, or post-route from Calcutta via Midnapore to Bombay. It is the centre of a widely extended region, containing many large towns and villages. It was occupied for a short time by the American missionaries Noyes and Phillips; but scarcely had they completed their habitations, ere they were visited with severe affliction,—all were ill. Mrs. Phillips, with her infant, and a daughter of Mr. and Mrs. Noyes, died; and the rest, extremely ill, escaped to Cuttack. These friends eventually resumed their missionary work at Balasore and Jellasore.

During the residence of Messrs. Noyes and Phillips at Sumbhulpoor, the importance of the district daily grew more apparent, while the prospect of extended usefulness was very cheering. They had inquirers visit them from beyond Ruttenpore, one hundred miles further to the north-west, who spoke the Oriya language, and who asserted that it was commonly spoken in their neighborhood. This station, moreover, borders on the wide, neglected field of Gandwana, the Khund districts, the whole Cole country, and several of the independent Oriya rajuaries.

It is a vastly important field, but it demands men of a special spirit of consecration, who will brave its dangers, endure hardships, and not count their lives dear unto themselves, so that they may preach the gospel. Englishmen live there, whose sole object is to gain wealth, and obtain civil appointments; why then should not the missionary of the cross venture?

At present, however, we have more land to occupy than we have laborers to appoint to the work; and we can only hope and pray, that God will enlarge our means and raise up the men who shall be able and willing to enter on this vast field, and thus connect our stations on the plains with those on the hills.

Here is a brief outline of our mission field, and the

stations we need to establish ere we can be said to occupy the land. It will be seen that our estimate calls for about twenty-four laborers from Europe and America. These laborers, thus located, would bring their efforts to bear on nearly eight millions of souls. And surely the charge is heavy enough for this number of missionaries to sustain. Suppose that Ireland was the field, and you were sending twenty-four men to grapple with the popery and bigotry and vice of its eight millions, would or could any Christian man say, that the force was too strong?

The editor of the Friend of India, when commenting on our China mission, makes the following observations: "It may be quite true, that the number of missionaries in Orissa (10) is larger than it has been at any previous period; but still it is inadequate to the field of labor which appears to have been entrusted to the agency of the Society; and if there were twenty additional laborers, there would be work enough for them all. In the position in which the Society stands in relation to Orissa and the surrounding provinces, which may be said to embrace a country as large as England,—that is, if we extend the circle of its exertions till its missionaries come in contact with those of other societies,—it seems the dictate of wisdom to concentrate its energies on this broad field, instead of dissipating them by the occupation of distant and unconnected stations. No other Society has, for so long a period, had so large a field entirely to itself; and we cannot but think that strong obligations arise out of this state of things, the due observance of which is incompatible with a mission to China, to which all other societies are hastening. Nor should the Society forget the extreme uncertainty of life in this tropical climate, and the necessity of having so strong a body of laborers on the spot, that no circle of missionary labors shall be left entirely destitute, by the death or departure of a missionary."

*Distribution and work of Missionaries.*

The right distribution of the missionary force, and a true idea of the work of a missionary, are matters of grave importance. All the friends of missions, of every denomination of Christians, are deeply interested in this matter. It is, in the opinion of the writer, a fundamental error of nearly all missionary societies, that they attempt with totally inadequate means, a too widely extended sphere for their operations ; and an error, too, which involves a great waste of missionary strength. It is so congenial with that spirit of enlarged benevolence which the gospel cherishes in the Christian heart, to wish to make known that gospel to every creature, that it is not surprising for missionaries, in the warmth of their first affections, and for societies, in the ardor of their desire for extensive usefulness, to embrace in theory a field of labor which they are practically unable to cultivate. It is one thing to take up a map of the world, and mark out a series of missionary stations, and a range of anticipated influences, but it is quite another matter to place men in these respective stations, at from a hundred to a thousand miles apart, with the expectation that they will soon christianize the whole intermediate space, and thus work themselves into each others neighborhood and co-operation !

Our elder brethren at Serampore commenced upon this plan. They reiterated the cry, so agreeable to friends at home, and so theoretically captivating, "spread the light;" forgetful that the light of missionary zeal and usefulness resembles that of live coals, which, if kept together, may long continue to burn bright and diffuse a genial warmth, but which, if scattered, will soon become dim and cold. On this principle we find them sending one man to Agra, another to Bornio, a third to Amboyna, a fifth to Ceylon, and so on. The failure of these efforts furnishes the best comment upon this plan.

The writer begs leave here to insert an extract from the writings of the junior Baptist brethren in relation to this matter.

"As to the diffusion of missionary effort recommended, I beg to offer a few observations, especially as we are much disparaged in the public estimation for adopting different ideas and pursuing another course. Generally speaking, I should submit, that better results might ultimately be expected from a union and consolidation of missionary efforts than from their wide diffusion, unless the laws which govern men's decisions upon all other subjects be in this case utterly inapplicable. The latter may possess the present advantage of kindling expectation and giving a momentary stimulus to exertion, but the former, by making good its aims and substantiating its promises, will gradually rise in importance, will make more effective and steady impressions, and create, ultimately, a more grateful and salutary feeling upon the public mind. If it were designed to conquer India, and to bring it under equal laws and improving institutions; or to clear away its pestiferous trackless jungles, dress the soil and plant it with all that could conduce to health and beauty, would the end be better attained by dividing the strength applicable to either purpose into feeble bands, to be widely detached and cut off from the possibility of contributing to each other's succor and completing their respective designs; or by consenting to move slowly, but in such union and strength as to make good their progress and assure themselves of perfect, though distant success? I allow we may err in pressing analogies too far; but to act in defiance of them would not be less erroneous. In the principles they cherish and the designs they meditate, Christians cannot deviate too widely from men of mere secular prudence; but in adapting means to ends, and proportioning their attempts to the resources they can command, it is a reproof to Christians, if the children of this world are wiser in their generation than the children of light. In the first twenty years of onr mission in India, we never had more than eight or ten brethren devoted to the preaching of the gospel to the heathen. If they had established themselves at contiguous stations in Bengal and Hindoosthan, where two or three languages would have been found adequate to all the purposes of intercourse with 40,000,000 of population, where an almost identity of religious and civil customs prevails, and nearly the same economical detail and scale of expenditure have been applicable to all, it is plainly to be perceived that much vigor, consistence, and ultimate extension had resulted to our labors abroad, great perplexity had been spared the executive at home, and great and fruitless expenses never incurred. Instead of this, our brethren have been scattered at different times over one third of the Asiatic world—from Agra and Sirdannah in the north, to Rangoon and Ava in the east. They have gone to Java, to Ceylon, to Amboyna, and to Sumatra. Some of them forfeited experience and acquisitions of no small importance to the scene they were then occupying, to encouter difficulties equal in magnitude to those which they had already overcome; then, after years of insulated and mere inceptive labor, they are compelled by political or other changes, to quit their undertakings, with disappointed hopes and ruined health; and return, perhaps, to the very scene from which they had departed many years before. The most obvious reflection, therefore, that must strike every one from this state of things is, that to gain success in missionay labors, to produce something which will last beyond the present generation, and to give the Society a certain and lasting footing in this country, a different course must be pursued."

It should, however, be remembered, that in the case of the immortal Serampore brethren, they not only acted in accordance with the general feeling of Christians, but that their extensive labors in Bible translations called for a wide dispersion of agents, in order to put these translations into circulation. Aad moreover, at that time the Baptists alone had entered sufficiently into the work, in India, to furnish such agents. The case is very different now. Their error, if error in their case existed, was that of miscalculating the means of filling up their magnificent outline of operations. As, however, the whole Christian church is now more or less engaged in missions, the same reason for a wide distribution of the agents of any one section of the church does not exist. It has indeed become a question of deep interest and importance, whether it is not high time that some friendly arrangement should be made between the various missionary societies as to the sphere of their respective operations. A vast deal of missionary strength is wasted, and Christian love put fearfully in jeopardy by the unnecessary proximity of missionary laborers of different denominations. While "the field is" still "the world," this surely ought not to be. Certain posts and emporiums may be considered as common ground, but the general field of labor, or site of any mission, should be chosen at a suitable distance from any other. The clash of denominational opinions need not come now; and there is at least the hope, that as the Millennial year draws on, the increased piety of the church, if it do not altogether avert such clash, will at least render it comparatively innoxious. Were some amicable division of the whole mission force thus effected, would not all feel a purer, deeper interest in the prosperity of each; and moreover be ready to say, as Joab to his brother Abishai, "If the Syrians be too strong for me, then thou shalt help me; but if the children of Ammon be too strong for thee, then I will help thee"?

But leaving these general views, which in all probability will be deemed chimerical, let us confine our attention to the propriety of limiting our own efforts to the sphere of labor so signally our own, until there shall be a far greater development of our denominational resources. It is hoped that the divisions of the field, here presented, and the number of laborers required to occupy them, may suffice to show that we need seek no other field; and that it must be wrong to do so, unless it can be shown, either from the labor hitherto bestowed no adequate results have been obtained such as shall justify our keeping sole possession of the field; or that our prospects for the future are so discouraging that we can have no hope of keeping up the interest of the mission in the minds of our friends and supporters. That neither of these alternatives is true, I dare boldly affirm. It is my conscientious belief, that no Indian mission, with the same amount of labor and efficient laborers, has been more prosperous, and no field in Eastern Asia presents a more encouraging aspect than does Orissa.

Earnestly and fervently would the writer plead with his brethren on either side the Atlantic, to arouse themselves to the high duty, the glorious privilege of evangelizing this whole province. They are well able to go up and possess the whole land. Orissa, with all her millions, looks to you for the means of her deliverance. Give us, for the present, ten more men—four from England, and six from America—and we can then take possession of this wide field. Not that we suppose any given number is essential, for the Lord can save by many or by few, but such on a very moderate computation human prudence requires, for the efficient conducting of our various missionary operations.

In connection with a right distribution of the missionary force at the command of any given mission must be considered the important question, What is the specific work which a missionary should seek to accomplish, or what is the true office of the minister who is sent out by distant churches to seek the evangelization of any foreign people? The writer begs, with unfeigned diffidence, to offer an answer. And in the right answering of this question, he feels his dearest interests to be at stake.

He must, then, express his conviction that the Scriptures recognize a class of ministers distinct from the pastors of churches, and who must take precedence of them. They are called in Scripture apostles, fellow-laborers with the apostles, or missionaries and evangelists. Such were Timothy, Titus, Barnabas, Silas, and others; and such an order of men the writer is convinced ought to be fully recognized and duly provided for by the church of Christ at large. Such a class of men should be our missionaries. Not our missionary physicians, schoolmasters, printers, or translators, but our missionaries properly so called, who are sent out to preach the gospel to the heathen. These men he conceives ought not to settle down as pastors of native churches, but spend their whole time in founding churches, appointing officers to such churches, watching over them both till able to stand alone, and in general itineracy to preach far and wide the glorious gospel.

Such being a missionary's special work, his efficiency in it demands that his sphere of labor should be circumscribed within such limits as he can traverse within the time required for a vigilant superintendence of his whole field. I have, in the foregoing remarks, pointed out what I deem such limits should be in the several divisions of the Orissa Mission.

The writer would thus assign to every missionary his own sphere of labor, and give him all the helps for the cultivation of his field the state of the general mission can afford. Thus he should have a suitable proportion of the native preachers; from among these he should select pastors for the infant churches he may be successful in forming; and others he should direct to the most eligible posts for evangelical labors. The missionary would usually live at the most commanding position in his district, but should, as already observed, never take sole charge of a native church. He might appoint native assistant pastors at first, so as to leave himself free from local ties, in order to be always at liberty to visit any part of his field, to instruct, encourage, reprove, or assist his native preachers as occasion might require. On this plan, the missionary would become well acquainted with his whole work, and so dispose of his native fellow-laborers, that with the help of a small bungalow, erected at suitable locations, he would be enabled to traverse the length and breadth of his field without the labor and expense of carrying tents and heavy baggage. Thus would he not only be spared the toil of extended missionary journies, but make these short perambulations far easier than can now generally be done.

The native preachers, moreover, would be better accommodated as this plan of operations became more systematic and thorough. More permanency in our operations would thus in all probability be secured, and inquirers after Christianity receive far greater assurance than they now have, that they would not be left as sheep without a shepherd, provided they joined the Christian flock. In case of the absence of a brother from his field, on account of sickness or any other cause, the work need not stop as it now must; for, either a junior brother might keep up his system of operations for a time, or a neighboring missionary might pay an occasional visit to encourage and direct the native preachers, or even take the general oversight of the district till the brother returned. The missionaries, too, having fewer local ties, would be able to leave their posts for mutual consultation or more frequent social intercourse; and so, though in some respects more isolated than on the present plan, they would really, as a body, oftener see each other and feel more intimately connected. This is a desideratum. The writer has been so confined to his own sphere of labors as scarcely ever to see some of his fellow-laborers in Orissa during the course of seven years, —their whole term of missionary service. And not to prolong these remarks, each missionary would, on this plan, have sole control of his own field of labor, while able to consult his brethren on equal terms. A matter, as experience shows, of first rate importance, and without which it seems impossible, in congregational missions, to secure mutual harmony and cordial coöperation.

## CHAPTER XIII.

The missionary a man of all work—Kind of men needed—Medical aid—Charitable efforts—Temporal improvement of native converts—Education—Literary labors—English preaching—Itineracy.

The benevolent, though eccentric Rowland Hill, when describing the qualifications of a missionary, is reported to have said, "He ought to be a man of all work; he should know how to preach a sermon and make a wheelbarrow." This description is more applicable to the laborers among the savage tribes of the Pacific, or of Africa and America, than to those laboring among the people of India, yet it is not without some point of application to the latter. Certainly it is not altogether inapplicable to the Orissa missionaries. The fact is, the field is so wide and the work to be done so various, that no talent or ability a man may possess can be useless, provided he have also a warm heart and a wise head to direct its employment. This remark bears on the inquiry so often proposed, as to "Who are suitable men for the mission field?" I answer, we need the best men in every sense. We require the most diligent and profound students; the most eloquent preachers; the most able expositors of Scripture; the most keen logicians; the ablest mathematicians; the very best linguists; men with great zeal and equal prudence; men of first rate physical and mental stamina; the most devoted Christians and the most accomplished gentlemen. None are too good to be the successors of apostles and prophets, and the ambassadors of the Son of God.

It will be no drawback, in many cases, to have a

knowledge of surgery, medicine, printing, mechanics; nor to be well skilled in botany, chemistry, or any other branch of physical science. But we do not expect to find all these combined in any individual, and we have reason for thankfulness that one talent along with love to Christ and a desire to do good, can be well employed; while, should we have many given us, full scope will be found for the employment of them all. We want good men rather than (as is usually understood) great men; men who are content to do the Lord's work in the Lord's way, leaving the worldly wise to experiment in all manner of novelties.

It is a grave question with the writer how far Missionary Societies are justified in sending out missionary physicians, and schoolmasters, and printers, and mechanics, and farmers, &c., &c.; and yet more so, whether they are justified in embarrassing their home deliberations with questions about mission property, houses, lands, and vessels. He is disposed to think that it will be the prelude to good times when such Societies shall confine themselves to the simple object of selecting and sustaining *preachers of the gospel to the heathen* and not stir beyond this; leaving the agents they send forth to originate and direct, though not to own, funds for the mental or physical improvement of the people among whom they labor. In short, to do the best they can to evangelize, and, then, by the help of the people, civilize the nation. The missionary himself, however, must, in most cases, be the centre of various benevolent operations, the main-spring which sets to work numerous important agencies. Hence he should not unnecessarily encumber himself with the details of matters which others may do just as well. As already observed, we would not have him take the oversight of any individual church, but be the overseer of all he can succeed in forming in his district. While he makes his influence felt in many ways, and becomes the friend of all that is true, honest, just, pure, lovely and of good report, great caution is necessary lest he be tempted to forget, or hold in subordination his one work, preëminently his, viz.,—to seek the salvation of the souls of the people. Let them become Christians, and all desirable advancement in most other things will be effected with comparative ease.

We shall devote this chapter to an enumeration of those miscellaneous efforts which missionaries are called upon to make; some of them we had intended to illustrate at greater length, but, as in other cases, we must study brevity.

1. The bodily ailments of the people demand a large portion of the missionaries' time and attention. Our earliest journals detail our daily attempts at alleviating the miseries induced by the car festival as well as ordinary calls upon us for the relief of the sick and afflicted. The late Mr. Peggs completely broke down in his attempts thus to alleviate the sorrows of suffering humanity. A large portion of the time of some of our missionaries is yet daily devoted to this matter.

Mr. Bachelor, at Balasore, being a medical man, has not only exceeded us all in systematic labors of this kind, but has undertaken the training of a class of medical students. His colleague, Mr. Phillips, at Jellasore, living by the side of the pilgrim road, where no assistance for the wretched wanderers can be had, has also established a small hospital. We insert a few passages from the report of each of these brethren.

Mr. Bachelor writes:—

Medicines have been dispensed to all who have applied, and surgical operations performed, for the last nine years. These applicants have usually been poor; such as were not able to pay for medical advice. The pilgrims, on their return from Jugernath, have usually afforded a large number of patients; and many come from remote parts of the district, as well as from the town and vicinity of Balasore. During the last year, the number of applicants has very much increased, in consequence, probably, of the introduction of chloroform. A few successful operations under its influence seemed to establish the confidence of the people to an extent never before known,—not only in regard to surgical operations, but also in the use of European medicines generally.

A small medical class was formed about the commencement of the year, composed of young men from different parts of the province. They are pursuing a course of study sufficiently thorough, it is hoped, to enable them to practice medicine and surgery with success, according to European principles.

In the absence of medical books, a lecture has been delivered daily, which each student has copied out for future reference; and these, when the course is completed, will embrace a sufficient amount of information to enable them to perform the duties of their calling with acceptance. They have rendered great assistance in the Dispensary,—most of the labor of preparing and dispensing the medicines having been performed by them.

Ten students composed the class last year. Of these, one has taken charge of the hospital at Jellasore, and three have left without completing their course of study. Three have also joined the class the present year, making the present number nine.

The expense of medicines was in former years defrayed by contributions received at this station; but in consequence of the increase of patients, and the additional expenses of the medical class, we have been under the necessity of soliciting assistance from the friends of the cause at neighboring stations, which has been most promptly rendered.

It is true that all this does not save the soul, neither, in itself considered, does it advance the sinner a single step in the way to heaven; but it affords many opportunities of communicating religious truth which could not otherwise be enjoyed, and that, too, when the heart is softened by affliction and sorrow. The comparative good that may result will only be known in eternity; and having done what seems to be our duty, we would wait with humility and patience for the blessing of Him who alone is able to render our feeble efforts for advancing his cause successful.

| | |
|---|---|
| Number of cases treated during the year, . . . | 2,407 |
| Surgical operations, . . . . . . . . . . . . | 126 |
| Operations under the influence of chloroform, . | 12 |

Mr. Phillips writes:—

The liberality of friends has enabled us to establish a small hospital at this station the past year. The need of an institution of this kind had long been felt. Numbers of sick and destitute pilgrims had yearly been sent to pine away and die by the way-side, unsheltered and unattended in the time of their greatest need. This was the more requisite at Jellasore, as, not being an European station, no provision is made by the public authorities for the relief of this class of sufferers; and the universal practice of Hindoo shopkeepers, to expel travellers from their premises when they fall ill, especially if they are in a state of destitution, greatly aggravates the evil. A small cottage, containing three rooms, has been erected in a dry, airy spot, which has afforded shelter to rather more than twenty sick pilgrims the past year. The number of pilgrims, and the amount of sickness among them, were much less than in ordinary years.

2. The poor we have always with us, and no Christian can refuse to do them good. Hence the missionary feels a special claim upon him for a portion of his time to be employed in benevolent societies, in obtaining and dispensing funds, and visiting the destitute.

For many years some of us had a weekly assembly of lame, halt, leprous, blind, &c., to whom we gave alms and preached the gospel. The writer was made the almoner of more than one generous individual, for the relief of poor Christians. A benevolent society has for years been well supported at Cuttack, (and probably at some of our other stations,) which has shared more or less of our services, though when a chaplain has been at the station, it has usually been consigned to his superintendence.

Mrs. Lacey has for many years taken a benevolent interest in poor Christian families, and while it has not been neglected by others, has probably done more in this especial department than all the rest. A stock of child-bed linen, &c., has usually been under her charge, with which she has supplied those needing such aid.

3. The temporal improvement of our native converts is a matter calling for much anxiety and effort on the part of the missionary. Converts who lose all for Christ's sake, cannot be left to starve unaided; but to assist them without cherishing improper motives; to foster habits of self-dependence and enterprise; and to adapt the improvements of the West to the circumstances of the East, is no small undertaking. Besides there are extremes to be avoided in this matter. It is not every European or American improvement that would be of advantage to a Hindoo, nor is their state of civilization the best for India. Most absurd notions are entertained on this subject by Christians in both these countries. The writer has been often amused and sometimes vexed at the ridiculous earnestness with which questions in relation to this matter are proposed. Let the people be evangelized, and they will readily make all desirable advancement in imitation of European manners and customs. The minister's great work is to seek to bring them to Christ.

4. The promotion of education among the people is another legitimate branch of missionary benevolence. He feels himself called upon to take a prominent place in this department. He is the friend of truth, and, therefore, all branches of learning should find a friend

in him, though religious truth, and consequently religious education, has his whole-hearted concurrence. The missionaries of India have probably furnished four-fifths of its school literature. The missionaries of Orissa have furnished every school book in the Oriya language. They established the first English school, which, as the report for 1842 says, is now merged in the Government school. "Thus after running its useful course for seventeen years, distributing the stream of knowledge through many parts of this desert province, the stream has swollen to a river, whose waters, if less limpid, will yet form a vaster body, swelling on we trust with increasing power, and bearing on their bosom the ark of knowledge through the length and the breadth of the land."

Reference is had elsewhere to our vernacular schools. One of the brethren has felt called upon to devote a portion of his time to the translating of various documents and legal enactments for Government, not as a matter of choice, but duty, under the circumstances of the case, and may yet continue to do so. Thus did Dr. Carey, the leader of the missionary band in India.

Again, the preparation of grammars and dictionaries, the translation of the word of God, the preparation and printing of religious tracts, are all so many departments of labor devolving on the missionary. The church has ever been the patroness of learning. Even the papacy, amidst all its bigotry and blindness, has proved the conservatory of what remains to us of ancient learning, and though it has destroyed much, has preserved, through the dark ages, most of what we yet have of classic Greece and Rome. "When the light of the Reformation penetrated her gloomy cloisters, it revealed her in the attitude of a fond mother pressing to her lifeless bosom this last cherished object of her fondest affection."

The Cuttack mission press was established in 1838. On this subject we furnish a few extracts from a report prepared for the Orissa conference.

Closely connected with the translating is the printing department. Our mission this year presents a new and interesting feature in the establishment of a printing office in connection with our mission, and in the centre of Orissa. It may not be deemed inappropriate in our first report of this department of missionary labor to quote the remarks of the "Friend of India."

"Orissa. — We have received a copy of a tract printed at Cuttack at the press which the missionaries have this year established at that station. It is printed in the Oriya character, and for neatness of execution is not exceeded by any similar brochure which has issued from the Metropolitan presses in Calcutta. It does no little credit to those to whose feelings of public spirit and Christian benevolence the district is now indebted for an efficient press. The establishment of a press in any province is an important era in its history. It is delightful therefore to contemplate the rapid increase of the means of intellectual and religious improvement through means of this mighty engine in the various and even remote provinces of this empire. We now witness the establishment of presses at the opposite extremities of the Bengal presidency through the spirited exertions of missionaries, but for whose labors those provinces might long have remained destitute of them. Looking down to the southernmost of the provinces, we find a press set up in the country of Orissa."

"We rejoice that a press has been established in that country, capable of executing any work in the Oriya language and character. The extent to which the language is used has only been discovered of late. We find that it is spoken and written through an extent of country three hundred miles in breadth from the sea, to one hundred miles in length west of Sumbhulpore, and more than two hundred miles in breadth from Midnapore, where it melts into Bengalee, to Ganjam, where it meets the Teloogoo. It was indispensable therefore to the completeness of missionary operation to that kingdom, that means should be provided on the spot for multiplying books in a language so extensively used. But why should the benefits of this local press be confined to missionary operations? Why should not Government avail itself of the means of communication with the people which have thus been provided, by publishing its own acts and notifications through the same channel? We know that a strong disposition exists in the highest quarter to provincialize the public service in Orissa. It is the wish of Government, that those who are appointed to this province should apply themselves earnestly to the acquisition of the vernacular tongue, and should move in a circle of promotion within the province itself. In this arrangement there is much wisdom. But to render it efficient, it is necessary to follow it up by the translation of all orders, which the people are required to understand and act on, into their own language, and by a liberal use of the press which has now been established in the province."

Two presses have ever since been kept in operation, and a large number of useful works published, under the management of Mr. W. Brooks.

5. Labors in English.

The cause of missions, apart from its direct object, which is the evangelization of the heathen, scatters numberless blessings in its track. Among these may be mentioned the benefits it incidentally imparts to our "kinsmen according to the flesh." Many a son and daughter of Christian parents, or those who have been born and nurtured in a Christian land, have gone forth hardened in sin and neglect of religion, to find in a heathen country the precious gospel they so long heard at home but to slight. At this moment there are before the throne a host of living witnesses to the value and importance of these incidental labors of missionaries, both in heathen lands and when travelling to and from their distant stations.

It has been already stated, that the Orissa missionaries early commenced preaching in English for the benefit of their own mission families and any residents at their stations who were disposed to attend their services. In this they have the sanction of the great apostle to the gentiles, who felt himself to be a debtor both to the Jew and to the Greek; and who ever seemed willing to make known the everlasting gospel to his fellow members of the stock of Israel. The precise course, however, which missionaries should follow in relation to English preaching, is by no means agreed upon by missionaries themselves, or by their fellow Christians in India. English preaching is doubtless a snare to some missionaries, and there is danger of their being either wholly or too much drawn away from their proper work by over attention to it. In ordinary cases, one service on the Lord's day is as much as they can with propriety devote to this purpose; but where there are several European missionaries at a station, and a considerable number of hearers unprovided for, another service may be afforded. It should, however, be kept constantly in mind, that to preach the gospel to the heathen are we sent, and while we should never allow English services to interfere with or lessen the efficiency of native services, there should be constant efforts made to raise the character and deepen the interest of native services. And in cases where there is a mixture of language, especial care should be taken not to throw the native portion of the service into the back ground.

When there happens to be a chaplain at the same station as the missionary, the difficulty of deciding as to the path of duty becomes more perplexing. Some, especially those who have adopted Puseyite sentiments, would join with the chaplain in saying, at once and decidedly, that the missionary ought not to preach in English; and certainly he should not do so when the chaplain is at the station, engaged in regular divine services. A brief statement of the case, however, will suffice to show that the path of duty for the missionary is, after all, not so clear. I cannot, perhaps, do better than state the facts of the case in relation to Cuttack.

The missionaries entered that city in 1822, and at once commenced their English services. Up to that time there had been no attention whatever paid to the outward observance of the Sabbath. In 1826, they built their first house of prayer for English worshippers. In the following year, or soon after, the first chaplain was appointed to the province. His sphere of labor as chaplain extended from Midnapore to Pooree, that is, four English stations, at which he was expected in turns to officiate. He was, moreover, though an able, it is no breach of charity to say, a profane man, and was subsequently unfrocked, and sent back to England in disgrace.

After an interval of several years, a second chaplain was appointed. A man of the old black letter school, who was not likely either to attract the people to church, or benefit them when there. The character I have given him is fully brought out in his subsequent quarrel with the bishop. Again, after an interval of years, a third chaplain was appointed, the best certainly that ever was stationed at Cuttack. He was more evangelical than any of his predecessors, and was desirous of doing good, but he unfortunately was not a popular minister, and his own people sought every opportunity of attending worship with us. Again, after his decease another interval of being without a chaplain occurred, when at last a fiery Puseyite appeared for a few times, denouncing us and our efforts, and in love with nothing, seemingly, but popery. He was followed by a stationary chaplain, also a Puseyite, whose intemperate living soon brought him to the grave. And, lastly, he was succeeded by a fashionable young sprig of divinity, also a rank Puseyite, but who fixed his head quarters at Midnapore, and paid Cuttack but an occasional visit. He was removed before the writer left and the station was again without a chaplain. Thus during a period of twenty years, the station was for nearly or quite ten years without a chaplain, and in the ten years in which it was supplied, there were half a dozen changes. Those who are acquainted with the importance of regularity in religion, and have had experimental acquaintance with the fact, that growth in piety is nothing more than a series of moral repetitions, will need no argument to prove that such fitful services will not suffice, even supposing that the chaplains had been all evangelical and able men.

Some of these men, however, as is the case at other stations, were decidedly opposed to the gospel, as an evangelical scheme, and to us as its ministers. With them neither ourselves or the spiritual portion of the lay community could have any fellowship. And, in most cases, the exclusive claims put forth by them declared too plainly that it was not to us, as laboring in English merely they were opposed, but to our whole ministerial character. We could not, therefore, "Give place by subjection" to such men, "no, not for an hour," lest the truth of the gospel should be sacrificed. For whatever may be a man's pretensions, if he have not the spirit of Christ, he is none of his. For the honor of divine truth, therefore, for our own sakes, our families' sakes, and the benefit of mankind, we felt constrained to continue our labors.

The purpose, however, with which this chapter was commenced, was not to justify the missionaries in their occasional or stated efforts to benefit their own countrymen, but to furnish some illustration of their usefulness in this department. It has already been stated that the church records contain a goodly list of individuals, European and East Indian, who have been benefited by their labors and added to the church at Cuttack. These are exclusive of those who have been baptized and added to our churches in other parts of the province. Among these names appear the civil servants of the Honorable Company, with the commissioned and non-commissioned officers of their army. Perhaps a still larger number have been benefited by our services, who have not embraced our views as Baptists; for proselytism has never been our leading purpose. The writer can assert for himself that he scarcely preached twice on baptism in the course of twenty years. Each of these mission chapels may be regarded as a spiritual fountain in a heathen desert. And here many a Christian pilgrim has paused to refresh his wearied spirit, and gathered fresh strength for the prosecution of his heavenward journey.

In the early days of the Cuttack mission, the fort, now dismantled and in ruins, was used as an arsenal, and an establishment of Europeans and natives kept up. On one occasion four individuals were appointed for this purpose, in the ordinance department, that is, two Europeans and their wives. They had been well known as leading men in the Dum-dum theatre, and one of them was a favorite performer, at least such was the report which preceded their arrival at Cuttack. The fears of the writer and his colleague were much excited as to the probable ill effects of their influence among our religious community, or at least those who appeared well disposed. Nor I trust were we forgetful that "in God was all our hope." The mother of one of these men,—the actor,—was a pious woman, and often in her letters said to her son, "Henry, if ever you are stationed near any of the missionaries, go and hear them preach." He did so; the word was quick and powerful; he became a new man in Christ Jesus, and ere he left Cuttack, not himself only, but his wife and the other two individuals also, were converted, baptized, and added to the church. So much better was God to us than our fears.

The wife of Mr. B. had been brought up as a Roman Catholic, and I have often heard her say that her father on one occasion held a drawn sword over her head, while he made her swear that she would never become a Protestant. This oath troubled her for some time after she experienced the truth as it is in Jesus; but at length she felt that taken as it was in ignorance and extorted by compulsion, it ought not to prevent her obeying the express command of Christ; accordingly she arose and was baptized.

Mr. B. soon gave evidence of talents for the ministry, and we at first hoped to see him unite with our department of the Baptist mission. Circumstances however prevented this, and he was received by our Calcutta brethren, and by them appointed to a station where for many years himself and wife have labored faithfully for Christ.

The writer has before him a pile of letters from which he had thoughts of making extracts, but he forbears. These letters are written by gentlemen and ladies in every grade of standing in the Indian community, and many of whose names would do honor to his pages. The sentiments of Christian liberality and of exalted piety which many of them breathe, along with the unostentatious generosity they disclose, are refreshing to the soul. But we know they were not written for the public eye, and we may not therefore gratify far distant readers by their publication. They shall be consigned to their long inherited privacy with the prayer, may we at length

> " On yonder green and flowery mount
> Through grace abounding, meet ;
> And with transporting joy recount
> The labors of our feet."

6. In our enumeration of the means employed for the evangelization of Orissa, missionary journeys were spoken of as occupying a prominent place. We would fain devote a chapter to this subject, but have barely room for a few paragraphs.

In Bengal, and other parts of northern India, much missionary itineracy may be performed in boats, and this is certainly by far the most comfortable mode of travelling. In Orissa, but few journeys can be so performed, though the writer has thus accomplished several of an interesting character. Some of the branches of the Mahanudi, of the Brahmunee, of the Subhanreeka, and especially the Chilka lake, afford facilities for such journeyings. Our boats are usually flat-bottomed, and either propelled by poles or dragged by ropes ; of course our progress is slow, and the route generally circuitous, while there is constant interruption for want of sufficient depth of water. Such journeys are, however, beneficial to the invalid and the man of sedentary employments. Still the shallowness of most of our streams, and the wide belt of sand over which the traveller must pass before he can reach the shore, are considerable drawbacks to this mode of travelling, Our usual plan is, for the missionary to ride on horseback, and his wife, if she accompany him, travels in a palanquin or tonjohn. Sometimes, however, as has been intimated, our ladies ride on horseback. We usually travel about eight or ten miles from stage to stage, unless we have any particular place we wish to reach. Our journey is made generally before breakfast, so that we rise early, strike our tent, send off our baggage, and start by day-break. We then rest for a day or two, as the circumstances of the neighborhood demand or invite. In long journeys we travel night and morning.

As there is rarely any shelter to be met with, and the natives will not, except in special cases, admit us to their houses, or even their out-buildings, we can seldom dispense with taking our tent. Our furniture and baggage generally consists of a cot, a couple of camp-stools or chairs, a small table, changes of clothes, cooking apparatus, provisions, knives, forks, plates, spoons, &c., a box of books, and a few medicines. Some carry a gun and ammunition; others of us depend on the supplies we meet with, or carry a few fowls, &c., with us. Sometimes our apparatus is conveyed on a native bullock-cart, at others it is carried by coolies on their heads. Our native preachers and servants go on foot. If there be opportunities of preaching on the road, the missionary often walks with them the whole or part of the way. In such cases the servants should go on and prepare breakfast, while the preaching party continue their perigrinations till about ten o'clock. If the wife be of the party, she usually goes forward, and superintends the needful preparation, so that the heartily wished-for meal is ready by the time the tired laborers can wash, and prepare for it. Then, unless there be any inducement to go out again, the party rest till the heat abates, when they sally forth and continue their labors till dark.

These labors are often very pleasant and useful. They bring the missionary in contact with classes of people he could never meet with elsewhere, or, if he could, he would be unable to address them as he can in their own villages and rural abodes. Often does he feel, in prosecuting his journey from hamlet to hamlet, through paddy fields and jungles, that he is treading in the footsteps of the Son of God. His heart is elevated, his conceptions of the moral dignity of his work are enlarged, and he rises superior to all the glare and glitter of earth, and man's false estimate of true greatness. Still, these journeyings are often very trying to flesh and blood—there is little poetry in them. The badness of the road, the difficulty of procuring supplies, the reluctance of the people to afford assistance, the inclemency often of the weather, the absence of all official authority to command needed aid, as changes of bearers, carts, coolies, or other means of conveyance, and many such things, often try the strength and patience of the itinerant. He therefore finds it necessary to dispense with all superfluities, to travel as light as possible and with very little dependence on others.

The Orissa missionaries have ever been characterized by their devotion to this department of missionary labor. Messrs. Lacroix and Mullins, in their lecture on the Orissa mission, remark — "The preaching of the gospel in the vernacular language, has been the great means employed by the missionaries in Orissa. They have not neglected the preparation of a Christian literature, the translation of the bible, the printing of tracts, or the education of youth ; but public preaching in all parts of the country has always been considered by them a first and chief duty." After other remarks, laudatory of our missionaries in applying the native language and mythology to the purpose of the evangelization of the people, they add—"The Orissa mission may justly claim the title of the great preaching mission of Bengal." "We mention

these things, not to unduly praise the instruments of God's mercy to a heathen land, but to show how successfully the native language, native illustrations and modes of thought, and a knowledge of the native system, may be acquired by English missionaries who take up this matter as their one great subject of study, and the one great vehicle of preaching the gospel to Hindoos." We cannot but be obliged to our brethren of another denomination for this generous testimony. The writer hopes, however, it is not so exclusively due to the Orissa missionaries. There are some in Bengal and other parts of India, he knows, who are like-minded, while several of his brethren of the American Baptist mission on the eastern side of the bay of Bengal have equalled, if not exceeded us, in this mode of evangelical labor.

[The writer's sentiments on this important matter are still further expressed in a paper in the Calcutta periodicals, headed, Desultory thoughts on Itineracy, and in another, entitled the Necessity for a Revival of Primitive Missionary Agency. He avows the authorship of the latter piece, as it has given rise to some controversy, and the character of the writer has been entirely misconceived.]

The following quotation, referring to the whole subject of preaching the gospel to the heathen in India, written by a missionary no longer in the field, contains sentiments so just and appropriate that we cannot forbear appending them to this chapter.

But let all know, who may henceforth embark in this work, that the simple and legitimate object of missionary pursuit in India, as in all other countries, will prove to be one essentially humiliating. It will not unfrequently be holden in light estimation by their fellow countrymen, though of enlightened minds and honorable deportment; while the natives, though commending you to adulation for other pursuits, will condemn this as unnecessary and futile; nay, disdain it as a ludicrous departure from all dignified and rational proceeding. A distaste to it is easily insinuated into the mind even of a missionary, especially in a country where other lines of occupation, not seemingly very alien to its success, solicit a portion of attention. The approach to it is very gradual, somewhat rugged and foiling. To submit, as every one beginning his work must do, to utter truths, or rather fractions of truth, in imperfect sentences; and to have these retorted in jibes and sarcasms, or abruptly encountered by objections subtilly conceived and proverbially expressed, will be found to supply no ordinary trial to some of those graces it is among the choicest purposes of the missionary office to inculcate. There is no pursuit, from the highest literary undertaking to teaching the meanest native school, or the composition of the humblest manual, that will not secure a readier countenance or an easier state of feeling.

It is a work, moreover, the results of which may prove more tardy and partial, and which it may be more difficult to estimate than those of any other. You may teach a child to read, and easily ascertain with what degree and with what kind of success. But to conflict single-handed with the darkness and the vices of adult heathens, who have been schooled in error and so perverted in moral sense, and obdurated in heart, that truth and falsehood, holiness and sin, heaven and hell, are mere sportive sounds, is a work commenced, sustained, and ended with toil. A thousand distinct and painful efforts may be required without producing a single instance of palpable or even apparent success. In reporting, it admits of little garnish and variety, and will supply but moderate interest to the page of missionary record at home; often not enough to gratify even the laudable anticipations of the Society that sent him forth, whose command of public patronage is generally more determined by showing the successful issues of missionary enterprise, than by describing those many and tedious efforts indispensable to their production. Hence a missionary, to avoid disappointment, should look for solace alone in his proper work, and in his Master's smiles, and suspend the smallest portion of his happiness upon the estimation in which he may be holden even by the wise and good. Instances might be adduced, of persons, not alone in one community, possessing excellent capabilities, and laboring to the utmost that time and strength allowed, yet little known or commended until death closed their career; while others, who were intent rather upon wide schemes which were more likely to be admired than achieved, and to dazzle than prove useful, have been seen riding upon their high places.

Santal House.

# CHAPTER XIV.

Choga and its surrounding scenery—Village scenes—Rural habits—Introduction of the gospel—Bamadeb—Pursua—Opening of a new chapel.

The establishment of Christian villages in the midst of a heathen population marks a decisive inroad upon the empire of darkness. It affords an opportunity for the exhibition of many of the characteristic social influences of the gospel which cannot otherwise be displayed. Such a stage of progress is exceedingly cheering to the missionary's heart, and affords him a sort of foretaste of the joy which his successors will realize in full measure. The brethren of the London Missionary Society, to whom reference has several times been made, visited Choga, or rather one of our Christian villages in that vicinity. They remark, "Choga is in more senses than one a lovely spot, standing out prominently from the wide cultivated plain, as the neat native houses appear embowered in trees with the little sanctuary in their midst, it involuntarily reminds the Christian journeying towards it of the church of Christ. 'A little spot enclosed by grace out of the world's wide wilderness.' While the clean, orderly and busy population; the neat and well-swept houses; the large store-houses for grain; the quiet Sabbath; the joyful assembly gathered for worship and listening to God's word, as expounded by a minister once a heathen like themselves, are proofs incontestible that the gospel can change the Ethiopian skin and make the miserable sinner happy. The name of this village is Oodoyapoor, the village of the dawn. May the broad light of day shine upon it and shine from it. May the Spirit of God

plant many an oasis like it among the abominations of Orissa."

Thus far our brethren. Now let a person imagine himself seated beneath the embowering shade which crowns the hill where the abovenamed chapel stands. He may from this elevation see spread around him, far as the eye can reach, numerous little villages and hamlets located amidst dank grass and brushwood and overshadowed by the mangoe, the tamarind, the banian, and various species of acacia. Here cluster the plantain and the castor oil tree, and there towers many a graceful palm. Far away stretches the interminable jungle, and so luxurious is its growth, that the comparatively sparse population can scarcely restrain its encroaches upon the limits of the professedly cultivated patches.

Should the observer pass through any one of these villages at early morn, he would hear, as he passes on, the heavy thump of the dhinkee, or rice pounder, at which the females of the family are already laboring in order to prepare the daily supply. A few lazy pariah dogs will perhaps rouse themselves from the ashes, where they have made their nightly bed, and annoy him by crabbed growls or yells. As he gains the outskirts of the village, he will see the men each with his lota or waterpot prowling about, or squatting by some neighboring pool or ditch cleaning his teeth. He cannot fail to remark on the dilapidated character of many of the houses, the strong smell of closely packed cattle, the general air of untidyness and an all-pervading appearance of discomfort.

Should there be an idol temple near the village, as there is at both ends of heathen Choga, most likely the officiating brahmun will be seen going or returning with a shuffling gait and dripping clothes, holding in his hand the sacrificial dish, or a few flowers, and muttering his morning formula as he proceeds.

Let us, however, suppose our observer reseated on the mount about the time of sunrising. Soon will he be struck with the dense mass of misty clouds gathering in layers over the paddy fields and anon moving majestically westward, lingering for a brief space over the interminable forest, and then rolling up the mountain side till here and there a solitary stray patch alone remains. The sun now gilds the mountain top, the pea fowl and jungle fowl begin to retreat to their wild home, and man goes forth to his labor from the morning until the evening.

It is worth while to linger here and notice a little more in detail the leading features and characteristics of the Oriya peasantry. The Oriya husbandman, or ryot, induces any thing but an idea of cheerful labor. He looks, poor, idle, spirit-broken and apathetic. The miserable yoke of oxen he drives before him, are the mere skeletons of quadrupeds, and scarcely have animation enough to drag the primitive apology for a plough, to which they are attached. The dogged master knows that his crop is mortgaged before it is ripe for the sickle, and that it will only be by a succession of shifts and abject duplicity he shall be able to secure such a scanty moiety as will suffice to feed his family. If by rare good fortune he obtain more than this, a hundred hungry applicants, in the shape of brahmuns, astrologers, shopkeepers, Government officers, and leeches of all sorts, will stick to him till the uttermost cowrie has been extracted.

About 10 or 11 o'clock he returns home and bathes preparatory to his first meal. He repairs to the nearest ditch, pond or stream, as the case may be, and dips himself, if water sufficient, all over. Perhaps he has wisdom enough to utter a few vain repetitions, and pour out a drink-offering to the sun, and then with folded hands bows down his head in adoration. Perhaps he calls at some neighboring temple of Mahadaiv and prostrates himself before the image, or it may be he does this to the village goddess, a mere heap of stones; or else he pours out half the contents of his waterpot at the foot of some banian or pipul tree, as his act of morning devotion.

His wife, then, in a very dirty cloth, first serves out his meal, next supplies the children, and, lastly, goes out to bathe herself, in order that she may take her own breakfast. The man then smokes his cigar, and lies down to sleep; unless, indeed, he is summoned away on some village duties, or to meet some importunate creditor.

While the observer is thus surveying from his elevation the movements of the ryot, his ears will be assailed by the most uncouth chant of the village school. At the very top of their voices he will hear the naked urchins vociferating Ka kha, ga gha, gnooa; kabba khabba gabba ghabba; ka ká, ki kee, ko kung, &c. &c., from treble to base and base to treble, making the strangest bedlam noise imaginable. Yet amidst all this confusion, the uproarious pupils make real progress in writing and enunciating the extremely artificial, yet consistent and complete collocation of vocables.

The middle of the day is its quietest part. When all who can, young and old, male and female, take a long, quiet nap, or recline leisurely in the coolest spot the house affords. A strange stillness every where prevails. The very birds and brutes seem to join with one consent in the general truce to all exertion, and retire to the neighboring jungle or thickest foliage.

As the heat abates, the husbandman again crawls forth to his work in the fields, or perhaps finds employ at home in preparing a load of corn, straw or wood for conveyance to the market in the early morning. Many, both men and women, may be seen at early dawn wending their zigzag way through paddy-fields or plots of tall grass, with such burdens on their heads, from the neighborhood of Choga towards Cuttack. The village schoolmaster now again resumes his noisy occupation, and continues it till dark. The Oriya wife, or widow, seats herself at the cottage door with her rude spinning-wheel. The younger branches of the family spread themselves over the neighboring fields or plains, to collect the all-important cow-dung, which is brought home, kneaded into cakes, and either stuck against a sunny wall or spread on the grass to dry. The cows then come streaming home to be shut up for the night, and milked next morning ere they are turned out for the day's rumination. The crows and birds of various kinds now cluster on some favorite bush or tree, and then file off for their roost. The fire-fly lights up his brilliant lamp, and flits through the trees in graceful though eccentric movements. The jackal's horrid yell is heard, and the shouts of the watcher in the surrounding fields, driving off the intruding wild beasts, announce that night has fully set in.

The people now eat their second, and usually their best meal, then stretch themselves on the mat for their night's repose. Occasionally, however, groups are formed to hear one of their number read some favorite legend or to unite in some uproarious ditty. In the temple, perhaps, the loud clang of pooja is long kept up, and the stentorian voice of the attendant brahmun is heard shouting Ram Ram, or Jugernath, or Hey Mahadaib, as the case may be. On special occasions, a party will assemble in the temple porch, and loud and long is the clangor and uproar, while doing honor to the god, or themselves.

But gradually the last sound dies away, and deep stillness every where prevails. It is a stillness which may be felt.

To such sounds and sights as these the writer has often been witness at Choga. Into this village and its neighborhood the gospel has been introduced. Its location is within the territory of the Athgur raja, subject to the general control of the Cuttack commissioner. The place, though not much more than six miles distant from Cuttack, is difficult of access, having to cross the river, travel through a dense jungle, and over paddy-fields and plots of beni grass in order to reach it. As one of the brethren remarks, "I rarely go without thinking, surely if God had not begun the work here, men would never have selected such a spot." The whole aspect of the country is wild in the extreme, and the people generally very ignorant and boorish in their manners. One of our earliest converts, Bamadeb, was from this neighborhood, and he has a number of relatives still residing there. Some of them are bitter enemies to the gospel, though others have of late manifested a change of feeling, and are on the eve of making a Christian profession.

We insert a few brief notices of this brother.

### *Brief Notice of Bamadeb.*

Bamadeb was a disciple of the old gooroo previously mentioned. From him he received his first imperfect acquaintance with Christianity, and a couple of Christian tracts. As in many other instances which have come to our knowledge, these little messengers of mercy to benighted man, broke up the foundations of Hindooism in his mind, and at once let in light that could not be again expelled. Their first effect seems to be to convey an idea of moral responsibility, of exposedness to condemnation, of provision made in the gospel for man's depravity, of which they never before could form any idea. And beginning with these elementary truths, they are led on gradually to higher attainments by every additional tract they obtain or discourse they hear, though they are so entangled with the fundamentally erroneous notions of Hindooism in its extended ramifications, that it is long ere they can wholly escape, and enjoy the liberty of divine truth. So it was with Bamadeb. He obtained other tracts, and at length the New Testament. The old gooroo sent him on a message to the missionaries at Cuttack, where he obtained further light. He sought out his old associates in the service of the gooroo, who had embraced Christianity, and at length resolved himself to embrace it. This determination aroused the enmity and zeal of his friends and neighbors. Having ascertained that he had gone to Cuttack to profess Christianity, they followed him in a body; and, failing by promises or threatenings to move him from his purpose, they carried him off bodily. As he himself graphically expresses it, "Just as men take a corpse by the arms and legs and head, so they, seizing hold of me, carried me off. In the struggle, they tore off my clothes; and thus naked they bore me away, now cursing and now abusing both me and the Saviour I loved." He was rescued, however, by the interposition of the magistrate, and allowed to do as he pleased. He therefore at once embraced the gospel, and joined himself to the little company of baptized believers at Cuttack. His wife and children soon joined him, though deterred at first; and he now ranks among our ordained preachers of the gospel.

Here is a man, born and reared in perfect heathenism, who with his own hand set fire to the pile which burnt alive his own mother with the dead body of his father, selected, by the grace of God, from his benighted fellow men, to be the first fruits to Christ in the land, and the harbinger of many others who should continue to follow him in the way to heaven.

A friend of Bamadeb, and also a disciple of the old gooroo, was Pursua-rout. He, in common with many others, received some rays of truth into his mind through the reading of our tracts, and felt a strong bias towards Christianity. His wife and family, however, were decidedly opposed to it, and he long stood aloof from us, though we occasionally had a glimpse of what was going on in his mind. While my colleague, Mr. Lacey, was in England, he called and had a long conversation with me, which greatly excited our hopes. He then said, his wife and son were the main obstacles to his avowing himself a Christian. After my colleague returned, he came again, and attended chapel ; when, in answer to some remarks by Mr. Lacey, he gave us reason to expect he would soon join us. He did so. His wife soon followed him, and his son entered our school and became at length a student for the ministry. While Pursua was in this transition state, the writer, with his colleague and others, visited heathen Choga, and he well remembers with what agreeable surprise we were awakened before day-dawn, by Pursua chanting, at the top of his voice, his Christian orison. Now reading the sacred page—then pouring forth his favorite hymns—and then closing with a long, fervent prayer for himself, his family, his country, and his neighbors. He certainly was not disposed to hide his light under a bushel, or cloak his profession. The whole village must have learned that Pursua was a Christian. He has since endured very harsh treatment from the raja's people. He has been severely pummelled, put in the stocks, and otherwise insulted; but he has borne all admirably.

Choga, from its pleasant associations, convenient distance from Cuttack, and other circumstances, has become a favorite place of resort for our Christians, and often for a sort of picnic parties for European Christians, who love our work and are interested in its progress. Several interesting wedding-parties have held their primitive feasts on Choga hill, beneath its mangoe-trees. Artificial lights are easily supplied by earthen pans of oil placed on split sticks, green boughs and plantain trees are placed around the space cleared for the entertainment, mats are spread for the guests to seat themselves tailor-fashion on the floor; plates, spoons, knives, forks, tables, chairs—are all dispensed with; and the guests eat with their fingers from heaps of smoking viands served up on plantain leaves. Many such feasts has the writer been privileged to enjoy. Perhaps the following account of the way in which Hindoos entertain their guests, may interest the reader.

### *Entertainment by Hindoos.*

The domestic economy of the Hindoos is at the very antipodes of European comfort and convenience; and notwithstanding the ample room there is for improvement, it is very questionable whether the former would be any gainers by adopting the manners and habits of the latter. It is said of Sir Philip Francis, when he saw the tribes of bare-legged Orientalists which thronged the ghat, as he stepped ashore at Calcutta, that he said emphatically to his fellow judge, "See, brother, the supreme court has not been established before it was needed. I hope in two years more we shall see these poor wretches comfortably clothed with shoes and stockings!" And just about as suitable would be the introduction of many other European customs in India. One leading difficulty in the way of making any extensive additions to the home comforts of the people, is the very limited means they possess, or are likely to possess. For instance, the daily use of meat, or bread, or tea, or wine, and similar articles of European diet, or luxuries, is utterly beyond the means of the mass of the people in Orissa; so also would be the use of many articles of furniture, as chairs, tables, bedsteads, earthen ware, and so on; while they would be inappropriate to their habits. And indeed, the difference of climate, and materials furnished by the country, call for a very different mode of living, were the means of the people much more ample in a pecuniary sense than they are.

The Oriyas, almost to a man, build their habitations of mud. The family residence, and its appurtenances, usually form a square, viz., two long buildings, standing parallel to each other, united at the side by two mud walls protected by a narrow thatched roof. The whole encloses an open area of from ten to twenty feet in diameter. The front building, through which the entrance lies, is commonly appropriated to the cattle, or the dhinkee for cleaning rice, or for a granary, or all these purposes united ; the inner building is the dwelling-house, chiefly employed as the domicil. The furniture consists of a few mats for sitting and sleeping on, a few brass vessels, as one or two lotas or watering-pots, two or three flat brass plates, a brass basin or two, a low stool, and perhaps one or two dirty bolsters or pillows. In the cooking room there will usually be a chuli, or fire-place, made in the floor, of earth; a curry stone, a knife fixed in wood to cut vegetables, several earthen pots of all sizes; and, either in this or the sleeping-room, a wooden chest to hold clothes, cash, or other valuables. In some houses we meet with a rough-made cot, or broad low wooden bedstead; but this is an exception to the rule.

The daily food of the people consists of rice admirably boiled in these earthen pots, a vegetable curry, or split pulse, cooked in various ways, with a pungent sauce, called chetna, salt, a few chillies, &c. The universal drink is water. Milk and ghee, viz., clarified butter, are luxuries, and so may generally be considered the various kinds of fruits which the country produces. The flesh of the wild hog, buffalo, deer, wild fowl, goat and different kinds of game, are occasionally eaten by most castes, that is, when they can obtain them, and fish is eaten by all excepting brahmuns. Meat and fish, however, are eaten in small quantities. A roast or boiled joint or a chop are, I believe, unknown; the universal custom, so far as the writer knows, is to mince the meat and fish and cook it with hot spices and condiments. Plantains and various kinds of vegetables are cooked in the same way, and eaten rather as seasoning than as the basis of a meal.

On occasion of a feast, or extra entertainment of guests, the mats are usually spread in the enclosed area or on some convenient spot before or near the house, and the meal is there served out to the party. On these occasions the host is by no means perplexed by the fact of his brass plates barely sufficing for his own family; he has recourse to his own or neighbor's garden and cuts a sufficient number of fresh plantain leaves to supply the whole party without any exceptions or distinctions. Knives, forks or spoons, he has none, but each man uses his own good right hand to supply the place of all these items of European refinement. Indeed the natives say that an European does not know what is good or he would never employ these articles, as food is far more relishing when eaten with the hand.

On special occasions of feasting, such as a wedding dinner or any similar occasion, a Hindoo will, if he can, spread an awning, under which the guests are to sit, and place around the spot, at convenient distances, a series of forked sticks or bamboos, to hold earthen saucers of fat or oil. A piece of cloth rolled up serves for a wick, and thus a splendid illumination is effected at small expense and in the most primitive manner. The writer has been present at many such entertainments among our Christian converts, where from fifty to 300 persons, men, women and children, have been thus feasted. The men usually seat themselves, tailor fashion, in rows, in one place, and the women and children in another. Half a dozen or more active male friends serve out the food from the cooking pots with their hands, whether it be rice, curry, thickened milk, pea soup, vegetables or fruit, and the whole company set to with right good will at their respective messes, usually, on these occasions, having the whole of these articles and any other the host can afford, all heaped up together on his leaf.

It is impossible for the writer to forget the first occasion on which he was invited to eat in the house of an Oriya. The occasion was as follows. Rama Chundra, the second convert baptized at Cuttack, had, a few days subsequently to his baptism, returned to his native village. His wife and family, though they admitted him within the family enclosure, refused to eat with him, or indeed have any kind of intercourse. Both from them and his neighbors he had to endure a great fight of afflictions, and it was with the hope of encouraging him, if not to soften the opposition of his family, and, at the same time, strengthen the minds of several inquirers in the village, that two of my colleagues and myself, accompanied by our first convert, Gungadhor, went over to his neighborhood. It was the rainy season, and our way lay, for three or four miles, through fields of flourishing rice plants, or the wide spreading thorny jungle.

After visiting Rama and succeeding to some extent in our mission respecting him, we were most agreeably surprised at being invited to dinner at the house of one of the inquirers. His name was Karana Sahoo, whom, with his wife, we had subsequently the pleasure to baptize. Our friend was by trade an oilman, and in his circumstances was at least as well off as his neighbors. The hall of entertainment was the cow house, the first building in the Hindoo mansion already described. Had it been fine weather, probably we should have been seated in the court yard or area referred to, but, as it was, the worthy host was fain to drive his bullocks as snugly as possible into one corner, and polish the saturated floor after his oriental fashion, and thereon spread, not the table-cloth, but the mats which were at once to serve for table, table-cloth, and chairs. On these he placed the plantain leaves, from which we were to eat our rice and curry with our fingers as best we might. There, while the good old lady was busy in the culinary department preparing our savory meal, the old gentleman entertained us with the most primitive cigars imaginable, with many apologies and some fears for his presumption in inviting us to come under his roof. No such thing had been done within the range of at least fourteen generations of his ancestors in Orissa. It was a bold stroke, a masterpiece of moral courage deserving of the most respectful memorial, and which at the time excited no less our admiration than our gratitude. True, there was much that might be revolting enough to the fastidious, and which, apart from *the occasion*, we might not have relished, but that sweetened and sanctified every thing, and I much question whether, amidst all the generous hospitality I have so largely and in so many parts of the world experienced, I could select an entertainment so grateful to my own feelings.

From the summit of Choga hill, or Oodoyapoor, the Christian philanthropist may survey the influence of the gospel among the people, in contrast with heathenism. A great part of the plain below is now well cultivated by Christian ryots; the cottages, for the most part, are surrounded by gardens, and an air of comfort, neatness, and prosperity distinguishes the whole. Near the spot where the thieves' goddess stood, the Christian children hold their village school; Christian women are seen seated at their cottage doors, singing the songs of Zion as they ply their spinning-wheels; and the Christian temple adorns the summit of the hill. The prosperity of the little church here, has been uninterrupted hitherto, and its ministers have chiefly been Pursua and Bamadeb. Each year continual accessions are being made to the little flock, and various pleasing incidents might be noticed. We have room only for a pleasing fact, related of a little girl.

When one of the men hesitated to come out at the time he had appointed, through fear of losing his farm, his little daughter, a nice girl about ten years of age, came to him, and looking him in the face, said, "Come, father, don't be afraid; let us leave these idols, and go to the Christians on the mount who worship God. Come, father, I will carry the basket with a panee kokharoo" (a kind of large fruit). The father looked upon his little girl and took courage. The little one was as good as her word; and I saw her, first in the group, and with a basket containing the panee kokharoo on her head. The kokharoo is a fruit needful for every meal.

The continued increase of converts rendered it desirable to provide them with a commodious house of prayer. A chapel was accordingly erected and opened on the 12th of March, 1846. The narrative of the opening, by Mr. Lacey, is very encouraging.

On the 12th of this month, our new chapel at Oodoyapoor, Choga, was opened for divine worship. It is entirely for the use of native Christians, and the ministrations in it will be in the Oriya language exclusively. I cannot depict the feelings of pleasure and hope which animated our minds throughout the day. The place being on a small mountain—being called, even by idolators, "the mount"—its outskirts being inhabited entirely by Christian converts from heathenism; its being surrounded by thick jungles and large mountains; the highly poetical descriptions contained in the sacred word respecting "Zion, the house of God,"—their appropriate application to Oodoyapoor; and the numbers of native Christians, clean and white, streaming over the surrounding plains to attend the opening services,—all these things fired our imaginations, and kindled feelings of sacred delight in our hearts.

Brother Sutton took for his text Isaiah ii. 2, 3. I had just seen the native Christians, and the school children, like a stream of whiteness, flowing from the further extremity of the cleared plain towards "the mount," and had been indulging in some very pleasurable reflections suggested by the sight; and the announcement of the text, so appropriate, was very pleasant. The chapel was more than filled. The front verandah, and a space beyond that, which had been shaded by a bower of green branches, were also fully occupied. The preacher caught the spirit of his theme, and uttered many encouraging truths, and made many delightful and appropriate allusions, in which all appeared to participate. Four years ago, this mount was the ambush of thieves and robbers—on its summit stood a small old temple containing an image of Koosalee, the patroness of thieves; the rest of the mount was covered with a dense and thorny jungle, where occasionally the hungry tiger lurked for his prey; and was, besides, the abode of noxious serpents and unclean reptiles, so as to be unsafe to enter. Koosalee, who the people told us could never be removed, as she sprang up through the ground from the nethermost regions, has been plucked up and cast away; her house demolished and burnt; her horses, elephants, children, and all her paraphernalia of worship scattered abroad, and destroyed. The jungles have been cut and cleared away; the tigers, which erst remained in the "mount," now pass by, wondering at the change.* If such a transformation has occurred in this "mount," now ornamented and blessed with the Lord's house, I will not despair of the Lord's house crowning the mightier hills and mountains around us. The native Christians sung with unusual spirit, and with considerable harmony, that pretty hymn by Rama Chundra, commencing,

> Beyond these heavens with ether filled,
>   Beyond unfathomed space,
> God dwells upon a throne of light,
>   And manifests his grace.
> Then come, my soul, and worship him;
>   In Christ salvation dwells.

We closed with a hymn in English, which I have often sung as I approached Choga; it is beautifully appropriate to the occasion.

> Messiah, at thy glad approach
>   The howling winds are still;
> Thy praises fill the lonely waste,
>   And breathe from every hill.

The day, till evening, was spent by the native Christians generally in visiting their friends; and by the native preachers, and some others, in groups, on the "mount," under the shade of the mangoe trees, chanting hymns, and conversing, or disputing with

---

* The footsteps of tigers have been traced all round the mount, since it was cleared, and depredations committed near it. These footsteps were imprinted evidently by brutes, which were in the habit of lurking in the place for prey. A cow was killed by a tiger, only five hundred yards from the mount, two days before the opening.

heathens who had been attracted to the spot. At seven o'clock in the evening I preached from Isaiah xxv. 6, "And in this mountain shall the Lord of Hosts make unto all people a feast of fat things," &c.; and the native congregation united in singing a translation of the hymn, commencing—

"The King of Heaven his table spreads."

The attendance was very good both times, and much pleasurable feeling prevailed. The chapel is twenty-seven feet long by eighteen feet wide, inside. It is prepared of burnt bricks, with tiled roof, and a verandah in front.

We intended to give a brief history of Khundittar, and the commencement of some other Christian villages, but our limits will not permit. In this brief account we have an illustration of the progress of our work in Orissa. That work will not be complete until what has been commenced in Choga shall be effected in every village of the province,—until the Christian chapel and the Christian school shall expel the last vestige of heathenism from the land; and, over all, the pure, unfettered influence of the gospel shall be spread.

"O, scenes surpassing fable, and yet true!
Scenes of accomplished bliss! which, who can see,
Though but in distant prospect, and not feel
His heart expand with foretaste of the joy!"

# CHAPTER XV.

Moral transformation of Orissa—Glance at heathenism—Change effected in Oriya converts—Death of heathen and Christian Hindoos.

When the Orissa missionaries commenced their work, the whole land might be called, in a spiritual sense, a waste, howling wilderness, a moral desert, "a land of darkness, as darkness itself and of the shadow of death, without any order and where the light was as darkness." A land where all that met the eye, or saluted the ear, or impressed the mind, gave awful intimation that Satan triumphed there. We have indeed disputed his right to reign, but, alas, how little abatement can yet be made from the foregoing description of what it was.

Behold its gods! Who are they? Not Jehovah, the living God, and Jesus Christ whom he hath sent; but Jugernath, Seeva, Krishna, Rama, Hunooman, Kalee, Radha, the sun, moon, stars, trees, rivers, beasts, birds, fishes, reptiles, yea, stocks and stones,—a literal fulfilment of Romans 1 : 23. "They have changed the glory of the incorruptible God into the likeness of corruptible man, and fourfooted beasts," &c.

Look at its temples! Are they like the Christian's house of prayer, all chaste and neat and grave, where serious men and devout women assemble with holy awe and humble hearts and pure desires; whence the sounds of sacred prayer and praise from spiritual worshippers ascend to heaven? Ah, no! They are fit residence for the gods they accommodate. Ere you enter these sinks of sin, in many cases the impure sculpture, the personifications of cruelty and lust, direct the mind to the character of the being worshipped, and seem to say, "Let no holy thought intrude." I remember on one occasion accompanying a missionary brother in Orissa to some celebrated temples at Jajipoor. We walked round them, followed by a train of priests and their deluded disciples. As we were examining some historical designs toward the base of the building, the brahmuns directed our attention to some figures above our heads, exclaiming, "Look up, sirs, at the glory!" But, oh, how ashamed we were,—there was lust and indecency so portrayed in all their disgusting odiousness, that we were abashed, and turned away in confusion, while the delighted crowd triumphed in their abominations; and such things are no strangers in Orissa.

What, then, is the character of the priests and servants of these idols? We hesitate not to assert that they are the wickedest of the people. Has it not been repeatedly said by judges and magistrates in India, that there is scarcely an act of enormous wickedness perpetrated in that country without a brahmun having something to do with it? Their pride, their covetousness, their sensuality and their idleness are proverbial. But such we might expect to be the case with men so intimately connected with gods, the very personifications of these vices.

From the temples to which I have alluded at Jajipoor several unhappy women of abandoned character came to us for books. These are a very common appendage to many of the temples. Their professed employment is to dance before the idols and to sing their abominable songs. Several of these degraded creatures are said to be connected with the temple of Jugernath. The statements of converted Hindoos on this distressing subject prove that many of these temples are in fact houses of ill-fame.* What, then, is the worship offered to these gods by such worshippers? It is just what might be expected from their well-known character. When we address ourselves to a superior being, we shall, if we are desirous of gaining his favor, endeavor to conduct ourselves agreeably before him. Just so the Hindoo idolator when addressing himself to his god. Most of the gods are said to have been overcome by flattery, hence a Hindoo endeavors to gain his cause in this way, and ascribes to his idol all the most extravagant attributes and outrageous excellencies he can imagine. Many of them are great sensualists, hence they are presented with the most excellent food, agreeable perfumes, golden couches, valuable jewels and gay clothing. Some of them are worshipped with the most obscene gestures and abominable songs, as at the car festival at Jugernath and the Doorga poojah in Calcutta. Others are malignant beings, and require to be propitiated with bloody sacrifices,—severe bodily mortifications,—penances and pilgrimages. Hence the immolation of human victims,—mutilations of fingers and toes,—swinging with hooks in their backs,—holding up their arms till they become stiff and dry as a withered branch,—drowning in sacred

* Testimony of Wesley Abraham, a convert at Madras :—"I was much scandalized by the profane and immoral service performed in our pagodas. At Supramanciam, a famous pagoda, three leagues from Goa, the image of a serpent with seven heads is worshipped. At a certain festival this serpent is said to move the head, and three girls of the most beautiful shape dance before him stark naked, in the sight of an innumerable crowd of spectators. At the sacrifice of Satty, (this is the Venus of the Romans,) men and women eat and drink together, and afterwards mix promiscuously. Daily are entertained in our pagodas the dancing girls, who are professed prostitutes, who sing at morning and evening sacrifices the impurest songs, and offer in the pagodas, with the obscenest language, their persons to the spectators and invite them to lie with them."

rivers, and all the endless series of painful ceremonies practised by these deluded people to win upon the attention of their gods.

You will perhaps be disposed to ask, "What blessings do the worshippers of these gods hope to gain by their self-denying services? We would reply both as to the principle which dictates their worship of the gods, and the purposes for which they worship them. First, as to the principle which dictates the worship of idolators, we would remark that it is in most cases either from fear or fraud.

While I was in America, I saw at the museum connected with the American Pedobaptist Board for Foreign Missions, an image of the poison goddess of the Sandwich Islands. It was a frightful looking figure, as is indeed the case with most heathen gods. The missionary who forwarded this image stated that the people in those islands supposed that most of the persons who died there had fallen under the malignant influence of this goddess, and this was particularly the case as it respects children; hence it was common for women who had children, to offer one of them in sacrifice to this poison goddess, hoping she would thus be prevailed upon to spare the rest. Similar views and feelings influence many of the Hindoos. How different is all this from what the Bible teaches. A Christian is taught to contemplate the blessed God as the best and most gracious of beings, looking down from heaven on the children of men with the tenderest compassion, and devising a thousand plans of love and mercy to make them happy. But a heathen regards his gods as malignant beings, ever envious of any degree of happiness he may enjoy, and watching about his path and around his bed with the intent of doing him some injury. If trial and misfortune overtake him, he supposes that he has incurred the displeasure of one of these gods, or that some enemy has been successful in obtaining the exercise of their power against him; hence by night and by day he is constantly in fear, and employs all sorts of tricks and charms and incantations to avert the malignant influence of these gods.

From beings such as these, what real good can be expected? The Hindoos neither wish or expect any, at least any spiritual good. They pray to them for wealth for a son, for deliverance from disease or difficulty; or for success in some undertaking, perhaps that undertaking is to circumvent or ruin a neighbor. Or if it be some future good they supplicate, it is for wealth and grandeur or civil power in another birth, or for some millions of years of happiness in one of the sensual heavens of the gods; or if the man be a devotee of the highest class, it may be for absorption into deity, that is, to amalgamate with the divine essence as a drop of water is lost in the ocean.

It is an awful fact, but one very common to heathenism, that the worshippers of idols separate, in most cases, morality from religion. They seem to have no conception that purity of motive and sincerity of intention and honesty in conduct and holiness of heart are necessary to the right performance of divine worship; nor, indeed, are they, for what *they call* divine worship. The prostitute and the reverend brahmun alike suppose that they offer an acceptable sacrifice. The thief returns thanks for his success in some nefarious exploit and divides the spoil with the god. And the adulterer proceeds from the temple to his mistress,—yea, we have remarked we fear that the temple itself is often little better than a house of ill-fame. Hence, in Hindoo worship, you hear no sighing of the humble, contrite heart; no self-abasing confessions of duty neglected, or sin committed; no penitent cry for pardon; no earnest prayer for preserving grace for the future.

Need we say that the tendency of Hindooism, then, is to debase the human mind, and corrupt still more the naturally depraved heart? It must be so. How can any thing else be expected from the adoration of beings whose "acceptable service" is a mere tissue of disgusting flattery, of bargaining and intrigue for selfish, sensual gratification? Whence can morality be learned? Certainly not from the gods. If it be learned at all, it must be by unlearning every thing connected with them. The whole tendency of their example, and their injunctions, too, is to make men as wicked as themselves,—a mere mass of sensuality and covetousness and cunning and falsehood and cruelty. Eighteen hundred years ago the Apostle Paul described the cause and consequences of idolatry,* and the picture is so striking, that modern idolators have accused the missionaries of forging it since their residence among them. Indeed I do not know of a sin mentioned in that chapter, which the heathen in India do not commit at this hour.

But it will be asked, Do not the Hindoos know that many of the above acts and practices are wrong? Have they no sense of sin, no admonitions of conscience? Most certainly the Hindoos do know that they are sinners. They have often "fearful looking for of judgment." They know in themselves the "judgment of God, that they who do such things are worthy of death, and yet not only do the same, but have pleasure in them that do them."

Many years ago did the author, while sitting under a

* See Rom. 1, 18—32.

tamarind tree at Pipplee, looking at Jugernath's pilgrims passing along the high way to and from his shrine, and meditating on the helpless spiritual condition of the people, write in his journal,—"Were the divine Saviour to travel through Orissa, as he did through Judea, it would doubtless be said of him that he had compassion on the multitudes because they were as sheep scattered abroad, having no shepherd. It is strikingly the case with these poor Oriyas, for though apparently the most religious people on earth, yet in reality they have no one to guide them; they have no faith nor confidence in any of their shastras; and as to all the consolations of even a false religion, they are eminently without God in the world, having no hope. One perhaps picks up a few sentences from the fragments of some old poem. Another gets hold of a few sage maxims from some celebrated gooroo. Another has sufficient strength of mind to see the futility of all the popular nostrums, and is constantly unhappy and unsettled till he settles down in infidelity respecting all religion. The majority go to the festivals, and receive the muntra from the gooroo because others do. But scarcely a man is to be found whose mind is at rest respecting even the hopes held out to him by his own system."

[For a further illustration of these views, let the reader turn to the accounts furnished by Rama, Seebo, Lukhein-das, and others, as presented in this little volume.]

It is this wretched system which has prevailed in India, till it has wearied its adherents, and left them "without hope," as they are "without God." It is this which has created so many weary wanderers after rest, who by some means or other have received light enough to perceive the futility of all the popular spiritual nostrums; and it is for them, as for others, the gospel alone brings a remedy.

There is, in the redemption by Jesus Christ, pardon for the guilty, accompanied by a moral power to renew the heart. It affords justification and sanctification. What neither divine or human law could do, in that it was weak through the flesh, God has accomplished by sending his Son for a sin-offering, and thus pardoning their sin while creating the desire to be saved from it.

"If any man be in Christ Jesus," saith the Scripture, "he is a new creature; old things have passed away, behold, all things have become new." It is only in heathen lands that the extent of this change can be appreciated. In many Christian lands, there has so long been going on a process of outward Christianization, that the outward form and semblance of a Christian man—a Christian family—or a Christian state, may frequently be seen, where nothing but the living, vital power is wanting. But in heathen lands, outwardly as well as inwardly, the form as well as the spirit, whether in individuals, families, or communities, has to be renewed. And the Christian leaven will do this. It will leaven the whole lump.

It is now beginning with individuals, and here and there is affording proof of its power to save. It is taking one from a city and two from a family, and displaying its wonder-working efficacy in bringing peace to the troubled conscience and hope to the despairing soul. It is teaching lying lips to speak the truth; the debauched votaries of the gods to be chaste, pure, and "holy in all manner of conversation." It teaches the people that there is a power and influence in Christianity for good, to which they have hitherto been strangers, and many a testimony to this effect is extracted from their lips.

But the gospel is doing more than this. It is not now confined to individuals. It shows its sweet influence in the family, teaching "husbands to love their wives," and "wives to reverence their husbands"—"children to obey their parents, and parents to train up their children in the way they should go." Christianity looks lovely in the family. It appears to advantage in the formation of the marriage union,—in the training of the Christian household,—at the family altar,—in the interchange of neighborly acts of kindness; and it comes like a ministering angel to the sick bed, and while administering present comfort, points to glorious hopes on high. And, when it can do no more on earth for the soul, it directs to a decent disposal of the deserted tabernacle of clay. These things have their influence in India, and will have yet more and more.

We may, however, "thanks be to God, who causeth us to triumph in Christ," advance yet farther, for we have not only Christian families, but Christian churches, and with them all the delightful associations of the house of God, the Sabbath day, and the means of grace.

Christianity, now in her Oriya garb, stands forth, and publicly attests her divine origin. She claims a hearing from all that pass by. Every church or chapel is a public testimony for the God of the Bible. Every hallowed Sabbath claims man's reverence and regard. Every public service of religion says, Come, and see; and every sermon says, "I speak as unto wise men, judge ye what I say."

The people now know there is a God, hitherto to them unknown. They know there is a Saviour, such as Hindooism does not reveal. They feel there are denunciations against sin, which they have not yet regarded aright; that there is a heaven and a hell, of which they have formed no right conceptions. And these truths and convictions are becoming general in the land. They are exciting, I am persuaded, a widely-extended influence; and there are twitchings of conscience and surmisings of the falsehood of Hindooism, and secret apprehensions that the gospel is from God, which former generations have not experienced.

Yes, I believe that the gospel will triumph gloriously in Orissa; that the Hindoos will adorn the gospel as much as any nation upon the earth. There is much in them that will beautifully become the gospel. Cast your eye upon the loveliest village in Christian England, or in New England, seated amidst all its lovely scenery and moral beauties, and I believe there will yet be numerous villages in Orissa that shall equal, if not far exceed it. Orissa needs nothing but the gospel, in its full influence, to make it one of the happiest lands beneath the sun. Then will its mild climate, productive soil, its mountains and its villages, all contribute to promote the comfort and prosperity of its people. May they but maintain much of their present simplicity of habit and inexpensiveness of living, and want need never be known, poverty may be driven far away, and peace and prosperity bless her coasts. Above all, then shall her pilgrimages cease, her idols be forgotten, her shastras rejected, her refuges of lies swept away; and, instead thereof, Christian temples, and schools, and books, and habits and influences bless the land.

I feel some difficulty in describing the change effected in Hindoo converts to Christianity, in its proper light, to those who have never lived in any other than professedly Christian society. And the difficulty is increased by the very contradictory statements put forth by individuals when professing to give correct opinions on this important subject. It must be admitted, that before a just opinion can be formed in the case, there must be a tolerable degree of accurate information, and a moral capacity to judge in this matter. Now it is notoriously the fact, that many of those who have volunteered their opinion, have been deficient in one or both of these essential preliminaries.

Many have been at no pains to obtain adequate information. They have perhaps touched at some principal seaport, or made a tour through the country, or, it may be, have resided for some time at a civil or military station, Cuttack for instance; and, as has been actually the case, have gone away and told their friends the missionaries were impostors; there were no native Christians there. I knew an old colonel, who stoutly maintained that no Hindoo brahmun had ever become a Christian.

An excellent, well-known missionary in Calcutta, mentioned that on one occasion, some native Christians, going down the Ganges, accidentally came in contact with some European gentlemen, and when they stated that they were Christians, could not obtain credit for their assertion. At last it was sagely concluded, that a certain test would be, to get them to eat meat, and drink a glass of brandy and water! There are many, alas! whose ideas of conversion to Christianity extend very little further.

A few days since, an intelligent young man in many respects roundly asserted, in my hearing, that the Catholic priests had done more good than all other Christians put together in Calcutta; and when asked, in what respect, replied, in converting many poor heathens to Christianity!

Now, admitting that all writers on the subject are not so incompetent as those referred to, yet it must also be admitted, that few exhibit adequate knowledge, combined with that personal acquaintance with Christianity, which alone can qualify them to give a just opinion.

Even among missionaries themselves, there is some considerable difference in statement, as to the character of native converts in India. Many of their discrepancies may be easily adjusted by first ascertaining of what native converts they are speaking; whether among the low tribes of the South or Roman Catholic converts, or those sects which do not make a moral change essential to baptism or church-fellowship,—or those who do both feel the need of this change themselves, and look for it as essential to real Christianity in their converts.

After all, it must be admitted, that in the purest native churches there are many and obvious defects ; much that tries the faith and patience of their teachers, and that requires to be covered with the mantle of charity.

It ought, however, to be distinctly apprehended, that, for whatever of real moral good is found in native Christians, they are indebted to Christianity alone. There are no subsidiary moral influences, as in Christian lands. No *tone* of public morals to assist, no moral *training*, but just the reverse. Every thing about and around them is adverse to purity, goodness and truth.

With these preliminary observations, I now proceed to point out in what the most obvious characteristics of a moral change, effected in our Hindoo converts, consists. And, first, I may notice the decisiveness of their conversion from idolatry to the worship of the true God. We may safely say of them, in this respect, in the words of the apostle to the Thessalonians, "For they themselves show of you what manner of entering in we had among you, and how ye turned to God from idols, to serve the living and true God." The change is entire, universal, and decided. No vestige of a hankering after their gods, or either of fear or love toward them, remains. I may say, that there actually appears much less of veneration for them than is manifested by many Europeans.

Poor old Erun, the first convert, earnestly desired, in his simplicity, to petition the court of Directors for authority to go about the conntry, and destroy the idols, for he thought they had deceived the people long enough.

There is a curious anecdote, too, of Gunga-Dhor, of the way in which he put Jugernath's divinity to the test, by piercing him with a sharp piece of iron. I have heard him repeat this circumstance, with infinite humor, more than once, though at the time he was perfectly sincere and earnest. I have frequently heard both Gunga and Erun offer to bring the idols to a similar test.

We may say the same of all the rest, unless, perhaps, it be in the case of some poor, ignorant old creature, connected with the Christian natives, who has grown too old in idolatry to shake off all associations connected with them.

The addresses of our native preachers abound with the most explicit denial of power, authority or divinity in the gods of the people. The danger is rather of their being too cutting in their remarks. And no wonder if, after the full conviction they have of the falsehood and impious character of the heathen gods, there should be this "clearing of themselves, this indignation," this zeal; yea, "this revenge."

Nor is this trait in the character of the Hindoo converts peculiar to Orissa. We see it exemplified in the first converts in Bengal, and in other parts of India.

2. Another characteristic mark of our native converts is, their decided renunciation of Hindoo shastras, and their reception of the word of God. Here too, with

great propriety may we adopt the words of St. Paul to the Thessalonians, "For this cause also thank we God without ceasing, because when ye received the word of God which ye heard of us, ye received it not as the word of man, but as it is in truth the word of God," &c.

Nothing can be more interesting than the progress of divine truth in the minds of our converts. I may refer to the effectual working of it in the minds of all, but especially as recorded by Rama Chundra, Bamadeb, Seebo Sahoo, Pursua, Abraham, &c. And the interest with which the sacred volume is perused, is truly delightful. I confess I had some fears lest there might be something in the style and plain prose of many parts of the volume, and especially as given in a translation, when compared with the very different character of their own shastras, which would make the Bible irksome and unattractive, as predicted by Dubois, &c. But this is not the case. On the contrary, many of our converts seem never weary of reading the Bible. They are scribes well instructed, considering their means, in the things contained in the Bible. I believe there are few of us, who have not been surprised and delighted at the extent and accuracy of the knowledge which many of our people manifest of the word of God.

And they abominate Hindoo books. There is no giving "place by subjection, no, not for an hour." The Bible is truly the man of their counsel, and in this mark of real conversion we have great reason to rejoice.

3. Another interesting feature in their general character as Christians, is the simplicity of their faith.

They profess themselves to be sinners, "looking for the mercy of our Lord Jesus Christ unto eternal life." And this is the universal confession of faith. It may be made by some improperly, and by others without an adequate feeling of what is here implied, but this is their faith,—by many certainly deeply felt and most cordially embraced. It is really "all their salvation and all their desire."

The love of Christ, in the redemption of fallen man, is the grand staple theme in their ministry—in their prayers—and their hymns. "We will preach Christ crucified," was the emphatic declaration of three of our native preachers at the last ordination service, and this pledge has been fully redeemed. The marrow of the gospel is every where current among them, and is the solid foundation on which they rest their hopes. We may advert to this point again at the close of our remarks.

4. The doctrine of the Holy Spirit in his person and work are fully recognized, and to a considerable extent practically improved among our people. This is a subject respecting which it is every where easy to run into extremes, and we cannot pretend that none of our native Christians have not done so. Still it is a doctrine identified with their religious experience, and exemplified in their confessions and prayers. In this view I have often felt the importance and applicability of the baptismal formula, "Baptising them in the name of the Father, and of the Son, and of the Holy Ghost." It is a sublime and comprehensive epitome of Christianity, which Hindoos know how to improve, and from which, to use their own phraseology, they milk out inexhaustible supplies of Scripture teaching. This is the focus where all the rays of divine truth centre, and whence they emanate and irradiate the mind.

Prayer is intimately blended with the doctrine of divine influence, and many of our converts are men and women of prayer. I have often asked our young people and others about what they pray, and it is a frequent answer, that we pray for the Holy Spirit,—for his guidance and for his strength.

I would not convey an idea that our native converts are as attentive to this duty as it is their duty and privilege to be; for I fear the number of Christians in any land is very few of whom this can be said. But we may safely say of many an Oriya convert, "Behold, he prayeth!"

It is no mean evidence that prayer is not a strange work to them, that very few when called upon refuse to pray, and they pray with great propriety and fervency too. Nor is this remark applicable to the male sex only; our females in their meetings engage quite as freely as the men.

5. But however correct in doctrinal views we may truly believe our converts generally to be, I am aware that this is not all the evidence that is required. It is faith that worketh by love, purifieth the heart and overcometh the world, that must afford us the most solid satisfaction on this subject. And to this test we are desirous our converts should be brought. All we ask is that these fruits of faith should be traced to their proper source. Here mistakes are easily made. As it is not all gold that glitters, so all we see in Christian lands are not genuine fruits of Christian knowledge, faith and love. A thousand other influences combine to make a professed Christian honest, benevolent, chaste, decent in all his deportment, a man of veracity, and whatever else may be of good report. It is not so, we again repeat, in India, and, therefore, we should not measure our converts by the standard of European attainments. It certainly would be infinitely to the disgrace of the latter, to suppose with all their means and helps, and long series of years of progressive improvement, they are no better

Christians than the converts of a few years in the midst of heathenism.

Of the love of benevolence, charity and good will to others, which Christianity inculcates, our Oriya Christians are not destitute. In this respect, as in many others, their means and circumstances should be distinctly considered.

Many of them were poor at first, though not all; but most were made still poorer by embracing Christianity. They were, in almost every case, turned out of house and home, and all their ordinary means of subsistence. The income of the richest does not exceed £80 a year, and of the poorest it is in several cases less than £1 sterling, yet they contribute quite as liberally as their richer brethren and sisters in England. It requires nothing but a proper system of training in this grace to elicit its full development. And this is saying a great deal for Hindoo converts, rescued from a grovelling system of corrupting covetousness and duplicity; and yet not *wholly* rescued from it, for it meets them every where as the established order of things and concentration of human wisdom.

They are hospitable. Many pleasing proofs of this have been from time to time afforded. They entertain friends and strangers generously. Much more so than might be expected for their narrow means; and there is, all things being considered, a good share of mutual, kind assistance and interchange of friendly offices.

Several of our converts have confessed that they were for a time deterred from embracing Christianity because they knew they must, if they became Christians, cease to cheat, lie and use false weights or measures; but at last, urged by conscience, they were obliged to do so at all hazards, and to their surprise found they prospered far more than before.

Old Erun has long been known by the appellation of the man of one word. He is a cloth dealer, and asks but one price for his goods, hence his cognomen. He is so well known as an upright man, that frequent applications are made to him to act as arbitrator in cases of dispute and litigation.

I cannot refrain from adding an anecdote of good old Krupa, deacon. It refers to a circumstance he mentioned while ill several years ago.

It appears that in the early part of his Christian course he was employed by a Mr. Beecher, as superintendent of a number of coolies while repairing the road. It is the practice of these superintendents of laborers to take what is called dustoori, a per centage, from every laborer in his gang, and for all articles bought. Krupa, with the rest, did so too, to the extent of some eight or ten rupees. Three or four years afterward his conscience continued to smite him for this transaction. And when very ill, he, after several attempts to speak, sent for and told me of this matter. He had got the money tied up, and wished to restore it, but to whom was the question, and begged me to make it over to Mr. Beecher. He was evidently much burdened, and said his only reason for not revealing the case sooner, was, that as he occupied the office of deacon, he was afraid of bringing religion into disrepute, but he could not die in peace till he had confessed his fault. I mentioned the matter to Mr. B., who said although the custom was reprehensible, yet as it was the custom, the old man was not particularly to blame, and refused to take the money. The burden of Krupa's trouble was, that as he was well paid for his office, he ought not to have taken this from the pittance allowed the laborer, and in this he judged rightly. The whole matter, however, served to endear him to our hearts, and few, if any, are the Christian converts I have seen, who displayed so much of the spirit of Christ. I will only add, he was the father of Anunta, our oldest scholar, who died in Calcutta, and the husband of the woman who compared the fragrance of the Saviour's name to the breaking open of delicious fruit.

Of those other graces of the Spirit, usually classed under the head of spirituality, we must, from the very nature of the subject, speak with caution. The kingdom of God cometh not with observation or ostentation. We can speak best of outward conduct as significant of the inward state.

As, then, it regards the sanctification of the Sabbath, attendance on the means of grace, and especially of a devout demeanor in the house of God, our testimony must be favorable. Few things are more cheering to a missionary's heart, or give rise to more sacred joy and satisfaction in his work, than our worshipping assemblies. The attentive ear, the glistening eye, the calm, serene repose of the soul, are often witnessed there. And with a meaning as deep and a satisfaction as intense as are experienced in England or America, do we often say in our hearts,

"My willing soul would stay
In such a frame as this;
And sit and sing herself away
To everlasting bliss."

We, too, have meetings intended especially for a detail of personal religious experience, and there, while listening to their respective accounts of their joys and sorrows, conflicts and defeats, victories and renewed resolutions, have we been constrained to say, that whatever may be the defects and deficiences of our converts, here is true Christian experience; these are manifest proofs that they are renewed in the spirit of their mind.

Referring to our Lord's day service in the chapel at Cuttack, the brethren of the London Missionary Society remark:—

The neatly dressed assembly, the orderly worship, the hearty voice of praise, the attention given to the preached word, the thought that so many souls are being fed with the bread of heaven, and that many of them will, through God's grace, enter into eternal life, cannot but excite great gratitude to that Saviour who has made a broad breach in the fortress of Hindooism and given such encouragement to his ministering church. We had the pleasure of preaching to this numerous flock (who, on the whole, understood Bengalee well), and of joining with them in celebrating the Lord's Supper. Three military officers, brethren in the church, joined them at the same time. Such opportunities are not soon to be forgotten.

We give a few specimens of the experience of some of our native converts, prefaced by the testimony of Mr. Lacey to their character. Mr. Lacey writes:—

In the majority of instances of native converts it is impossible to attribute their conversion to other than sincere motives. They were men of caste, credit and consideration among their countrymen; and in embracing Christianity, they have become, in the estimation of their countrymen, the offscouring of all things; they have become absolute outcasts; persons with whom no one would hold communication, whom no one could touch. This loss of credit and character was not a result with which they were unacquainted; they came to it with a full knowledge of it; and with a keenness of feeling and apprehension respecting it, of the extent of which we can comparatively be no judges. They have approached the crisis nevertheless, steadily and resolutely. The importance and excellency, as well as the necessity of Christianity, have gradually developed themselves to their minds, till they have overcome and overborne every obstacle and every opposing consideration and consequence. The same remark is true as to their means of subsistence. Many of them were respectably situated in life,—some not necessitated to work at all. They had, therefore, to renounce the means of easy and comfortable subsistence for an uncertainty. At the time they became Christians they knew not how they should live, and their teachers knew as little how they would be able to subsist. They could only tell them, that as God provided for sparrows and lilies, he would in some way or other provide for them, in connection with labor and industry: so that gain can never be justly imputed to them as the motive which induced them to embrace the gospel. Besides, many of the native converts have suffered the loss of all things for the gospel's sake. The dearest ties and connections of life they have severed for Christ's sake. The love of wife, and children, and parents, and brothers, and sisters, and friends, dwells as warmly and as strongly in their bosoms as in any other bosoms; yet these they have forsaken, when called upon to do so for the sake of professing Christ and uniting with his people. It is true these relations have, in many cases, been recovered by process at law; but at the time they became Christians they knew not, nor had any hope that they should recover them. What more, I ask, can be required as marks of sincerity in any people professing Christ?

And apart from these considerations, the declared experience of the native converts evinces the possession of Christian principles. Those who know their characters best, and are witnesses to the expression of their experience, are the only credible judges of their sincerity; and I can solemnly testify that I never heard Christian exercises more clearly expressed than by the native converts in Orissa.

### *Gunga's address at an experience meeting.*

[It should be prefaced, that Gunga has for a number of years been troubled with a swelling of the right knee; all methods have been tried in vain to cure it; it now seems coming to a crisis, breaking out in holes, and making him so lame that he was obliged to sit while speaking. Still there was the same bodily action, and no sensible diminution of his usual fervor. It was my turn to preside, and I had no easy task to command my feelings as I listened to him, with the fearful foreboding that this disease might prove fatal. I am not at all aware that he has any such apprehensions.

After sitting silent for some time, Gunga arose and tried to stand; I, however, begged him to be seated, when he proceeded.]

"During the past month, my mind has been exercised with many things, new and old. Among the old things I mention with sorrow, my own fierce evil nature has been raving and bellowing like a roaring lion against one and another. Now it said, Up, run and bite and devour such a one, uproot him—quick, kill him, destroy him. Thus did my hateful passions rise; but, thank the Lord, I have obtained some calmness of spirit. I beg forgiveness of any I have injured. I also forgive.

Again, my mind has been much exercised in reviewing my experience from the first until now. I have thought of the time when I first became a Christian. I was alone, dark, feeble. I remember my old nature and sins—how I often sat alone in my dark house, (viz., in spiritual darkness,) almost in despair, while the tears, like the thick fast-falling drops of rain, would flow. [Here followed a striking expression I cannot fully recollect.] Then did my spirit seem to pass from me and stand in the presence of the all-seeing God, waiting for his sentence upon my conduct.

My mind also has been much tempted to laziness in my work. O, it said, you have preached so much, sung so many hymns, labored in so many places, now sit still and rest. Never mind; if you get something to eat and drink, well; if not, there are multitudes dying of hunger all around; you can but die also.

Then I learned a new thing, not that it is not in the holy book, but new in its force and application to my mind. While poring over my old nature and experience, I thought the Lord said, "If you will adhere to what you have heard from the first until now, you shall be my son. If you can but follow Christ, who now wandered on the mountains, now travelled through the jungles, now in the cities, now in the villages, now on the sea, now on the rivers. O if you could in some small degree (but like the end of your nails) imitate him, as he was followed by blessed brother Paul, you shall be saved."

Then did I think of the crowds by whom I have been surrounded in the bazar, who listened to the words of everlasting life,—wretched, sinful beings!—only to reject them. I said, Well, these have refused, but there may be others who will hear the good news. The conduct of the religious beggars from the west occurred to my mind ; they take their dish, and go from house to house and door to door begging—[here Gunga gave a specimen of their doggrel poetry, which they sing at each door, done to the life, and of which it is hopeless to attempt a specimen,]—and I thought, what if I should thus go and preach the gospel ; or, standing at the head of the streets and villages, proclaim aloud for three or four days,—who can tell, but some wretched, rotten in sin, ill-favored, bone-eating sinner may repent, and turn to drink of the flowing waters of immortality !

Again, I have thought much of the state of the church, pondering upon the unfavorable signs. As a person looks at a fracture in a pillar or wall, and says to himself, "If this be not repaired it will soon fall," so have I looked at the church. We read of many churches which were once flourishing, but they fell —peradventure such may be the case with this.

He then went on to describe the manner and guilt of apostacy, especially in reference to the excluded and unworthy members, in a strain of fervent and striking eloquence. I can give but a faint idea of it.

The Lord sometimes looks with an eye of mercy upon ill-favored sinners on the dunghill,—he sees them disgusting and naked, like a putrifying corpse, but with his own hands he takes them up, washes off their filth, cleanses their sores, covers them with white and beautiful garments, brings them into his house, and places them on a chair midst his sons and daughters to hear His good word. All this he does for them ; but they, after a time, return to their deadly poison, scratch open again their filthy ulcers, pollute the chair on which they sat, then slide down to the ground and sit on the floor, then roll out to the verandah, then remove to the high road, and at last return to their old ways, pouring forth from their lips the foul and hateful putridity of their hearts !—Can such wretches ever dwell in the heavenly mansion of God? An expressive silence answers, No !

Thus he went on, pouring forth one striking observation after another, which we attempt in vain to recall and record with any thing like justice. Indeed, what is written appears ineffably tame compared with what it was in the delivery. If, then, a power to command the feelings, make even enemies forget their enmity and listen with interest, excite now smiles, now tears, yet leaving an abiding impression, that whatever may be the man's faults, he is deeply sincere, open, generous and earnest, while we are brought to assent to the truths he utters, and admire the cause he advocates,—if this be eloquence, then Gunga stands in the first rank of orators.

At this meeting, Sodanunda, the son of Rama Chundra, who threatened to hang or drown himself if his father were baptized, but who is now a worthy deacon of the church, thus related the feelings of his chequered pilgrimage:—

It is now just nine years since I joined the church, and I can witness before all my brethren and sisters, of a truth God has blessed me. I have frequently been wayward and erring; I have strayed from God's truth, but he has in mercy brought me back to his paths. I have often fallen, if not into gross and open sin, yet into private and secret sins, yet has God been very gracious to me, and has not permitted me finally and irretrievably to fall away. He has not cast me off, but has corrected me for my transgression and humbled me for my sin. O how often have I felt a negligent spirit in the means of grace, and especially in prayer to God; yet he has borne with me, and has stirred me up to seek his face. At this time I feel much devotedness to God; I am very happy in the enjoyment of his love. I am confirmed in my faith of his word. I have lately been constant in prayer to God. I have love to, and much enjoyment in the means of grace; I feel that they are sweet to me. I have great love to my Christian brethren, and to the church of Christ. In this way does God bless me. This is my experience. This I testify before God and before my Christian friends.

Bunamalee said,

He was unable to speak of the Lord's goodness to him. At first, he understood but little, and his mind at that time was very unsettled and restless. As one wave succeeded another on the great sea, such was the state of his mind; he had no rest. At length obtaining the knowledge of Christ, he found a settled confidence. After briefly referring to his conversion, and the time he spent at Khundittar, he passed on to notice his appointment to the work of the ministry, and his being sent to Berhampore. He ascribed it to the abounding grace of God, that he should have been called to preach the gospel, and that he should have been called to preach it at so great a distance from his native place. (Berhampore is one hundred and sixty or one hundred and seventy miles from Khundittar, and nearly as distant from his native village.) For the work of the ministry he felt himself utterly unworthy, but he daily prayed to the Lord for strength, that he might perform it in a proper manner. These and similar observations were made with all that meek humility and transparent sincerity, for which, as a man and a Christian, our brother is distinguished. I have always admired his humility and desire to be instructed.

Hurree Paree, the deacon of the church, and one of the early converts, next rose.

He was not able, in his own strength, to speak properly of what the Lord had done for him. He referred to the time, now many years ago, when he obtained his first light on Christianity, to his conversing with one of the preachers, (Bamadabe, I believe,) and to his obtaining the important knowledge that salvation was to be obtained through the death of Christ. He afterwards went to Cuttack, conversed with Mr. Lacey, and saw Christianpoor: there were then only a few Christians. After all he had seen and heard, the conviction was settled in his mind that this was the religion; and he resolved to embrace it. He knew that he should have to bear reproach, lose caste, &c., but he was willing to bear it all. He referred to the love of Christ. In the sight of God he was like an ant, but yet such wondrous love had been displayed to him!

Ras Douri, a member of some standing, with great deliberativeness gave utterance to some important sentiments.

Like his brethren, he said, he was once in the region of darkness, but the Lord had brought him to see the light of life: he was once without understanding—altogether without understanding—concerning religion; he heard the shastras and trusted in the gods, but of the way of salvation he knew nothing. By the gospel, however, he had been led to see and know what he did not know before: he had been brought to know his own heart; he had been led to see the evil of sin, and the gospel had revealed to him the doctrine of salvation through Christ. For a time after he had received some Christian light, his mind was unsettled; but one night, he said, when the hour of sleep had arrived, bending my knees I made known my mind to the Lord. At that time I said, O Lord! all these refuges are false; this I know, and from this day I leave them. I will trust in them no more. Whether it be for joy or for sorrow, whether it be for good or for evil, as respects this world, I have done with them forever. I will be thy servant. Thou hast said, "Take up thy cross and follow me;" this, Lord, I desire to do. Having done this, my mind was at rest, and my confidence was settled. I was happy, and gave thanks to the Lord, that I was counted worthy to take His yoke upon me, and that he had brought me out of the region of darkness and introduced me into the kingdom of light.

At another meeting of this kind, Rama Chundra spoke of the delightful contrast that was exhibited between what he then witnessed of the progress of the gospel, and the gloomy and discouraging scenes of the early part of his pilgrimage.

I bless God for what my eyes have seen and my ears have heard; things which I never believed I should see, yea, of which I always despaired. When first Gunga brother became a Christian, and Krupa followed, and next, by the grace of God, I was brought in, how few and feeble we were. Of knowledge we had very little, of right conceptions how few! We met with our instructors and tried to profit, but all our services were in so small a way! All around seemed dark; there were none but ourselves to speak to—none to bid us God speed. Whenever we passed the door of those we knew, they pointed, and said, Che! che! fie! fie! I used to have a thousand fears whether I was right. Sometimes I wondered what was before us,—how our families would be preserved,—where I should get a wife for my son,—to whom I should give my daughter! No others seemed to come forward, and I despaired of their coming. If I went to a distance I used to have a thousand fears. Satan disturbed my peace by suggesting, your wife is dead, your house is burned, some misfortune has befallen your children; while every where, from every body, we met with opposition. But God has been better to us than all these apprehensions. Here I can meet with two or three hundred brethren and sisters, a thing I could not have believed would ever be. We can read and pray, and tell of our experience, and help each other. The gospel has brought down our pride and levelled our distinctions; and we can marry our children without difficulty, and as we please. I see our young folks growing up to succeed us old ones. Yea, I have heard our children* preach to me the gospel, and seen them go forth with us to the work. Again, then, I bless God for what my eyes have seen and my ears heard.

Gunga thus described the comforts that he enjoyed while watchful and prayerful, and the anguish of soul that he had suffered in consequence of becoming involved in a quarrel.

Last month I said something about the state of my mind at the experience meeting, and then in the afternoon I met with the church around the table of the Lord, to remember the Saviour's death. On that occasion I was much comforted, instructed, and edified. I went from the Lord's table with my good resolutions and vows renewed, and my inward joy was very great. I took my Lord home with me to my house, and there, in the citadel of

* Younger members coming forward and engaged as preachers.

my heart, I had sweet communion with him. O, I was fed. I was fat,—I was filled with joy!—I was glorious! Well, so I remained for fifteen or sixteen days. I placed my watchmen at every door:—a watchman at the door of my lips, a watchman at the door of my eyes, a watchman at the door of my ears—a watchman at every door. And all my watchmen were wakeful and vigilant, and Satan could find no entrance into the citadel of my heart. O how happily my days passed! I went to the bazar to preach, and I spoke with affection, freedom and boldness. I attended the preaching of the Word, and it did me good and fed me. I attended to my domestic engagements with great delight. Thus for sixteen days did I enjoy uninterrupted pleasure with the Lord, in the citadel of my heart, while my watchmen with sleepless vigilance guarded all the avenues to my soul. Thus passed the first half of the past month. Well, at the expiration of sixteen days, why I know not, but at the expiration of sixteen days, the enemy made a vigorous and sudden attack upon me, and this attack was by means of a word of angry abuse from a certain person. O, this word was one of his fiery darts. This fiery arrow fell into, and burned in my ear. This arrow was so fiery and dreadful that my watchman became afraid, and fled from his post. This fiery arrow burned its way to my heart, and set me all on fire! Immediately I snatched up similar arrows, and returned arrow for arrow, word for word, till I became as bad as the aggressor, till I became defiled with sin and filled with burning rage, and was on fire of the devil. And now I lost my peace; my Lord was gone from the citadel of my heart, and I went and sat me down under the lime tree in my garden, and there I mourned. So soon as the heat of the contest was over, alas! to what a miserable condition I was reduced! I looked here, and I looked there, but could find no rest; my pleasure and my Lord were gone! My sweet experience was burned to ashes. For several days I was very sorrowful and wept much, and I went into my garden and sat down under my lime tree, and there I tried to pray. The enemy now came to me, and said, What are you weeping about?—you sob and cry like a child. You are utterly fallen, you are gone; give it up, and cease to weep. I now went heavily about all I did, and I stayed from the bazar for three days. I was overwhelmed with gloom and dejection. At length my Saviour sent me a promise by a special messenger, and this promise struck light into my dark mind, and in part I recovered my comfort. Yet it was not till a few days ago that I regained full comfort of mind. I sought pardon of the Lord with diligence and importunity; and that pardon I at length obtained. My Saviour has now fully restored my peace; I am to-day very happy. I am glad to be here. To-day I shall appear around the Lord's table with my Christian friends, and remember my Lord's love. Thus I have told you my experience through the past month; and I close by telling the church that my Lord is again in the citadel of my heart, and that my watchmen are again at their posts. When my Lord came back, he said to me, Why did you allow the watchman at your ear to run away? God has forgiven me, let all my brethren forgive me.

6. I must hasten to a close, and in doing so should notice, in the last place, the dying experience of our converts, but this I shall reserve for another section. Hindooism affords but poor consolation for its deluded votaries; an escape from greater evils is well nigh the summit of happiness the best can hope to reach. It speaks of endless transmigrations, of accumulated evils treasured up in numerous former births yet unendured, and then, far on beyond all these, there may remain a definite period of happiness in the heaven of some sensual god; or for the anchorite the sublime hope of annihilation,—that is, of absorption into the universal spirit! I never saw our native Christians manifest any fears of the threatened evils of Hindooism, or any hope of attaining to its promised good; but many have died in calm, and firmly expressed hope of a glorious immortality. Sometimes there has been strong consolation, and remarkable words of exalted hope and the triumphs of faith have fallen from their dying lips, and all this in de-

lightful contrast to the sullen silence or strong alarm of the Hindoo idolator.

If, then, the views here presented of the moral transformation effected in Orissa by the gospel be correct, if it be in our hands, even in these high places of idolatry, "mighty to save," shall we not regard the past as the pledge and earnest of a mightier change yet to be effected? May we not look on beyond present discouragements to the time when the victory shall be won, and Orissa become Immanuel's land? It will be then, as now, filled with temples, but they will be temples dedicated to the living God. It will be thickly populated with worshippers, but they will worship God in spirit and in truth. It will have its highways thronged with pilgrims, but they will be travellers in the way to heaven. It will have its shastras, but they will be the Sacred Scriptures, or books deriving their subject matter from them. It will have its songs, but they will be sweet songs of praise to God and the Lamb. Its fathers and mothers, as numerous as now, will be all Christians; its youth, of both sexes, all will be taught the lessons of early piety; the land shall have its Sabbaths; it shall feel the full influence of truth and peace; the earth shall yield its increase, and heaven receive successive generations of its ransomed multitudes, then shall the word be fulfilled, "The wilderness and the solitary place shall be glad for them; and the desert shall rejoice and blossom as the rose. It shall blossom abundantly, and rejoice even with joy and singing; the glory of Lebanon shall be given unto it, the excellency of Carmel and Sharon; they shall see the glory of the Lord, and the excellency of our God." Isa. 35, 1—2.

### *The dying Hindoo as affected by Heathenism and Christianity.*

Religion derives its main importance from its relation to a future state of existence, and by the character of that future state and the hope of happiness in it which any system of professed religion imparts, may its claim to be a revelation from God be satisfactorily tested.

"There is a divinity which stirs within us, and points out immortality to man." So says the poet, and to this sentiment all nations, unless sunk in the most brutal ignorance, respond. Endlessly diversified may be the character of their immortality, and strangely diverse, too, the means by which they hope to be made partakers of the blessedness such immortality affords, yet still there is a hope of something better than earth and time can give.

The Hindoos vary exceedingly in their views respecting the future destiny of man, still the leading characteristics of their faith, especially as held in Orissa, may be stated with tolerable accuracy in few words. They all but universally believe in the transmigration of souls, and the Pooranas on the most venial occasions denounce myriads of such transmigrations through every imaginable form of being. Of course, just in proportion as these denunciations have power to affect the mind of individuals, will their apprehensions in a dying hour be awakened. Mr. Ward thus describes the fears and anxieties of the dying Bengalee. "Among other similar expressions, he exclaims, alas! how dark and dreadful is the cloud that envelopes me; is there no ray of light from the shastras to guide me in yon unknown world? What shall I become in another birth? Shall I enter the body of a bird, or of a snake, or of a jackal, or what is to become of me?" And thus, in perplexity and despair, he steals out of existence.

Another specimen is furnished by Ram Mohun Roy from the Veds.

A person at the point to die addresses the sun,—" Thou hast, O sun, concealed by thy illuminating body the way to the true *being* who rules in thee. Take off that veil for the guidance of me, thy true disciple." Then, within himself, he says, " Why should I entreat the sun, as I am what he is ;" that is, the being who rules in the sun, rules also in me. Let my breath be absorbed after death into the wide atmosphere, and let this, my body, be burnt to ashes. O, my intellect, think now on what may be beneficial to me. O, fire, remember what religious rites I have hitherto performed. O, illuminating fire, observing all our religious practices, carry us by the right path to the enjoyment of the consequences of our deeds, and put an end to our sins ; we being now unable to perform thy various rites, offer to thee our last salutation.

Such are the best expectations of Hindooism, while for those who neglect the wretched system of the Veds, there is held out the terror of, after death, " assuming the state of demons." The hope of the ignorant is endless transmigration; of the learned, annihilation.

It has not fallen to my lot to witness precisely such scenes, though I have in numberless instances heard Hindoos when in health avow similar apprehensions. The fact is, that as a large proportion of mankind, of all creeds, live in a state of indifference and practical infidelity respecting futurity, so they die in a sottish state of insensibility to the momentous change which awaits them. In this state of sottish indifference, or sullen despair, I have seen a great many die. The Hindoos are especially disposed to this state of mind. They believe that every man's destiny is irreversibly decided by some supposed previous good or evil conduct, and that no wit or skill of man can possibly alter it. It is true, that the hope of reward or dread of evil does arouse him to the performance of astonishing acts of penance or devotion, yet in the very midst of these, he displays the same apathetic spirit, and yields, with scarcely the shadow of resistance, to the most adverse decisions of fate.

Still the writer's experience has presented him with many most affecting illustrations of the dreary character of the Hindoo mind in prospect of death. Many a poor pilgrim has he seen summon the last energies of expiring nature to direct one last look to the idol and pronounce the name Jugernath, Jugernath, ere that eye closed and that tongue became silent in death; or else, with sullen moan, has he rolled himself in his mat or blanket and yielded up his spirit. But never has he heard any expression of hope beyond the gloomy valley, nothing of faith which triumphs over death, no ardent longings after such immortality as Hindooism reveals. The only instance of any thing like consolation amidst the pangs of death, he has met with, was the satisfaction expressed by Dr. Carey's head pundit, the man who served him so zealously and faithfully for so long a period, yet remained a staunch idolator, celebrated alike for his orthodoxy and his learning till the last. And what were the grounds of rejoicing of this distinguished individual? It was simply this, that he had accomplished his purpose in becoming a learned and celebrated man,—had amassed sufficient property to leave his family comfortable,—that all the rites and ceremonies of his creed had been duly performed; and now, said he, the aspect of the heavens is propitious, the sun is in his northern tract, let the last ceremony be performed. That was, to choke him with the mud and water of the Ganges, by the side of which river he was brought out to die.

There was not one word of sins forgiven,—of peace with God,—of glorious hope,—but all was cold, worldly, puerile, and at best but a negation of all rejoicing in a glorious immortality. The case was a melancholy one, and shows how mechanically he had for so many years prosecuted his daily work in transcribing and translating the Scriptures.

Hindooism has no "strong consolation" to impart, and the highest reach, both of Brahmunism and of Buddhism, is absorption. It remains, however, for the gospel to throw light upon immortality.

> "Hail glorious gospel, heavenly light! whereby
> We live with comfort, and with comfort die."

When Doytari, one of our native preachers, was, as he supposed and we supposed, upon his dying bed, I went with Mrs. Sutton to pay him a visit. The old man was tender, resigned, thankful; and while referring to his children, he spoke very feelingly of the contrast in his own circumstances and theirs in his youthful days. He spoke of the excess of riot and immorality to which he had run, and how his children had neither the wish nor power to do as he had done; so delightfully had Christianity changed the whole course of their lives. He then sobbed out (literally so) his thanks for the gospel, emotion almost choking utterance, saying how he was enveloped in gross darkness, and that we had come 18,000 miles to show him the way to heaven. "You," he exclaimed, "are apostles to me just as much as Paul was to the Corinthians, Galatians, and others." He, after a pause, added, "I often think, when I first became a Christian, of the time spent in travelling with you and James Sunder. I then knew not how to pray, and was so ignorant I knew not what to do or say; but blessed,

blessed, blessed be the Lord," he would have added, for the change, but he could not.

Here, I remarked at the time, I would rest my appeal for missions. Let a man who can appreciate the change, look at the contrast between a living and dying heathen, and a living and dying Christian Hindoo; and he must exclaim, O what a precious boon to sinful men, is the glorious gospel of the blessed God!

One of the earliest of our converts, who was gathered into the heavenly garner, was Lutchmee-bai, a Mahratta female, and wife of Rama Chundra, our native preacher.

### *Death of Lutchmee-bai.*

On the evening of Tuesday she took her meal as usual, and then attended to her family and private devotions. Almost as soon as she came out of her room, where she had been engaged in prayer, she was taken with looseness in her bowels. She lay down again on her cot; but was soon obliged to rise, and so on through the night. The cholera was heavy upon her. On Wednesday, Padree Lacey came and felt her hand and said, "This is the cholera," and gave her some medicine, which she was unwilling to take, observing, "I shall not stay long." She said to Padree Sahib, "Pray for me." He did so, and into the Lord's hand committed her. "To the Christian brethren and sisters," she said, "my son, Sodanunda, and my daughter, Bochanabie, I commit, under God, to your care, for I shall not survive to care more for them." She was asked how she felt in her mind, to which she replied, that her heart was with the Lord, and she was quite happy. Her mind now wandered again, but soon she recovered, and exclaimed, "O how happy I am!" Sodanunda read a portion of the New Testament, when she said, "My Saviour is in heaven; I know him! He will save me. I am not afraid, but willing to depart." Her symptoms relaxed, and she appeared much better; this improvement lasted not long, for presently her eyes turned upwards and became fixed. She was unable to speak, but lifted up her hand, to intimate she was happy. In the afternoon, the Padree, and Gungadhor, and other Christian friends came, and while they prayed her spirit departed. The Padree remained and consoled our minds and settled our grief. Thus lived and died Lutchmee-bai. She was a good mother to her children, instructing them in the word of God. She was a good neighbor, for she sought the good of all around her ; but more especially was she useful to the native Christian females. She was diligent in her household, and, as far as her abilities extended, compassionate to the widow, the fatherless, and the poor. In her religious duties, she was faithful and constant. In prayer she had an excellent gift, and used to pray in her family and in her closet with great punctuality. She grew daily in the knowledge and experience of the word of God. At public worship she was always present, and the first that was ready to go. When the heathen people around heard of her death, they placed their hands on their foreheads and exclaimed, "Ah ! ah !" for they all respected her.

Bochanee-bai, daughter of the above honored sister, was early converted and died in great peace about two years since. We have the following notice of her death in our Annual Report for 1848.

In April, last year, Bochanee-bai, a daughter of Rama Chundra, died. She had been a consistent member of the church. Her illness was long and painful,—she had suffered much, but the last scene was very tranquil and happy. To her father she said, "This is a world of trouble ; I have suffered much, but it will soon have an end, and then in heaven there will be no suffering." Her father inquired whether she had any fear of death. In the true spirit of Christianity she answered, "Why should I fear death ? I am a Christian. Christ conquered death, why should I fear it ?"

To the last she remained sensible. Shortly before her death she desired her father to give her farewell salutation to all her friends, and she hoped that wherein at any time she had grieved them, they would, in the spirit of Christian love, forgive her. She then expressed her humble hope in Christ, and calmly gave up the ghost. Thus another, who owed her knowledge of Christ and hope of salvation to your missionaries, has passed away from this scene of trial, to, it is trusted, a heavenly home. Let such pleasing instances encourage our dear friends to continue their efforts to benefit this degraded people. They will never see those who are so deeply indebted to their kindness upon earth, but they will recognize them and rejoice over them in the day of the Lord. But for that blessed truth which your missionaries proclaim, where would Bochana-bai have been now? By that gospel she is, we cannot doubt, a happy saint in light. Let us go forward. How striking her dying language. "Why should I fear death: I am a Christian. Christ conquered death, why should I fear it?"

### *The Mother of Rama Chundra.*

Another who slept in Jesus was an aged convert, who was called the mother of Rama Chundra, and was more than ninety years old when she died. She was very aged when she first listened to the gospel, and for a time appeared hardened and indifferent, through the influence of idolatry; at length her heart became the subject of converting grace, though the enfeebling effect of age prevented her displaying a high degree of Christian knowledge and experience. She, however, felt her depraved and sinful condition, and sincerely loved and firmly trusted in the Saviour. She was always deeply affected by reference to his dying love, as was attested by the tears that trickled down her cheeks. Latterly her mental powers seemed to brighten. She spoke freely of the dying love of Jesus, and rejoiced greatly at the prospect of going to be with him.

The testimony she bore to the supports which the gospel gives in death, was very pleasing. The day before her death, she said, that she was going to heaven; that she had no hope but in Christ; that the Lord called her, and she was going to be with him. Those who witnessed her dying hours were surprised and much affected by the fearless and joyful manner in which she entered the gloomy vale that all must tread; so peacefully and happily did she bid farewell to mortal things. She had been a consistent member of the church about thirteen years. A brother states that the scene at her interment was interesting, and well fitted to impress the mind with the vast importance of missionary labors. The sun had just sunk below the horizon, the moon and the more conspicuous of the starry host had risen. A select company of the disciples of Jesus, all of whom but one, it was believed, had once bowed to gods that could not save, gathered round the grave. All was quiet, orderly and becoming. Words of hope and comfort were spoken. The confidence which our holy religion inspires in the hour of death, and the blessed portion of those who sleep in Jesus, were adverted to. An appropriate hymn was softly and sweetly sung, of which the chorus is,

"Merciful Jesus be gracious to me at the last."

Solemn thanksgiving and prayer were offered, the body was conveyed to its last resting place, till the Lord shall bid it rise, and the little company departed. But for the introduction of the gospel into Orissa, no scene so bright with hope would ever have been witnessed.

### *Radhoo-das.*

This brother, when about eighteen years of age, appeared in our premises as a byraggee, covered with ashes. He was then a disciple of the old gooroo, and probably was the first who obtained the tracts which influenced the minds of both teacher and disciples. Radhoo was one of the earliest converts, and immediately gave up his vagrant habits, and earned his living by a course of industry. He sank under the operation of having a large wen cut from his neck.

When he found himself dying, he called his brethren around him, and begged them to join with him in prayer. He then sent for his wife, and asked her to sing him a favorite hymn, and joined himself in trying to utter the chorus of "I have no hope in this world but in the death of Jesus Christ my Lord." He then in a most affecting manner took leave of his wife and children, commending them to the God of the widow and the Father of the fatherless, and charged his Christian brethren to be her guardian and friend. He continued to utter sweet words of faith and hope, till he expired, with his brethren kneeling around him. They glorified God in him, and many said, May my death be like the death of Radhoo.

The last moments of Krupa deacon are thus described.

Some years ago, he was chosen and appointed a deacon, and he conducted himself in that office with much honor, and the church paid him great deference and respect. In settling disputes and differences among his Christian brethren, he had a large degree of influence; and the coolness and solidity of his character produced great effect. He was employed in instructing inquirers and candidates with advantage, and had the character of a father in the church. About three weeks previous to his death, Krupa Sindhoo was despatched with one of the native preachers into the rajuary of Atthgar. He spent eight or nine days there, and his companion spoke of him as talking very earnestly and affectionately to the people; he did so particularly to the Christian natives at Choga. During this journey he inhaled the seeds of a jungle fever, which attacked him on the second day after his return. I saw him that day in the evening, and he expressed his confidence that God would not forsake him in what he thought would be his last sickness. On the next day he became speechless, but by signs and intimations expressed his faith in Jesus Christ, and his freedom from fear of death. Half an hour before he died, when prayer was offered on his account, he raised his hands over his breast, and, turning his eyes toward heaven, united his supplications with those around him. After prayer the symptoms of immediate dissolution came on, and he soon expired. Krupa Sindhoo is now one added to the church in heaven, who have their robes washed and made white in the blood of the Lamb. He decks the Saviour's crown, and exhibits the reward of his travail from the dark and idolatrous tribes of Orissa. He was poor as to this world's riches; but though poor in this world he was rich in faith. He was unknown to the great and famed among the sons of men, but he is high in honor both by God and by his people. He will always be remembered with respect and love. Few, who have had superior advantages compared with his, have finished their course so well or left a sweeter testimony behind them, that they are now forever with the Lord.

### *Makoonda.*

Makoonda was an unlettered convert, who received the gospel at Khundittar. He, in common with the rest at that station, endured affliction for the sake of the gospel. But he still held on his way. On one occasion, when returning from Cuttack with his hackery, he was seized with cholera on the road. Rundentilly, another brother, was with him. He sank rapidly; and, as death drew on, he made a dying effort to send an affectionate message to his wife, and then, with his last expiring energies, raised his clasped hands to his head, and said—"Give my loving salutations to all the brothers and sisters of the church;" and thus he died.

### *Jagapa.*

Jagapa was a member of the church at Berhampore. He too was an unlettered man—by trade a milkman. The change produced in him by the gospel excited the wonder and admiration of his Christian friends. Eighteen months afterwards, he finished his short but consistent course. In his last illness he appeared in a pleasing state of mind. He said, I am nothing but sin, but Jesus Christ is an all-sufficient Saviour. In him I trust, through him I shall obtain salvation. I have no other hope. Just before his death, he said three times over to his weeping wife, "Weep not for me. My Father calls me. I am going to his heavenly kingdom." He then desired his loving salutations to be given to the Mission family, and hoped that wherein he had grieved any he should be forgiven. To his native brothers and sisters also he desired to be affectionately remembered. He again entreated his wife not to weep, for it was better for him to depart. He then began to pray, O my merciful God! my merciful God!—but could say no more ere his happy spirit winged its flight, to be with Him, whom, having not seen, he loved.

The following instance is taken from the nineteenth report of the eastern division of the London Society, mission, in the Madras Presidency.

Vatha-Nayakum was a valuable native preacher, attached to the above mission. He died October 13, 1846, aged 37 years.

After much opposition from his family, and eight months preparation, he was received into the church by baptism. His faith and love were clearly manifested by his zeal for Christ and the good of souls. He labored and travelled much as a teacher of the gospel for about fifteen years, and earned the general esteem of all classes. Nine days before his death, he returned home from addressing the people in the town, and complained of being unwell, but nothing serious was apprehended by others. He with cheerfulness took the medicines and nourishment provided for him, but at the same time he distinctly stated that the means used would be of no use, for that he was fully *convinced he was going " to his heavenly Father's house."* He had no pain, and even walked about the house within an hour of his death, exhorting all around him to attend to the salvation of their souls; then, lying down, he quietly breathed out his life into the hands of that Redeemer whom he loved and faithfully followed to the last period of his existence. He was followed to the grave by numbers of heathen, as well as Christians, who manifested real sorrow at his removal.

This list might be greatly extended, but we forbear. These are but specimens of a class every day becoming more numerous — a class which we humbly hope will form our joy and crown in the presence of our Lord Jesus Christ, at his coming.

The gathering into the garner of the first fruits of our mission, is an eminently interesting part of our missionary proceedings. There they are, safe and blessed forever, just where we wished to conduct them, and where we, too, ere long, hope to join them. Here is all our salvation and all our desire; and it is only as, by our humble agency, the great multitude before the throne is augmented, that we realize the results on which, from the commencement of our labors, our eye was fixed. Never can we forget with what intensity of interest and what joy of faith did we long regard the declaration, that this great multitude should be from all nations, and kindred, and tongues and people, and all alike should wash their robes and make them white in the blood of the

Lamb. Then, our hearts had not been cheered by a single conversion, but often had incipient hopes been blasted. Still we felt, this ample enumeration must include the sons and daughters of India, yea, of Orissa, and on that were we satisfied to rest our faith.

And surely, the rapturous songs of praise, so cordially sung in heaven by the redeemed multitude, may administer a rebuke to the opponents of missionary efforts. So far from these converted gentiles being deemed intruders there, it would seem to require no great stretch of imagination to suppose, that as each party of ransomed spirits, from any newly-established mission, enter the heavenly courts, a louder shout of triumph is heard, and louder congratulations offered to these new arrivals. And in perfect accordance with this remark may we suppose, that when, from the polluted site of Jugernath and the bone-strewed plains of Orissa, the first company of Christian pilgrims reached the eternal throne, there would be a still louder chorus reverberate through the whole domain of glory; and "Worthy is the Lamb, who has prostrated the vile idol of Pooree," would form a new stanza in the rapturous song.

And if a contemplation of these results of missionary labor may serve to rebuke the opposers of missions, does it not furnish a lesson to the apathetic and faltering class of our supporters? Is it no glory, thus to deck the Redeemer's crown? Is it no joy, thus to swell the anthems of Heaven? Is it no privilege, thus to spoil the idols of India, and guide their deluded pilgrims into the path of life? Does the hope of distinguishing, among the "great multitude," one and another of those we have been instrumental in introducing there, afford no sacred pleasure to your soul? If so, with such Christians we can have no fellowship, we wish to have no sympathy. May it be ours to know the blessed Saviour for ourselves, and then live and die proclaiming HIM to others.

## CHAPTER XVI.

**Motives for returning to India—Appeal to the friends of the missioñ—Last requests to Christian friends.**

The writer must hasten to the close of this volume. The ship which he expects will convey him and his faithful partner to India, gives notice of a speedy departure, and the busy season of preparation for a final adieu to all we love in this land of Christian privileges has come. Again and again is the writer asked, what can induce you, after so many years of labor, at your advancing stage of life, to reëmbark in the missionary cause? I answer, in brief, first, my own personal obligations to the Saviour; all I have and all I am are his. Next, my views of the privilege of being employed in this work. And, finally, my conviction that our cause will ultimately triumph in Orissa, and the whole land be won to Christ.

"I see a hand you cannot see, that beckons me away,
I hear a voice you cannot hear, forbidding me to stay."

And yet the heart flutters, the tongue falters, and the mind for a moment seems unwilling to turn away from you for ever. Accept of the missionary's apology.

O say not that his heart is cold
Because he goes far hence to dwell;
That parting hour can ne'er be told
When last he sighs farewell, farewell.

And as he yet pursues his way
O'er dark blue wave or foreign strand,
Oft does he dash the tear away
At thoughts of home and native land.

'Tis love to Jesus bears him on,
'Tis love to souls that fires his breast;
Beyond the cross he sees the crown,
And light he deems of all the rest.

Fain would he on some heathen shore
Plant the first church, in Christ, its head;
Then watch it branching into more,
And die beneath its spreading shade.

And thus, beloved ones, would I
See earth's dear, fondest ties, all riven,
And in far India's jungles die,
In hope to meet and love in heaven.

I must, ere I close, appeal to the venerated men and beloved friends who sustain and direct this mission. When, let me remind you, when you chose Orissa as the field of your labor, when you selected, ordained and sent forth your missionaries to cultivate that field, you either understood the nature of the undertaking or you did not. To suppose the latter, is to impeach the wisdom of men we love and revere; but to suppose the former, implies a sense of responsibility which must overwhelm all who put their shoulder from under the burden, or who refuse to sustain to the utmost a cause to which they are so solemnly pledged. Perhaps, however, many of those who engaged to pray for and support the Orissa mission, had but a very inadequate idea of the extent and responsibility of that pledge, and hence it may be as much justice to them, as to our cause, here to call their serious attention to it.

Taking into account all the circumstances of the case, I think it may be said, in general terms, that you pledged yourselves *to seek the evangelization of the whole province of Orissa*, nor are you at liberty to slacken in your work, much less retire from it, without evident intimations from on high that you are unequal to the task, and without, in that case, doing your utmost to induce some other body to undertake the enterprise of which you deem yourselves unworthy. For your entrance into this field was a virtual exclusion of all others, and such I suppose you would wish your occupancy of it to be understood. What is more, the Christian church has with one consent, during almost thirty years, ceded to us this province as our undisputed field of labor. Now I think it may be shown that you are not only fully equal to the work which you have undertaken, if you have the will, but that you have also most abundant encouragement to prosecute it with renewed vigor. We, as your missionaries, share with you in the solemn responsibilities of this vast undertaking, and groan under the task of urging you to duty in this matter. I had thought I had discharged my share of this duty by my many letters and personal appeals; but, as my thoughts rest on the still hapless condition of that dark land, the burden rolls afresh upon my conscience, and I feel that I must again and again plead with you and continue to do so till I die. And, then, if I were permitted, I would on my dying day visit your Committee-room, and placing myself at your feet, plead with my last breath for Orissa; yea, in that last effort of expiring nature, I would utter one loud, solemn warning that should ever thrill through your souls, REMEMBER YOU ARE PLEDGED TO SEEK THE SALVATION OF ALL ORISSA.

But leaving the more immediate directors of our mission affairs, I turn, with gratitude for the past and hope for the future, to our friends and supporters generally. There have indeed been times when your zeal seemed to flag and your love to wax cold; it is still the case that a large portion of the denomination do nothing, or next to nothing, for the Orissa mission; but I cannot believe that, as a body, you will ever cease to pray for and support this mission. You will not, cannot raise by the hands of your missionaries the water of immortality, the cup of salvation to the lips of the perishing multitudes of Orissa, and then dash it to the ground forever. Oh, no! I feel as if I could sooner die than believe this. I will not think it can ever be. Those eyes which I have so often seen overflow at the detail of the miseries we witness, those ears which so eagerly received our statements, and which seemed so to thrill through your crowded assemblies, those hands which have been raised up as a pledge to pray for and support the mission, dwell in my fond remembrance as the sure guarantee that you will never cease to feel for Orissa, to pity its sorrows, to contribute toward their removal, and to pray that a most abundant blessing may rest on all your missionaries.

And, finally, to you, American Christians, I make one last appeal. Seventeen years ago, when I first became acquainted with your churches, you received me with a favor and cordiality I had no reason to expect. You listened, with deep interest, to my plea for the benighted and perishing millions of Orissa, and warmly welcomed me to your country, your assemblies and your homes. When I left, after two years laboring among you, you not only gave me your silver and gold, but far more precious to me, your sons and daughters to be fellow-laborers in evangelizing Orissa. Others have since been sent to join us, and now you share the responsibility of bringing that province to the feet of Christ. All therefore I write in this book, is as much addressed to you as to the churches of our denomination in my native country. I cannot visit you personally, for the time of my departure for India is at hand; but I thus ask you, if you are not become far too cold and apathetic in this noble enterprise? Must I adopt the language of another, and say, half reproachfully to you, "Where are your love and zeal, if you can make no further effort to spread the knowledge of salvation in Orissa?" What mean those strong expressions of interest, those flowing tears, those hands uplifted in solemn pledge to pray for and support the mission? Must I conclude that all this was the mere sympathy of excitement, a feeling akin to that produced by the novel or the drama—the interest of an hour? No, I cannot, dare not, will not, till obliged, think this of you.

Nor will you I trust complain, "We have labored in vain and spent our strength for nought and in vain." True it is, we have not seen all the success we wished for and hope yet to see, for then we should see Orissa converted to God; but I believe it may, without fear of contradiction, be asserted, that the Orissa mission, considering the amount of actual labor and expense bestowed upon it, has been as successful as any mission in India; and that missionaries of all denominations who are acquainted with us, will cordially admit this assertion. Will you then, can you then, think of lessening your exertions for this important field? I would remind you of your early cherished sentiments regarding it, and beseech you to consider that those sentiments are as becoming now as then, inasmuch as they have been tested and proved.

The Indian banian tree presents no unfit illustration of our mission to Orissa. That useful and beautiful product of India's plains affords a grateful shelter to many a wayworn traveller, and few thoughtful minds can contemplate this kind provision of the munificent Creator without some thoughts of his goodness. Yet how much more precious is the cultivation there of that tree of life, beneath whose shade many of these same weary pilgrims have taken refuge, and there found that even in Orissa its leaves are for the healing of the nations. Yes, we have witnessed even there abundantly sufficient of such instances to prove that there is vitality in the tree we plant; that it contains within itself the power of self-extension; and while its even now spreading branches afford a shelter for many a weary wanderer after rest, like the banian alluded to, these branches are taking root downward, and surrounding the parent stem with a number of thriving daughters, which give promise of still wider, yea, of indefinite extension. So may our sister churches multiply and strengthen, till they overshadow the whole land!

But I must check myself; my wishes are that our mission should be devoutly cherished by you; that it be prosecuted far more zealously; that it be associated with your most fervent prayers, desires and hopes; and when you die, that you would hand it down to your children and successors as your most precious bequest. Be you faithful to your trust at home, and pray for your missionaries that they may have grace to be faithful abroad, to finish their course with joy, and to lay a broad and firm foundation for the conversion of all Orissa to Christ.

FINIS.